EMERGENCY MANAGEMENT FOR LAW ENFORCEMENT

EMERGENCY MANAGEMENT FOR LAW ENFORCEMENT

Strategies, Operations, and Tactics

By

JAMES F. PRESCOTT, JR.

CHARLES C THOMAS • PUBLISHER • LTD.
Springfield • Illinois • U.S.A.

Published and Distributed Throughout the World by

CHARLES C THOMAS • PUBLISHER, LTD.
2600 South First Street
Springfield, Illinois 62704

ISBN 978-0-398-09430-0 (paper)
ISBN 978-0-398-09431-7 (ebook)

Library of Congress Catalog Card Number: 2023040599 (print)
202040600 (ebook)

With THOMAS BOOKS *careful attention is given to all details of manufacturing and design. It is the Publisher's desire to present books that are satisfactory as to their physical qualities and artistic possibilities and appropriate for their particular use.* THOMAS BOOKS *will be true to those laws of quality that assure a good name and good will.*

Printed in the United States of America
MX-C-1

Library of Congress Cataloging-in-Publication Data

Names: Prescott, James F., Jr., author.
Title: Emergency management for law enforcement: strategies, operations, and tactics / by James F. Prescott, Jr.
Description: Springfield, Illinois : Charles C Thomas, Publisher, Ltd., [2024] I Includes bibliographical references and index.
Identifiers: LCCN 2023040599 (print) | LCCN 2023040600 (ebook) | ISBN 9780398094300 (paperback) | ISSN 9780398094317 (ebook)
Subjects: LCSH: Emergency management. | Threats. | Public safety. | Law enforcement--Psychological aspects. | Preparedness.
Classification: LCC HVSSl.2 .P748 2024 (print) | LCC HVSSl.2 (ebook) | DDC 363.34/8--dc23/eng/20230901
LC record available at https://lccn.loc.gov/2023040599
LC ebook record available at https://lccn.loc.gov/2023040600

PREFACE

Law enforcement officers have always been involved as first responders to road accidents, chemical spills, evacuations, rendering aid after hurricanes, tornadoes, and floods, terrorist attacks, train derailments, mass shootings, and a litany of other emergencies and disasters. Emergency management and law enforcement have a close historical relationship. Since the United States was attacked by the coordinated actions of terrorists on September 11, 2001, a renewed interest in both emergency management and homeland security has become manifest. Disproportionate attention and resources have been focused on terrorist threats although natural hazards pose a far greater risk of death, injury, and property damage to the typical American jurisdiction. Hurricanes, floods, and tornadoes cause billions of dollars in damage and substantial numbers of deaths and injuries each year. Greater attention should be focused on these natural hazards.

Law enforcement officers are on call 24 hours per day, 365 days per year. Few other emergency responders possess the versatility and availability to respond to every type of hazard, disaster, attack, or emergency than police officers. Law enforcement personnel officers are on the "front line" of emergency management because they are among the first to respond to every type of manmade and natural disaster. Police officers render aid and secure the scene rapidly in all conditions. Few textbooks recognize this reality and fewer still focus on the linkage between law enforcement and emergency management. One of the purposes of *Emergency Management for Law Enforcement: Strategies, Operations, and Tactics* is to better integrate law enforcement officers with other first responder agencies as they work together to resolve critical incidents.

Emergency Management for Law Enforcement: Strategies, Operations, and Tactics pulls together important information obtained from empirical research and disaster experience. This knowledge is designed to help law enforcement officers deal with disasters and emergencies more effectively as important players in emergency management. Learning evidence-based practical applications can assist police officers in making better decisions and taking more effective actions at critical incident scenes. This book draws from criminal justice, psychology, public administration, emergency management, public health, meteorology, leadership, and management in an effort to synthesize a wealth of knowledge to better prepare police officers to respond to the complete range of emergencies and disasters they encounter on the job.

J.F.P.

CONTENTS

EMERGENCY MANAGEMENT FOR LAW ENFORCEMENT

Chapter 1

LAW ENFORCEMENT, EMERGENCY MANAGEMENT, AND HOMELAND SECURITY

Emergency management is a field designed to assist in providing the knowledge and skills necessary to deal with all hazards that may be encountered by a community. Emergency management has grown in stature and relevance in the years since the terrorist attacks against the United States on September 11, 2001. Members of the general public typically hear about emergency management primarily in connection with major disasters such as tornadoes, hurricanes, earthquakes, or pandemics. Mass shootings, acts of terrorism, and other attacks involve emergency management as well.

Law enforcement officers and agencies are intimately involved in emergency management as first responders to disasters and attacks. In most jurisdictions, law enforcement officers play the primary role in critical incident and disaster response due to the nature of their mission and due to the fact that police agencies operate 24 hours per day.[1] Law enforcement agencies are required to respond to service calls including disasters as part of their protection mission. The state government's "police power" to protect the health, safety, and welfare of their communities is the legal basis for emergency response.[2] The heaviest burden of calls for service falls upon municipal police departments due to population density in cities and due to the fact that they comprise the majority of American police.[3] However, there has been a tendency of many law enforcement agencies to deemphasize emergency management and to focus instead primarily on human-caused problems such as crime.[4] This book examines the linkages between emergency management, homeland security, and law enforcement.

Law enforcement refers to "the agencies and employees responsible for enforcing laws, maintaining public order, and managing public safety. The primary duties of law enforcement include the investigation, apprehension, and detention of individuals suspected of criminal offenses."[5] In terms of emergency management, the law enforcement duties of managing public safety and maintaining public order are paramount.

Law enforcement agencies do much more than enforce criminal law: they are also *first responders* to crises caused by human beings or natural disasters during times of need. A **first responder** is the initial emergency services government employee or agency to arrive at the scene of an accident, disaster, fire, crime scene, or call for assistance. First responders include police, firefighters, and paramedics.[6] First responders respond directly to the disaster by attacking the threat to reduce death, injury, and property damage. Law enforcement officers focus on closing dangerous areas and control at the scene of disasters, while firefighters and paramedics deal with extinguishing fires and medical emergencies.[7]

First responder agencies and personnel such as law enforcement are *local* and are thus close to the places where disasters, accidents, and crimes occur. They are also community members and have a vested interest in carrying out their oaths and rendering aid. For this reason, law enforcement personnel have major roles to play in the implementation of emergency management functions. Law enforcement personnel are often the first to arrive at the scene of a disaster, crime, or accident. They are familiar with local conditions, people, and geography. Law enforcement personnel are generally uniformed and highly visible in crisis situations. They help to provide immediate aid to those injured or in crisis, and help to secure the scene and assist others involved in the disaster or attack.[8] Due to their training, experience, and on-call availability, first responders are the first line of defense in emergency incidents. Law enforcement officers in particular possess the skillsets to provide rapid response to a wide variety of critical incidents.[9] The linkage between law enforcement and emergency management is the focus of this book.

Since the terrorist attacks of September 11, 2001 upon the United States, law enforcement agencies have moved strongly towards a *homeland security* focus. Indeed, it has been convincingly argued that American policing has since that time entered what Oliver calls the **Era of Homeland Security**.[10] Due to the fact that law enforcement officers are among the first responders to both terrorist attacks and natural disasters, this is arguably the typical means by which police officers and agencies become involved in both homeland security and emergency management.[11] The emphasis on homeland security has resulted in the situation in which there has been an unduly heavy concern with terrorist attacks while the more likely natural and human-made disasters have been deemphasized.[12] While homeland security and emergency management are not identical, emergency management is a vital component of homeland security.[13]

The connection between emergency management and homeland security is made manifest in the original **National Strategy for Homeland Security** issued by the federal government in 2002. The National Strategy for Homeland Security contains six essential missions, three of which deal with homeland security and three of which deal with emergency management. The first three essential missions deal with homeland security: (1) Intelligence and Warning, (2) Border and Transportation Security, and (3) Domestic Counterterrorism. The last three essential missions focus on emergency management: (4) Protecting Critical Infrastructure and Key Assets, (5) Defending Against Catastrophic Threats, and (6) Emergency Preparedness and Response.[14] While law enforcement agencies deal in some capacity with all six essential missions, the focus of this book is upon the three essential missions (4, 5, and 6) that deal with emergency management.

Areas 4, 5, and 6 recognize that natural disasters such as earthquakes, tornadoes, and hurricanes result in escalating losses of life and property in the United States. Property damage in particular continues to escalate due to population growth, increasing concentration of people in cities and vulnerable coastal areas, and deterioration of aging infrastructure such as roads, bridges, and tunnels. This requires a greater recognition of an emphasis on emergency management. The collective knowledge of emergency management must be better connected with first responders.[15]

Climate and weather-related events alone (fires, hurricanes, tornadoes, etc.) have resulted in a series of multi-billion-dollar disasters in the United States during the past ten years. For example, in 2017 such losses exceeded $300 billion. Increasing disaster preparedness utilizing emergency management approaches could significantly reduce these losses.[16] However, achieving disaster preparedness nationwide is difficult in part due to the existence of federalism in the United States.

Federalism

The American system of government is based upon **federalism**, in that political powers are divided between the national government and the state governments. The national government in Washington, D.C. operates under the enumerated powers contained in the U.S. Constitution. Thus, Congress, the federal courts, the president, and military and civilian personnel under the authority of the president operate on the basis of federal constitutional and statutory authority. Local governments (cities, counties, special districts) operate under state government authority. State governments possess all powers not delegated to the federal government and not prohibited by the U.S. Constitution. For this reason, the vast majority of law enforcement officers in the United States serve at the local and state levels of government.

American Law Enforcement: Number of Personnel

In 2018, there were a total of 17,541 state and local law enforcement agencies in the United States. These agencies collectively employed 1,214,260 employees, of which 787,565 were full-time sworn law enforcement officers.[17] City police officers comprise the majority of American police (465,891 full-time sworn officers in 11,824 agencies). County sheriff's deputies comprise the second largest group of 192,380 full-time sworn officers in 3,051 agencies. The 49 states that maintain state police forces collectively employ 60,451 full-time sworn officers. Special jurisdictions, such as colleges, universities, public schools, airports, tribes, etc., collectively employ a total of 68,843 full-time sworn officers.[18]

Since all disasters and critical incidents are ultimately local in impact, city, county, and state police are on the "front lines" of protecting and serving the public as first responders in emergency management and homeland security. This is why patrol officers must learn the skills necessary to assess the situation, maintain the perimeter, render aid, and perform rescue operations pending the arrival of supporting units.[19] Due to the fact that local law enforcement officers are usually the first responders to disasters and critical incidents, they are a vital component of emergency management.[20]

In 2016, the federal government maintained 132,110 full-time sworn law enforcement officers in 83 agencies.[21] Compared to local and state law enforcement, federal law enforcement officers comprise only a small percentage of police in the United States. In addition, federal law enforcement is focused more heavily on homeland security with a national focus rather than on the local focus of emergency management. Therefore, the involvement of federal law enforcement in emergency management tends to be much less than that of local and state police forces.

The U.S. Department of Justice employs the most visible federal law enforcement officers, including the FBI (Federal Bureau of Investigation), the U.S. Marshals Service (USMS), the DEA (Drug Enforcement Administration), and the Bureau of Alcohol, Tobacco, and Firearms (ATF). When the U.S. Department of Homeland Security was created after 9/11, several federal law enforcement agencies were placed under its administration. These include the TSA (Transportation Security Administration), U.S. Customs and Border Protection (CPB), U.S. Immigration and Customs Enforcement (ICE), and the U.S. Secret Service (USSS).[22]

The U.S. Department of Homeland Security recognizes the primacy of local and state law enforcement agencies in emergency management in their training materials. "Incidents typically begin and end locally and are managed on a daily basis at the lowest possible geographical, organizational, and jurisdictional level. However, there are instances in which successful incident management operations depend on the involvement of multiple jurisdictions, levels of government, functional agencies, and/or emergency responder disciplines. These instances require effective and efficient coordination across this broad spectrum of organizations and activities."[23] In addition, the Federal Emergency Management Agency (FEMA) maintains the Office of Law Enforcement Engagement and Integration (OLEEI), which "seeks to integrate the law enforcement, private sector security, and emergency management communities by enhancing communication and coordination between FEMA, private sector security, and state, local, tribal, and territorial law organizations."[24] This can be achieved by developing "an operating model for all facets of emergency management response (i.e., law enforcement personnel, firefighters, medical personnel, etc.) to delineate responsibilities during federally declared disasters."[25]

FEMA also supports state and local law enforcement agencies in emergency management training through its Emergency Management Institute (EMI), its Center for Domestic Preparedness (CDP), and its Federal Law Enforcement Training Centers (FLETC).

Both emergency management and homeland security are heavily interdisciplinary. This means that many different fields of study have coalesced to form these fields. Emergency management and homeland security draw from the knowledge created from criminal justice, public administration, public health, political science and law, engineering, geography, sociology, psychology, and the physical sciences of biology and chemistry. This book draws from all of these fields of study in order to distill meaningful knowledge each as contributed towards relating emergency management to law enforcement.[26]

It is important to clearly define the terminology discussed in this examination of the linkage between homeland security, emergency management, and law enforcement. Clear definitions reduce ambiguity between and among concepts. Good definitions assist in the meaningful transmission of knowledge and in recognizing the linkages between different fields of academic and practitioner research.[27] The body of knowledge that comprises emergency management consists of definitions, concepts, typologies and theories.[28] This body of knowledge is a resource that law enforcement professionals can draw upon to more effectively carry out their mission.

Terminology

Terminology deals with important definitions to provide a frame of reference to examine a particular field of study. Law enforcement as used in this book was defined above. Emergency management must also be clearly defined as part of applying emergency management to law enforcement.

The U.S. Department of Homeland Security defines **emergency management** as "the coordination and integration of all activities necessary to build, sustain, and improve the capability to prepare for, protect against, respond to, recover from or mitigate against threatened or actual natural disasters, acts of terrorism, or other manmade disasters."[29]

Emergency management is the application of technology, science, management, and planning for the purpose of effectively handling natural and manmade events that can cause injury or death to large numbers of people and cause extensive property damage to property accompanied by community disruption.[30] The task or job of the emergency manager is to prevent or reduce the impact of hazards, emergencies, and disasters. To this end, emergency management is about identifying and assessing risks accompanied by developing and implementing strategies for reducing these risks.[31] According to the National Governors Association, emergency management involves the integration of community stakeholders into the four phases of emergency management (mitigation, preparedness, response, and recovery) related to natural, and manmade hazards.[32]

The fundamental objectives of emergency management are to prevent injury and loss of lives and to protect property. Participants in emergency management should include local, state, and federal governments in addition to private sector organizations, entities, and private citizens.[33] Emergency managers should ideally serve to coordinate community resources to best deal with disasters and emergencies. This includes first responders, utility providers, public health agencies, charities, and private businesses.[34]

Emergency managers try to coordinate people, resources, and systems in relation to disasters and hazards by means of a collaborative, multidisciplinary process.[35] Emergency management focuses on **consequence management**, which deals with preparation for disasters, recovery operations, responses to disasters, and restoration.[36] For that reason, emergency management is not entirely within the purview of law enforcement or first responders. It is not entirely about emergency services or homeland security. It is both different from these things and similar to these things. Emergency management is more proactive and comprehensive than law enforcement or firefighting. Emergency management also involves the integration and coordination of public and private sector organizational risk reduction efforts.[37]

Emergency management's overall focus is on the administration of and *planning* for disasters, rather than a narrow focus on *response* to disasters. For that reason, emergency management is focused more on management than on first response. However, emergency managers need to have a basic understanding of first response principles and protocols in order to perform their jobs most effectively as emergency *managers.* Thus, emergency management is less about the study of emergencies than about the management of emergencies by reducing risk and solving problems.[38] It is thus much broader than homeland security.

All fifty states and all of the approximately 3,000 counties in the United States have a designated emergency management agency. However, there are fewer than 11,000 emergency management directors in the United States. Most local emergency management agencies have two or fewer full-time employees. Thus, the number of actual emergency management personnel is substantially smaller than the number of law enforcement officers.[39]

Each state government maintains a full-time emergency management director, most of whom are appointed by the governor. Major cities also typically employ full-time emergency managers. Counties, towns, and cities with less population typically do not maintain full-time emergency management personnel, choosing instead to utilize a part-time or volunteer emergency management workforce. Many jurisdictions with relatively low populations delegate their emergency management responsibilities to their EMS (Emergency Medical Services) agency.[40]

In the past, emergency management was viewed narrowly as a response function rather than as a proactive, "all-hazards" endeavor. This was reflected in low budgetary support from governments. Emergency management was seen as an adjunct or "add-on" function of local governments and was typically managed by someone from a first responder agency, such as police or fire service personnel. These personnel typically did not possess specific training or expertise in emergency management *per se.*[41]

As the field of emergency management has become more professionalized over the years (moving beyond conceptualizing the field as an extension of the duties of first responders), professional organizations in the field have defined the term. According to the IAEM (International Association of Emergency Managers), an emergency manager is an individual who possesses the skills, abilities, and knowledge to effectively operate a comprehensive emergency management program. Such an individual has a strategic vision regarding disasters and hazards and how to deal with them effectively and is able to communicate this to others inside a jurisdiction.[42]

Recognizing this, one way that emergency management has become more professional has been through professional organizations such as the IAEM, which supplies both continuing education and professional certification. The IAEM offers the Certified Emergency Management (CEM) credential. The Emergency Management Accreditation Program (EMAP) is offered by a private agency and has professionalized emergency management through common minimum standards for the profession.[43] The National Emergency Management Association (NEMA) is designed for state emergency management directors.

IAEM and NEMA do important work in the field of emergency management, but they possess relatively little visibility, influence, and political support.[44] Homeland security organizations generally have more influence over policy and usually receive more resources. The Disaster Preparedness and Emergency Response Association is an organization with members from both the public and private sectors. It offers both school-based educational programs and training. These and other groups provide practitioners with opportunities for learning and networking.[45]

Professional training by FEMA is another way that emergency management has increased in professional stature and visibility. FEMA maintains an Emergency Management Institute in Emmitsburg, Maryland to assist academics and practitioners of emergency management to increase their professional skills.[46] In addition to on-site training, FEMA operates online certification and certificate programs.

Another way that emergency management has become more professional is due to the expansion of emergency management course offerings at colleges and universities. There are more than 180 academic programs offering majors, minors, and courses in emergency management.[47] Academic courses, degrees, and certifications confer increased legitimacy to emergency management as a field. Emergency management courses organize materials from the social and physical sciences and orient this information into a body of substantive knowledge to effectively address crises faced in the field. In this way, professional degree programs assist students and practitioners in acquiring substantive knowledge in emergency management. This knowledge can be utilized to solve problems caused by natural and manmade forces.[48]

One of the goals of the study of emergency management is to take the body of knowledge that applies to the field and synthesize it in such a way as to provide the skills and competencies necessary to help law enforcement students and practitioners integrate this knowledge to be more effective on the job. **Education** is broader than **training**. Neither is a substitute for the other. Education is broader and deeper than training. Education focuses on theories and principles, while training focuses on teaching individuals how to perform specific tasks. Education teaches the theoretical principles of a profession and in so doing makes the individual better able to adapt to unforeseen circumstances.[49] Both education and training are necessary in order to be an effective emergency manager.

The study of emergency management enables law enforcement officers to develop or acquire the following skills: (1) knowledge of the full range of natural and technological threats facing the United States, (2) awareness about systems and techniques for managing community vulnerabilities, (3) knowledge of hazard vulnerability analysis, hazard mitigation, recovery, and response, (4) communication skills inside and outside organizations,

(5) organizational (management) skills, including strategic planning, human resources, and political management skills.[50]

Obtaining these skills helps to make those who possess them more valuable than the average emergency responder. The ability to integrate substantive knowledge contributed by many different disciplines is the mark of a professional. Although it is not required that a professional be competent in all technical skill areas, he or she must understand how these skill areas apply to emergency management overall. This will enable law enforcement officials with this background know-how to locate and to request services from other agencies when needed.[51]

Homeland security has become closely related to emergency management during the past twenty-two years. **Homeland security** is a focused national endeavor to prevent terrorist attacks within the United States and to reduce the vulnerability of the United States to terrorism. Homeland security also involves efforts to reduce the impact of terrorist attacks that cannot be avoided and to expedite recovery from terrorist attacks.[52]

Homeland security is concerned with *crisis management.* **Crisis management** deals with the prevention and protection from terrorist violence and the prosecution of perpetrators. It is primarily a law enforcement function.[53] However, it is also an intelligence function in that crisis management as part of prevention obtains information about the capabilities and intentions of terrorists and terrorist groups.

Both emergency management and homeland security deal heavily with disasters. FEMA defines **disaster** as "an occurrence of a natural catastrophe, technological accident, or human-caused event that has resulted in severe property damage, deaths, and/or multiple injuries."[54] Disasters can be natural or man-made. *Man-made disasters* are caused by the actions of human beings and can be either *accidental* (chemical incidents, airplane crashes) or *deliberate* (terrorism, riots, bombings, cyberattacks, etc.). *Natural disasters* occur independently from the actions of human beings and include floods, hurricanes, tornadoes, ice storms, etc. Deliberate man-made disasters are the main focus of homeland security. Emergency management focuses primarily on accidental man-made disasters and natural disasters.

Although emergency management pre-dates Homeland Security by more than fifty years, the concern with the terrorist threats posed to the United States since 2001 has resulted in emergency management being subsumed into Homeland Security. Emergency management though is far broader in scope and purpose than homeland security.[55] Statistically, hurricanes, earthquakes, and pandemics are much more likely than terrorist attacks to result in deaths and property damage. However, terrorism has been over-emphasized as a threat when compared to natural disasters.[56]

Natural disasters and man-made disasters are interdependent. Large numbers of people in urban areas are more susceptible to tornadoes, earthquakes, floods, hurricanes, mass shootings, and terrorist attacks than are persons living in rural communities. These are complex threats that overlap with each other.[57] Disasters emanate from relatively predictable interactions between risk and population density. Protecting the public from disasters and responding to them requires sophisticated processes. Emergency management endeavors to provide these processes based on accumulated knowledge.[58]

Emergency response is different from emergency management. Emergency response is narrower and more designed to deal effectively with immediate crises. Emergency management is broader and is focused upon a more holistic view – prevention, mitigation, response, recovery and the management methods (budgeting, planning, directing, staffing, coordinating evaluating, etc.) needed to reduce and respond to risks and damages from all causes. Emergency management also requires broad-based problem-solving skills and substantive knowledge of the causes of both man-made and natural disasters.[59]

Emergency management and law enforcement overlap. This book examines strategies, operations, and tactics with which to more effectively connect law enforcement with emergency management. Thus, strategy must be examined. It is important that law enforcement personnel have an understanding of the strategic objectives behind emergency management so that operations and tactics can be geared toward dealing more effectively with disasters and emergencies.[60] Strategy provides the objectives behind planning for law enforcement-based emergency management efforts. **Strategy** is defined as a mechanism that law enforcement agencies can utilize to determine *how to act* and *where to act*.[61] There are multiple sources of strategy regarding law enforcement in emergency management, including FEMA, the U.S. Department of Homeland Security, the Police Executive Research Forum, and the International Association of Chiefs of Police (IACP).[62] Chapter 8 examines law enforcement strategies in emergency management.

Law enforcement **operations** involve specific actions and activities in the field.[63] Operations are thus specific action plans based upon the strategy of a law enforcement endeavor. Police operations are plans of action based upon solid law enforcement strategy.[64] Operations involve selecting the best ways to deploy law enforcement personnel to improve emergency management. Operations also involve optimizing decision-making.[65] Chapter 9 examines law enforcement operations as related to emergency management.

Tactics in law enforcement deal with how personnel are deployed in a given situation and for a particular purpose. Tactics are utilized to put the overall plans developed during operations into action to fulfill the strategy. Action at the incident scene, such as a disaster is the primary focus of law enforcement tactics.[66] Tactics also involve utilizing the appropriate training and equipment on the scene of the critical incident.[67] Chapter 10 covers important emergency management law enforcement tactics.

Theory

Once terminology has been clarified to create a common set of definitions, **theory** (a coherent set of knowledge and principles with which to orient action) can be developed, understood, and utilized. Theory is based upon the recognition that in order to be most effective, there needs to be a link between a coherent set of knowledge and principles and practice. *Theory orients action* and provides a framework for understanding disasters and emergency management. Practice is based on both training and experience. Theory cannot take the place of practice, just as practice cannot take the place of theory. These principles apply very much to both emergency management and law enforcement. For example, patrol procedures (theory) establish the basic expectations of officers on the street. However, these patrol procedures may need to be modified in a given encounter with a member of the public based on actual practice in terms of the experiences and training of an officer.

Professionals learn from experience how to draw upon stored knowledge, including the body of knowledge presented in this book. The ability to make generalizations from past experience and past training and to apply them to emergency situations is a mark of an effective law enforcement professional. Emergency management knowledge represents a synthesis of first responder experiences, science, and management."[68] It is hoped that the knowledge presented in this book will reinforce the theoretical idea that law enforcement officers are *force multipliers* in effectively responding to critical incidents at the *intersection* of emergency management, homeland security, and policing.[69]

Theory is also comprised of **concepts** (mental "shortcuts" that assist in quickly understanding complex phenomena), **classifications** (ways to quickly differentiate between complex phenomena), and **typologies** (ways to analyze things of a different type, such as natural disasters versus human-caused disasters).[70] An important theoretical construct in emergency management is the Emergency Management Cycle.

Emergency Management Cycle

The **Emergency Management Cycle** is the basis for emergency management efforts and serves as a framework for understanding the emergency management process. The Emergency Management Cycle involves the steps that personnel involved in emergency management take in planning for and responding to disasters. The four-phase emergency management cycle is used both domestically and internationally by first responders, academics, and practitioners associated with the emergency management community.[71] The Emergency Management Cycle consists of four phases: (1) Mitigation, (2) Preparedness, (3) Response, and (4) Recovery.[72]

The first phase is **mitigation**. This is about efforts to prevent disasters from happening in terms of stopping disasters before they occur or at the minimum to reduce the impact of disasters that do occur.[73] For example, nailing boards across windows before a hurricane or placing sandbags around a house will reduce or eliminate property damage from a hurricane. This is mitigation in action: "An ounce of prevention is worth a pound of cure."

The second phase of the Emergency Management Cycle is **preparedness**. This means taking steps to get ready for a disaster in the event that a disaster occurs. For example, stockpiling bottled water and non-perishable food before an ice storm because you know the power will likely be out for several days is preparedness. Making plans and setting aside resources in advance is preparedness.[74]

In addition to supplies being obtained in advance, preparedness in emergency management also means that law enforcement, fire, and emergency medical services personnel should be properly trained in advance of a disaster occurring.[75] To facilitate this emergency management preparedness, the Federal Emergency Management Agency (FEMA) provides substantial training opportunities to law enforcement officers as well as emergency responders as part of preparedness for disasters. FEMA provides both face-to-face and online training either on site or at its training facility in Emmitsburg, Maryland.

In terms of mitigation and preparedness, there are FEMA subdivisions that provide support and assistance. FEMA's Mitigation Directorate maintains resources designed to take action before a disaster hits for the purpose of identifying risks in order to assist in reducing injuries, property damage, and to expedite recovery. FEMA operates analysis programs for floods, hurricanes and tropical storms, dams, and earthquakes. Also, the National Flood Insurance Program and its requirements about buildings in flood plains also support the mission of mitigation and preparedness.

Mitigation and preparedness are very important, but they have received less attention than they should. Historically, greater resources have been allocated to response and recovery than to mitigation and preparedness.[76]

The third phase of the Emergency Management Cycle is **response**. Response is about reaction to a disaster or catastrophic event. For example, the actions "on the ground" engaged in by first responders do in the aftermath of a major event, like a tsunami, mass shooting, earthquake, or hurricane. This includes taking actions such as securing the impact area, conducting search and rescue of survivors, providing emergency medical care, and sheltering victims and evacuees. Taking such response actions protects the affected population and limits damages as much as possible.[77]

This involves securing the impact area, conducting search and rescue of survivors, providing emergency medical care, and assisting with the sheltering victims and evacuees. The goal of response is to protect the population, to limit damages as much as possible, and to deal with the effects of **secondary impacts** ("disasters caused by the disaster") such as chemicals leaking into the floodwaters (Houston and Hurricane Harvey), mold and mildew diseases caused by flooding, outbreaks of illness caused by overflowing sewers and lack of clean water, etc.[78]

Law enforcement officers and other first responder agencies work with emergency managers to assess damage and coordinate the deployment of sullies and equipment. This also involves working with volunteers. At the site, these activities are often managed through an **Emergency Operations Center (EOC)**. Local law enforcement personnel and local emergency responders are the most visible players during the response period.[79]

In terms of federal government support to local law enforcement and first responders, realize that most of FEMA's resources are oriented towards response. To do this, FEMA utilizes a subdivision called the **NRCC (National Response Coordination Center)**. The NRCC is located in Washington and coordinates overall federal support for major disasters. The NRCC is activated by the FEMA administrator whenever he feels that a disaster is about to strike or has already struck. The NRCC activates FEMA's emergency support functions. The NRCC coordinates with the affected geographical areas and provides vital resources to support critical incident response. In this way, the NRCC provides emergency management coordination and resource deployment to the disaster.

Based on the overall situation and the NRCC assessment, FEMA's emergency response may utilize small teams trained in various areas including disaster medicine (National Disaster Medical System and the Disaster Medical Assistance Team), search and rescue in densely populated areas (Urban Search and Rescue), management of large numbers of dead bodies (Disaster Mortuary Operations Response Team), and donations management. It is easily apparent why FEMA is the nation's lead emergency management agency.

The fourth and final traditional stage of the Emergency Management cycle is **recovery**. Recovery deals with efforts to get the impacted area back to normal – to restore it as close to possible to its pre-disaster state. The most immediate goal of recovery is to restore the critical infrastructure (electricity, gas, potable water, functional roads, etc.) to the community. Restoring critical infrastructure and rebuilding may take an extended period.[80]

Recovery is both short-term and long-term. Short-term recovery is about "rehabilitation and relief" which sets up temporary solutions to make life easier and to bring about basic community functioning. For example, debris cleanup to allow transportation to occur; temporary housing, food, and clothing; restoring government services, etc. Long-term recovery is about reconstruction, such as rebuilding houses, businesses, roads, and bridges, and getting the economy functioning normally again. Achieving things requires many resources from outside the local areas such as insurance companies, private organizations, and state and federal governments.[81]

Since the events of 9/11, some academics and practitioners have argued that a fifth stage of the Emergency Management cycle has been added: **prevention**. Prevention deals with efforts of first responders and emergency managers on the job taking active measures to reduce the impact of disasters that are likely to happen, such as chemical spills, mass shootings, hurricanes, etc.[82] Taking actions to prevent terrorism, mass violence, etc. by means of intelligence operations is an example of prevention. Thus, prevention is a combination of preparedness and mitigation.

The Emergency Management cycle assists law enforcement agencies in planning for disasters. Planning for future disasters is vital for law enforcement agencies. Failing to do so can lead to unnecessary deaths and property damage within the jurisdiction. Law enforcement agencies should have plans in place for responding to disasters. This plan should be practiced through training, drills, etc.[83] These plans can be achieved through EOPs (Emergency Operations Plans) and by means of an Integrated Emergency Management System.

An **Emergency Operations Plan (EOP)** is a document that describes how an organization, such as a police department, will respond to and recover from all possible hazards, including disasters.[84] All organizations, both public and private, should have an EOP in place as part of sound management practice. Many law enforcement agencies, for example, have EOPs in place available for inspection on their websites. EOPs should take an "all hazards" approach to emergency management to address every known disaster scenario. An organization's EOP should incorporate all four phases of the Emergency Management cycle.

An **Integrated Emergency Management System** is a framework designed to increase emergency management capability of an area or jurisdiction by establishing a mechanism that enables first responder and emergency management agencies to work together in a coordinated way. This involves partnerships, coordination, and networking between and among agencies involved in emergency management.[85]

Most disasters will result in some degree of property damage, injury, or death. Disruption in traffic flow, electricity, communications systems, and water supplies may occur.[86] Planning by means of EOPs and Integrated

Emergency Management systems is essential to mitigate and respond to these possible effects.[87]

There are *three (3) levels of severity for disasters*: **Level I** (least severe – local resources can handle), **Level II** (moderate severity – involves both local and regional resources) and **Level III** (most severe – requires state and federal assistance).[88]

Planning for disasters will lessen the impact of disasters, both natural and man-made. However, plans can and do fail. It is impossible to plan for every contingency. In addition, resources are limited. Nevertheless, it is important for a community or a jurisdiction to have a disaster plan in place due to the potential consequences of a disaster.

Stakeholders in Emergency Management

Law enforcement agencies involved in emergency management should be aware of the environment in which government organizations operate. Although it is true that disasters affect everyone in society, some individuals and institutions have more influence than others.

A **stakeholder** is an individual or group with an interest in an emergency management endeavor and who is impacted by and cares about how an emergency management function turns out.[89]

A stakeholder is somebody affected by what an emergency management agency does–it is someone with "skin in the game" with regard to emergency management. Stakeholders matter, because we live in a republic or representative democracy. Government in the U.S. responds to the organized articulated demands brought to bear upon it. This means that what emergency management does is influenced by many stakeholders at the national, regional, and local levels. Emergency managers can go further and get more accomplished with stakeholder support than without it.

Thus, emergency management does not exist in a vacuum. Emergency management is affected by the political and economic environment. Working with stakeholders and getting their approval for what you are doing is much better than having stakeholders working against you. It is easier to do your job with stakeholder cooperation.

In order to be most effective, individuals and institutions working in emergency management should involve as many stakeholders as possible in making and implementing plans.[90] This includes doing things such as encouraging and maintaining relationships among stakeholders. When they know each other, it is more likely that they will cooperate. This applies to all four phases of the Emergency Management Cycle. This also applies to emergency management drills and practice exercises. This principle applies to emergency operations and recovery operations as well. FEMA training can be used not only to gain substantive knowledge, but to build relationships between agencies, jurisdictions, and individuals.

There are many ways to do this. One obvious way is in public meetings. Cities and counties have open public hearings on zoning. This is a chance to meet with stakeholders and to address their concerns. There are various citizen advisory committees as well. This gives an opportunity for emergency management and first responder personnel to interact with stakeholders.

With regard to community stakeholders, law enforcement and emergency management agencies should speak to schools and community organizations as well. Doing these things makes the agency visible to stakeholders. Emergency management and first responder personnel should be willing and able to answer questions and to come across as helpful and interested in stakeholder concerns. Recognize that stakeholders have different needs and different agendas. Working with stakeholders can serve two purposes: (1) it can give the emergency responder or emergency management agency a base of support in the community, and (2) it can derail opposition to agencies, which amounts to cooperation. Both of these things are beneficial to the emergency manager and first responder community.[91]

The objective is to obtain the cooperation of the community for what agencies are doing in the community. Agencies should paint a positive picture to the stakeholders. This will make the tasks of emergency management and first responder agencies easier.

There are types and categories of community stakeholders that should be understood by law enforcement agencies involved with emergency management. These are (1) **social groups**, (2) **economic groups**, and (3) **governmental groups**. There are subcategories within each.[92]

First are **social groups**. A **social group** is a collection of two or more people who interact and share common goals. The basic social group is the household (people who live together). It is certainly true that households do things such as attempting to prevent accidents, prepare for disasters, evacuate, and suffer losses. But a social group can be broader than this. It can also encompass clubs and voluntary associations.

Social groups can take actions to reduce their exposure to disasters, such as choosing to live in less hazard-prone locations and choosing to live in residences that are more resistant to disasters (such as an apartment rather than a trailer). Actions such as these are called **hazard adjustments**. Social groups can also certainly purchase hazard insurance and can choose to take mitigation measures, like boarding up their windows after receiving a hurricane warning. Doing many of these things requires economic resources that not all social groups possess. Even those with financial resources may choose not to take precautions due to laziness, lack of knowledge, etc.[93]

Moving beyond household social groups, there are **private sector groups** that involve more people. These include religious organizations, nongovernmental organizations, nonprofit organizations, and community-based organizations. These groups serve many different purposes. However, some private sector groups are involved with emergency management. For example, some religious organizations open up their facilities to disaster victims. Some nongovernmental organizations (like the American Red Cross) play significant roles in disaster response. Some community-based organizations also play a major role in emergency management.[94]

One type of community-based organization is called a **CERT (Community Emergency Response Team)**. These are usually seen in rural areas – those areas that possess few emergency medical services or fire services. A CERT is a group of homeowners that has organized to provide emergency services in their communities. These are trained emergency response volunteers at the neighborhood level. They can provide emergency services such as firefighting, first aid, search and rescue, and assisting first responders. For example, rural communities and rural subdivisions with private water, sewer, and neighborhood watch services outside city limits often maintain CERTs.[95]

There are also *economic groups* that are community stakeholders. **Economic groups** are closely related to businesses: they exist to make a profit for their owners. Businesses can be small (run directly by their owners) all the way up to multibillion-dollar international corporations. Small businesses, because they are locally owned and operated, are typically more cooperative with local emergency managers.[96]

There are exceptions to this: some large corporations are very cooperative with emergency managers for their own self-interests. These include mortgage banks, insurance companies, real estate developers, and home improvement stores. For-profit utility companies are also cooperative with emergency managers (power, solid waste, telecommunications companies, etc.). For-profit utilities want services restored as soon as possible after a disaster because it negatively impacts their revenues and thus their profits. But all businesses are afraid of and affected by disasters due to the very real possibility of **business interruption** and the resulting economic losses caused by a disaster.[97]

Another stakeholder consists of **governmental groups**. Governmental groups are part of the public sector. *Public sector* organizations are established by the government through the passage of laws by the legislature and are funded by taxes. Public sector agencies are placed under the executive branch of government (bureaucracies) for the purposes of coordination and control. In the United States, government agencies exist at the federal level, the state level, and the local level (counties and cities). These are local (city and county), state, and federal government agencies. These give law enforcement officers and emergency managers their budgets, training, and legal authority.

Local government first responders are the most initially visible public sector employees connected with emergency management. In a large-scale disaster involving FEMA, state and federal government employees become visible as well.[98]

City police and county sheriff's departments are the first to respond to emergencies and disasters because they are part of the *local government.* A local government is a county or city organization that performs services on behalf of the public. This includes law enforcement, firefighting, emergency medical services, and local emergency management.[99]

An important emergency management concept relating to governmental groups is mutual aid. **Mutual aid** involves the sharing of equipment and personnel between jurisdictions during times of disaster or large-scale emergency. Mutual aid is necessary due to the fact that disasters and emergencies often cross local jurisdictional boundaries and because local personnel and equipment resources are often insufficient to deal with a large-scale disaster or emergency.[100]

Many local governments maintain emergency managers as well. Their task is to engage in mitigation and preparation activities before disasters and to liaise with first responders and other emergency management agencies during disasters. Local emergency managers also issue warnings, share information with the community through media outlets, and assist in damage assessment and in the determination of the priorities of recovery and response efforts.[101]

Obviously, local police, emergency medical technicians, firefighters, and local emergency managers are stakeholders in terms of comprising a governmental group. But there are also **regional and national stakeholders** in terms of governmental groups. In terms of **regional stakeholders**, state emergency management agencies are the primary stakeholders. The majority of emergency management policies that affect first responders and state-level emergency managers are set at the state level. Such agencies provide the legal framework for emergency management agencies along with state legislatures.[102] For example, city police, county sheriff's personnel, and state police all enforce state statutory law.

State governments maintain emergency management agencies. These are called by a variety of names, including the state Dept. of Homeland Security, the state Emergency Management Agency, or the state Homeland Security Agency. These state agencies work with local and federal emergency management agencies during times of disaster. State emergency management agencies are often affiliated with the governor's office, though some are operated as independent agencies.[103]

As the chief executive of the state government, state governors have the authority to declare both disasters and emergencies within their states. In addition, state governors possess the authority to call up and deploy the

National Guard. The **National Guard** is a military reserve force maintained under the authority of state governments under the control of the governor. During times of emergency or disaster, National Guard personnel can be deployed to assist local and state law enforcement personnel to maintain law and order, provide medical aid, conduct rescue operations, or provide other services.[104]

During public health emergencies (such as COVID-19), some state constitutional provisions and laws give the governor expansive authority in the event that such an emergency is formally declared to order quarantines and suspend state statutes.[105] For example, New York allows for extensive business closings, area quarantines, and curfews.[106] This was observed during the initial year of the COVID-19 outbreak in 2020-2021.

In the event that a state is overwhelmed by the scope and magnitude of a disaster or emergency, the governor can request mutual aid from other states through the **EMAC (Emergency Management Assistance Compact)**. The EMAC is maintained by the National Association of Emergency Managers. Aid and assistance can be requested from the federal government in the event that pooled state resources are insufficient to deal with the situation.[107]

All fifty states, Washington, D.C., and the U.S. Virgin Islands, Puerto Rico, and Guam are members of EMAC. Congress recognized EMAC in federal law in 1996. State-level mutual corporation during the aftermath of Hurricane Katrina in 1995 was considered to be successful under EMAC.[108]

With regard to national stakeholders and governmental groups, officially the U.S. Department of Homeland Security is the biggest stakeholder. In reality, its FEMA subdivision is the major federal government stakeholder. Other national stakeholders are the Environmental Protection Agency (EPA), the National Weather Service, the U.S. Army Corps of Engineers, and the U.S. Geological Survey (earthquakes and volcanoes).[109]

The president of the United States has the authority under federal law to declare a federal disaster. If such a presidential declaration is made, federally funded resources can be dispatched to states and localities.[110]

Individuals working in the field of emergency management need to know the different types of stakeholders and their roles at all levels of American government.[111] Keep in mind that most law enforcement officers are employed by local governments. Local governments have discretion in terms of the resources that they devote to emergency management. However, FEMA and state agencies also impact these local decisions.

As noted previously, city and county governments request aid from the state in the event of a major disaster. If a state believes that its own resources will be insufficient to deal with the disaster, it will request aid from the federal government following a presidential disaster declaration. These requests are usually approved. About 75% of state requests are granted by presidents.

Those that are denied are usually because FEMA does not agree that the state has exhausted its resources on the disaster in question.[112]

Most presidential disaster declarations are in response to natural disasters. Tornadoes, hurricanes, floods, and earthquakes accounted for more than eighty percent of disaster declarations between 1964 and 2011.[113]

Emergency management has been handled and implemented differently by governmental stakeholders over the years. The federal government has tended to emphasize plans, conceptual frameworks, and hierarchy. Local first responder agencies have shown a preference to emphasize their own duties and command structures (police, fire, etc.) without extensive coordination. In addition, local law enforcement and fire agencies have tended to view emergency management as a "subset" of their primary tasks. This works against the holistic "all hazards" approach advocated by the emergency management profession.[114]

These are some of the major stakeholders in emergency management. Emergency managers and first responders must deal with stakeholders. They can either be an asset to the emergency manager or a hindrance. The most effective emergency managers know how to deal with constituents as allies. When constituents and emergency managers are on the same page, things go more smoothly in terms of the four phases of emergency management, and also in obtaining more resources to support the emergency management effort.

Stakeholder Power and Influence

Stakeholders vary in terms of power and influence. The effective emergency manager and first responder needs to know what power is and the types of power available to both the emergency manager and to various stakeholders in order to affect governmental decisions related to emergency management.

Stakeholders possess different degrees of power with regard to how well they are able to influence the emergency management process. Some stakeholders have more power than others, in other words. "**Power** is the capacity to influence the behavior of others." A person does not need to be your boss in order to have power over you. Power does not depend entirely upon one's job title or official position. Due to human nature, many people attempt to utilize power to influence the behavior of others in the workplace and at home.

In terms of the emergency management process, stakeholders possess varying levels of power. The ultimate goal of using power is to influence the behavior of others – to get others to do what you want them to do.

There are many types of power, including reward power, coercive power, legitimate power, expert power, referent power, and information power.[115]

In addition, realize that *power* can operate *upward or downward.* **Upward** involves trying to influence those with more resources and authority than you have. **Downward** deals with a situation in which someone with more resources and authority tries to get someone to do their bidding.[116]

The most primitive forms of power are *reward power* and *coercive power.* First is **reward power**: this is someone's ability to influence others by providing something desirable in compensation for doing what the giver wants – rewarding desirable behavior. For example, a pay raise or more resources for an agency. Reward power is closely associated with coercive power.[117]

Coercive power is an individual's ability to influence others by means of punishment for undesirable behavior. Ex: firing an employee for failing to perform the job; the federal government making the decision to cut off grants to states that do not comply with federal policies, etc. One potential problem that can arise from the use of coercive power occurs when people retaliate by behaving passive-aggressively, falsifying documents, etc.[118] The other types of power are more subtle and sophisticated.

Legitimate power is the ability to influence others to do one's bidding because others see the holder of power as entitled to being obeyed because of his/her position or rank.[119] For example, managers have official authority to supervise employees and to hold them accountable for performance. We expect this as part of the job. In government, we might give legitimate power to a first responder because we respect his or her position, status, etc.

Expert power is related to legitimate power. This is a person's ability to exert power over others due to his or her technical expertise or specialized skills.[120] For example, a police officer might defer to the opinion of an emergency medical technician about the likely cause of a stab wound on a crime victim. Having special skills, knowledge, or training that the average person lacks can give an individual expert power.

Next is **referent power**. Referent power is an individual's ability to influence the behavior of others as a result of being liked or admired. It is about a person's desire to be like the power holder or simply to please the power holder.[121]

Finally, we have **information power**. This is power a person can have over others due to the ability to provide important factual information about a situation – information that others lack.[122] For example, a coworker went to an important meeting and found out things that were about to happen to the emergency management organization that had not yet been made publicly available. The person with this information has power and influence over others, who are likely to listen to the information provider's opinions and recommendations. It is a short-term power. However, people who have good "gossip connections" on the job tend to keep information power over time.

Remember that power can be used *upward or downward.* Human beings often engage in the use of power to advance their own agendas and to attempt to better their own situation. People want to get the most for themselves. This is not a secret! But emergency managers need to keep these things in mind.

Power can be used on the job by first responders and emergency managers. Power can also be utilized at the macro level to affect the emergency management policy process.

Emergency Management Policy Process

Because first responders and most emergency managers work for government agencies, it is necessary to discuss what public policy is and the policy process. This is needed because the stakes are high in terms of shaping what governments do with regard to emergency management. Stakeholders want what is best for themselves. One way they can get it is by trying to influence public policy and the policy process.

It is necessary to possess a basic knowledge and understanding of both *public policy* and the *public policy process.* **Public policy** is essentially the actions and activities that a government chooses to do or not to do.[123] In other words, public policy deals with the actions and decisions made by a government.

These definitions to public policy illustrate that American governments respond to real or perceived problems by means of taking actions designed to "do something" about the problem or issue. Elected officials give money and legal authority to government bureaucracies to "handle" or to "deal with" an issue or problem of public policy. For example, in emergency management, government responds to real or perceived problems in this area by establishing and paying for bureaucratic agencies (FEMA, police, firefighters, etc.) for the purpose of having such agencies "do something" about disaster response.

How government organizations "handle" the problem or issue has a "real-world" effect on society. For example, first responders attempt to render aid at the scene of a disaster. FEMA provides training on handling water contamination after a tsunami. How emergency managers, first responders, and other bureaucratic organizations implement public policy has a significant impact.

One should also have knowledge of the *public policy process.* The **public policy process** explains how issues become identified as problems to be addressed that later become public policy. Getting something, such as emergency management, part of the law or public policy is important because then the government will concentrate resources (money, personnel, etc.) on it. This is one of the goals of exercising stakeholder power. Law enforcement stakeholders can influence the public policy process in several ways. They can advocate for or against specific policies. They can testify and share their practical experience as first responders to critical incidents.[124]

The public policy process consists of five steps: (1) agenda setting, (2) policy formulation, (3) policy adoption (4) implementation, and (5) policy evaluation.[125] Each step will be briefly examined in turn for the purpose of demonstrating the points in the process in which emergency management stakeholders exert power and influence.

A precursor to beginning the policy process is **problem identification**. Before anything else can occur, an issue that should be appropriately addressed by government must be identified. Here, interest groups, government employees, or the media bring an issue to public attention, where it is discussed. Interested or concerned individuals or groups communicate their desire to have government "do something" about the issue to elected officials.[126]

Agenda setting is the first major step of the policy process. In **agenda setting**, a particular policy issue that has been identified is selected as a priority from among other competing issues.[127] Because there are many competing issues and many persons attempting to influence elected officials, not all issues that have been identified as problems can be addressed due to the lack of time and other resources. Thus, advocates of a policy must employ various strategies, such as media campaigns, protests, and letter-writing campaigns, in order to persuade elected officials to place the issue on the agenda. A tried-and-true strategy in agenda setting is to wait for a disaster to occur. This will get media attention. Using a **focusing event** like this to provide a **window of opportunity** to get noticed by government decision-makers is an intelligent strategy and an effective use of power. Once this has occurred, the policy issue moves to the next steps.

Policy formulation and policy adoption are the next steps of the policy process. In **policy formulation and policy adoption**, proposed solutions to deal with the issue or problem are created, discussed, and debated.[128] The decisions about how to achieve the policy are made in terms of what changes to laws must be made and which government bureaucracy will be delegated the authority and resources necessary to implement the policy are selected and created. This includes writing the bills (proposed laws) for consideration by the legislature, gaining the necessary majority votes, and persuading the executive to sign the bill into law.

Because the federal government has the greatest ability to raise revenue among all governments in the United States, it often chooses to establish grant programs (such as FEMA's Emergency Management Performance Grant) to distribute federal funds to state and local law enforcement agencies. The local and state law enforcement agencies must agree to follow federal mandates and guidelines regarding how the grant is to be implemented. Because state and local funding sources are much more limited than federal funding sources, it has been convincingly argued that the "carrot" of federal grants for emergency management and crime control functions is the area in which federal public policy can have the most impact upon local and state law enforcement agencies.[129] In a similar way, state governments can also distribute state grants to local law enforcement agencies.

With regard to major policy formulation and policy adoption, if a law is not successfully made or changed, the policy process ends here. However, if and when a law is made or changed, the next step of the policy process begins.

Implementation is the fourth step of the policy process. **Implementation** consists of the concrete actions of executive branch government bureaucracies to carry out the policy that was made through law.[130] Implementation by government organizations is necessary to make change occur by putting the policy into effect because elected officials cannot implement the policies that they make by themselves. Doing so requires the efforts of government employees. Bureaucracies then must, through the chain of command, take the steps necessary to make change occur by implementing the policy. Bureaucrats have the greatest influence over policy implementation because legislatures typically enact vague laws, delegating discretion to government agencies to "fill in the details" through implementation efforts. When bureaucrats interpret and apply vague laws, they are making what amounts to policy.[131] How a policy is implemented makes all the difference with regard to its effectiveness in dealing with a policy issue.

Local and state law enforcement agencies can serve as "proving grounds" to evaluate the efficiency and effectiveness of state and federal public policy initiatives in emergency management. This is true because how a policy works "on the ground" may very well be different from how it was intended to work "on paper." If grant-funded programs are determined to be effective, they may be increased or at least maintained.[132]

Once a policy has been implemented, the fifth step of the policy process can occur: evaluation. **Policy evaluation** examines the extent to which a policy actually achieved its intended results.[133] Did the policy achieve its objectives and goals? This is important to determine, because only in this way can it be discerned if the money and effort that was expended were worth the cost in political terms.

Stakeholders and Government organizations, through their employees, affect all phases of the policy process. They can affect problem identification by contacting the media, elected officials, etc. about issues or problems that they want to be addressed in the emergency management arena. Similarly, government employees can write letters to elected officials or give media interviews in which they express a preference for a particular policy. Doing so impacts agenda setting.

In addition, stakeholders and government employees can affect policy formulation by testifying before legislative committees about their views regarding the pros and cons of particular policies being considered. Government employees possess their greatest influence over policy implementation.[134] Finally, policy evaluation is conducted by bureaucratic agency personnel, because they are charged with determining the effectiveness of their implementation efforts. The results of these policy evaluations can result in the continuation, modification, or termination of the policy in the future.[135]

When a stakeholder gets something on the public policy agenda, he or she is using power to the maximum extent. This is true because the government has made a law or policy to give the stakeholder what he or she seeks. Even after a policy is made, how the agency uses its discretion to emphasize certain things gives stakeholders new opportunities to use power. An effective law enforcement agency involved in emergency management must be aware of "how the game is played." If he or she, or if his or her organization wants things to change and to be effective in his or her role, they have to play by these rules.

Notes

1. Jay Levinson and Hayim Granot, *Transportation Disaster Response Handbook*, San Diego, Academic Press, 2002: 111.
2. William C. Banks, *The Legal Landscape for Emergency Management in the United States*, New American Foundation, February 2011: 8.
3. Nancy E. Marion and Willard M. Oliver, *The Public Policy of Crime and Criminal Justice*, 2nd Edition, Boston, Pearson Prentice-Hall, 2012: 323.
4. Karen M. Hess, Christine H. Orthmann, and Henry Cho, *Police Operations: Theory and Practice*, 6th Edition, Clifton Park, NY, Delmar Cengage Learning, 2014: 290.
5. bjs.ojp.gov/topics/law-enforcement
6. David E. McEntire, *Introduction to Homeland Security: Understanding Terrorism With an Emergency Management Perspective*, New York, John Wiley and Sons, Inc., 2009: 319.
7. David A. McEntire, *Disaster Response and Recovery: Strategies and Tactics for Resilience*, 2nd Edition, Hoboken, John Wiley and Sons, Inc., 2015: 45.
8. Jason R. Jenkins, "Foreword: Law Enforcement: A Key Role During Disasters and Crisis," in *The Role of Law Enforcement in Emergency Management and Homeland Security*, Mark R. Landahl and Tanya E. Thornton, Eds., Bingley, United Kingdom, Emerald Publishing, Ltd., 2021: xvii.
9. Tonya E. Thornton, Patrick R. Baxter, and C. Tyler Goodwin, "Introduction: Exploring the Role of Law Enforcement in Emergency Management Throughout 2020" in *The Role of Law Enforcement in Emergency Management and Homeland Security*: 3.
10. Willard M. Oliver, *Policing in an Era of Homeland Security*, New York, Oxford University Press, 2020: ix.

11. Marion and Oliver, *The Public Policy of Crime and Criminal Justice*: 336.
12. David A. McEntire, "The Historical Challenges Facing Emergency Management and Homeland Security," *Journal of Emergency Management*, Vol. 5, No. 4, July/August 2007: 17.
13. McEntire, *Introduction to Homeland Security*: 11.
14. Office of Homeland Security, *National Strategy for Homeland Security* (2002): https://www.dhs.gov/sites/default/files/publications/nat-strat-hls-2002.pdf
15. B. Wayne Blanchard, "The New Role of Higher Education In Emergency Management," *Journal of Emergency Management*, Vol. 1, No. 2, Summer 2003: 30.
16. Corey Olszewski and Laura Sibeneck, "Emergency Management Collaboration: A Review and New Collaboration Cycle," *Journal of Emergency Management*, Vol. 19, No. 1, January/February 2021: 57.
17. U.S. Department of Justice, Office of Justice Programs, Bureau of Justice Statistics, *Census of State and Local Law Enforcement Agencies, 2018-Statistical Tables*: 4.
18. Ibid.
19. Lewis Eakins, "Integrating Law Enforcement & Emergency Management," January 21, 2015: https://domesticpreparedness.com/articles/integrating-law-enforcement-emergency-management
20. Ibid.
21. U.S. Department of Justice, Office of Justice Programs, Bureau of *Justice Statistics, Federal Law Enforcement Officers, 2016-Statistical Tables*: 1 and 3.
22. Marion and Oliver, *The Public Policy of Crime and Criminal Justice*: 314.
23. *National Incident Management System*, Washington, DC: Department of Homeland Security, Federal Emergency Management Agency, 2008: 5.
24. U.S. Department of Homeland Security, Federal Emergency Management Agency, Office of Law Enforcement Engagement and Integration: https://www.fema.gov/about/offices/law-enforcement
25. Ibid.
26. McEntire, *Introduction to Homeland Security*: 11.
27. McEntire, "Emergency Management Theory: Issues, Barriers, and Recommendations for Improvement," *Journal of Emergency Management*, Vol. 3, No. 3, May/June 2005: 45.
28. Ibid.
29. *National Incident Management System*, Washington, DC: Department of Homeland Security, Federal Emergency Management Agency, 2008: 5.
30. T. E. Drabek, *Introduction to Emergency Management: Principles and Practices for Local Government*, Edited by T.E. Drabek and G.J. Hoetmer, Washington: ICMA, 1991: xvii, cited and quoted in Michael K. Lindell, Carla Prater, and Ronald W. Perry, *Introduction to Emergency Management*, Hoboken: John Wiley and Sons, Inc., 2007: 6.
31. Lindell, Prater, and Perry, *Introduction to Emergency Management*: 7.
32. B. Wayne Blanchard, "Background 'Think Piece' For the Emergency Management Roundtable Meeting EMI, March 5-6, 2007 On What is Emergency Management and What are the Principles of Emergency Management," FEMA EMI Institute, Emmittsburg, MD, March 2, 2007: 5.

33. Michael J. Fagel, Editor, *Principles of Emergency Management: Hazard Specific Issues and Mitigation Strategies,* Boca Raton, CRC Press/Taylor and Francis Group, 2012: 6.
34. Maureen Long, "Just What Is It Emergency Managers Do, Anyway," *Journal of Emergency Management,* Vol. 1, No. 1, Spring 2003: 13.
35. Olszewski and Siebeneck, "Emergency Management Collaboration: A Review and New Collaboration Cycle": 59-60.
36. McEntire, *Introduction to Homeland Security*: 12 and 21.
37. Fagel, *Principles of Emergency Management*: xiv-xv.
38. Blanchard, "Background 'Think Piece" for the Emergency Management Roundtable Meeting," quoting Robert Freitag: 5.
39. Walter S. Topp, "Making the Transition From Law Enforcement to Emergency Management: Organizational, Occupational, and Cultural Issues," *Journal of Emergency Management,* Vol. 17, No. 1, January/February 2019: 48.
40. Jerome H. Kahan, "Emergency Management and Homeland Security: Exploring the Relationship," *Journal of Emergency Management,* Vol. 13, No. 6, November/December 2015: 486.
41. Robert O. Schneider, "An Overview of the 'New' Emergency Management", *Journal of Emergency Management,* Vol. 2, No. 1, Winter 2004: 26.
42. R. Ditch, *Professionalism in Emergency Management*: Falls Church, IAEM, 2003: 12, cited and quoted in Lindell, Prater, and Perry, *Introduction to Emergency Management*: 445. Emphasis added.
43. William A. Waugh, Jr., Emergency Management Today and Tomorrow," *Journal of Emergency Management,* Vol. 1, No. 1., Spring, 2003: 6.
44. Richard Sylves, "Why Revolutionary Change is Needed in Emergency Management," *Journal of Emergency Management,* Vol. 3, No. 6, November/December 2005: 15.
45. R. Ditch, *Professionalism in Emergency Management,* cited and quoted in Lindell, Prater, and Perry, *Introduction to Emergency Management*: 453.
46. Ibid.
47. Waugh, Foreword to *Principles of Emergency Management*: xv.
48. Lindell, Prater, and Perry, *Introduction to Emergency Management*: 460.
49. Ibid.
50. Ibid: 452.
51. Ibid: 452-453.
52. McEntire, *Introduction to Homeland Security*: 7.
53. Ibid: 12 and 21.
54. https://www.fema.gov/pdf/plan/glo.pdf
55. Kahan, "Emergency Management and Homeland Security: Exploring the Relationship": 483.
56. William L. Waugh, Jr., "The 'All-Hazards' Approach Must Be Continued," *Journal or Emergency Management,* Vol. 2, No. 1, Winter 2004: 11-12.
57. Schneider, "An Overview of the 'New' Emergency Management:" 25-26.
58. Attila J. Hertelendy and Frederick M. Birkle, Jr., "The New Normal: A Catalyst for Leadership Adaptation in a Tumultuous World-Let's Stop Applying 20th Century Solutions to 21st Century Problems in Emergency

Management," *Journal of Emergency Management,* Vol. 19, No. 4, July/August 2021: 323.
59. William L. Waugh, Jr., "The Principles of Emergency Management," *Journal of Emergency Management,* Vol. 5, No. 3, May/June 2007: 16.
60. Willard M. Oliver, *Policing In An Era of Homeland Security,* New York: Oxford University Press, 2020: 103.
61. Ibid: 104.
62. Ibid: xi.
63. Karen M. Hess, Christine H. Orthmann, and Henry Cho, *Police Operations: Theory and Practice,* 6th Edition, Clifton Park, NY, Delmar Cengage Learning, 2014: 3.
64. Oliver, *Policing In An Era of Homeland Security:* 139.
65. Ibid: xi.
66. Ibid: 187.
67. Ibid: xi.
68. Waugh, Foreword to *Principles of Emergency Management*: xii.
69. Thornton, Baxter, and Goodwin, "Introduction: Exploring the Role of Law Enforcement in Emergency Management Throughout 2020": 8
70. McEntire, "Emergency Management Theory: Issues, Barriers, and Recommendations for Improvement": 45.
71. Matt Rosenberg, "The Disaster Cycle" at ThoughtCo, https://www.thoughtco.com/the-disaster-cycle-1434979
72. Thornton, Baxter, and Goodwin, "Introduction: Exploring the Role of Law Enforcement in Emergency Management Throughout 2020": 2.
73. Lindell, Prater, and Perry, *Introduction to Emergency Management*: 10.
74. Ibid.
75. Ibid.
76. Ibid: 14.
77. Ibid: 12.
78. Ibid.
79. Ibid: 13.
80. Ibid.
81. Ibid.
82. Kahan, "Emergency Management and Homeland Security: Exploring the Relationship": 487.
83. Hess, Orthmann, and Cho, *Police Operations: Theory and Practice*: 290.
84. http://www.calhospitalprepare.org/emergency-operations-plan
85. Fagel, *Principles of Emergency Management: Hazard Specific Issues and Mitigation Strategies* 6.
86. Ibid: 3.
87. Ibid: 2.
88. Ibid: 4.
89. Lindell, Prater, and Perry, *Introduction to Emergency Management*: 21.
90. Ibid: 29.
91. Ibid: 21-30.
92. Ibid: 21-28.

93. Ibid: 21-22.
94. Ibid: 22-23.
95. Ibid: 22.
96. Ibid: 24.
97. Ibid.
98. Ibid: 25-26.
99. McEntire, *Disaster Response and Recovery*: 45.
100. Ibid: 46.
101. Ibid.
102. Lindell, Prater, and Perry, *Introduction to Emergency Management*: 25-26.
103. McEntire, *Disaster Response and Recovery*: 49.
104. Ibid: 51.
105. Banks, *The Legal Landscape for Emergency Management in the United States:* 25.
106. Ibid: 27.
107. McEntire, *Disaster Response and Recovery*: 51.
108. Banks, *The Legal Landscape for Emergency Management in the United States:* 27-28.
109. Lindell, Prater, and Perry, *Introduction to Emergency Management*: 27.
110. McEntire, *Disaster Response and Recovery*: 52.
111. Ibid.
112. Ibid: 28.
113. Daniel W. Martin, "The Shifting Paradigms of a Profession: Calming Conflicts Between Homeland Security and Emergency Management," *Journal of Emergency Management,* Vol. 9, No. 5, September/October 2011: 13.
114. Sylves, "Why Revolutionary Change is Needed in Emergency Management": 17.
115. McEntire, *Disaster Response and Recovery:* 31.
116. Ibid: 32-34.
117. Ibid: 31-32.
118. Ibid.
119. Ibid: 32.
120. Ibid.
121. Ibid.
122. Ibid.
123. Joseph Losco and Ralph Baker, *Am Gov 2017-2018,* 5th Edition, New York, McGraw-Hill Education, 2017: 419.
124. Marion and Oliver, *The Public Policy of Crime and Criminal Justice:* 67 and 336.
125. Losco and Baker, *Am Gov 2017-2018:* 419-422.
126. Ibid: 419.
127. Ibid: 420.
128. Ibid: 420-421.
129. Marion and Oliver, *The Public Policy of Crime and Criminal Justice:* 326.
130. Losco and Baker, *Am Gov 2017-2018*: 421.
131. Ibid.
132. Marion and Oliver, *The Public Policy of Crime and Criminal Justice:* 326-327.
133. Losco and Baker, *Am Gov 2017-2018*: 422-423.
134. Marion and Oliver, *The Public Policy of Crime and Criminal Justice:* 79.
135. Ibid: 79-81.

Chapter 2

HISTORY AND DEVELOPMENT OF EMERGENCY MANAGEMENT

To understand where emergency management is today, we need to learn something about the history of emergency management. Today we think in terms of the Federal Emergency Management Agency (FEMA) as the lead emergency management organization in the United States. But this has only been the case since FEMA began operations in 1979. The federal government has been "late to the game" of emergency management in historical terms since the United States began under our present constitution in 1789.

Emergency Management Before FEMA

Historically, emergency management was seen a more or less strictly a matter for local communities (towns, villages, counties, cities) to handle. Prior to the 20th century, the federal government had little involvement with disaster response or what we would today call emergency management. The federal government got involved in disaster relief only rarely. For example, in 1803 the federal government appropriated funds to aid Portsmouth, New Hampshire following a devastating fire.[1] In 1889, the newly-formed American Red Cross engaged in disaster recovery following the deaths of more than two thousand people as a result of the Johnstown, Pennsylvania flood. Following the 1906 San Francisco earthquake, the U.S. Army engaged in direct actions to fight fires and to provide law enforcement assistance. The American Red Cross also participated in disaster recovery. In this way, the American Red Cross became a primary relief agency in emergency management.[2]

Before 1900, emergency management was almost entirely a local government and individual responsibility. Towns, cities, counties, and states were basically "on their own" with the exception of sporadic federal appropriations and interventions to deal with specific disasters. During World War I, the federal government began to engage in emergency management in terms of what would later be called civil defense. In 1917, the U.S. Council of National Defense (consisting of federal cabinet secretaries and a presidentially appointed advisory committee) led state and local efforts to practice safety drills, establish civilian civil defense patrols, and deploy air raid sirens.[3] This served as a model for civil defense efforts leading up to World War II. In 1941 the Office of Civilian Defense (OCD) was established. The OCD served as a liaison between federal and state civil defense efforts during World War II. However, the OCD was eliminated in 1945.[4]

Civil Defense (CD): The Forerunner of Emergency Management

During the Cold War between the U.S. and the former Soviet Union, emergency management efforts shifted towards Civil Defense (CD) designed to mitigate the effects of a nuclear war. 1950s legislation caused federal emergency management responsibilities to be fragmented across dozens of federal agencies.[5] The Civil Defense Act of 1950 was designed to establish a national civil defense policy that was to be implemented by the states. This led to the development and dissemination of nuclear shelter building plans in suitable buildings, the placement of black and orange Fallout Shelter signs, the stockpiling of food (consisting of crackers and hard candy), canned water, other survival supplies, and an attack warning system.[6] Local Civil Defense agencies recruited volunteers and trained them to manage fallout shelters and operate radiation detection devices. Civil Defense was very active during the 1950s and early 1960s but diminished in importance under the Johnson administration. What remained of the Civil Defense system was absorbed into the U.S. Department of Defense's Defense Civil Preparedness Agency during the Nixon administration.[7]

Federal Involvement in Natural Disaster Recovery

With regard to natural disasters, it was not until the late 1920s that the federal government began any systematic or regular involvement in emergency or disaster management. Following a devastating multi-state flood that occurred along the Mississippi River in 1927, Congress enacted the Lower Mississippi Flood Control Act. In 1933 Congress created the RFC (Reconstruction Finance Company) to provide loans to repair and reconstruct state and local government buildings damaged by earthquakes. The U.S. Army Corps of Engineers also began work on dams and levees to control flooding (as part of mitigation efforts) during that decade.[8] Between 1803 and 1950, Congress enacted more than one hundred separate laws related to providing federal aid for disasters. Congress thus chose to deal separately with most disasters in an uncoordinated and piecemeal fashion.[9]

The Federal Disaster Act of 1950 was enacted to provide federal relief to local communities. This law set an important precedent for modern patterns of federal-state disaster relief, gave the president the authority to declare a major disaster, and enabled state governors to request federal disaster aid through the president.[10]

In the aftermath of the extensive damage caused to Louisiana and Florida by Hurricane Betsy, Congress enacted the National Flood Insurance Act (1968). This important law made federally-backed flood insurance available as a risk reduction strategy.[11] Following Hurricane Camille, a catastrophic Category 5 hurricane that hit Mississippi, Congress enacted the Disaster Relief Act of 1969. This law created an official called a Federal Coordinating Officer (FCO), who was appointed by the president to manage federal disaster assistance "on the ground" at affected areas.[12]

In 1970 the Disaster Relief Act was intended by Congress to consolidate federal disaster recovery programs.[13] The law was amended in 1974 to provide expanded resources to individuals and communities impacted by disasters through grants to local and state governments, nonprofit organizations, and unemployment insurance compensation to those left unemployed due to a disaster.[14] However, neither the 1970 law nor the 1974 amendments achieved their intended purposes in that by the late 1970s, more than one hundred federal agencies were involved in different aspects of emergency management.[15]

Congress granted the president the authority in 1976 to declare a national emergency and to activate federal disaster response capabilities in the National Emergencies Act. Under this law, presidents have the sole discretion to determine what constitutes a national emergency. Presidents simply declare the presence of such a national emergency, notify Congress, and announce which federal laws will be invoked.[16]

The Creation of the Federal Emergency Management Agency

Prior to the 1970s, there existed a piecemeal federal effort of disaster relief services. Dozens of federal agencies dealt with emergency relief and disaster services in an uncoordinated manner. Following the impact of four major hurricanes and the Three Mile Island nuclear incident during the 1970s, the federal government finally saw the need for centralized disaster coordination.[17] To this end, The Federal Emergency Management Agency (FEMA) was created in 1979.[18] FEMA was given two missions: (1) emergency management and (2) civil defense. The creation of the agency brought the

Federal Preparedness Agency from the General Services Administration, the Federal Disaster Assistance Administration from the Department of Housing and Urban Development, and the Defense Civil Preparedness Agency from the Department of Defense into FEMA.[19]

FEMA is the lead emergency management agency in the United States, and law enforcement officers should be aware of the scope of its history, responsibilities, and organizational structure. The purpose of FEMA is to coordinate disaster relief efforts at the federal level.[20] "FEMA's creation in 1979 was the first step in unifying federal emergency management activity and building a comprehensive approach to national emergency management."[21]

When FEMA was established in 1979, it was intended by former President Carter to focus almost entirely on natural disasters. His successor, Ronald Reagan, disagreed with this exclusive focus and required that FEMA become a "dual-use" organization and to prepare for and respond to both man-made and natural disasters and attacks. FEMA ultimately developed its first all-hazards plan known as the **Federal Response Plan** (FRP) designed to address how federal agencies and the American Red Cross would respond to local and state government needs following a disaster.[22] The first FRP was issued in 1992 under former President George H.W. Bush.

When Bill Clinton became president, he appointed James Lee Witt to be FEMA director. This is significant because Witt was the first FEMA director who actually had experience in emergency management. In part due to the poor federal response to Hurricane Andrew in 1992, the first World Trade Center bombing in 1993, and the Oklahoma City truck bombing of the federal building in 1995, in 1996 Clinton made FEMA a cabinet-level agency whose director reported directly to the president.[23] Nevertheless, FEMA has not been without its problems. The agency has been criticized for poor response to natural disasters, especially hurricanes. Following the creation of FEMA, the federal government continued to refine disaster response by creating several new federal laws and issuing many new presidential executive orders.[24]

An important federal law affecting FEMA is the **Robert T. Stafford Disaster Relief and Emergency Assistance Act (1988)**. Technically, the Stafford Act is both an amendment to and a re-naming of the 1974 Disaster Relief Act. The Stafford Act was designed to establish systematic methods of bringing federal disaster assistance to state, local, and tribal governments. This law stipulates the processes and programs used by the federal government to provide support and coordination to local and state governments, tribal nations, certain nongovernmental organizations (NGOs), and individuals impacted by declared emergencies and disasters. The Stafford Act covers both natural disasters and terrorist events.[25] The law "establishes the current statutory framework for disaster response and recovery through Presidential disaster declarations."[26] Further, "the Act defined the disaster declaration process and provided the statutory authority for federal assistance during a disaster."[27] For these reasons, the Stafford Act is FEMA's primary legal mandate.[28]

Under the Stafford Act, state governors may request federal disaster aid from the federal government in the event of a major flood, fire, or explosion. Thus, both natural disasters such as hurricanes and earthquakes and man-made disasters such as terrorist attacks could trigger the Stafford Act. If the president agrees and declares that a major disaster has occurred, federal aid is deployed. The president also has the authority to deploy federal troops for up to ten days. The Stafford Act was invoked by former President Clinton following the Oklahoma City bombing in 1995 and by former President Bush following the 9/11 attacks.[29]

The Stafford Act also gives the president the authority to engage in disaster response at the state level even without the request or consent of state governments when strictly federal aid is deemed necessary to carry out delegated national powers, though this authority has never been used.[30] However, the possibility exists that it could be used in the event that a state government was deemed by the president to fail to protect its citizens. The Stafford Act provides the president the authority to declare an emergency (rather than a disaster) without the request or consent of the state government in subject matter areas in which the federal government possesses preeminent authority, such as to protect federal property.[31]

Federal Process for Disaster Declarations

Under the Stafford Act, a process for state governments to receive federal disaster funding exists. First, local resources must be exhausted and local government officials request aid from the state government. The state government in turn responds with state resources, which includes state emergency management agencies and often the National Guard. Damage assessments are conducted to examine the scope and magnitude of the disaster. If the governor issues a major disaster declaration, he or she commits to providing state funding and other resources to facilitate response and recovery. The governor then can request federal aid under the Stafford Act. FEMA personnel evaluate the state request. FEMA makes a recommendation to the president based on the damage assessments and their expertise. The president considers these requests and recommendations and then makes a decision to accept or reject the state request.[32]

A **major disaster** under the law exists when the president determines that federal aid to supplement state and local disaster response and recovery efforts is warranted. This could be caused by fires, floods, hurricanes, tornadoes, etc.

If a major disaster is declared, money is disbursed from the Disaster Relief Fund, which is administered by FEMA.[33]

A **presidential major disaster** declaration under the Stafford Act is declared when the magnitude of the disaster is more severe than the supplemental funding disbursed under a major disaster declaration. Presidential major disaster declarations are used to fund long-term recovery programs maintained by the federal government. These programs assist state and local governments, businesses, and the victims of disasters.[34]

Under the Stafford Act, an **emergency declaration** is utilized to provide federal funding and assistance to meet a narrow disaster need in a particular area or for a particular item in the infrastructure. An emergency declaration provides limited funding for this specific purpose and does not include any long-term recovery funding.[35]

Folding Civil Defense Into FEMA

In 1994, Congress repealed the Civil Defense Act (1950) and transferred all remaining civil defense authority to FEMA. "This completed the evolution of civil defense into an all-hazards approach to preparedness. FEMA now had the statutory responsibility for coordinating a comprehensive emergency preparedness system to deal with all types of disasters."[36] In 1996 FEMA was elevated to cabinet-level status under former President Bill Clinton. During the six years that FEMA held this status, the agency had a direct line of access to the president. In 2000 Congress took further steps to facilitate the work of FEMA by enacting the Disaster Mitigation Act. Among other things, the 2000 law mandated that local and state governments make plans for mitigation and to engage in risk assessment as a condition to receive federal mitigation grants.[37]

The Creation of the U.S. Department of Homeland Security

Following the terrorist attacks of 9/11, Congress created the Department of Homeland Security. The **Department of Homeland Security Act** of 2002 was passed to create an explicit national defense strategy. As part of this, the law was designed to put mechanisms in place to both prevent terrorist attacks upon the United States and to reduce the impact of damage and foster recovery in the event that terrorist attacks occur.[38]

The law substantially and significantly reorganized the American homeland security community.[39] The Department of Homeland Security (DHS) became a cabinet-level department under the president, making the DHS the third largest federal agency. Only the Department of Veteran's Affairs and the

Department of Defense are larger.[40] FEMA became a component part of DHS and thus lost its previous cabinet-level status.

Under the 2002 law, the U.S. Customs, U.S. Coast Guard, FEMA (Federal Emergency Management Agency), many functions of the INS (Immigration and Naturalization Service), and the U.S. Secret Service were placed under the DHS.[41] The TSA (Transportation Security Administration) was also placed under DHS. However, the FBI remained under the Department of Justice, and the CIA kept its status as an independent agency.[42] These reorganizations in theory helped agencies to better coordinate their activities.

The greatest relevance of this for emergency management was the placement of FEMA under DHS. The primary objectives of DHS relate to the prevention of terrorism, with emergency management functions receiving less emphasis. This is evidenced by where emergency management has been placed within the Department of Homeland Security's five core missions: (1) prevention of terrorism and the enhancement of security, (2) securing the borders of the United States, (3) enforcing immigration laws, (4) safeguarding cyberspace, and (5) ensuring resilience to disasters that impact the United States.[43] Emergency management is thus listed as the *last* priority of DHS.

Under the 2002 law placing FEMA under DHS, a direct line of report between the FEMA administrator and the DHS secretary was established. However, the direct access to the president by the FEMA director was lost. The Preparedness Directorate consolidated assets related to preparedness from across the Department of Homeland Security by facilitating grants and overseeing nationwide preparedness efforts. These include first-responder training, citizen awareness, public health initiatives, cyber security, and infrastructure.[44]

One of the reasons that the U.S. Department of Homeland Security was formed was to consolidate federal emergency management agencies. However, FEMA employees actually represent less than two percent of the Department of Homeland Security personnel. This situation has subsumed FEMA under Homeland Security to a significant degree.[45]

FEMA has only approximately 2,500 full-time employees. However, it maintains "on call" 5,000 "standby disaster assistance employees" that can be deployed after disasters. Due to the low level of staffing, it is necessary for FEMA to maintain and engage in partnerships with other organizations in both the public and private sectors. Some of these organizations include local and state emergency management agencies, other federal agencies, and the American Red Cross. FEMA also utilizes private sector contractors during times of disaster deployments.[46]

Federal Emergency Management Plans and Initiatives

In 2004, FEMA published the **National Response Plan (NRP)** which replaced the 1992 Federal Response Plan.[47] The National Response Plan was designed to establish a single national framework with which to manage emergency responses to domestic emergency incidents. The National Response Plan encompassed an all-hazards approach to critical incident response across both public and private sector organizations (law enforcement, fire, non-government organizations like the American Red Cross, public health, etc.). It was presumed by the National Response Plan that critical incidents would be managed at the local level when possible, but that emergency response could be escalated to state and even to the federal levels based upon the scope of the disaster.[48]

The National Response Plan contained innovative ideas of special relevance to law enforcement and other first responders in emergency management. It recognized the vital roles played by those who were the first to arrive at a critical incident site. In addition, the National Response Plan anticipated that local incident command structures at a critical incident would be responsible for on-site emergency management activities and control over providing aid and the deployment of resources. The chief executive of the local jurisdiction (city manager or mayor) was tasked with the responsibility of requesting state or ultimately federal assistance if the magnitude of the disaster exceeded local capabilities. Similarly, state governors are responsible for supervising disasters within a state that exceed the capabilities of local jurisdiction. The governor can order the mobilization of state police forces and the national guard depending upon the scope of the critical incidents. Further, the governor can request federal aid and assistance if the magnitude of the disaster exceeds state capabilities.[49]

In 2008, the National Response Plan was replaced with the **National Response Framework (NRF)** due to criticisms that the former was not actually a *plan*, but rather a conceptual *framework* for emergency management response. The NRF contained much of the same materials as the National Response Plan, but with updated emergency response and operations plans. Guidelines are provided to first responders at all levels about "best practices" in critical incident response based upon a comprehensive all-hazards approach to both man-made and natural disasters. To support the National Response Framework, FEMA created a National Response Framework Resource Center. The National Response Framework Resource Center maintains a website to provide first responders with access to information needed to perform their assigned duties and responsibilities.[50] Essentially, the NRF delineates what governments at all levels should do following a major disaster.[51]

The NRF established a National Operations Center (NOC) to serve as the collector and disseminator of information regarding incident management operations among federal response agencies during disasters. The NOC transmits situational data through the NRCC (National Response Coordination Center) and the NICC (National Infrastructure Coordinating Center). The NRCC is FEMA's primary center of operations, while the NICC monitors the nation's key resources (KR) and critical infrastructure (CI).[52]

In 2005, Hurricane Katrina impacted Louisiana and Florida. In addition to the direct deaths of nearly two thousand people, Katrina caused billions of dollars in property damage and extensive human suffering. Following the poor governmental response to the effects of Hurricane Katrina, Congress modified both the Stafford Act and the Homeland Security Act with the **Post-Katrina Emergency Management Reform Act** (2006) (**PKEMRA**). The 2006 law was designed to improve DHS and FEMA operations and disaster responses. PKEMRA modified and clarified both the Stafford Act of 1988 and the Homeland Security Act of 2002 regarding the organizational structure, authority, and responsibilities of FEMA and the FEMA administrator during disasters. PKEMRA resulted in the transfer of a significant portion of the DHS Preparedness Directorate into FEMA, including the United States Fire Administration, the Office of Grants and Training, the Chemical Stockpile Emergency Preparedness Division, the Radiological Emergency Preparedness Program, and the Office of National Capital Region Coordination.[53]

PKEMRA allows the president to declare a major disaster and to deploy federal resources to disaster-impacted areas even without formal state requests under limited circumstances.[54] Organizationally, the law re-named the FEMA director's position into the FEMA administrator's position and made the administrator and undersecretary of the U.S. Department of Homeland Security, which requires Senate confirmation. The statute mandates that the FEMA administrator must possess a background in emergency management. In addition, the law set up a ten-region FEMA system dividing the United States and created a National Integration Center (NIC). The purpose of the NIC is to maintain the National Response Framework and the National Incident Management System.[55]

PKEMRA also mandated that FEMA establish IMATs (Incident Management Assistance Teams) to support local incident command during disasters and emergencies. IMATs are composed of emergency management personnel with specific disaster and emergency training and skills and are capable of rapid deployment. IMATs help to deliver federal support in crisis situations and provide coordination with state and local emergency responders.[56]

In 2012, Hurricane Sandy impacted the eastern seaboard of the United States, causing billions of dollars in damage and destroying thousands of homes. In response, Congress enacted the Sandy Recovery Improvement Act

(2013) to improve recovery efforts for infrastructure. In addition, the legislation allowed federally recognized tribes to directly request a presidential disaster declaration.[57]

The Department of Homeland Security published the second edition of the **National Preparedness Goal** in 2015. The National Preparedness goal is stated as "A secure and resilient Nation with the capabilities required across the whole community to prevent, protect against, mitigate, respond to, and recover from the threats and hazards that pose the greatest risk."[58] To achieve this, FEMA maintains a National Preparedness System, which consists of online resources designed to assist stakeholders in (1) identifying and assessing risk by utilizing the National Risk and Capability Assessment, (2) estimating capability requirements by examining core capabilities and mission areas, (3) building and sustaining capabilities through utilization of the National Incident Management System, (4) planning to deliver capabilities through the National Planning System, (5) validating capabilities by means of emergency planning exercises, and (6) reviewing and updating.[59] The National Preparedness System was established by PKEMRA to provide a statutory foundation to facilitate coordination between emergency management and homeland security agencies based upon the all-hazards approach.[60]

In 2016, the Department of Homeland Security published the second edition of the **National Disaster Recovery Framework (NDRF)**.[61] The first edition had been published in 2001 prior to the terrorist attacks. The National Disaster Recovery Framework provides a detailed set of protocols for facility restoration and reconstruction of communities harmed by major disasters.[62] The NDRF "establishes a common platform and forum for how the whole community builds, sustains, and coordinates the delivery of recovery capabilities."[63]

In 2017, severe fires in California and the impact of three hurricanes (Maria, Irma, and Harvey) caused extensive damage. Congress enacted the Disaster Recovery Reform Act in 2018. This law was designed to support disaster mitigation efforts and to increase the capacities of state and local governments to prepare for and reduce the impact of future disasters.[64]

Implementation of Emergency Management Laws and Initiatives

These and other laws enacted by Congress require implementation in order to go into effect. For this reason, the president, as the chief executive of the federal government, must then implement and enforce the laws made by Congress. In order to do this, the president has the federal bureaucracy under his chain of command. The president implements emergency management and homeland security laws under his *chain of command authority* and his *authority to issue executive orders.*

An **executive order** is a formal written directive from the president to administrative agencies or officials. An executive order can either stipulate the policy direction of agencies or require agencies to do or refrain from doing certain things. It is said that executive orders "have the force and effect of law" because they are valid and legal unless overturned by a federal court or Congress limits this power in a particular instance.

Presidential executive orders that deal broadly with the national security of the United States are called **Presidential Decision Directives**. Former President Clinton issued **Presidential Decision Directive 39 (PDD-39)** following the deadly domestic terrorist bombing of the federal building in Oklahoma City in 1995. PDD-39 is entitled "U.S. Policy on Counterterrorism" and contains a three-part strategy: (1) threat/vulnerability management, (2) crisis management, and (3) consequence management. The directive delineated the specific responsibilities of several federal agencies regarding these three elements.[65]

Following the passage of the Homeland Security Act in 2002, presidential executive orders that deal specifically with homeland security have been called **Homeland Security Presidential Directives (HSPDs)**. The HSPDs issued since that time have either supplemented or replaced the PDDs issued by former President Clinton.[66] The two HSPDs of most relevance to emergency management and law enforcement are HSPD-5 and HSPD-8.

HSPD-5 is entitled "**Management of Domestic Incidents**." HSPD-5 was issued in February 2003 and established a comprehensive national incident management system.[67] This is called **NIMS or National Incident Management System**, which is a vitally important part of both emergency management and homeland security. NIMS comprises a standardized system for managing emergency response.[68] It consists of command and management, preparedness, resource management, communication and information management, supporting technologies, and ongoing management and maintenance. HSPD-5 designated the secretary of the Department of Homeland Security as the primary federal official for domestic incident management. It also recognizes the statutory authorities of the secretary of defense, the secretary of state, and the attorney general with regard to the management of domestic incidents.[69]

"**HSPD-8** is entitled **National Preparedness**." It was issued in December 2003 and set up policies designed to strengthen the preparedness of the United States for the purpose of preventing and responding to threatened or actual domestic terrorist attacks, major disasters, and other emergencies. HSPD-8 requires a national domestic all-hazards preparedness goal and set up mechanisms for improved delivery of federal preparedness assistance to local, state, and tribal governments. It also outlined initiatives to bolster the preparedness capabilities of governments at all levels inside the United States.[70]

These directives are implemented also through what is known as the chain of command authority. **Chain of command authority** refers to either oral or written orders given to administrative agencies by the executive of lesser formal stature than that stipulated in executive orders. Administrative agencies are designed and managed on the basis of *hierarchy*. This means that higher-level officials supervise the work of lower-level officials in a defined chain of command. In other words, bureaucracies metaphorically "look like" a pyramid. The personnel who staff administrative agencies must obey lawful orders from their appointed superiors, including the president with regard to federal agencies.

Thus, when a governor (state agencies) or president (federal agencies) gives either written or oral orders to a bureaucracy, these orders are communicated to the political appointees who head these agencies. Then these top officials in turn issue orders to their subordinates below them in the hierarchy. In this way, the collective actions of the bureaucracy are controlled from the top down to the bottom. As long as such orders are legal (do not violate the constitution or the laws of the jurisdiction), they must be obeyed by government employees, including law enforcement officers. Failure to obey lawful orders can and does result in dismissal or other sanctions. Law enforcement and other first responder agencies are set up and run along bureaucratic lines.[71] The chief of police or the sheriff issues orders to his or her subordinates through the chain of command. These orders are then supposedly implemented by law enforcement officers "on the ground."[72]

However, the theory sometimes does not neatly follow reality. In other words, how an organization appears on paper does not always correctly identify how it operates in reality. In order to better understand how emergency management agencies have actually operated over time, it is necessary to examine how agencies tasked with emergency management have evolved at the organizational level.

The Evolution of Emergency Management Operations: Management by First Responders (Police, Fire, and Military)

Historically, what is now called emergency management received relatively little status, recognition, or funding.[73] In the past, emergency management was an "appendix" to other government projects and initiatives. The advent of Civil Defense during World Wars I and II gave emergency management greater support from American governments. Civil Defense, coupled with the first federal legislation to support ongoing disaster response and relief during the 1950s, led to increased stature and visibility for emergency management. By the 1970s, more than one hundred federal agencies were involved in emergency management, and FEMA was formed in 1979.[74] Despite FEMA's creation, it was not until 9/11 that emergency management received widespread support and recognition as a needed function of American government.[75]

While emergency management received additional support and recognition at the federal level, local governments still considered emergency management to be a low priority. Emergency management was viewed generally as an annoying federal mandate. In most jurisdictions, emergency management was an "add-on" duty for first responder agencies such as fire and police departments. Local government employees appointed to emergency management positions typically had no training or expertise in the field.[76]

Elected officials have shown the tendency across the decades to view emergency management in a reactive way as a means to respond to disasters. Accordingly, elected officials determined that government employees with fire, police, or military backgrounds were most suitable to operate emergency management agencies at the local level. The traditional method to staff local emergency management agencies has been to recruit personnel with training, expertise, and experience in the military, fire service, and law enforcement due to their experience with "on-the-ground" response. Plus, many members of first responder organizations have worked with emergency management personnel in their jobs.[77]

This is especially true of law enforcement personnel. For more than one hundred years before any emergency management agency was formed, law enforcement officers responded to disaster-related emergencies and calls for service. Maintaining law and order, transporting the injured for medical care, and distributing relief supplies have always been associated with police response.[78]

Due to traditional recruitment practices, many retired first responders found positions in local emergency management agencies. It was believed that those with first responder backgrounds would be best suited to deal with emergency management. However, this created several problems and issues, including confusion between the reactive focus of first responder duties an the more proactive focus of emergency management.[79]

One problem has been the excessive focus upon response to disasters in emergency management rather than the prevention of disasters during past decades. The argument is made that the "saturation" of local and to a degree, state emergency management agencies in the past with retired first responder personnel (especially police and fire) led to subsuming preparation and mitigation in emergency management. In addition, it has been noted that local and state emergency management agencies have operated with an over-emphasis upon "command and control" management techniques that are not well suited to the overall mission of emergency management's more open and collaborative organizational approach.[80]

Significant differences exist in orientation between first responders (especially law enforcement) and emergency managers. The argument has been made that fire service personnel are the first responders most suited to step into an emergency management role. This is due to their experience in recovery and rescue missions and due to their familiarity with working in team-based approaches. Similarly, former military personnel often perform well in emergency management roles due to their culture of learning new skills and frequent changing of job tasks.[81]

However, former law enforcement officers often face challenges in shifting to an emergency management role. This is attributed to the substantial differences that exist between law enforcement culture and organizational design and those found in modern large emergency management agencies.[82] For example, law enforcement officers are trained and socialized into the "command and control" authoritative management structure. This is the default orientation when responding to critical incidents.[83] In addition, most law enforcement officers are used to working with other first responder agencies where hierarchy is valued. In addition, most law enforcement officers have worked in that profession for their entire career.[84]

This paints a picture of past local (and many state-level) emergency management employees with the following characteristics: (1) middle-aged to late-aged male; (2) on a second or third career; (3) knowledge of first response extensive and learned on the job but little knowledge of emergency management; (4) has a reactive approach; (5) job experience is primarily with first responder agencies; (6) little access to elected officials and other government decision-makers; (7) working a part-time job or a full-time job with emergency management duties added; (8) never prepared a risk analysis or disaster plan nor is familiar with such plans.[85]

All of these characteristics have worked against the effort to "recreate" emergency management into a better-recognized profession in recent decades.[86] Under the modern conceptualization of emergency management, the field is much broader than emergency response. The modern emergency manager should focus on and maintain the holistic, all-hazards framework to assist communities to prepare for, mitigate, respond to, and recover from disasters. This means moving away from the mentality and limited first-responder focus that emphasizes being oriented toward proactive preparation and mitigation. Working with organizations, communities, and individuals outside the first responder community thus requires decentralization and a focus on collaboration and cooperation rather than the use of authority.[87]

According to this conceptualization, the ideal emergency manager should exemplify the following characteristics: (1) younger than in the past with more diversity represented; (2) first-career chosen deliberately; (3) knowledge of emergency management obtained through higher education credentials based upon empirical research into disasters; (4) has a proactive approach; (5) job experience is primarily with emergency management agencies; (6) access to government decision-makers; (7) working a full-time job focused upon emergency management; (8) familiar with disaster plans; may have prepared them.[88]

Law enforcement personnel wishing to transition to emergency management requires the individual to adapt. Individuals that desire to transition to emergency management should familiarize themselves with appropriate concepts and terminology, such as the all-hazards approach, the phases of the emergency management cycle, and various plans such as the NRF (National Response Plan). Formal education at colleges and universities in emergency management would be helpful, as would free non-credit training in emergency management offered by FEMA's Emergency Management Institute both online and in-person.[89]

To help facilitate this transition, in addition to its Emergency Management Institute, FEMA operates an Emergency Management Professional Program (EMPP) that provides training in functional areas of emergency management. Certificates are issued for those that successfully complete the EMPP training. In addition, FEMA operates the CDP (Center for Domestic Preparedness) and the NTED (National Training and Education Division). The CDP provides training for emergency managers and emergency response providers. NTED offers courses (approximately one hundred) to assist emergency managers and first responders in building critical skills for significant events.[90]

While substantial components of emergency management remain focused on response, this has been changing. The four-phase all-hazards approach where emergency management employees do not take direct part in critical incident response activities is the modern paradigm. Emergency managers are called upon to take a broad, holistic approach to disasters and hazards. This requires practicing the four phases of the emergency management cycle and participating with stakeholders.

Notes

1. Willard M. Oliver, *Policing in an Era of Homeland Security*, New York, Oxford University Press, 2020: 47.
2. Ibid: 48.
3. Ibid: 49.
4. Ibid: 50.

5. Michael K. Lindell, Carla Prater, and Ronald W. Perry, *Introduction to Emergency Management*, Hoboken, John C. Wiley and Sons, Inc., 2007: 8.
6. Oliver, *Policing in an Era of Homeland Security*: 51.
7. Ibid: 54.
8. Lindell, Prater, Perry, *Introduction to Emergency Management*: 8.
9. U.S. Department of Homeland Security, Federal Emergency Management Agency, *We are FEMA: Helping People Before, During, and After Disasters* (Publication 1), 2016: 16.
10. Ibid.
11. Ibid: 16-17.
12. U.S. Department of Homeland Security, *Civil Defense and Homeland Security: A Short History of National Preparedness Efforts*, September 2006: 15.
13. David A. McEntire, *Disaster Response and Recovery: Strategies and Tactics for Resilience*, 2nd Edition, Hoboken: John Wiley and Sons, Inc., 2015: 332.
14. Homeland Security Digital Library, "Disaster Relief Act of 1974", https://www.hsdl.org/c/tl/disaster-relief-act-1974
15. U.S. Department of Homeland Security, Federal Emergency Management Agency, *We are FEMA: Helping People Before, During, and After Disasters* (Publication 1), 2016: 17.
16. William C. Banks, *The Legal Landscape for Emergency Management in the United States*, New America Foundation, February 2011: 9-10.
17. Michael J. Fagel, Editor, *Principles of Emergency Management: Hazard Specific Issues and Mitigation Strategies*, Boca Raton: CRC Press/Taylor and Francis Group, 2012: 10.
18. Lindell, Prater, and Perry, *Introduction to Emergency Management*: 8.
19. U.S. Department of Homeland Security, Federal Emergency Management Agency, *We are FEMA: Helping People Before, During, and After Disasters* (Publication 1), 2016: 17-18.
20. Fagel, *Principles of Emergency Management*: 10.
21. U.S. Department of Homeland Security, Federal Emergency Management Agency, *We are FEMA: Helping People Before, During, and After Disasters* (Publication 1), 2016: 14.
22. Oliver, *Policing in an Era of Homeland Security*: 54-55.
23. Ibid: 55.
24. Fagel, *Principles of Emergency Management*: 10.
25. Ibid: 11.
26. U.S. Department of Homeland Security, Federal Emergency Management Agency, *We are FEMA: Helping People Before, During, and After Disasters* (Publication 1), 2016: 18.
27. U.S. Department of Homeland Security, *Civil Defense and Homeland Security: A Short History of National Preparedness Efforts*: 21.
28. Royce Saunders, "FEMA: Change or Die," *Journal of Emergency Management*, Vol. 4, No. 3, May/June 2006: 6.
29. Banks, *The Legal Landscape for Emergency Management in the United States*: 10-11.
30. Raymond K. Shin, "The Federal Government's Potential Power to Coordinate or take State Assets During Emergencies," *Journal of Emergency Management*, Vol. 9, No. 3, May/June 2011: 7.

31. Banks, *The Legal Landscape for Emergency Management in the United States*: 12.
32. Roger L. Kemp, Editor, *Homeland Security: Best Practices for Local Government*, Washington, D.C., ICMA Press, 2010: 276-277.
33. Ibid: 276.
34. Ibid.
35. Ibid.
36. U.S. Department of Homeland Security, *Civil Defense and Homeland Security: A Short History of National Preparedness Efforts*: 23.
37. Ibid: 21.
38. Fagel, *Principles of Emergency Management*: 200.
39. Gus Martin, *Understanding Terrorism: Challenges, Perspectives, and Issues*, 5th Edition, Thousand Oaks: Sage Publications, 2016: 420.
40. Ibid.
41. Ibid: 422.
42. Ibid: 420-421.
43. Oliver, *Policing in an Era of Homeland Security*: 82-83.
44. Fagel, *Principles of Emergency Management*: 11.
45. Ricard Sylves, "Why Revolutionary Changes is Needed in Emergency Management," *Journal of Emergency Management*, Vol. 3, No. 6, November/December 2005: 17.
46. Jeff Nelson, Kiril Hristovski, and Danny Peterson, "Mission Possible: A Failure Mode and Effect Analysis of the Federal Emergency Management Agency," *Journal of Emergency Management*, Vol. 5, No. 6, November/December 2007: 17.
47. U.S. Department of Homeland Security, Federal Emergency Management Agency, *We are FEMA: Helping People Before, During, and After Disasters* (Publication 1), 2016: 23.
48. Oliver, *Policing in an Era of Homeland Security*: 113.
49. Ibid: 114.
50. Ibid: 118.
51. McEntire, Disaster Response and Recovery: 52.
52. Banks, *The Legal Landscape for Emergency Management in the United States*: 14.
53. Fagel, *Principles of Emergency Management*: 11-12.
54. William C. Banks, *The Legal Landscape for Emergency Management in the United States*, New American Foundation, February 2011: 12.
55. Ibid: 13.
56. Ibid: 18.
57. U.S. Department of Homeland Security, Federal Emergency Management Agency, *We are FEMA: Helping People Before, During, and After Disasters* (Publication 1), 2016: 25-26.
58. U.S. Department of Homeland Security, *National Preparedness Goal*, Second Edition, September 2015: 1.
59. U.S. Department of Homeland Security, Federal Emergency Management Agency, "National Preparedness System" https://www.fema.gov/emergency-managers/national-preparedness/system

60. Banks, *The Legal Landscape for Emergency Management in the United States*: 13.
61. U.S. Department of Homeland Security, *National Disaster Recovery Framework*, Second Edition, June 2016.
62. McEntire, Disaster Response and Recovery: 52.
63. U.S. Department of Homeland Security, *National Disaster Recovery Framework*, Second Edition, June 2016: i.
64. Ibid: 27.
65. Fagel, *Principles of Emergency Management*: 12.
66. Ibid.
67. Ibid.
68. Lindell, Prater, and Perry, *Introduction to Emergency Management*: 284.
69. Fagel, *Principles of Emergency Management*: 13.
70. Ibid.
71. Edward A. Thibault, Lawrence M. Lynch, and R. Bruce McBride, *Proactive Police Management*, 6th Edition, Upper Saddle River, NJ, Pearson-Prentice-Hall, 2004: 61-63.
72. Walter S. Topp, "Making the Transition From Law Enforcement to Emergency Management: Organizational, Occupational, and Cultural Issues," *Journal of Emergency Management*, Vol. 17, No. 1, January/February 2019: 47.
73. William L. Waugh, Jr., "Emergency Management Today and Tomorrow," *Journal of Emergency Management*, Vol. 1, No. 1, Spring 2003: 5.
74. Thomas E. Drabek, "Emergency Managers as Change Agents: An Expanded View of the Profession," *Journal of Emergency Management*, Vol. 12, No. 1, January/February 2014: 10.
75. Daniel W. Martin, "The Shifting Paradigms of a Profession: Calming Conflicts Between Homeland Security and Emergency Management," *Journal of Emergency Management*, Vol. 9, No. 5, September/October 2011: 12.
76. Robert O. Schneider, "An Overview of the 'New' Emergency Management," *Journal of Emergency Management*, Vol. 2, No. 1, Winter 2004: 26.
77. Topp, "Making the Transition From Law Enforcement to Emergency Management: Organizational, Occupational, and Cultural Issues:" 45.
78. Ibid: 48.
79. Martin, "The Shifting Paradigms of a Profession: Calming Conflicts Between Homeland Security and Emergency Management:" 15.
80. Ibid: 15-16.
81. Topp, "Making the Transition From Law Enforcement to Emergency Management: Organizational, Occupational, and Cultural Issues:" 45.
82. Ibid.
83. Martin, "The Shifting Paradigms of a Profession: Calming Conflicts Between Homeland Security and Emergency Management:" 16.
84. Topp, "Making the Transition From Law Enforcement to Emergency Management: Organizational, Occupational, and Cultural Issues:" 46-47.
85. B. Wayne Blanchard, "The New Role of Higher Education in Emergency Management," *Journal of Emergency Management*, Vol. 1, No. 2, Summer 2003: 31.
86. Martin, "The Shifting Paradigms of a Profession: Calming Conflicts Between Homeland Security and Emergency Management:" 11.

87. Topp, "Making the Transition From Law Enforcement to Emergency Management: Organizational, Occupational, and Cultural Issues:" 47.
88. Blanchard, "The New Role of Higher Education in Emergency Management:" 32.
89. Topp, "Making the Transition From Law Enforcement to Emergency Management: Organizational, Occupational, and Cultural Issues:" 50.
90. Kahan, "Emergency Management and Homeland Security: Exploring the Relationship:" 492.

Chapter 3

UNDERSTANDING THE ROLE OF ICS AND NIMS IN EMERGENCY MANAGEMENT

Law enforcement and emergency management personnel utilize **NIMS (National Incident Management System)** and ICS **(Incident Command System)** frequently. It is imperative that those who work in the fields of emergency response and emergency management have a strong background in NIMS and ICS. This is required as a condition of receiving federal funding, and it is a vital part of the connection between emergency management and law enforcement. Chapter 3 is designed to provide a detailed overview and analysis of NIMS and ICS.

The ICS and NIMS are designed to help first responders more effectively work with other emergency services agencies during incidents. In particular, NIMS and ICS better facilitate the resolution of *critical incidents.* A **critical incident** is an unusual event that places human lives and property in danger and necessitates the deployment and coordination of resources to resolve.[1]

A critical incident is beyond a *typical* accident or event. A critical incident requires *additional resources* to resolve. For example, terrorist activities involving WMDs (Weapons of Mass destruction), major natural disasters (hurricanes, earthquakes, etc.), epidemics, pandemics, mass-casualty transportation accidents, serious criminal activities, major fires, and hazmat (hazardous materials) incidents are all examples of critical incidents. When and if the initial first responders are not capable of resolving the incident, additional resources from other agencies and outside parties are necessary.[2]

Now that we know what is meant by critical incident, we now need to turn to critical incident *management.* **Incident management** is "the broad spectrum of activities and organizations providing effective and efficient operations, coordination, and support applied at all levels of government, utilizing both governmental and nongovernmental resources to plan for, respond to, and recover from an incident, regardless of cause, size, or complexity."[3]

Critical incident management involves working with other emergency responders—both within one's agency and in different agencies. The larger and more complex the situation on the ground, the more responders and resources will be required. Large-scale emergencies require greater resources and a complex way of organizing different emergency response agencies. This led to the development of NIMS broadly, and to ICS more particularly.

The ICS is an organizational structure designed to effectively resolve the management of critical incidents. First responders and emergency managers must understand ICS for this reason. A combination of education, training, and experience will allow the emergency manager and first responder to manage and handle critical incidents effectively and efficiently. None of these alone is sufficient: a combination is necessary for maximum effectiveness.

NIMS contains broad principles that can be applied to first responder and emergency management agencies. NIMS is designed to assist first responders and emergency managers to better collaborate in incident management. NIMS is comprised of doctrines, concepts, and principles and thus is not a specific method to resolve critical incidents.[4]

NIMS and ICS evolved from earlier systematic efforts to make emergency response more rational and effective. As early as the 1970s it was recognized that large-scale critical incidents that require the deployment of first responders from different jurisdictions created significant problems with coordination and control. This situation was made worse when fire and law enforcement personnel were required to interact in a complex critical incident due to the lack of a standardized mechanism with which to coordinate their activities.

Historical Background

The first significant effort to standardize critical incident response was the **ICS (Incident Command System)**, which was originally developed during the early 1970s following a series of wildfires in Southern California. ICS was developed out of practical necessity: because different fire jurisdictions used different organizational structures, names, procedures, and positions, it seriously hampered coordination to fight large-scale fires. Southern California firefighting organizations joined together to address this problem. They concluded that something had to be done to address:

- Inadequate emergency assessments/lack of standardization
- Lack of common organizational structure
- Poorly coordinated planning and resource allocation
- Inadequate interagency coordination at fire scenes[5]

Addressing these things led to the creation of the **Incident Command System (ICS)**. The ICS is "a standardized approach to the command, control, and coordination of on-scene emergency management, providing a common hierarchy within which personnel from multiple organizations can be effective."[6]

ICS is based upon seven vitally important elements critical to emergency first responders. These are:

1. **Standardization**. This means all agencies involved in an incident must use a common emergency response organizational structure with common names and uniform functions for subunits.
2. **Functional specificity**. This is based on division of labor–each unit and subunit has a specific task and function to perform.
3. **Manageable span of control**. This deals with the ratio of supervisors to subordinates. Under ICS, the ratio should be 1:5 but it can range between 1:3 and 1:7.
4. **Unit integrity**. This means assigning personnel from the same professional discipline to the same unit during a response. Ex: firefighters with firefighters; police with police, etc.
5. **Unified Command**. Here, someone is in charge of the incident response, no matter how large or small the incident is. A single **Incident Commander (IC)** manages and directs most incidents. A unified command team manages response when multiple agencies have responsibility for a given incident.
6. **MBO (Management by Objectives)**. Here, the IC and/or senior incident managers develop action plans to deal with the incident that have specific *measurable* objectives. They evaluate "where they are" in terms of effectiveness by comparing the present situation against the objectives.
7. **Comprehensive resource management**. This means that the IC or the unified command team is responsible for allocating all available resources at the incident site. This includes personnel, equipment, vehicles, etc.[7]

ICS is primarily a command and control system for managing standard, on-scene, day-to-day operations.

ICS represents a major step forward in the management of large incidents, especially those that require the joint coordination and interaction of several first responder agencies. A problem with the original version of ICS was that it was region-specific. It spread from California to other jurisdictions, but it still was not completely standardized. Some fire agencies, even within California, used different versions of ICS.

During the 1980s, fire departments advocated for a common ICS to increase response effectiveness in large-scale incidents.[8]

This led to an organization called FIRESCOPE developing a more advanced ICS system in an effort to increase standardization. FIRESCOPE stands for Firefighting Resources of Southern California Organized for Potential Emergencies. This is an organization comprised of several large and small California firefighting agencies.

They developed **FIRESCOPE ICS** during the mid-1980s in cooperation with FEMA. FEMA paid for much of the development costs and adopted FIRESCOPE ICS as FEMA's own ICS system in 1987.[9]

FIRESCOPE ICS was designed for large-scale incidents. It was a planning-based response system that combined planning functions with the functions of an Emergency Operations Center (EOC). "An **Emergency Operations Center (EOC)** is a physical central location from which local governments can provide interagency coordination and executive decision-making in support of incident response and recovery operations. The purpose of the EOC is to provide a centralized location where public safety, emergency response, and support agencies coordinate planning, preparedness, and response activities."[10]

FIRESCOPE ICS also implemented a **Multiagency Coordination System (MAC)** in order to integrate the operations of several agencies and departments into a unified whole. FIRESCOPE ICS was more advanced than the older ICS, but it still needed improvement. This led to the IMS.[11]

The **IMS (Incident Management System)** was developed during the late 1980s by firefighting organizations and implemented during the early 1990s. The IMS is "the combination of facilities, equipment, personnel, procedures, and communications operating within a common organizational structure, designed to aid in the management of resources during incidents."[12]

IMS guides how personnel, facilities, equipment, procedures, and communications may be coordinated during an incident. Under IMS, in every incident, the functions of command, operations, planning, logistics, and finance and administration must be carried out regardless of incident size. IMS helps to quickly initiate emergency operations. Incidents can be handled by first responders guided by an incident commander (IC) that can be adapted to different situations.[13]

What is the *major* difference between IMS and the original ICS? First, IMS is more advanced and comprehensive than ICS. ICS is primarily a command and control system for managing standard, on-scene day-to-day operations. IMS expands ICS by incorporating into a single system MACs (Multiagency Coordination System) at the incident site and within the EOC (Emergency Operations Center) for use at all levels of response.

Today, ICS has essentially "absorbed" IMS. For this reason, some people use IMS and ICS interchangeably. One reason for the confusion between IMS and ICS is that firefighters have historically used IMS. Police agencies have more often employed ICS. It is argued that IMS is simply a "more advanced" version of ICS. In any event, they have both similarities and differences. Both have the same goal: a rational, structured, universal approach to dealing with disaster incidents.

The major advantage of IMS is to make all organizational resources available for every incident, both large and small, if needed. IMS can coordinate resources from an incident command post. In addition, the incident commander can escalate the response as conditions at the critical incident scene warrant.[14]

In this way, IMS is premised on the assignment of specific responsibilities to fit standardized positions. When first responder agencies train their personnel according to their job descriptions, any responder can potentially take on the role of incident commander. Based upon the unity of command concept, there can be only one incident commander at a critical incident site. This position should be held by the most senior officer present.[15] IMS allows the number of personnel and their specialized duties to expand based on the size and complexity of the critical incident.[16]

The terms *sections*, *branches*, and *sectors* are used under IMS to describe different groupings of equipment and personnel.[17] A **section** is a broad area, such as *operations* or *logistics*. Section chiefs direct and monitor personnel activities within their area and work with the incident commander to devise a strategy to best deal with the critical incident.[18]

A **branch** is underneath a section. A *branch* implements tactical operations and includes things like rescue, transport, fire, and medical. Branches comprise tactical and functional expertise at the critical incident site based on the activity in which they are engaged. Branches are named based on the activity that they perform.[19]

Sectors are the most specialized functions performed at the incident site. **Sectors** are specialized subsections of branches. For example, the hazmat (hazardous materials) branch might have several sectors underneath it, such as decontamination and monitoring. The Medical branch might have several sectors under it, such as triage and treatment. This is the tactical level of incident response.[20]

Under IMS, the IC (Incident Commander) must establish a command post (CP). During the critical incident, the IC performs the following tasks:

1. Conduct initial situation evaluation and continual reassessments of the situation
2. Initiate, maintain, and control communications

3. Identify the incident management strategy, develop an action plan, and assign resources
4. Call for supplemental resources, including EOC activation
5. Develop an organizational command structure on the scene
6. Continually review, evaluate, and revise the incident action plan as the situation on the ground warrants
7. Provide for continuing, transferring, and terminating command[21]

Here, the command staff delegates authority to the section chiefs to implement the response.[22] Large critical incidents typically require several sections, which typically include (1) the *planning section*, (2) the *operations section*, (3) the *safety section*, (4) the *administration section*, and (5) the *logistics section.* Under each section are typically branches.

The **planning section** handles predicting the resources needed to deal with the incident and conveys vital information to the command staff.[23]

The **operations section** has, as its main duty, to set up branches. The number of branches depends upon the severity of the critical incident. Rescue, fire, hazmat, and medical are typically established at most large-scale critical incidents.[24]

The **safety section's** purpose is to maintain safe operations for responders at the incident scene. This includes environmental cleanup at the conclusion of first responder operations.[25]

The **administration section** is charged with procurement, cost recovery, liability, and risk management. These things generally involve purchasing items and contracting for services that the first responder agencies are not able to provide. In addition, the administration section documents property damages, deaths, and injuries.[26]

The **logistics section** deals with accounting for and overseeing all equipment. In addition, the logistics section oversees the initial arrivals of unassigned units, tracks them, monitors deployed personnel, and provides food, fluids, and debriefing to them.[27]

In large incidents with many sections, branches, and sectors, incident commanders are often supported by a *senior advisor* and a *support officer.* These individuals generally arrive at the critical incident scene after the command post has been established and initial operations have commenced.[28]

The **senior advisor** provides high-level advice and assessment regarding the situation to the incident commander. This is an emergency manager or a high-ranking first responder. He or she often makes recommendations about involving other agencies or organizations and helps the incident commander to determine the appropriate scope of the response.[29]

The **support officer** assists the incident commander in determining response priorities. He or she also focuses on safety, accountability, and control.[30]

IMS design recognizes that in a major critical incident, extra effort must be expended. A public information officer (PIO), a police liaison, and an emergency operations center (EOC) liaison can be assigned to assist the command staff.[31]

The great value of IMS lies in its ability to make emergency response operations more rational based on structured planning. IMS is considered to be more effective than the earlier ICS in that it is more sophisticated and recognizes that many response-related activities must be performed at locations other than the critical incident scene.[32]

IMS can be executed effectively only if first responder personnel have been properly trained in IMS. Emergency managers must also receive training if they are to be effective partners in critical incident management.[33]

The National Incident Management System (NIMS)

Now that we have been exposed to ICS and IMS, we are ready to examine the latest manifestation of these concepts: NIMS. **NIMS (National Incident Management System)** is "a systematic, proactive approach to guide all levels of government, NGOs, and the private sector to work together to prevent, protect against, mitigate, respond to, and recover from the effects of incidents."[34]

NIMS was created by the federal government as a result of the terrorist attacks of September 11, 2001. NIMS is intended to lead to a standardized system for managing both emergency response and emergency preparedness based on ICS and IMS principles.[35]

NIMS is presently in its third edition. NIMS is issued by FEMA through the U.S. Department of Homeland Security. The first edition of NIMS was developed in 2004 and formally issued in March 2006. The second edition of NIMS came out in December 2008 and superseded the first edition. Finally, the third edition of NIMS was issued in October 2017 and superseded both earlier editions.

A primary purpose for establishing a national system of incident management (NIMS) is to standardize procedures across all jurisdictions in the American federal system. Many different first responder agencies in many different jurisdictions operated different procedures for critical incident response based upon ICS or IMS. Standardization is possible only if all jurisdictions utilize the same incident response system.[36]

FEMA indicates that NIMS is "a comprehensive, nationwide, systematic approach to incident management, including the command and coordination of incidents, resource management, and information management."[37] In addition, NIMS is "a set of concepts and principles for all threat, hazards, and events across all mission areas (Prevention, Protection, Mitigation, Response, Recovery)."[38] It contains "essential principles for communications and information management."[39] NIMS provides "standard resources management procedures that enable coordination among different jurisdictions or organizations."[40] FEMA emphasizes that NIMS is not "a response plan"[41] or "a static system."[42]

In 2004, the U.S. Department of Homeland Security mandated the adoption of NIMS by all federal agencies. State and local EM and first responder agencies must also adopt NIMS as a condition of receiving federal funding, including FEMA grants. This is required by federalism, in that the national government cannot compel other levels of government to comply unless funding is dependent upon such compliance.[43]

NIMS is similar in intent to ICS and IMS, but it is broader than incident response. NIMS also encompasses emergency preparedness.[44] Nevertheless, NIMS incorporates substantial parts of both IMS and ICS, IMS in particular.

Research has demonstrated that NIMS is quite effective for fire service operations. However, it is less effective in law enforcement work. This is because typical law enforcement incidents are resolved by one or two officers at the scene. The complex organizational structure of NIMS does not function at optimum efficiency when first responders must deal with a sentient adversary or with unfolding attacks.[45]

The terrorist attacks on 9/11 created a state of "new normal" in which a strong focus on Emergency Management became an important public policy. As we have seen, following the terrorist attacks of 9/11, Congress created the Department of Homeland Security (DHS). The **Department of Homeland Security Act** of 2002 was passed to create "...a national defense strategy, prevent terrorist attacks within the United States, and minimizing the damage and assisting in the recovery from such attacks."[46]

The law substantially reorganized the homeland security community.[47] The Department of Homeland Security became a cabinet-level department under the president, making the DHS the third largest federal agency. Only the U.S. Department of Veteran's Affairs and the U.S. Department of Defense are larger.[48]

Under the law, the U.S. Customs, U.S. Coast Guard, FEMA (Federal Emergency Management Agency), many functions of the INS (Immigration and Naturalization Service), and the U.S. Secret Service were placed under the DHS.[49] The TSA (Transportation Security Administration) was also placed under DHS. However, the FBI remained under the Dept. of Justice, and the CIA kept its status as an independent agency.[50] These reorganizations helped agencies to better coordinate their activities.

The greatest relevance of this for emergency management was the placement of the Federal Emergency Management Agency (FEMA) under DHS.[51] This resulted in a diminished role for emergency management and a correspondingly increased profile for terrorist-related law enforcement and intelligence tasks.

Several presidential executive orders have been utilized to implement laws passed by Congress relevant to Emergency Management. Following the passage of the Homeland Security Act in 2002, presidential executive orders that deal specifically with homeland security have been called **Homeland Security Presidential Directives (HSPDs)**. The three HSPDs of most relevance to emergency management are HSPD-5, HSPD-7, and HSPD-8.

HSPD-5 is entitled "**Management of Domestic Incidents**." HSPD-5 was issued in February 2003 and established NIMS as the single comprehensive national incident management system intended for use by American jurisdictions.[52] This makes HSPD-5 a vitally important part of both emergency management and homeland security. NIMS is a mechanism to manage emergency preparedness and emergency response as part of a standardized system.[53] It consists of command and management, preparedness, resource management, communication and information management, supporting technologies, and ongoing management and maintenance. HSPD-5 designated the Secretary of Homeland Security as the principal federal official in charge of domestic incident management.[54]

The creation of NIMS moved the nation away from discipline-specific critical incident response systems (police only; fire only) to a multiagency approach. All jurisdictions in the United States (federal, tribal, local, state, etc.) are intended to utilize NIMS. In addition, NIMS is adaptable to civilian public service and health care agencies.[55]

Another Homeland Security Presidential Directive is **HSPD- ("Critical Infrastructure Identification, Prioritization, and Protection")**. HSPD-7 is a presidential executive order that prioritizes the protection of *critical infrastructures* and *key resources*."[56] Under the Homeland Security Act (2002), The Department of Homeland Security (DHS) was given the responsibility for developing a comprehensive national plan to secure critical infrastructure and key resources (CIKR).[57] **Critical Infrastructure (CI)** refers to "assets, systems, and networks, whether physical or virtual, so vital that the incapacity or destruction of such may have a debilitating impact on the security, economy public health or safety, environment, or any combination of those matters."[58]

Closely related to CI sectors are **Key Resources (KR)**. A Key Resource is "any publicly or privately controlled resources essential to minimal operations of the economy and government."[59] These include agriculture and food, banking, water, chemicals, and government facilities.

Attacks on CI or KR could result in significant disruption of both government and the economy. Terrorist attacks, human error, and natural disasters could produce catastrophic losses resulting in death, injury, property damage, and economic harm. Such a situation would also likely result in negative psychological impacts on the general population.[60]

It is for this reason that the **National Infrastructure Protection Plan (NIPP)** was published by the Dept. of Homeland Security in 2006. The NIPP is a comprehensive document that seeks to integrate efforts to protect CIKR.[61]

HSPD-7 mandates important facilities, such as Emergency Operations Centers (EOCs), dispatch centers, and other command facilities be identified and protected through hardening. Efforts are made to enhance key resource protection, or hardening. Because communications and information technology are defined by HSPD-7 as critical infrastructure, their protection is vital.[62]

HSPD-8 is entitled "**National Preparedness**." It was issued in December 2003 and established federal policies and initiatives designed to increase the preparedness of the nation. Natural disasters and terrorist attacks are the primary focus of HSPD-8. Increased preparedness can be achieved through an all-hazards focus and by improving federal preparedness assistance to state, local, and tribal governments.[63] HSPD-8 established preparedness-related objectives for federal agencies are specified and mandated federal support requirements for first responders at the state and local levels of the American government.[64]

Interoperability and *compatibility* are terms one often encounters as part of NIMS. FEMA defines **interoperability** as the "Ability of systems, personnel, and equipment to provide and receive functionality, data, information, and/or services to and from other systems, personnel, and equipment, between both public and private agencies, departments, and other organizations, in a manner enabling them to operate effectively together."[65] **Compatibility** deals with systems being able to co-exist without conflict. Together, interoperability and compatibility mean that "systems operating in an incident management environment must be able to interact smoothly across disciplines and jurisdictions. Interoperability and compatibility are achieved through the use of tools such as common communications and data standards, digital data formats, equipment standards, and design standards."[66]

NIMS is based on the premise that utilization of the common incident management terminology and approaches provides emergency management and emergency response personnel a predictable standard with which to operate.[67] The 9/11 Commission Report noted that the inability of multiple police, fire, and other emergency workers to effectively communicate in New York City and at the Pennsylvania crash site of United Flight 93 seriously hampered critical incident response. Even first responders within the same jurisdiction sometimes lack interoperable communications. For this reason, the U.S. Department of Homeland Security has distributed billions of dollars in grants to improve interoperability.[68] In addition to radios, wireless technology has shown great promise in facilitating communication during emergency situations.[69]

NIMS is adaptable in theory to any incident encountered by first responders. This can include routine incidents and large-scale critical incidents that require the assistance of other agencies.[70] In other words, in complex critical incidents, state, federal, and local emergency management and first responder agencies will have to work together to achieve resolution. Although each agency is operated by different levels of government and each agency has different legal authority and differing chains of command, the utilization of NIMS allows them to work together to effectively respond.

NIMS allows flexibility and scalability of critical incident response. It also provides a set of standardized organizational procedures that improve the interaction and integration of different first responder disciplines and jurisdictions. Importantly, NIMS provides common technology. A body of common terminology enhances communication between responding agencies at an incident site.[71]

NIMS incorporates substantial parts of both IMS (Incident Management System) and ICS (Incident Command System). It has changed and evolved since 2004 to reflect problems encountered during implementation.

In the first edition of NIMS published in 2006, there were six components: (1) *command and management,* (2) *preparedness,* (3) *resource management,* (4) *communication and information management,* (5) *supporting technologies,* and (6) *ongoing management and maintenance.*

The 2008 second edition of NIMS contained five components: (1) *preparedness,* (2) *communications and information management,* (3) *resource management,* (4) *command and management,* and (5) *ongoing management and maintenance.*

The present (2017) edition of NIMS contains four components (1) *fundamentals and concepts of NIMS,* (2) *resource management,* (3) *command and co-ordination,* and (4) *communications and information management.*

Fundamentals and concepts of NIMS is the first component. It emphasizes that the effort to protect property, save lives, and deal effectively with critical incidents requires collaboration and cooperation between first responder and emergency management agencies. "NIMS provides stakeholders across the whole community with the shared vocabulary, systems, and processes to successfully deliver the capabilities described in the National Preparedness System."[72] This section covers the applicability and scope of NIMS, guiding principles (flexibility, standardization, and unity of effort), and the background of NIMS.

Resource management is the second NIMS component. This requires federal, state, and local EM and first responder agencies to identify and type their available resources according to the standardized mandated by NIMS. This is complex and extensive. It has generated complaints from EM and first responder agencies due to the expansive documentation requirements.[73]

Command and coordination is the third component of NIMS. This utilizes the command and management structure of ICS (Incident Command System) as its primary tool. The EOC (Emergency Operations Center), JIS (Joint Information Systems), and MACS (Multiagency Coordination Group) are also utilized to provide scalable coordination and command of critical incident scenes.

Communication and information management is the fourth NIMS component. This establishes standards for incident communication. It also sets up processes and protocols for managing incident information.[74]

Keep in mind that NIMS is not itself an incident management plan. Rather, NIMS provides broad principles that are intended to be applied to first responder and emergency management agencies. These broad principles are designed to assist first responders and emergency managers to better collaborate during critical incidents. NIMS is composed of concepts, principles, and doctrines and is therefore not a specific method to resolve critical incidents.[75] NIMS contains broad principles that can be applied by emergency management and first responder agencies to integrate their work and tasks during critical incidents and planned events. ICS, on the other hand, is a much more specific methodology to achieve these purposes.

Incorporation of the Incident Command System into the National Incident Management System

As was noted previously, ICS was developed *much earlier* than NIMS. NIMS has *incorporated* ICS. Thus, ICS is a *part* of NIMS. Specifically, ICS is the *major part* of the *command and coordination component* of NIMS. ICS is the most commonly utilized part of NIMS to the first responder community.[76]

NIMS has absorbed and incorporated the older components of the ICS.[77] ICS is taught so extensively to emergency management and first responder personnel because it is a standardized system that allows for **multidisciplinary** (emergency response provided by different organizations within a single jurisdiction, such as city police and fire) and **multijurisdictional** (emergency response provided by different organizations simultaneously, such as local fire, state hazmat, or federal agencies such as FEMA). Federal, state, local, police, fire, emergency medical, and emergency management agencies work for different organizations and in some cases different levels of government. NIMS requires the ability to integrate the work performed by personnel in these different agencies. This is the goal of NIMS broadly and ICS in particular.

In order to be effective, ICS requires common definitions and conceptual frameworks.[78] This is true because although most critical incidents are handled by local emergency response personnel in a single jurisdiction, more extensive and complex critical incidents require additional agencies from other jurisdictions to intervene. ICS provides a common methodology with which to coordinate incident management (regardless of scope) across emergency response jurisdictions and disciplines.[79]

The ICS system is very useful as a methodology. Widespread use of ICS helps to develop skills at the local level that can be expanded for large-scale critical incidents. For that reason, ICS is used by all levels of government and all emergency response disciplines.[80] Communications in ICS are improved by the use of common terminology as incorporated by NIMS.[81]

The organizational structure of ICS should unfold in a modular fashion depending upon the size, magnitude, and hazard profile of a particular critical incident. Separate functional elements can be established when needed in this modular structure. Incident Command (IC) established and expands the ICS modular structure.[82]

If the complexity of a given critical incident increases, the ICS structure allows for expansion vertically and horizontally as functional responsibilities are assigned by the IC. Management positions expand under ICS as needed depending upon the requirements of the incident.[83]

Incident Command begins with the Incident Commander himself or herself. The individuals exercising the command function must be clearly identified from the beginning of the incident operation. When a more senior officer arrives, the command should be transferred following a briefing that summarizes and captures all essential information about past and present critical incident operations. Effective use of Incident Action Plans (IAPs) facilitates the transfer of incident command.[84]

IAPs are plans that lay out general objectives for managing a given type of critical incident. They are prepared by the Planning System Chief and address both operational and support activities of first responder agencies.[85] They are a summary of current actions taken to address the critical incident, objectives, ICS position assignments, a communications plan, and incident safety and medical plans.[86]

The more complex the critical incident, the more likely that (A) command will need to be transferred to Unified Command or (B) Area Command.

Unified Command (UC) is "an ICS application used when more than one agency has incident jurisdiction or when incidents cross political jurisdictions."[87] UC allows first responder agencies in different disciplines and jurisdictions to work together effectively during a critical incident.[88]

If and when a critical incident is more complex than Unified Command can handle, the overall mission must be transferred to **Area Command**: "an organization that oversees the management of multiple incidents or oversees the management of a very large or evolving situation with multiple ICS organizations."[89] For example, earthquakes, tornadoes, tsunamis, volcanic eruptions, pandemics, and mass casualty terrorist attacks. would require Area Command. Complex, widespread, and geographically dispersed incidents are amenable to Area Command because they require extensive coordination from a higher jurisdictional level. In addition, Area Command is also utilized when several critical incidents of the same type in the same geographical area all require the same resources, such as multiple fires or chemical spills.[90]

Command and Coordination Functions of ICS

The command and coordination component of NIMS is based upon ICS and is designed to enable effective and efficient incident management.[91]

Command in this context refers to the structure and pattern of authority relationships under ICS at a critical incident scene. Under ICS, command is about **Incident Command,** which is the ICS element that deals with the overall management of the critical incident. Incident Command is comprised of the Incident Commander and the assigned supporting staff.[92]

Command can be *single* or *unified* under ICS. **Single command** is the most common—here a single first responder possesses overall incident management responsibility. Single command is most appropriate in critical incidents involving a single discipline (such as the police) in a single jurisdiction is responsible for managing the incident.[93]

Unified Command (UC) is less common under ICS. It is used when more than one agency has ins involved in a critical incident. This can occur when police, fire, and EMS are deployed to a critical incident or when critical incidents cross jurisdictions. First responder agencies work together through UC, which is often comprised of the most senior officers on the scene.[94]

Unified Command represents an important component of the ICS system. Unified Command recognizes that many critical incidents involve multiple jurisdictions and agencies. UC establishes a framework that allows agencies with different functional and jurisdictional authority to interact effectively.[95] The more complex the critical incident, it is unlikely that any particular individual would possess the ability to effectively manage that incident alone.[96]

Although UC has proven to be effective, making it work in reality can sometimes be difficult. This is due to bureaucratic territoriality. Some first responder agencies resist sharing decision-making with other organizations, especially at other levels of government. This resistance can be overcome through interaction between agency representatives prior to a critical incident, and through explaining the rationale behind Unified Command during training and educations sessions.[97]

ICS *command staff* and *general staff* must be differentiated. **Command staff** refers to those critical incident personnel who report directly to the Incident Commander. These personnel include the PIO (Public Information Officer), SO (Safety Officer), and LNO (Liaison Officer). They may have an assistant or assistants, as needed."[98] These are the top or senior officers under Incident Command.[99]

The **Safety Officer (SO)** is responsible for monitoring the health and safety of emergency responders during a critical incident.[100] The **Liaison Officer (LNO)** coordinates critical incident response activities between agencies on the scene.[101] His or her role is especially crucial for critical incidents involving the integration of the efforts of state, local, and federal agencies and responders. The PIO or **Public Information Officer** interacts with the media and the public and media regarding the progress made in dealing with the critical incident.[102] Thus, the PIO is the "face and voice" of the critical incident response team operating under ICS to the news media and the public.

General Staff refers to "groups of incident personnel organized according to function and reporting to the Incident Commander or Unified Command. The ICS General Staff consists of the Operations Section Chief, Planning Section Chief, Logistics Section Chief, Finance/Administration Chief."[103] In law enforcement operations, an Intelligence/Investigations Chief may be established.[104] The general staff is composed of sections under ICS.

ICS Operations Section

The **Operations Section** of ICS is the most important section. The Operations Section is part of the General Staff, which is below the Command Staff in the Incident Command System.

The *Operations Section* manages tactical operations at the critical incident site. These tactical operations generally are aimed at reducing the immediate hazard. This involves establishing situational control, saving lives, reducing property damage, and making other efforts to resolve the critical incident. The Operations Section usually has the greatest number of functions at a critical incident scene and often has the largest number of personnel.[105] Thus, the Operations Section is considered to be the most important section, because it handles tactical critical incident operations and implements the Incident Action Plan. It includes branches, divisions, and sometimes groups.[106]

The Operations Section supervises the units that are responsible on the scene for incident stabilization and resolution. The scope and magnitude of the critical incident determines the makeup of the Operations Section. If the critical incident was caused by criminal activity, Operations will be composed of criminal investigators and other law enforcement personnel. If the critical incident is a hazmat scene or a fire, this section will be composed of hazmat or fire.[107]

As a member of the General Staff, the **Operations Section Chief (OPS)** directly manages all tactical critical incident endeavors. He or she also implements the Incident Action Plan (IAP) in terms of the objectives established by the Incident Commander.[108] Because the Operations Section Chief has such vital responsibilities, the OPS should be the first responder who possesses the most technical expertise and the most tactical critical incident experience available.[109]

The OPS is assigned responsibilities more extensive than most personnel at the incident site. He or she must also assist in developing the IAP. The OPS must also supervise the Operations Section, conduct briefings, and assess the need for additional resources. The OPS must constantly review deployed resources and maintain a unit/activity log.[110]

In a large and complex incident involving death, injuries and property damage, the number of first responders arriving at the critical incident site can become overwhelming in terms of the OPS's span of control.[111] **Span of control** is about the ratio of subordinates for each supervisor. Because the most dangerous activities at a critical incident scene usually occur in the operational area, it is vitally important for the Operations Section Chief to maintain an optimal span of control.[112] A ratio of 1:3 to 1:7 is considered the most appropriate. Beyond this, coordination and control over the first responders is likely to occur.[113]

For this reason, ICS should be utilized to add additional resources to the Operations Section. Doing so will help maintain a suitable span of control."[114] This means delegation of authority through the Incident Command System structure in terms of divisions, groups, and branches.[115]

The term *operational period* is often used in ICS and NIMS. An **operational period** is "the time scheduled for executing a given set of operational actions, as specified in the Incident Action Plan. Operational periods can be of various lengths, although they usually last 12 to 24 hours."[116]

Divisions in ICS are utilized to geographically divide a critical incident. Supervisors are in charge of each division.[117]

Groups refer to "an organizational subdivision established to divide the incident management structure into functional areas of operation. Groups are composed of resources assembled to perform a special function not necessarily within a single geographic area."[118] The official in charge of each group is also designated as a Supervisor. The names or labels assigned to each group are made according to the job that they are assigned, such as Traffic Control Group.[119]

Both Groups and Divisions and Groups can be jointly assigned at a critical incident. Division and Group Supervisors are responsible for reporting status to the OPS.[120] The Operations Section can operate both Divisions and Groups.[121]

ICS also recognizes something called **Resources** that can be utilized and operated under both Groups and Divisions. A **Resource** refers to "Personnel, equipment, teams, supplies, and facilities available or potentially available for assignment to incident operations and for which status is maintained. Resources are described by kind and type and may be used in operational support or supervisory capacities at an incident or at an EOC."[122] Resources can be organized and deployed as needed at a critical incident.[123] Resources in this context can include *single resources, task forces,* and *strike teams.*

A **Single resource** is "an individual, a piece of equipment and its personnel complement, or a crew/team of individuals with an identified work supervisor that can be used on an incident."[124] Single resources are generally used on a specific mission.[125]

Task Forces refer to a combination of resources assembled to accomplish a specific mission or to support an operation. Task forces have designated leaders. For example, a Task Force could be three police units, an EMS unit, and a rescue unit, and two EMS units working together under a single leader to carry out a given mission.[126]

Strike Teams are similar to Task Forces in organization and mission. However, Strike Teams are said to possess more specific proven skills than Task Forces. A Strike Team is "a set number of resources of the same kind and type that have an established minimum number of personnel, common communications, and a leader. In the law enforcement community, strake teams are referred to as resource teams."[127] An example of a Strike Team is four police units under the command of a team leader.[128]

Branches under ICS will now be discussed. A branch is "the organizational level having functional or geographical responsibility for major aspects of incident operations. A branch falls between the Section Chief and the division or group in the Operations Section and between the section and units in the Logistics Section. Branches are identified by Roman numerals or by functional area."[129] Branches may or may not need to be created as additional subdivisions of an Operations Section. It depends upon the size and characteristics of a critical incident. If a critical incident expands in size or complexity, larger subdivisions of the Operations Section need to be created. This can be achieved by creating Branches, which can be used to manage the span of control more effectively.[130]

Because Branch Directors supervise substantial numbers of personnel and resources, they possess much responsibility. They attend Operations Section meetings, supervise Divisions and Groups assignments and assign and modify work tasks to Divisions and Groups. The Branch Director resolves logistical problems and ensures that documentation is completed and submitted from each area under his or her supervision.[131]

ICS Planning Section

The Planning Section is one of the components of the General Staff, along with the Operations Section, the Logistics Section, and the Finance/ Administration Section.

The **Planning Section** is "the Incident Command System Section responsible for the collection, evaluation, and dissemination of operational information related to the incident, and for the preparation and documentation of the Incident Action Plan. This Section also maintains information on the current and forecasted situation and on the status of resources assigned to the incident."[132]

The Planning Section collects and evaluates information utilized to measure the size and magnitude of the critical incident. The Planning Section is also involved in the development and implementation of the Incident Action Plan. It locates technical specialists to plan incident resolution activities.[133]

The **Planning Section Chief (PSC)** is in charge of gathering and analyzing all critical incident-related data on operations and assigned resources. The PSC also engages in planning for tactical operations and conducts planning meetings. He or she is also responsible for preparing the Incident Action Plan for each period of operations.[134]

The PSC runs the **Planning Meeting**, which is "a meeting held as needed before and throughout the duration of an incident to select specific strategies and tactics for incident control operations and for service and support planning. For larger incidents, the Planning Meeting is a major element in the development of the Incident Action Plan."[135]

The Planning Section is comprised of five (sometimes six) units. Remember that a **unit** is a subset of a section or of a branch. "The unit can be staffed by a number of support personnel providing a wide range of services."[136] The units contained within the Planning Section are the *Resources Unit*, the *Situation Unit*, the *Demobilization Unit*, the *Documentation Unit*, and the *Technical Specialist Unit*. In the event that the Intelligence/Investigations Section was not established earlier, its duties can be covered by establishing an *Intelligence/ Investigations Unit* within the Planning Section.[137]

First is the **Resources Unit**. The task of the Resources Unit is to ensure that all dispatched and assigned personnel and other resources have reported to and have officially checked in at the critical incident scene.[138] This unit is in charge of **Resources**, which refers to "Personnel and major items of equipment, supplies, and facilities available or potentially available for assignment to incident operations and for which status is maintained. Resources are described by kind and type and may be used in operational support or supervisory capacities at an incident or at an Emergency Operations Center."[139]

The Resources Unit must implement and maintain a system for keeping track of the physical location and status of all assigned resources and personnel. A master list of all personnel and other resources located at the critical incident should be maintained. The master list should be categorized in terms of functional discipline and by capability and capacity.[140]

This monitoring system indicates whether a resource is classified as *assigned, available,* or *out-of-service.* An **assigned resource** has been officially checked in and is presently engaged in incident operations. An **available resource** has officially checked in and is located at the staging area waiting for deployment. **Out-of-service resources** are located at the incident scene but are unable to be deployed due to mechanical or rest reasons.[141]

Next is the Situation Unit. The **Situation Unit** prepares the status of current operations in real time. In order to do so, the Situation Unit receives real-time information. Part of this involves preparing maps of the critical incident and the gathering of intelligence and other information for use in the Incident Action Plan.[142]

The word of the Documentation Unit is another part of Planning under ICS. The **Documentation Unit** has the task of maintaining written records of the steps taken to manage the critical incident. In addition, the Documentation Unit provides duplication services to critical incident personnel. The Documentation Unit also stores incident files for legal purposes. These stored documents can also be used to analyze and improve future performance.[143]

The fourth unit is the Demobilization Unit. **Demobilization** is about "the orderly, safe, and efficient return of an incident resource to its original location and status."[144] Thus, the Demobilization Unit develops an Incident Demobilization Plan for these purposes. Specific demobilization instructions for resources and personnel are included. that includes specific instructions for all personnel and resources.[145]

The fifth unit under the Planning Section is the **Technical Specialist Unit**. Technical specialists are not generally traditional first responders. Rather, they are persons that contribute specialized skills to dealing with a given critical incident. These technical specialists are notified and activated by first responder organizations when needed to address specific critical incident situations.[146] Such technical specialists are often used in hazmat incidents, hostage situations, or epidemics.[147] The Technical Specialist Unit identifies such technical specialists to assist in the resolution of certain critical incidents. 'incident resolution' strategies. Examples of such technical specialists could include environmental scientists, structural engineers, psychologists, and chemists.[148]

If the technical expertise is needed for only a single incident for a short period of time, the individual should be assigned to the Situation Unit. On the other hand, if the technical expertise will be required for an extended period of time and requires several personnel, they should be made part of the Technical Unit.[149]

In some situations, a sixth unit should be added to the Planning Section: the **Intelligence/Investigations Section**. In critical incidents involving a crime, the incident site is both a crime scene (for which evidence and intelligence information must be collected) and a critical incident site. Sometimes a separate Intelligence/Investigations Section is established at some critical incident sites for this reason.[150]

These units work together under the Planning Section to collect vital information on the incident and to update the Incident Action Plan to resolve the critical incident in the best way possible.

Remember that Incident Action Plans (IAPs) are oral or written plans containing general objectives reflecting the overall strategy for managing an incident. It is prepared by the Planning Section Chief.[151]

The IAP usually includes a summary of the particular incident details (along with a map). The IAP also generally includes established incident objectives, a communications plan, specific ICS position assignments, and incident safety information.[152]

At the beginning of the response to the critical incident, planners should develop a basic plan that is disseminated through short oral briefings. This basic plan is typically developed "on the spot" and sometimes incomplete. As more personnel arrive and a more complete picture of the critical incident emerges, more detailed planning becomes possible.[153] Note that the incident objectives are determined by Incident Command, while other parts are prepared by the Planning Section.

It is important to recognize that the IAP provide clear direction about the overall goals of the operation and also include a listing of tactical objectives. The IAP should be as complete as possible and indicate the steps needed to resolve the critical incident.[154]

The best IAPs are clear and concise. The IAP is essential for coordination and planning.[155] IAPs made according to the NIMS-approved planning process are considered to be the most effective.

NIMS-approved Planning Process Phases

There are five phases to the NIMS-approved planning process, which include *understanding the situation, establishing incident objectives and strategy, developing the plan, preparing and disseminating the plan,* and *evaluating and revising the plan.*[156]

The first phase is to **understand the situation**. This is about gathering and analyzing information about the critical incident and the capabilities of available resources. Doing so will enable the planner to develop a clear picture of the seriousness and complexity of the critical incident. Once this assessment has been made, the planner will be able to develop an appropriate response to dealing with the critical incident based on logic and factual information.[157]

The second phase requires the Planning Section and other decision-makers to **establish incident objectives and strategy**. This is about determining priorities: what must be done first, second, third, and so forth. The objective is to determine the most appropriate strategy to resolve the critical incident. Establishing objectives and strategy requires that health and safety factors, number of casualties, environmental impact, and legal considerations be examined.[158]

The third phase involves actually **developing the plan** to achieve the incident objectives and strategy. This is about the tactics that should be utilized at the critical incident site in terms of resources by operational period. The Incident Commander or the Unified Command develops this plan based on the available information.[159]

Personnel must then **prepare and disseminate the plan** to responders "on the ground" in order to implement the plan. The plan must be communicated in a format that is suitable to the incident and the available resources and personnel. For the initial response that can be handled during one operational period, a concise oral briefing would be sufficient. For more complex critical incidents that span multiple operational periods, the plan should be disseminated in writing according to ICS protocols.[160]

The final step requires decision-makers to **evaluate and revise the plan** as needed depending upon changed circumstances as events unfold at the incident site. The ICS General Staff should constantly compare what has been achieved on the ground with the plan. If problems emerge or new information becomes available, the plan must be modified. Such modifications must be communicated to those working the critical incident.[161]

In summary, The Planning Section utilizes information to help the Incident Commander or Unified Command to develop IAP and a backup plan. Beyond this, the Planning Section also prepares a template for the return to normal operations.[162]

Logistics Section of the General Staff

The **Logistics Section** is "responsible for providing facilities, services, and material support for the incident."[163] **Logistics** itself deals with mechanisms for providing services and resources in order to support critical incident management.[164]

The job of the Logistics Section is to help ensure that critical incident responders have the equipment and other resources needed to perform their jobs. Logistics is a critical part of ICS.[165]

The Logistics Section is responsible for obtaining all resources and equipment needed to effectively resolve a critical incident. It is a proactive function that may involve obtaining resources from sources distant from the critical incident site. Logistics is also about the provision of transportation, facilities, food, fuel, medical services for first responders, supplies, communications equipment, and so forth. The ability of first responders to sustain operations depends upon effective logistics.[166]

The Logistics Section is led by a Section Chief. The Section Chief may have a deputy at large critical incident. At major critical incidents that require the deployment of assets from several facilities, the Logistics Section is divided into Support and Service Branches for span of control purposes.[167]

Logistics is especially important when a critical incident is large enough to exceed the capacity of the equipment brought to the scene by first responders. Major critical incidents consume resources quickly. It is for this reason that ICS operates and supports the Logistics Section: critical incident management operations must be supplied in order to be maintained.[168]

Unified logistics is often seen in ICS. Unified logistics is the combined utilization of the resources of two or more jurisdictions or agencies in the ICS Logistics Section. Unified logistics is used in complex critical incidents in which the equipment and supplies of a single jurisdiction or agency are insufficient to support ongoing incident response.[169] In addition, different emergency management disciplines require different supplies and equipment. Police agencies, fire agencies, and emergency medical agencies require very different supplies. Unified logistics can be achieved by assigning two or more Logistics Section Chiefs from different agencies or jurisdictions to a newly created unified Logistics Section under on-scene ICS.[170]

In order to understand ICS logistics, one must also know the distinction between *push logistics* and *pull logistics.* **Push logistics** is used for routine critical incidents. Push logistics is based on the supplies and equipment that first responders routinely carry with them to critical incident sites. Push logistics is usually part of the standard equipment list of police, firefighters, and EMS workers. This standard equipment is based on supplies and equipment typically needed and is based upon the collective experience of an agency assembled over a long span of time.[171]

Pull logistics involves ordering or bringing in supplies and equipment from outside the responding agency.[172] In large-scale disasters and critical incidents, first responders quickly consume their supplies. In order to sustain operations, resources must be sent to the critical incident site.[173]

Pull logistics makes the logistics function much more complicated for first responder agencies. Supplies and equipment must be located and ordered.[174] The ability of an agency to do so involves EMAPs (Emergency Management Assistance Compacts) and contracting from vendors.[175]

Under ICS, Logistics Sections are typically set up with two branches: the *Support Branch* and the *Service Branch*. Each branch has three units.

The **Support Branch** provides facilities, transport, supplies, and equipment and equipment maintenance in order to support first responders.[176] There are three units under the Support Branch: (1) the *Supply Unit*, (2) the *Facilities Unit*, and (3) the *Ground Support Unit*.

The **Supply Unit** processes, orders, receives, and stores the resources of a first responder agency. **Resources** refer to the equipment and supplies, needed to support critical incident operations.[177] The Supply Unit procures tactical and support resources in addition to expendable and nonexpendable supplies required to support the incident. Examples of **tactical resources** include ambulances, fire units, tools such as saws, and equipment like electrical generators. **Support resources** include fuel for motor vehicles and generators and food for personnel. **Personnel resources** include police officers, firefighters, and emergency medical workers. **Expendable supplies** are items that are consumed at the critical incident scene and cannot be reused, such as gloves, bandages, ammunition, water, and oxygen. Nonexpendable supplies can be cleaned and reused, including body armor and fire hoses.[178]

Next is the Facilities Unit. The **Facilities Unit** sets up and takes down temporary structures used to support critical incident operations such as the EOC, trailers, sleeping areas, showers, and sanitation.[179] In addition, the Facilities Unit sets up areas used to provide food and water services for deployed personnel.

The third unit under the Support Branch is the Ground Support Unit. The **Ground Support Unit** repairs and maintains tactical equipment and motor vehicles at the critical incident site. The unit also records usage time and supplies gasoline or diesel fuel for all motorized equipment assigned to the incident. In addition, the Ground Support Unit provides ground transportation and develops and implements the incident traffic plan. The incident traffic plan delineates routes for motor vehicles entering or exiting all areas of the incident site.[180] The Ground Support Unit also maintains a motor pool for official uses at critical incident sites.

The second branch of the Logistics Section established at major incident sites is the Service Branch. The **Service Branch** provides medical service, food and water, and communications to incident personnel.[181] There are three units under the Service Branch: (1) the *Communications Unit*, (2) the *Food Unit*, and (3) the *Medical Unit*.

First is the **Communications Unit**, which provides communications planning for the ICS. Keep in mind that complex critical incidents require an incident communications plan in order to effectively coordinate on-the-ground activities. The Communications Unit determines radio frequencies and sets up telephone equipment. The Communications Unit also sets up and maintains other communications links between the critical incident site and the outside world.[182]

Communications plans are prepared by the Communications Unit. The Communications Unit sets up the vital radio networks for large incidents, including the *command net, tactical nets, support net, ground-to-air net, air-to-air nets,* and *marine nets.*

One of the major themes of NIMS is to standardize communications between all agencies. Therefore, experts advise, based on critical incident experience that codes should not be used for on-site for radio communications. Rather, the use of NIMS-based a clear spoken message will reduce misunderstanding between first responders from different disciplines.[183] For example, law enforcement personnel utilize "10-codes" routinely. These should be avoided in multidisciplinary and multijurisdictional critical incidents.

It is noted that the failure of communications is a common factor in disasters and terrorist attacks. For example, police and fire personnel did not communicate effectively with each other in the 9/11 attacks on the World Trade Center. For that reason, a **communications failure protocol** should be developed and maintained. This is a plan that specifies major communications networks and backup systems in the event of infrastructure failures.[184]

The second subdivision of the Service Branch is the Food Unit, which provides meals to on-scene incident responders. The **Food Unit** determines the nutritional and hydration requirements of deployed personnel, orders and prepares food, serves food, and maintains the hygiene of food service areas.[185]

The third subdivision of the Service Branch is the **Medical Unit**. It provides needed medical care to critical incident personnel.[186] Working in a hazardous and stressful incident scene may lead to health problems for responding incident personnel. Dealing with these needs is the task of the Medical Unit. The Medical Unit is usually staffed by a local EMS agency.[187] Keep in mind that the Medical Unit is for *incident personnel only.* It is not intended to be used to assist disaster victims. Providing civilian/victim medical care is a task for the Operations Section.

In the event of a disaster of such magnitude that mass care and sheltering is required, a considerable strain will be placed upon the Logistics Section. Mass sheltering functions should be transferred from the Logistics Section Facilities Unit to the Operations Section when a disaster or attack is of such magnitude to require mass sheltering. In such a situation, sheltering demands expand dramatically. If this occurs, the ICS structure should be used to redirect operations to respond to public needs for shelter, food, water, and sanitary facilities.[188]

A final potential task of the Logistics Section lies in its role in dealing with donations and volunteers following a major disaster. Many individuals and organizations donate clothing, food, time, and talents for the purpose of helping disaster victims. Both donations and volunteers result in challenges to management. The Logistics Section and the Planning Section help to coordinate both.[189] In other words, food and clothing must be evaluated, sorted, and distributed. Volunteers must be organized. Medical volunteers must be credentialed and deployed.

The Finance/Administration Section of ICS

The **Finance/Administration Section** performs all money-related recordkeeping and cost analysis of a large-scale critical incident. This is an important function because government services are paid for with tax dollars. Both the public and elected officials require and demand accountability for the use and expenditure of public funds. Under NIMS and ICS, this accountability for critical incident management expenses is provided by the Finance Section.

Funding and reimbursements are vital and significantly affect the ability of first responder agencies to respond to and recover from incidents. Incident response has a high dollar cost. For that reason, these costs must be properly recorded. This is the job of the Finance/Administration Section. This Section manages the accounting done to keep track of costs for supplies and services. This is necessary for reimbursement by government bodies.[190]

Every incident incurs monetary costs. That is why a Finance/Administration Section is established under ICS. However, not all first responder agencies require reimbursement. Serious disasters and critical incidents that involve several jurisdictions and levels of government require good record keeping. That is handled by the Finance/Administration Section in ICS.[191] Realize that many activities of the Finance/Administration Section are not necessarily performed at the incident scene. Rather, these accounting functions are often conducted off-site.[192]

The Finance/Administration Section is managed by the **Finance/ Administration Section Chief**. This official reports to the Incident Commander or Unified Command as a member of the General Staff.[193] In addition to monitoring expenditures and funding sources. the Finance/ Administration Section must also keep a running tally of current available funds to the agency and federal and state disaster relief funds from grants. This information must be reported periodically to the Incident Commander so that he or she can make decisions about what resources to order and deploy without running out of funding.[194]

The Finance/Administration Section Chief must monitor expenditures. This is necessary to ensure that statutory laws and administrative regulations are met.[195] In other words, there are "strings" attached to receiving taxpayer funding for critical incidents that are complex, "out of the ordinary," and that cause extensive deaths, injuries, and property damage. Spending by a city or county local government is usually limited by law. Major critical incidents cost more than budgeted. New legislation making additional appropriations will then be needed, or grant funding from other levels of government must make up the additional cost.[196]

Section Chiefs determine if subordinate units should be established. In major critical incidents, a Deputy Section Chief can be appointed. The subunits of the Finance/Administration Section are managed by a Unit Leader and are comprised of the *Time Unit*, the *Procurement Unit*, the *Compensation/Claims Unit*, and the *Cost Unit*.[197]

The **Time Unit** records and maintains the number of hours of personnel working hours at the critical incident and often the number of hours of equipment usage.[198] Keeping accurate records of the number of hours employees at the incident scene is a vitally important function. Overtime hours worked must also be calculated and recorded. This documentation is vital as part of the reimbursement process and can be utilized when grant funding becomes available to agencies after the incident has been resolved.[199] The Time Unit and the Logistics Section work together to maintain records on equipment usage.[200]

The second unit under the Finance/Administration Section is the **Procurement Unit**. The Procurement Unit purchases goods and services from private sector vendors.[201] The **Procurement Unit** deals with vendor contracts in terms of locating and renting equipment. It also deals with supply contracts.[202]

The **Compensation/Claims Unit** deals with on-the-job injury compensation and claims related to other types of incident activities.[203] This unit thus deals with worker's compensation claims and documentation for responders injured on the job. In addition, the Compensation/Claims unit handles documentation and investigations for claims for monetary damages from civilians who claim that they suffered losses as a result of incident response activities. Because some injuries and damages may lead to lawsuits, it is especially important for the unit to maintain good records.

The **Cost Unit** is the last of the four units under the Finance/Administration Section. It collects and reports the monetary costs that stem from a critical incident.[204]

In summary, the Finance/Administration Section deals with administrative and financial considerations surrounding a critical incident.[205] These things involve procurement, cost recovery, liability, and risk management.

Intelligence/Investigations Section of ICS

The four sections that have been examined thus far under ICS are *minimally* required when ICS is implemented. If the incident is the result of a crime (mass shooting, terrorism, arson, etc.), then it will also be necessary to establish a separate **Intelligence and Investigation Section**. This is true because these types of critical incidents are both a crime scene and an emergency response scene. The victims must be assisted, the scene must be controlled, and evidence must be preserved to support criminal investigation and criminal prosecution in these types of critical incidents.

The **Intelligence/Investigations Function** provides Incident Command or Unified Command with information about a criminal adversary in the operational environment. The Intelligence/Investigations Function supports management decision making by helping to reduce uncertainty about a potentially hostile environment.[206]

However, in a "normal" critical incident such as an accident, a hazmat incident, etc., the necessary intelligence functions performed, such as risk assessment, weather information, and building floorplan and utilities information can be performed by an intelligence/investigation unit located inside the Planning Section.[207] But in atypical critical incidents such as terrorist attacks, the Incident Commander may assign the Intelligence/Investigations Function to another area.[208] This is done by establishing a separate Intelligence/Investigations Section under the General Staff at a critical incident scene.

If this occurs, the objectives of the Intelligence/Investigations Function become more specialized. Intelligence gathered within the Intelligence/Investigation function is used to support criminal investigation and criminal prosecution. This is different from the normal operational information gathered by the Planning Section.[209]

Some critical incidents may involve sensitive information that does not need to be disseminated to all first responders on the scene. In addition, this information should not be discussed over nonsecure communications networks because doing so may compromise operations.[210] This is especially true in hostage situations, barricaded gunman scenarios, and the initial stages of terrorist investigations.

This is why a "best practice" principle is that disclosure of certain kinds of intelligence information should occur with the approval of Incident Command or Unified Command to those that have the proper clearance and need to know.[211]

Multiagency Coordination Systems under NIMS

Thus far, we have examined ICS (Incident Management System) in some detail. Remember that ICS is *one* component of the command and management structure of NIMS.

In review, the command and management structure of NIMS utilizes the Incident Command System as its primary tool. FEMA points out that

"The Incident Command System (ICS), Multiagency Coordination System (MACS), and Public Information are the fundamental elements of incident management. These elements provide standardization through consistent terminology and established organizational structure. Taken together, these elements of Command and Management are the most visible aspects of incident management, typically executed with a sense of urgency."[212]

"A **Multiagency Coordination System (MACS)** is a system of facilities, equipment, personnel, procedures, and communications integrated into a common system that is responsible for coordinating and supporting domestic incident management activities. A MACS is not simply a facility or physical location...."[213] Rather, a MACS is best conceptualized as an acronym that stands for "a process that allows all levels of government and all [emergency management] disciplines to work together more efficiently and effectively. Multiagency coordination occurs across the different disciplines involved in incident management, across jurisdictional lines, or across levels of government."[214]

MACS exist to provide multiagency coordination for complex events that involve several jurisdictions. MACS greatly enhance multiagency coordination activities. MACS also enhance effectiveness and safety of the response when multiple agencies respond.[215]

In short, "the primary function of MACS is to coordinate activities above the field level and to prioritize the incident demands for critical or competing resources, thereby assisting the coordination of the operations in the field."[216] In other words, MACS function at a *higher* "management" level than incident response. The MACS coordinates relationships and provides policy direction and support to emergency management and first responder agencies.

If a major terrorist attack or natural disaster occurs, EMS, fire, police, and public works personnel will be present at the critical incident location. Their activities must be coordinated. It is especially important when critical incidents cross disciplinary or jurisdictional boundaries to have such coordination.[217]

MACS entities are usually comprised of the principals from agencies with direct incident management responsibility. MACS entities can be called *crisis action teams*, incident *management groups*, or *executive teams.* [218]

Generally, emergency responder and/or emergency management personnel respond to what they at first believe will be a "typical" incident. Further investigation and assessment demonstrate, however, that the critical incident may be much more complex than first believed. In this situation, the initial response "transitions" from being a matter that can be handled entirely by Incident Command to requiring MACS.

The two most commonly seen used elements of MACS in action are **Emergency Operations Centers (EOCs)** and MAC Groups.[219] "An EOC is a physical central location from which local governments can provide interagency coordination and executive decision making in support of incident response and recovery operations. The purpose of the EOC is to provide a centralized location where public safety, emergency response, and support agencies coordinate planning, preparedness, and response activities."[220]

An EOC does not direct on-scene response efforts. Rather, an EOC helps to coordinate responses from different agencies.[221] The decisions made inside an EOC are broad-based and designed to guide priorities. Tactical decisions are made at the incident site. The EOC serves as a link between the Chief Elected Officer (CEO) of the jurisdiction and the first responders at the critical incident site.[222] An EOC is necessary to effectively coordinate critical response actions and to coordinate with other jurisdictions.[223]

As noted previously, one notch below an EOC is the Command Post (CP) which operates at the incident level. A **CP** is a **Command Post**, which is an "on scene" incident management facility for small-scale events and incidents. In small-scale critical incidents, the CP functions as a "miniature" EOC.[224]

In law enforcement contexts such as mass shootings, research has shown that rapidly unfolding events can interfere with establishing a command post. For example, in the Virginia Tech mass shooting of 2007, a command post was not established until the shooting had ended. Similarly, police and fire personnel have been known to establish separate command posts during the same incident. This occurred at during the I-35 bridge collapse in Minnesota the same year.[225]

Most larger cities and counties in the United States have an EOC. All fifty states have an EOC.[226] Keep in mind though that most of the time these EOC facilities are used for other purposes and are located in government buildings. In any event, the primary functions of the EOC are data and information management and resource support for critical incident sites. The majority of information that is transmitted to and from an EOC involves resource requests, resource tracking, weather, damage assessment, public information, and situation status.[227]

EOCs are a part of the critical infrastructure. For this reason, it can be at risk due to natural disasters and is a potential target for terrorist attacks. For these reasons, an EOC has to be located in a strong building and properly secured. Access to EOCs should also be controlled. In terrorism scenarios, armed teams should be deployed. In addition, communications coming to and from an ECO should be secured.[228]

It is noted that an EOC is an appropriate place to maintain the **Common Operational Picture (COP)**, which is a real-time view of the status of the situation from multiple sources. This can include situation and resource status. The COP provides an overview of a critical incident. The COP is a function of the ICS Planning Section. Due to complexity, the EOC is often the only location in the jurisdiction that maintains a COP.[229] COP communications, in addition to other EOC information, must be secured.

EOCs are often advised by a **Policy Group**. The EOC is usually operated at local or state levels by a Director of Emergency Management. The Policy Group consists of both chief executives and elected officials. The Policy Group should not be involved in operational decisions due to the fact that few members possess first responder training. A Legal Advisor is also recommended for the Policy Group due to the potential for litigation involving response activities.[230]

MAC Groups (Multiagency Committees) are another common way to operate MACS. A Mac Group is composed of administrators or executives (or their designees) that possess the authority to commit agency funds and resources. A MAC Group can make decisions in a coordinated manner between different agencies. A MAC Group can also establish response priorities between incidents and provide guidance to support incident management efforts.[231] Keep in mind that conceptually, a MAC Group is comprised of officials with decision-making authority equivalent to an EOC in authority and status. MACs may be used in conjunction with an EOC or independent of an EOC.

Both EOCs and MACs utilize ICS forms. Eleven common ICS forms are used. NIMS has adopted these forms.[232] The forms are part of the necessary bureaucracy to document actions taken by responding agencies.

As is the case with EOCs, MAC Groups are not directly involved in incident involvement. MAC Groups are usually located at a distance remote from the incident site. With modern technology such as Zoom, a MAC Group can meet and function virtually.[233]

Next is *Area Command.* **Area Command** is a temporary organization established to oversee the management of several organizations (each of which is utilizing ICS) responding to either a large incident or multiple separate incidents.[234] Area Command is only activated under these scenarios.[235] For example, earthquakes, tornadoes, tsunamis, volcanic eruptions, pandemics, and mass casualty terrorist attacks might require Area Command. Complex, widespread, and geographically dispersed incidents are amenable to Area Command because they require substantial coordination from a higher jurisdictional level. In addition, Area Command can also be established when several incidents of the same type in the same geographical area occur. Such a situation results in competition for the same resources.[236]

Keep in mind that Area Command does not possess direct operational control over response activities.[237] An Area Command integrates with EOC functions. MACS actually support Area Command. For this reason, MAC Groups can be confused with Area Command.[238] Public heath emergencies that cover a wide geographic are relevant to Area Commands.[239] Remember that Multiagency Coordination Systems go beyond Area Command.

In terms of organization, The Area Command is administered similarly to ICS. The key positions in an Area Command are Area Commander, Area Logistics Chief, Area Command Planning Chief, and Area Command support positions.[240]

The **Area Commander** supervises the overall direction of incident management teams assigned to the same incident. He or she also supervises the work of first responders to multiple incidents in the local community.[241] **The Area Command Logistics Chief** is in charge of the provision of services, facilities, and materials to Area Command level and allocates supplies and resources.[242]

The **Area Command Planning Chief** establishes incident strategies and objectives based upon information obtained from incident management teams.[243] As necessary, Area Command support positions such as the Resources Unit Leader, the Situation Unit Leader, the Public Information Officer, the Liaison Officer, and the Aviation Coordinator are established.

No matter whether an EOC or a MAC Group is established during a complex incident, all MACS entities include common system elements. Next is public Information, which is the third "organizational construct" of the Command and Management component of NIMS. In review, the other elements are ICS and multiagency coordination systems.

The Public Information Component of NIMS

Remember that the command and management structure of NIMS utilizes the Incident Command System as its primary tool. The command and management component of NIMS was developed as a standardized methodology with which to manage critical incidents effectively. The NIMS structure is based upon ICS, multiagency coordination systems like MACs, and public information.[244]

FEMA points out that "The Incident Command System (ICS), Multiagency Coordination System (MACS), and Public Information are the fundamental elements of incident management. These elements provide standardization through consistent terminology and established organizational structures.... Taken together, these elements of Command and Management are the most visible aspects of incident management, typically executed with a sense of urgency."[245]

Public information is designed to communicate accurate and timely facts regarding an incident's size, progress toward resolution, and causes to the public and other stakeholders.[246]

The dissemination of effective public information is essential following a disaster or attack. The public expects immediate and truthful information. The news media quickly report on attacks and disasters. Media personnel are entitled to access to information from public officials. Messages that recommend and instruct local citizens in the affected area with regard to the actions and precautions to take are an essential element of public information, which must be rapidly communicated.[247]

The key ICS and NIMS player in public information is the **Public Information Officer (PIO)**. The PIO is the official responsible for communicating with the public and media regarding critical incidents.[248] Thus, the Public Information Officer is the "face and voice" of the critical incident response team operating under ICS to the news media and the public.

The Public Information Officer (PIO) is a member of ICS Command Staff. He or she advises Incident Command or Unified Command on public information matters relating to the management of the critical incident.[249] The PIO deals with media relations, emergency warnings and public information, and rumor monitoring and response. He or she also handles inquiries from the public, the media, and elected officials.[250]

Emergency managers and Incident Commanders must understand that working with the media effectively is an important component of critical incident management. An important part of an overall emergency management system. Failing to maintain effective public information can lead to serious consequences for first responder agencies.[251]

The duties of the Public Information Officer are performed both during emergencies and as part of day-to-day organizational operations.[252] PIOs provide "public information" to those outside the first responder or emergency management organization. Public information can be used to protect property and to reduce deaths and injuries in addition to providing news about the critical incident. For this reason, information must be both timely and accurate.[253]

Due to the importance of the PIO's role in representing emergency management and first responder agencies to the media, FEMA engages in training and development for Public Information Officers. FEMA's Emergency Management Institute (EMI) offers Public Information Officer (PIO) training. The training program helps to provide PIOs with the abilities and skills to deliver correct and appropriate messages to the public. The PIO training program offered by EMI provides PIOs with the skills needed to gather, verify, and disseminate public information.[254] FEMA operates five courses for PIOs.

An emergency management or first responder agency's PIO must communicate with several constituencies including the public, the media, the agency, and other responding agencies. In order to be effective, Public Information Officers need excellent interpersonal skills and extensive substantive knowledge of the organization that they represent.

PIOs provide the vital connection between the emergency management or first responder agency and the public (members of the population and the media). Examples include warnings to the public in terms of hazards and protective measures, the current status of the incident or emergency, agency responses to the incident, specific evacuation actions or directions, important locations (shelters, water, food), closing information (roads, schools, etc.), and status of the grid (water, electricity, etc.).

Emergency managers should realize that the public "face" of the agency is represented by the Public Information Officer. For that reason, he or she must be media savvy. In communicating with the public through and with the media, the PIO forms a trust-based relationship with the jurisdiction. In order to be effective, a PIO should have knowledge of both traditional and social media. As an agency representative, the PIO should positively portray the critical incident response activities of the agency they represent.[255]

In an incident involving injury, death, or property damage, the media follows a predictable pattern, which includes dispatching reporters, obtaining or trying to obtain access to the incident scene, talking with agency officials including the PIO, dramatizing the situation, and expecting briefings and press releases.[256]

In small-scale local incidents and disasters, the local agency's Public Information Officer can usually deal efficiently with the media. However, large-scale incidents typically result in the necessity to engage the Joint Information System (JIS) under NIMS (National Incident Management System). Thus, the PIO must learn how to function in the JIS environment.[257]

Under NIMS, the **JIS (Joint Information System)** "Provides the mechanism to organize, integrate, and coordinate information to ensure timely, accurate, accessible, and consistent messaging across multiple jurisdictions and/or disciplines with nongovernmental organizations and the private sector."[258]

The JIS operates through the use of **Joint Information Centers (JICs)**, which "...is a physical location used to coordinate critical emergency information, crisis communications, [and] public affairs functions. JICs may be established at each level of incident management – local, state, regional, or national – as required. The JIC includes representatives of each jurisdiction, agency, private-sector entity, and nongovernmental organization involved in incident management activities."[259]

The broad system is referred to ta the Joint Information System, and the actual location where the process occurs is referred to as the Joint Information Center.[260] In other words The JIC is a mechanism used to help facilitate what happens within the Joint Information System.[261]

Reporters from major news networks can be aggressive in obtaining information. Emergency managers and first responder personnel should realize that refusing to cooperate with the media will not likely keep the story from being broadcast. An effectively operated JIS helps to provide the media with the information that they seek. Cooperation with the media helps to produce an accurate and favorable story about the agency.[262] In addition, the proliferation of social media has increased media interest for information.

Emergency response agencies have the duty to disseminate accurate public information. Doing so can be a challenging goal in major incidents, especially those that involve different jurisdictions and levels of government.[263] Information must be *gathered, verified, coordinated,* and *disseminated.*[264]

First, information must be **gathered**. This means that information must be obtained as the first step.[265] Information should be gathered from the Incident Commander, the news media, the public, and elected officials. The Incident Commander can provide "real-time" information about the status of the critical incident. Elected officials can provide additional information. Monitoring the news media can tell you the accuracy of the reporting, as well as providing a "larger-scale" picture of events.[266]

Valid information must be **verified** for accuracy. This is done by continuous contact with the Incident Commander and with the EOC and JIC. Such verified information should be **coordinated** with the EOC and other Public Information Officers so that the same message is **disseminated** (distributed) to the public and other stakeholders.[267] Keep in mind that monitoring what is reported about the agency and the critical incident is important. It helps to ensure that the information is understood correctly by the media and reported accurately. PIOs should address inaccuracies with the media as soon as possible.[268]

The goal is to allow the emergency management agency to *control the message* during the critical incident as much as possible. The major categories of information are narrative information, advisories and warnings, and action messages.[269]

Narrative information provides and overview of a critical incident or event. Narratives are usually in the form of video clips, audio sound bites, or articles. Narrative This information provides a picture of how a critical incident is being managed and helps to keep the public informed.[270] For example, "A train containing 26 cars derailed at approximately 10:05 AM."

Advisories and warnings notify members of the public about an emergency or hazard and can provide instructions recommending that actions be taken. These are time-sensitive and must convey accurate information.[271]

Action messages direct members of the public to take immediate action to protect their health and safety. Here, accuracy and timeliness are imperative. Action messages require aggressive media messaging by television, radio, and public warning systems. Nonmedia systems like reverse 911 are very helpful in disseminating action messages as well.[272] For example, "An evacuation has been ordered for Dauphin Island."

To help ensure accurate and timely information, JIS protocols require written procedures. These messages can come from many official sources at different levels of government and can be made by JICs, PIOs, or from EOCs.[273]

During an emergency, disaster, or critical incident, not all information flows into the JIC through official or formal channels. It may be the case that members of the public contact the EOC with information or to make inquiries. Such notifications or inquiries can include rumors that must be investigated and dispelled if necessary. In addition, the JIC may receive frequent calls from media reporters asking questions about the information they received from the public. Due to the pervasiveness of the media, it is not unusual for ICS staffers to learn incident information from national news networks rather than initially through official channels.[274]

When a local critical incident receives national media coverage, the pressures increase on the JIS. Reporters from national media organizations have an expectation that decision makers will afford them access, time, and preferential treatment. Major media news vans and equipment can interfere with local communications systems. During a major disaster or critical incident, cellular telephone systems can become quickly overloaded. The same can occur with computer bandwidth. As a sound practice, JIS procedures should plan logistics support for national media operations in the event that a major disaster, attack, or critical incident occurs in their jurisdiction.[275]

A final consideration with regards to public information deals with *operational security* and *force protection.*

Operational security (OPSEC) deals with procedures designed to prevent sensitive information that might compromise response operations from being disclosed or released intentionally or unintentionally. OPSEC is especially important during terrorism-related or criminal critical incidents. Response personnel should not broadcast information about strategy, tactics, protective equipment, or weapons. This is true because terrorists and criminals monitor the media as does the general public.[276]

Force protection is the safeguarding of facilities and key personnel to prevent or reduce losses in the event of an attack. The EOC and JIC must especially be protected. State, local, and federal law enforcement agencies should design and implement force protection procedures that can be implemented immediately in a large-scale attack or disaster.[277]

The Communications and Information Management Component of NIMS

Communication and information management is one of the NIMS components. This establishes standards for incident communication. It also sets up processes and protocols for managing incident information.[278]

The primary goals of the Communication and Information Management NIMS component are to develop and utilize common communication standards and technologies to support incident management organizations and operations.[279]

"Effective emergency management and incident response activities rely on flexible communications and information systems that provide a common operating picture to emergency management/response personnel and their affiliated organizations.... Properly planned, established, and applied communications enable the dissemination of information among command and support elements and, as appropriate, cooperating agencies and organizations."[280]

"The underlying concepts and principles of this component reinforce the use of flexible communications and information system in which emergency management/response personnel can maintain a constant flow of information during an incident. These concepts and principles emphasize the need for and maintenance of a common operating picture; interoperability; reliability, scalability, and portability; and resiliency and redundancy of any system and its components."[281]

Common Operating Picture (COP) is another phrase that refers to the more commonly used concept of **situational awareness**. Personnel involved with incident management should be exposed to the same information on the scene.[282] FEMA defines COP as "an overview of an incident by all relevant parties that provides incident information enabling the Incident Commander/ Unified Command and any supporting agencies and organizations to make effective, consistent, and timely decisions."[283]

Emergency managers and first responders must utilize standardized communication types in order to facilitate successful communications and information management.[284] There are four standardized communication types: (1) *strategic communications*, (2) *tactical communications*, (3) *support communications*, and (4) *public address communications*.

Strategic communications deal with overall incident response courses of action and determinations about roles and responsibilities at the site.[285] **Tactical communications** involve "on-the-ground" interchanges between commanders and first responders on the scene.[286] **Support communications** deal with interchanges involving coordination of tactical and strategic communications.[287] Finally, **public address communications** involve warnings, emergency alerts, and press conferences.[288]

NIMS stresses the necessity of engaging in a comprehensive planning process to develop and maintain involving interoperable communications.[289] The interoperable communications methodology should incorporate the information needs of the jurisdiction and organization in addition to procedures for the dissemination of warnings and public communications. Information management technologies such as computer networks should be inline in order to integrate incident management functions to enable the sharing of critical information during critical incidents.[290]

The information management technology selected must be understood by the users in order to be effective. Information is vital to decision-making by Incident Command or Unified Command at the critical incident scene.[291] In addition, the same incident information can be used in multiple ways to accomplish aiding the planning process, providing information to the Finance/ Administration Section to determine cost, and identifying information.[292]

Information is used to improve decision making at the incident site. It can be used effectively for incident notification, situation, and status reports. Situation reports (called **SitStat** within ICS) provide information about the past operational period. Situation reports also contain information about specific details of the critical incident and how it was resolved. Status reports also contain information about resource status. This can also be utilized later for assessment and analysis.[293]

This includes **geospatial data**. Geospatial data pertains to the geographic location and characteristic objects and terrain in the natural and built environments. It identifies features of the terrain and structures and can be used to enhance COP.[294]

A vital part of communications and information management involves communications standards and formats. Communications standards are necessary to enable agencies from different jurisdictions and functional disciplines to work effectively together. Common identifiers for locations and facilities, common typing, and standard functions and elements facilitate incident operations.[295]

Different jurisdictions and disciplines should develop plans for interoperability so that they will be ready prior to a critical incident. Protocols and procedures for communications are important to establish in advance. In order to make these plans effective, agencies and organizations must distribute this information to their employees.[296]

Beyond this, common terminology must be employed in complex critical incidents by responding personnel. Common terminology allows first responders personnel to effectively communicate with each other and to properly coordinate activities. This can be facilitated through the use of plain language rather than codes. When multiple agencies are involved in incident response, it is especially important not to use either acronyms or codes.[297]

While this is generally true, it is sometimes necessary to use encryption or tactical language, such as in a critical incident involving terrorism or certain types of crimes.[298] Internet resources should be used as needed and appropriate during critical incidents, especially with regard to situational awareness. Social media use and internet use must conform to standards and protocols, however.[299]

Finally, information security must also be established. Procedures must be developed and maintained for this purpose. Failing to do so can lead to public safety issues due to the release of incomplete or untimely information about the critical incident. The release of sensitive information about a criminal investigation or public health information can harm ongoing investigations, national security, or public health.[300]

The Resource Management Component of NIMS

The *resource management* component of NIMS is very complex and extensive. Local jurisdictions are required by NIMS to inventory resources according to a standardized system instructions (typing). Specific definitions for each type of resource is specified by the NIMS resource typing system. NIMS contains rules for determining which specific resources are deemed to be needed for an incident. How these resources are to be ordered, mobilized, tracked, reported, and recovered are also specified by NIMS. There is also a section requiring personnel credentials.[301]

Resource management deals with the oversight, coordination, and processes that provide timely and appropriate resources to emergency responders during an incident.[302]

Resources are comprised of the personnel and equipment that are activated, in service, out of service, or available for assignment. "Resources are described by kind and type and may be used in operational support or supervisory capacities at an incident or at an Emergency Operations Center."[303]

Resource management is used to provide suitable resources to first responders during all types of critical incidents. Resource management is a complex task. This is especially true when a critical incident is large in size and involves multiple jurisdictions.[304]

Incident commanders first establish incident priorities. Then resources needs are identified and ordered. Resource management systems are employed to process the orders. In the typical scenario, most resources are obtained through local channels or mutual aid agreements. In large-scale incidents, competition may ensue for resources and resources may need to be obtained from other levels of government and private vendors.[305]

The Unit Leader of the Resources Unit within the Planning Section of the General Staff under ICS is in charge of resource management.[306] Remember that one of the tasks of the Resources Unit is to ensure that assigned critical incident personnel and other resources have checked in.[307] A system is maintained by the Resources Unit to track the status and incident location of all resources at a critical incident scene. Each resource should be categorized by capacity and capability and the status of each should be tracked continuously.[308]

This monitoring system indicates whether a resource is classified as *assigned, available*, or *out-of-service*. An **assigned resource** has been checked in and are actively engaged in supporting incident operations. An **available resource** has checked in and is waiting for deployment at the staging area. **Out-of-service resources** are located at the incident scene but cannot function due to mechanical or rest reasons at a given time.[309]

NIMS requires that certain principles be followed to guide the resource management process. This standardization is designed to help ensure that resources move efficiently and effectively to support critical incident personnel.[310]

The NIMS resource management process employs a credentialing system. This credentialing system is linked to standardized training and certification standards. The objective is to help ensure that personnel resources will be successful in supporting incident operations.

The **Resources Unit Leader** is in charge of monitoring the status of all resources at an incident.[311] The simplest way to accomplish this task is to checking in and check out the resources at an incident. This can be done for typical or small-scale critical incidents. For more complex critical incidents, a master list of all resources that contains each resource's current location and status should be used.[312]

To help achieve rationality, NIMS bases resource management upon five principles: (1) *planning*, (2) *use of agreements*, (3) *categorizing resources*, (4) *resource identification*, and (5) *effective management of resources*.[313]

Planning involves taking steps to envision the future and to take steps in preparation. Planning, training, and exercises helps to achieve interoperability of resources during critical incidents. Agencies and jurisdictions should collaborate to develop plans for managing and employing resources at critical incidents. This should include identifying likely resource needs and developing plans to obtain these resources.[314]

Use of agreements deals with arrangements made between emergency management agencies prior to critical incidents. For example, mutual aid agreements can greatly increase the capabilities of all agencies involved.[315] Because most agencies do not possess the resources to respond to every critical incident, the use of agreements is necessary.

Categorizing resources is done to make resource management more efficient and effective during critical incident response.[316] By categorizing resources by capability, size, and so forth, emergency management personnel are able to know in advance the resources that are capable of performing a given task or function during specific types of critical incidents.

In terms of **resource identification and ordering**, NIMS stipulates that Resource Unit Leaders use a standardized process to order, identify, mobilize, and track the resources used in critical incident response.[317]

The final resource management principle is the **effective management of resources**. This involves following NIMS training and protocols to acquire and deploy resources. This deals with acquisition procedures used to obtain resources. This can include contracting, purchasing, and mission tasking. [318] Acquisition decisions also involve inventory. Much inventory is kept (stockpiled) at the emergency response or emergency management agency. Other resources are obtained when needed. The decision about which inventory to stockpile and to order as needed depends upon the present needs of the agency.[319] **Management information systems** can be used to facilitate the effective management of resources as well.[320]

Because so much is at stake in a critical incident, **redundant information systems** are necessary. Backup systems should be utilized by resource managers as well if the primary resource management information system becomes unavailable.[321]

The final component of effective management of resources involves **ordering, dispatching, and demobilization protocols**. This involves tracking systems that delineate the location and status of resources along with procedures to deactivate resources to return them to their original locations and status.[322]

These then are the *principles* of NIMS resource management. Next is an examination of the *process* of NIMS resource management. In order to implement the principles of resource management, NIMS includes standardized processes as part of its seven-step resource management process.[323]

The seven steps of the NIMS resource management process are: (1) *identifying resource requirements*, (2) *ordering and acquiring resources*, (3) *mobilizing resources*, (4) *tracking and reporting resources*, (5) *recovering and demobilizing resources*, (6) *reimbursing resources*, and (7) *inventorying resources*.[324]

The first step (**identifying resource requirements**) involves determining which resources will be needed to support predictable critical incidents by the jurisdiction or agency.[325] This is about the "what, where, and who" at a critical incident: what resources are needed, where the resources are needed, and who needs the resources. This can include equipment, supplies, or personnel.[326]

The second step **concerns ordering and acquiring resources**. Established ordering procedures are used to obtain necessary resources locally. Ordering items that cannot be obtained locally should be submitted through the local Emergency Operations Center. If the local EOC is unable to assist, the request should be forwarded to the regional level. ICS forms have been standardized for this purpose.[327]

The next step in the NIMS resource management process is **mobilizing resources**. This is about deploying resources to incident scenes. Response personnel are notified to deploy to critical incident sites. NIMS has a standardized process utilized to mobilize resources.[328]

The mobilization and resource tracking processes are linked. When resources arrive at a critical incident site, they are required to check in with the correct unit of the command. Formal check-in begins and validates order requirements. Appropriate channels are utilized to notify command on scene.[329]

The fourth step in the NIMS resource management process is closely related: **tracking and reporting resources**. Tracking resources provides incident command with a clear view of resource location and their current status (available, in service, out of service). Resource tracking information should be displayed in real time in a manner accessible to everyone on the scene.[330]

Recovering and demobilizing resources is the fifth step in the NIMS resource management process. During and after a critical incident, resources are recovered and prepared for future use. Every resource that was activated and deployed must be recovered, restored, and returned to the correct jurisdiction and agency. Part of this process involves replenishing and rehabilitating the resource. Some resources also must be disposed of and retrograded. Doing these things is related to resource inventory maintenance.[331]

Demobilization refers to the safe return of a resource to its original status and location. The Planning Section maintains a Demobilization Unit for this purpose. The Demobilization Unit develops and maintains an Incident Demobilization Plan (part of the Incident Action Plan), which is composed of demobilization instructions. Demobilization Plans have a process for tracking resources and notifying the appropriate agency of the return. The plan also addresses reimbursement if appropriate.[332]

There are two categories of resources that must be handled as part of recovering and demobilizing resources: *expendable resources* and *nonexpendable resources.* **Expendable resources** are generally consumed in service. Examples of expendable resources include bandages, water filters, and medical gloves.[333] Examples of nonexpendable resources are weapons, fire trucks, and fire hoses. **Nonexpendable resources** are durable and generally not consumed in service at a critical incident.[334]

Reimbursing resources is the sixth step in the NIMS resource management process. Remember that resources must be paid for. Reimbursement is the mechanism utilized to recover funds for resources expended resolving critical incidents. Reimbursement protocols should be included in mutual-aid agreements and other plans.[335]

The final step in the NIMS resource management process is **inventorying resources**, which consists of *inventory management systems, credentialing personnel,* and *identifying and typing resources.*

Inventory systems are tools utilized to assess the assets available for use in a critical incident. First responder organizations should enter the resources they have available for activation into their resource tracking system.[336]

Credentialing personnel is part of the inventorying of resources process. The credentialing process for personnel involves the evaluation and documentation of a worker's certification, license, experience, training, and degree, as appropriate. The credentialing process also documents the employee's ability to meet national standards and/or to perform specific tasks during a given type of critical incident. Under NIMS, this involves validating personnel qualifications and the provision of authorization to perform specific functions.[337]

The rationale for credentialing personnel is to help ensure that emergency responders are able to document their qualifications. There is a need to demonstrate that emergency response personnel possess the training, expertise, and fitness to perform their assigned tasks.[338]

Identifying and typing resources is another component of inventorying resources. Resource typing deals with categorizing the resources utilized in critical incidents by capability. The basis for typing categories are standards that measure resource capabilities and performance levels.[339] Resources are usually identified by four properties: category, kind, type, and additional information.[340]

Implementation of NIMS in American Jurisdictions

For NIMS to function as intended, local jurisdictions at the city and county levels must effectively implement the system.

State and local law enforcement agencies must implement NIMS for several reasons. Substantial federal grant funding is linked to NIMS compliance. In addition, the failure to implement NIMS makes a community more vulnerable to disasters, hazards, and attacks.[341] In other words, *studying* NIMS is one thing. *Implementing* it in a local organization is another.

Emergency management agencies and fire departments have taken the lead with regard to NIMS implementation. This is true because fire departments and emergency management agencies have experience with both ICS and multiagency operations. Plus, NIMS compliance is a mandated condition for receiving federal emergency preparedness grants in our federal system of American government.[342]

Local first responder and emergency management agencies are always challenged for funding. Federal grants are a good way to supplement local budgets. To set the example elected officials and chief executives should complete a NIMS introductory course offered by FEMA that also includes basic ICS concepts.[343]

In addition, when local legislative bodies adopt NIMS, it transforms it into a legal standard for critical incident management and operations within the jurisdiction.[344] Once this is done, local agencies should prepare a NIMS implementation plan.[345] Such a NIMS implementation plan should contain concrete steps towards achieving the objective, such as certification of the department heads of first responder agencies in the fundamentals of ICS.[346]

In addition to the plan and legislation, NIMS training is vitally important in order for successful implementation. Personnel must train in NIMS because a "paper picture" will not work in the "real world" of critical incidents unless they learn how NIMS works in practice. A combination of web-based training and exercises is vitally important in this effort.

Agency employees with previous ICS experience facilitate NIMS training.[347] In addition, FEMA web-based training is a major available resource, which is free. The FEMA NIMS training curriculum begins with courses designed to teach the fundamentals to field command officers. Several ICS training courses are available online from the Federal Emergency Management Agency (FEMA) training website (www.training.fema.gov).[348] Seven popular FEMA online ICS training courses should be completed by first responder and emergency management personnel. These include ICS 100a, Introduction to Incident Command System. There are eight additional courses that supplement ICS training, including IS 700A (National Incident Management System, an Introduction).

Personnel in local first responder and emergency management organizations should complete FEMA training, beginning with the basic ICS introduction in order to learn important terminology. In addition, government employees that are not first responders that may receive EOC assignments need training as well.[349]

Advanced ICS courses (such as ICS-300, Intermediate ICS for Expanding Incidents; and ICS-400, Advanced ICS Command and General Staff – Complex Incidents) cannot be completed online and must be taken in a classroom. These classroom-based courses are taught by state emergency management agencies and at some state fire academies.[350]

Training must be supplemented with exercises in order to successfully implement NIMS in a local jurisdiction. Classroom instruction is less effective than hands-on simulations and activities.[351] It is for this reason that the NIC (National Integration Center) developed a **NIMS 5-year training plan** based on three objectives: (1) *obtaining NIMS education and training for stakeholders*, (2) *applying NIMS to agency personnel training and credentialing programs*, and (3) *establishing minimum personnel credentials for service in complex incidents.*[352]

FEMA-administered personnel qualifications for named ICS positions are the final step in NIMS training.[353] After completing introductory courses in ICS and NIMS, individuals may progress in their learning in stages (with documented on-scene experience recording in task books) through FEMA, from Single Resource Leader, then Unit Leader, then Branch Director, and then Section Chief, and finally Incident Commander.[354] There are nine training courses for ICS positions. Individual agencies and preparedness organizations can assist in NIMS implementation.

Using NIMS in daily organizational activities inside emergency management and first responder agencies is another way to implement NIMS effectively. NIMS implementation is facilitated when it is used daily by first responder agencies in a variety of critical incidents. Ongoing exposure to NIMS terminology and ICS filters through the organization and becomes part of the workplace culture.[355] This language should be used in both emergency response and in covering major events.

ICS forms are teaching tools as well.[356] Doing these things will not only integrate NIMS and ICS more effectively into the organization but will simultaneously meet reporting and documentation requirements. Further, emergency management and first responder organizations should adopt NIMS resource management terms and procedures. If and when disasters or attacks occur, this internalized training will then make the response effort easier.[357]

NIMS exercises must be held in order to fully integrate the system inside agencies. Theoretical knowledge is not a substitute for real-world training and experience.[358] To this end, it is recommended that local emergency management and first responder agencies conduct at least one full-scale field exercise with complete EOC activation at least annually. Such exercises should include as many other agencies, especially at the state and federal level as possible. Concrete objectives should be simulated and the results should be measured.[359]

When exercises are held, they should involve multijurisdictional and multidisciplinary incidents and cover preparedness plans, including mutual aid agreements. Exercises should also include participation by NGOs and private sector organizations. In order to maximize effectiveness, exercises must also contain feedback mechanisms that can be used to improve agency performance in the future.[360]

The great potential of NIMS and ICS has been noted and extensively discussed. However, this potential has not been entirely realized, especially in making law enforcement critical incident response entirely rational. NIMS and ICS are more effective in the fire service than in law enforcement due to organizational culture. Fire service personnel are generally dispatched in crews along with a commander. At the incident scene, fire personnel respond to the incident without an armed and unpredictable adversary. Law enforcement is different. Most calls for service are resolved by one or two officers, and supervisors are not present at most routine incidents. Thus, law enforcement is more decentralized than fire services.[361]

In addition, NIMS and ICS have been criticized for being too complex and formalized to deal effectively with unfolding "real-world" events. This is especially true in mass shootings and terrorism-related critical incidents. In addition, the assumption of Incident Command by rank-and-file law enforcement officers that arrive on the scene of a critical incident can interfere with the performance of needed tactical actions. Establishing communications quickly with multiple agencies and jurisdictions coupled with the immediately establishment of a command post are serious obstacles to ICS at the initial deployment of law enforcement officers at a critical incident.[362]

After the initial response phase has concluded, NIMS has been found to work more effectively. In addition, NIMS works well with planned events and fire operations.[363] However, due to the differences between law enforcement and other emergency services, the full effectiveness and implementation of NIMS and ICS remains limited.

Notes

1. Vincent Faggiano, John McNall, and Tom Gillespie, *Critical Incident Management: A Complete Response Guide*, 2nd Edition, Boca Raton, CRC Press/ Taylor and Francis Group, 2012: 1.
2. Ibid.
3. U.S. Department of Homeland Security, Federal Emergency Management Agency, *National Incident Management System*, December 2008: 140.
4. Donald W. Walsh, Hank T. Christen, Jr., Christian E. Callsen, Jr., Geoffrey T. Miller, Paul M. Maniscalco, Graydon C. Lord, and Neal J. Dolan, *National Incident Management System*: Principles and Practice, 2nd Edition, Sudbury, Jones & Bartlett Learning, 2012: xxv.
5. Michael K. Lindell, Carla Prater, and Ronald W. Perry, *Introduction to Emergency Management*, Hoboken: John Wiley and Sons, Inc., 2007: 271.
6. U.S. Department of Homeland Security, Federal Emergency Management Agency, *National Incident Management System*, Third Edition, October 2017: 64.
7. Lindell, Prater, and Perry, *Introduction to Emergency Management*: 271.
8. Ibid.
9. Ibid.
10. www.chathamemergency.org/eoc/. Emphasis added.
11. Lindell, Prater, and Perry, *Introduction to Emergency Management*: 272.
12. https://www.ready.gov/incident-management
13. Lindell, Prater, and Perry, Introduction to Emergency Management: 272.
14. Ibid.
15. Ibid: 273.
16. Ibid.
17. Ibid.
18. Ibid: 274.
19. Ibid.

20. Ibid.
21. Ibid: 275.
22. Ibid.
23. Ibid: 276.
24. Ibid.
25. Ibid: 277.
26. Ibid.
27. Ibid: 278.
28. Ibid: 274.
29. Ibid.
30. Ibid: 274-275.
31. Ibid: 275.
32. Ibid: 278.
33. Ibid.
34. U.S. Department of Homeland Security, Federal Emergency Management Agency, *National Incident Management System*, Third Edition, October 2017: 67.
35. Lindell, Prater, and Perry, *Introduction to Emergency Management*: 284.
36. Ibid.
37. U.S. Department of Homeland Security, Federal Emergency Management Agency, *National Incident Management System*, Third Edition, October 2017: 2.
38. Ibid.
39. Ibid.
40. Ibid.
41. Ibid.
42. Ibid.
43. Brett Bailey, "The Impact of the National Incident Management System on Law Enforcement" in *The Role of Law Enforcement in Emergency Management and Homeland Security*, Mark R. Landahl and Tanya E. Thornton, Eds., Bingley, United Kingdom, Emerald Publishing, Ltd., 2021: 225.
44. Ibid.
45. John K. Nichols and Magdalena Denham, "Implementation and Effectiveness of the National Incident Management System's Incident Command System in Law Enforcement Since 2003," *Journal of Emergency Management*, Vol. 19, No. 4, July/August 2021: 388.
46. Michael J. Fagel, Editor, *Principles of Emergency Management: Hazard Specific Issues and Mitigation Strategies*, Boca Raton: CRC Press/Taylor and Francis Group, 2012: 200.
47. Gus Martin, *Understanding Terrorism: Challenges, Perspectives, and Issues* 5th Edition, Thousand Oaks: Sage Publications, 2016: 420.
48. Ibid.
49. Ibid: 422.
50. Ibid: 420-421.
51. Fagel, *Principles of Emergency Management*: 11.
52. Ibid.
53. Lindell, Prater, and Perry, *Introduction to Emergency Management*: 284.
54. Fagel, *Principles of Emergency Management*: 13.

55. Walsh, *National Incident Management System*: 4.
56. Ibid: 5.
57. Fagel, *Principles of Emergency Management*: 166.
58. U.S. Department of Homeland Security, Federal Emergency Management Agency, *National Incident Management System*, Third Edition, October 2017: 62-63.
59. U.S. Department of Homeland Security, Federal Emergency Management Agency, *National Incident Management System*, December 2008: 142.
60. Fagel, *Principles of Emergency Management*: 168-169.
61. Ibid: 166.
62. Walsh, *National Incident Management System*: 5.
63. Fagel, *Principles of Emergency Management*: 13.
64. Walsh, *National Incident Management System*: 5.
65. U.S. Department of Homeland Security, Federal Emergency Management Agency, *National Incident Management System*, December 2008: 141.
66. Ibid: 79.
67. Walsh, *National Incident Management System*: 5.
68. Lori R. Stone, "The State of Interoperability in the States," *Journal of Emergency Management*, Vol. 10, No. 1, January/February 2012: 7.
69. Pamela McCauley-Bush, et. al., "Assessment of Communication Needs for *Emergency Management Officials in High-Consequence Emergencies*," *Journal of Emergency Management*, Vol. 10., No. 1, January/February 2012: 15.
70. Walsh, *National Incident Management System*: 6.
71. Ibid.
72. U.S. Department of Homeland Security, Federal Emergency Management Agency, *National Incident Management System*, Third Edition, October 2017: 1.
73. Ibid: 285.
74. Ibid.
75. Walsh, *National Incident Management System*: xxv.
76. Ibid: 12. Emphasis in original.
77. Ibid: 20.
78. Ibid: 12.
79. Ibid.
80. Ibid.
81. Ibid: 13.
82. Ibid: 14. Emphasis in original.
83. Ibid.
84. Ibid: 17.
85. Ibid: 16.
86. Ibid.
87. U.S. Department of Homeland Security, Federal Emergency Management Agency, *National Incident Management* System, Third Edition, October 2017: 71.
88. Walsh, *National Incident Management System*: 18.
89. U.S. Department of Homeland Security, Federal Emergency Management Agency, *National Incident Management System*, Third Edition, October 2017: 71.
90. Walsh, *National Incident Management System*: 13.

91. Ibid: 7.
92. U.S. Department of Homeland Security, Federal Emergency Management Agency, *National Incident Management System*, December 2008: 140.
93. Walsh, *National Incident Management System*: 25.
94. U.S. Department of Homeland Security, Federal Emergency Management Agency, *National Incident Management System*, December 2008: 149.
95. Walsh, *National Incident Management System*: 25.
96. Ibid.
97. Ibid: 26-27.
98. U.S. Department of Homeland Security, Federal Emergency Management Agency, *National Incident Management System*, December 2008: 137.
99. Walsh, *National Incident Management System*: 27.
100. Vincent Faggiano, John McNall, and Tom Gillespie, *Critical Incident Management*: A Complete Response Guide, 2nd Edition, Boca Raton, CRC Press/ Taylor and Francis Group, 2012: 146.
101. Ibid: 142.
102. Ibid: 145.
103. U.S. Department of Homeland Security, Federal Emergency Management Agency, *National Incident Management System*, Third Edition, October 2017: 84.
104. FEMA, *National Incident Management System*, December 2008: 139.
105. Walsh, *National Incident Management System*: 36.
106. U.S. Department of Homeland Security, Federal Emergency Management Agency, *National Incident Management System*, December 2008: 144.
107. Faggiano, *Critical Incident Management*: 88.
108. Walsh, *National Incident Management System*: 37. Emphasis in original.
109. Ibid. Emphasis added.
110. Ibid: 37.
111. Ibid: 38.
112. Ibid: 39.
113. Ibid.
114. Ibid.
115. Ibid.
116. U.S. Department of Homeland Security, Federal Emergency Management Agency, *National Incident Management System*, December 2008: 144.
117. Walsh, *National Incident Management System*: 41. Emphasis in original.
118. U.S. Department of Homeland Security, Federal Emergency Management Agency, *National Incident Management System*, Third Edition, October 2017: 64.
119. Walsh, *National Incident Management System*: 41-42.
120. Ibid: 42.
121. Ibid.
122. U.S. Department of Homeland Security, Federal Emergency Management Agency, *National Incident Management System*, Third Edition, October 2017: 69-70.
123. Walsh, *National Incident Management System*: 42-43.
124. U.S. Department of Homeland Security, Federal Emergency Management Agency, *National Incident Management System*, Third Edition, October 2017: 70.

125. Walsh, *National Incident Management System*: 43.
126. Ibid.
127. U.S. Department of Homeland Security, Federal Emergency Management Agency, *National Incident Management System*, Third Edition, October 2017: 70.
128. Walsh, *National Incident Management System*: 43.
129. U.S. Department of Homeland Security, Federal Emergency Management Agency, *National Incident Management System*, Third Edition, October 2017: 62.
130. Walsh, *National Incident Management System*: 44.
131. Ibid.
132. U.S. Department of Homeland Security, Federal Emergency Management Agency, *National Incident Management System*, December 2008: 144.
133. Vincent Faggiano, John McNall, and Tom Gillespie, *Critical Incident Management*: A Complete Response Guide, 2nd Edition, Boca Raton, CRC Press/Taylor and Francis Group, 2012: 90.
134. Walsh, National Incident Management System: 52. Emphasis in original.
135. U.S. Department of Homeland Security, Federal Emergency Management Agency, *National Incident Management System*, December 2008: 144.
136. Ibid: 149.
137. Walsh, *National Incident Management System*: 52.
138. Ibid: 53.
139. U.S. Department of Homeland Security, Federal Emergency Management Agency, *National Incident Management System*, December 2008: 146.
140. Walsh, *National Incident Management System*: 53.
141. Ibid.
142. Ibid.
143. Ibid.
144. U.S. Department of Homeland Security, Federal Emergency Management Agency, *National Incident Management System*, December 2008: 138.
145. Walsh, *National Incident Management System*: 53. Emphasis in original.
146. Ibid.
147. Ibid: 54.
148. Faggiano, *Critical Incident Management*: 89-90.
149. Walsh, *National Incident Management System*: 54.
150. Ibid: 52.
151. Ibid: 16.
152. Ibid.
153. Ibid: 55.
154. Ibid.
155. Ibid: 54-55.
156. Ibid: 55.
157. Ibid.
158. Ibid.
159. Ibid.
160. Ibid: 56.
161. Ibid.

162. Faggiano, *Critical Incident Management*: 90.
163. U.S. Department of Homeland Security, Federal Emergency Management Agency, *National Incident Management System*, December 2008: 142.
164. Ibid.
165. Faggiano, *Critical Incident Management*: A Complete Response Guide: 91.
166. Walsh, *National Incident Management System*: 60.
167. Ibid: 61.
168. Ibid: 60.
169. Ibid: 61.
170. Ibid.
171. Ibid: 65.
172. Ibid: 65-66.
173. Ibid: 65.
174. Ibid: 66.
175. Ibid.
176. Ibid: 62.
177. Ibid.
178. Ibid.
179. Ibid.
180. Ibid.
181. Ibid: 63.
182. Ibid.
183. Ibid.
184. Ibid: 64.
185. Ibid.
186. Ibid: 65.
187. Ibid.
188. Ibid: 62.
189. Ibid: 68.
190. Ibid: 72.
191. Ibid.
192. Ibid.
193. Ibid.
194. Ibid.
195. Ibid.
196. Ibid.
197. Ibid.
198. Ibid: 76.
199. Ibid: 73.
200. Ibid.
201. Ibid: 76.
202. Ibid: 73.
203. Ibid: 74.
204. Ibid.
205. U.S. Department of Homeland Security, Federal Emergency Management Agency, *National Incident Management System*, December 2008: 139.

206. Ibid: 80.
207. Ibid.
208. Ibid.
209. Ibid: 141.
210. Ibid: 81.
211. Ibid.
212. U.S. Department of Homeland Security, Federal Emergency Management Agency, *National Incident Management System*, December 2008: 45.
213. Walsh, *National Incident Management System*: 86.
214. U.S. Department of Homeland Security, Federal Emergency Management Agency, *National Incident Management System*, December 2008: 64.
215. Ibid.
216. U.S. Department of Homeland Security, Federal Emergency Management Agency, *National Incident Management System*, December 2008: 64.
217. Walsh, *National Incident Management System*: 86.
218. Ibid.
219. Ibid: 88.
220. www.chathamemergency.org/eoc/. Emphasis added.
221. Ibid.
222. Ibid.
223. Fagel, *Principles of Emergency Management*: 297.
224. Walsh, *National Incident Management System*: 88.
225. Nichols and Denham, "Implementation and Effectiveness of the National Incident Management System's Incident Command System in Law Enforcement:" 390-391.
226. Walsh, *National Incident Management System*: 89.
227. Ibid: 90.
228. Ibid: 92.
229. Ibid.
230. Ibid: 89.
231. U.S. Department of Homeland Security, Federal Emergency Management Agency, *National Incident Management System*, December 2008: 143.
232. Walsh, *National Incident Management System*: 92.
233. Ibid: 91.
234. Ibid: 20.
235. Ibid: 12.
236. Ibid: 13.
237. Ibid: 94.
238. Ibid: 93.
239. Ibid.
240. Ibid: 94.
241. Ibid.
242. Ibid: 95.
243. Ibid.
244. Ibid: 7.
245. U.S. Department of Homeland Security, Federal Emergency Management Agency, *National Incident Management System*, December 2008: 45.

246. Walsh, *National Incident Management System*: 100.
247. Ibid.
248. Faggiano, *Critical Incident Management*: A Complete Response Guide: 145.
249. Walsh, *National Incident Management System*: 100.
250. Ibid.
251. Fagel, *Principles of Emergency Management*: 493.
252. Ibid: 502.
253. Ibid.
254. https://training.fema.gov/programs/pio/
255. Ibid: 502.
256. Ibid: 499.
257. Ibid: 502.
258. https://emilms.fema.gov/IS702A/PIO0103summary.htm
259. https://emilms.fema.gov/IS702A/PIO0105summary.htm
260. Fagel, *Principles of Emergency Management*: 504.
261. Ibid: 506.
262. Walsh, *National Incident Management System*: 102.
263. Ibid.
264. Ibid.
265. Ibid.
266. Ibid.
267. Ibid.
268. Ibid.
269. Ibid: 103.
270. Ibid.
271. Ibid.
272. Ibid.
273. Ibid.
274. Ibid: 104.
275. Ibid.
276. Ibid.
277. Ibid.
278. Lindell, Prater, and Perry, *Introduction to Emergency Management*: 285.
279. Walsh, *National Incident Management System*: 132.
280. U.S. Department of Homeland Security, Federal Emergency Management Agency, *National Incident Management System*, December 2008: 23.
281. Ibid.
282. Walsh, *National Incident Management System*: 123-124.
283. U.S. Department of Homeland Security, Federal Emergency Management Agency, *National Incident Management System*, December 2008: 137.
284. Ibid: 125.
285. Ibid.
286. Ibid.
287. Ibid.
288. Ibid.
289. Ibid.

290. Ibid.
291. Ibid: 126.
292. Ibid.
293. Ibid.
294. Ibid.
295. Ibid: 127.
296. Ibid.
297. Ibid: 128.
298. Ibid.
299. Ibid: 129.
300. Ibid.
301. Lindell, Prater, and Perry, *Introduction to Emergency Management*: 285.
302. U.S. Department of Homeland Security, Federal Emergency Management Agency, *National Incident Management System*, December 2008: 31.
303. Ibid: 146.
304. Ibid.
305. Ibid.
306. Ibid.
307. Ibid: 53.
308. Walsh, *National Incident Management System*: 53.
309. Ibid.
310. Ibid: 136.
311. Ibid.
312. Ibid.
313. Ibid: 137.
314. Ibid.
315. Ibid: 137-138.
316. Ibid: 138.
317. Ibid.
318. Ibid: 138-139.
319. Ibid: 139.
320. Ibid.
321. Ibid.
322. Ibid.
323. Ibid.
324. Ibid.
325. Ibid.
326. Ibid.
327. Ibid: 141.
328. Ibid: 142.
329. Ibid.
330. Ibid.
331. Ibid: 143.
332. Ibid.
333. Ibid.
334. Ibid.

335. Ibid.
336. Ibid: 144.
337. Ibid.
338. Ibid: 145.
339. Ibid.
340. Ibid: 146.
341. Ibid: 174.
342. Ibid.
343. Ibid.
344. Ibid.
345. Ibid.
346. Ibid.
347. Ibid
348. Ibid: 175.
349. Ibid.
350. Ibid.
351. Ibid: 175-176.
352. Ibid: 176.
353. Ibid.
354. Ibid.
355. Ibid: 177.
356. Ibid.
357. Ibid: 178.
358. Ibid.
359. Ibid.
360. Ibid.
361. Nichols and Denham, "Implementation and Effectiveness of the National Incident Management System's Incident Command System in Law Enforcement Since 2003:" 393.
362. Brett Bailey, "The Impact of the National Incident Management System on Law Enforcement:" 224-228.
363. Nichols and Denham, "Implementation and Effectiveness of the National Incident Management System's Incident Command System in Law Enforcement Since 2003:" 393.

Chapter 4

MANAGING AT-RISK POPULATIONS IN EMERGENCY SITUATIONS

The chapter examines ways in which law enforcement personnel can assist at-risk populations in emergency situations. For that reason, these and related terms must be defined and related to emergency management more broadly.

Managing at-risk populations in emergency situations is a component of *public health emergency preparedness and response.* Public health is different from traditional medical care because public health focuses on interventions and policies to improve health outcomes and minimize disease for populations rather than simply focusing on the health of a particular individual.[1]

Public health emergency preparedness and response involves prevention, protection against, and response to widespread health emergencies. **Public health emergencies** are critical events that due to either unpredictability or widespread scale either overwhelm or threaten to overwhelm routine health care capabilities.[2]

These emergencies are severe, have the potential to cause illness, injury, or death, and cannot be managed effectively with routine resources. Public health emergencies can involve a substantial range of disasters and emergencies, including natural disasters, acts of biological or radiological terrorism, and large-scale infectious disease outbreaks.[3] Both natural and man-made disasters can be causes of public health crises for the entire affected population.

Law enforcement agencies are connected to public health emergencies in several ways. For example, police officers provide crowd control, traffic control, and security during public health emergencies. In the event of a terrorist attack involving chemical, biological, and radiological weapons, law enforcement agencies will be involved in joint investigations with public health providers.[4]

Some segments of the population are more vulnerable than others to disasters. These are referred to as the **at-risk populations**. Recognize that social vulnerability is unevenly distributed in American society. Some parts of the population are more vulnerable than others based on age, education, gender, income, and ethnicity.[5] While all individuals are at risk when exposed to natural and man-made disasters, at-risk populations are potentially at **greater** risk due to their particular situations and characteristics. This chapter will examine how to plan for and deal with at-risk populations in various emergency situations as part of emergency management.

Public Health Preparedness and Emergency Management

This section looks at history and policy relating to public health preparedness and emergency management.[6] **Public health emergency preparedness** involves the preparation for, prevention of, response to, and recovery from health emergencies that impact the citizenry. **Public health emergencies** are emergencies of sufficient sale, timing, and scope that have the potential to overwhelm routine healthcare capabilities in a jurisdiction.[7]

Public health emergency preparedness did not become well established until shortly after the 9/11 terrorist attacks against the United States. Public health preparedness involves preparedness planning, training, and exercises between medical and first responder disciplines.[8]

Public health preparedness is designed to bring American health care, first responders, and emergency managers together to better protect the public from health-related disasters. To understand how to manage at-risk populations in emergency situations, we must first learn about the American public health infrastructure and how it relates to the emergency management community.

Public Health Officials and Their Roles

This section examines the role of the **Public Health Official (PHO)**, a government official charged with promoting and protecting the health of individuals and communities. Public health officials work to track disease outbreaks and to prevent injuries. They provide science-based solutions to health problems. Public health officials include public health physicians, epidemiologists, and occupational health professionals.[9]

The genesis of the U.S. Public Health Service was the 1798 establishment of maritime hospitals.[10] During the 1870s, the Office of the **Surgeon General** was created. In 1944, the **U.S. Public Health Service** was formally established. It was later placed under the U.S. Department of Health and Human Services.

At the federal level, the Department of Health and Human Services operates the **Centers for Disease Control and Prevention (CDC)**, which is the leading public health organization in the United States. State governments maintain state-level Departments of Public Health. At the county level, there are county Departments of Health. All these organizations maintain physicians, scientists, and disease specialists for the purpose of monitoring public health and assisting with health care and disease interventions.

The United Nations maintains an organization called the **World Health Organization (WHO)**. The WHO is the health arm of the United Nations. It was established in 1948.

Biological incidents especially require the services and expertise of public health agencies. County public health departments routinely monitor hospital and clinic records for evidence of epidemics. Health departments work to identify and control biological agents. They also recommend preventive measures for persons exposed to biological agents. For these reasons, local public health personnel should be a component part of Emergency Operations Center staff during large-scale disasters. Local public health department personnel provide expertise regarding the two unique powers that have been legally delegated to public health departments.[11] These powers are (1) to **quarantine** and (2) to administer **mass prophylactic measures**.

A **quarantine** involves the confinement of persons due to a public health threat. Quarantine and isolation are often confused. **Isolation** is the confinement of symptomatic individuals. On the other hand, *quarantine* is the confinement of individuals exposed to a contagious disease but are asymptomatic.[12]

Quarantine and isolation are one special power of public health agencies. Another is the authority to order *mass prophylactic measures.* Prophylactic measures refer to substances such as immunizations designed to prevent disease. Generally, state or local health departments possess the authority to order the administration of prophylactic measures in the event of an epidemic.[13] For example, the COVID-19 vaccines were distributed under this authority in 2021-2022.

In response to terrorist attacks that occurred during the 1990s, the federal government began the process of linking public health with emergency management and law enforcement. Presidential Decision Directive (PDD) 39 clarified the role of both public health and medical preparedness and response.[14] A distinction was made between **crisis management** and **consequence management**.

In the context of public health, crisis management is viewed as a law enforcement and intelligence function focused on actions taken to prevent terrorist attacks.[15] **Consequence management** refers to measures designed to protect public health, deliver emergency aid to persons affected by terrorism, and restore essential government services.[16]

Public Health Officials must also work within the Emergency Management cycle. Planning and training help PHOs to respond to critical incidents. Law enforcement officers should realize that PHOs do not become involved in routine emergencies typically resolved by local EMS and fire responders.[17] Rather, PHOS will generally become involved only with *serious, widespread, and catastrophic* health incidents, such as epidemics, pandemics, chemical, biological, radiological attacks, or large-scale hazmat incidents.

In 1997, Congress funded what would become the **MMRS (Metropolitan Medical Response System**). The MMRS facilitates homeland security health preparedness by providing federal grants to local jurisdictions to help integrate health, emergency management, and medical systems in order to more effectively respond to a mass casualty disaster.[18] The MMRS was a milestone in US public health and healthcare system preparedness. The threat of weapons of mass destruction in particular prompted new planning for public health emergencies between various agencies.[19]

The 9/11 terrorist attacks brought a new era to American public health.[20] Specifically, the bioterrorism threat brought public health into partnership with emergency management stakeholders, including law enforcement.[21] As time has passed, the emphasis has moved from bioterrorism preparedness towards "all hazards" preparedness with a special emphasis on protection of at-risk populations. Emergency management, public health, and healthcare are now linked.

In 1998, the **National Domestic Preparedness Consortium (NDPC)** was established pursuant to a federal law designed to prepare the United States for the possible terrorist uses of Weapons of Mass Destruction (WMD). The NDPC maintains seven training institutions across the nation to prepare law enforcement officers, firefighters, EMS workers, and public health professions for WMD threats. Training is provided at minimal cost to first responders and public health officials. NDPC training institutions include the Center for Domestic Preparedness (Chemical, Ordinance, Biological, and Radiological training), and the National Center for Biomedical Research Training.[22]

In 2006, the **Police Executive Research Forum (PERF)** published *The Role of Law Enforcement in Public Health Emergencies: Special Considerations for an All-Hazards Approach* through the U.S. Department of Justice's Bureau of Justice Assistance (BJA). This document describes the interaction between law enforcement officers and public health in the United States.[23] It contains information about risks to law enforcement officers from disease, PPE (Personal Protective Equipment) information, and the role of law enforcement in mass casualty planning, quarantines, mass vaccination, and working with other agencies on public health matters. Police officers and administrators should become familiar with this document, as it covers both law and policy relating to law enforcement and public health.

In 2011, a **capabilities-based approach** to public health was established by the CDC. This resulted in the present national standard for public health preparedness.[24] The 15 Public Health Emergency Preparedness (PHEP) Capabilities standard include Emergency Operations Coordination, Fatality Management, Mass Care, and Responder Safety and Health.[25] The public health preparedness capabilities linked emergency management, public health, and healthcare in the United States.[26]

In order to be effective, public health infrastructure must exist and be sustained prior to emergencies. Public health and healthcare systems preparedness are vital to national security.[27]

Public Health Infrastructure and Preparedness Capabilities

This section examines the ability and capacity of the American public health system to effectively deal with the impacts of emergency situations.[28] **Public health emergencies** are unfolding and dynamic events that overwhelm existing public health facilities and capabilities and also result in adverse health effects on a jurisdiction's population.[29] Public health emergencies are severe and cannot be effectively managed with routine resources. Public health emergencies have the potential to cause increased illness, injury, or death to the population. These emergencies can encompass a broad range of disaster situations, including diseases and injuries resulting from natural hazards, terrorism, and large-scale outbreaks of infectious diseases.[30] Public health preparedness, response, and recovery efforts are required to sustain the health of the population. Resilience is also required.[31]

Resilience is a term that is often used in emergency management. Resilience involves the ability to prepare for and recover from both natural and man-made disasters.[32] Resilience also requires a functioning public health infrastructure to deal with emergencies.[33] The public health infrastructure of the United States will now be discussed. The most obvious components of the public health infrastructure are health departments, hospitals, and emergency responders. It includes both public and private agencies and how they interact. The public health infrastructure includes healthcare providers, social services, first responders, pharmaceutical companies, insurers, and elected officials.[34]

Emergency management is related to essential public health services. Students of emergency management are familiar with the **Comprehensive Emergency Management Model**, also called the Emergency Management Cycle or Model. The Comprehensive Emergency Management Model consists of **mitigation**, **preparedness**, **response**, and **recovery**. Public health has three core functions: (1) assessment, (2) policy development, and (3) assurance. **Assessment** involves evaluation and analysis of the health needs of a community at a given time. **Policy development** concerns setting priorities and developing plans to provide for health needs. **Assurance** involves the implementation of public health programs and resource management.[35]

The functions of emergency management and public health interact. The core functions of public health alternate places according to the phase of each emergency. Individuals working in both emergency management and public health positions should understand the ongoing interaction between emergency management and public health during emergencies and disasters.[36] It is important for emergency responders and emergency managers to understand the nature of the connection between public health and emergency management.

The public health capabilities that are required to deliver healthcare services and public health in each phase of the emergency management cycle have improved though the development of a set of standards based on the capabilities approach. The Public Health Emergency Preparedness (PHEP) standards came out in 2011 and have improved the management of public health functions and capabilities.[37] In 2012, the U.S. Department. of Health and Human Services issued *Healthcare Preparedness Capabilities: National Guidance for Healthcare System Preparedness.*

These documents set up a mechanism with which to better understand the connection between emergency management, public health, and healthcare.[38] Together, these documents established comprehensive standards for preparedness in public health.[39] Further, the publications facilitate public health planning across American jurisdictions.[40]

Public health preparedness programs are related to emergency management by taking actions designed to reduce injuries and deaths resulting from a disaster or public health emergency.[41]

Emerging Infectious Disease Threats

This section looks at the impact of infectious diseases upon the population, especially the potential impacts of an *emerging* infectious disease. An **Emerging Infectious Disease (EID)** is defined as an illness caused by pathogens that show an increasing incidence in human beings. These pathogenic organisms include recently evolving pathogens or recognized pathogens that have been discovered in new geographic areas.[42]

EIDs have the potential for catastrophic morbidity and mortality across all populations. Increased globalization resulting from travel and commerce is associated with the wide dispersal of infectious diseases. Widespread geographic interaction exposes human beings to many diseases. Some of these diseases are novel to particular populations. Thus, natural immunity may not be present. Free movement and modern transportation can result in disease transmission at rapid rates.[43]

In addition to COVID-19, we have heard media accounts of West Nile Virus, Ebola, H1N1 flu, and other emerging infectious diseases. These and other diseases can be viewed as a national security threat in addition to presenting emergency management challenges.[44] If and when infectious disease outbreaks become widespread, the healthcare infrastructure is significantly impacted.[45]

Realize that many EIDs are **zoonotic**, which are diseases that originate in animals but are transmissible to human beings. For example, mosquitoes are well-known carriers of disease.[46] In addition, so-called "super-bugs" or "drug-resistant diseases" are susceptible to microbial adaptation.[47] Epidemiological surveillance assists prevention and preparedness for EIDs. The maintenance of the public health infrastructure helps to make society more prepared for disease outbreaks.[48]

Epidemiology plays a vital role in prevention and preparedness. *Epidemiology* is the study of the causes and origins of diseases in human beings and the communities in which they live in terms of patterns and frequency of occurrence.[49] Epidemiology is of paramount importance in prevention and preparedness. Epidemiology overlaps with the need for *surveillance* of disease outbreaks, along with their morbidity and mortality. In this context, **surveillance** examines disease occurrence through the collection, analysis, and dissemination of data.[50] Surveillance data comes from several sources, including hospitals, medical practitioners, and zoonotic information.[51]

To facilitate epidemiology surveillance, the **LRN (Laboratory Response Network)** was formed in 1999. The LRN is composed of approximately 150 surveillance laboratories in a national system. Federal, state, and local public health laboratories, veterinary laboratories, environmental testing laboratories, and food testing laboratories are part of the LRN national system.[52] The LRN plays an important role in prevention and preparedness.[53]

In terms of response and recovery, a major priority is to determine the transmissibility of a pathogen.[54] Public health authorities then take action to prevent transmission.[55] Ways to achieve this objective include hygiene practices, social distancing, and quarantine.

Remember that public health agencies possess the legal authority to take certain actions during a public health crisis, including quarantine, isolation, mandatory vaccines, and travel limitations. Some of these measures have political and economic implications, as was vividly illustrated during the COVID-19 pandemic.

Public health practitioners strongly argue that if an EID can be diminished through antibiotics or vaccines (medical countermeasures), rapid distribution and dispensing must occur. In addition, if the EID is highly contagious, aggressive actions designed to prevent transmission must also be taken.[56]

Both of these measures require appropriate public messaging. Such public messaging must contain information about the EID, actions to be taken to protect individuals and health treatment advice. Some EIDs may rise and fall in waves. Therefore, ongoing public health efforts must be made to deal with subsequent outbreaks after the crisis is over.[57]

Although preparedness efforts cannot stop a future emerging infection, the impact can be reduced through the ongoing development of healthcare and public health capabilities and the accumulation of knowledge and experience from prior outbreaks.[58]

Epidemics, Pandemics, and Preparedness

This section examines pandemics and pandemic preparedness in emergency management and response. An **epidemic** is an outbreak of disease that impacts more than the expected number of cases of the disease in a region during a given time period. A **pandemic** is a widespread sudden disease outbreak in a region, a continent, or the world. A pandemic can evolve from an epidemic. Both epidemics and pandemics are based on the geographic area impacted by the disease rather than on disease severity.[59]

Pandemics are viewed as historical events[60] such as the Black Death (1300s) or the Great Plague of London (1600s). In more recent times, the COVID-19 pandemic of 2020-2022 comprised such a historical event.

For example, the European Black Death of 1334-1347 killed an estimated 75% of the population. The Spanish Flu Pandemic of 1918-1919 killed between 20 and 40 million people worldwide, including 675,000 in the United States. These events exacted a psychological toll on the population due to treating the sick and dying. Mass burials also had a strong mental health effect.[61] Health care providers and institutions were affected quite negatively by past pandemics, as were families, communities, and nations.[62]

Pandemics differ from other types of natural disasters. Tornadoes, floods, and earthquakes are usually limited to local areas. But pandemics affect much wider geographical areas and many more people. This geographic dispersal interferes with preparedness planning. During a pandemic, aid from outside the local area cannot be assured due to the fact that the entire region or nation is also dealing with the disease as well.[63]

The effects of a pandemic can be catastrophic. All of society is affected. Society can be disrupted. The social fabric can be torn. Much stress is placed on first responders and government institutions. The infrastructure can be profoundly disrupted due to absenteeism.[64] There are also *psychosocial concerns* of pandemics. This refers to the fear and mental health issues that a pandemic may occur. Pandemics result in fear due to uncertainty.[65]

While 675,000 people died in the United States during the Spanish Flu Pandemic (1918-1919), the population of the nation was much smaller than it is today. If the same pandemic were to hit today, it is estimated that 1.7 million deaths would occur in the United States and 180-360 million deaths worldwide.[66] COVID-19 did not result in such a high proportion of deaths. We should keep in mind that this is within the realm of possibility for a new disease or a disease with limited immunity.

Many people overestimate the capabilities of our healthcare infrastructure. A nationwide mass casualty epidemic would likely overwhelm the nation's medical capacity. COVID-19 demonstrated the fragility of our healthcare infrastructure in a pandemic. In a severe pandemic with mass casualties, the American healthcare system could not adapt. It is estimated that five to ten million sick individuals could be expected, which would greatly exceed 970,000 staffed hospital beds and 100,000 ventilators available presently.[67] Even the relatively mild 2009 Swine Flu epidemic used up fully 25% of the federal government's antiviral drug stockpile.[68]

Although a planner can consider and assess aspects of the community population in terms of culture of the group, and the policies and strategies in place, we must remember that human behavior is unpredictable and nonlinear.[69] In mass casualty epidemics, it is unknown how well the social fabric would function.

Due to the potential severity and magnitude of a pandemic, *planning* is crucial. Several tools exist with which to measure the pandemic threat to the United States.

The first is the **World Health Organization's (WHO) Pandemic Alert Level Tool**. WHO is the health arm of the United Nations. WHO divides pandemic alerts into three phases (Interpandemic Period, Pandemic Alert Period, and Pandemic Period). Within the Interpandemic Period (no pandemic), there are two stages. In both Stage 1 and Stage 2 there are no new virus subtypes detected in humans. In the Pandemic Alert Period, a virus subtype has been detected in humans, but it either does not spread or spreads in localized areas. There are three stages within the Pandemic Alert Period: Stage 3 (human infection with no spread), Stage 4 (human infection with limited transmission), and Stage 5 (human infection spread into larger clusters). Finally, there is the Pandemic Period. Here, there is sustained transmission of the disease in the general population. Stage 6 is synonymous with the Pandemic Period.[70]

The **U.S. Department of Health and Human Services (HHS)** maintains the **Response Stage Tool** that mirrors the WHO Pandemic Alert Level Tool. This also has three phases and six stages. In the HHS Response Stage Tool, stage 0 means that a disease has not been identified in humans. Stage 1 involves a suspected human outbreak overseas. Stage 2 is a confirmed human outbreak overseas. Stage 3 involves widespread human outbreaks overseas. Stage 4 is the first human case in North America. Stage 5 involves the spread throughout the United States. Stage 6 is recovery and preparation for subsequent waves. In this framework, Stages 3-6 are pandemics.[71]

The WHO methodology quantifies the *transmissibility* of a disease rather than the *severity* of a pandemic.[72] However, the HHS does measure severity with the **HHS Pandemic Severity Index**. This index is based on fatality rates.[73] The severity of a pandemic can range from Category 1 (less than 90,000 deaths and less than 0.1% fatality rate) to Category 5 (greater than 1.8 million deaths and greater than 2% fatality rate).[74]

An important part of planning is monitoring the WHO and HHS pandemic tools. Planners should also remember that pandemics typically occur in waves of severity separated by times in which outbreaks decline.[75]

The pandemic planning of the federal government in this regard emphasizes the following elements: (1) support for international efforts to contain contagious and harmful viruses and to control their evolution, (2) build stockpiles of vaccines and improve antiviral drugs, and (3) improve health care capacity to better deal with a pandemic.[76] State and local government agencies have goals that are congruent with (2) and (3).

The federal government has devoted substantial resources to pandemic preparedness planning. Homeland Security Presidential Directives made under the authority of laws enacted by Congress serve as the basis for **disaster response plans**. These are comprehensive and detailed protocols designed to focus resources on reducing the effects of a catastrophic event. The most well-known federal disaster response plan is the **National Response Framework (NRF of 2008)**.[77]

The NRF utilizes **Emergency Support Functions (ESFs)**. An ESF provides the structured mechanism used to coordinate federal response to a critical incident.[78] At present, there are 15 Emergency Support Functions (ESFs) recognized by the federal government, ranging from transportation to public health and medical services to search and rescue.

The NRF stipulates that federal support will be implemented through the activation of 15 emergency support functions (ESFs) as needed. Four ESFs are relevant to pandemic planning: Mass Care, Emergency Assistance, Housing, and Human Services (ESF #6); Public Health and Medical Services (ESF #8); Public Safety and Security (ESF #13); and Long-Term Community Recovery (ESP #14). Each of these ESFs contains details about planning, training, implementation, and exercising.[79]

The federal government has also developed specific and detailed national strategies and implementation plans for dealing with pandemics. In 2005, the U.S. Homeland Security Council developed the **National Strategy for Pandemic Influenza** specifically to have a plan in place to deal with the Avian Flu. The National Strategy for Pandemic Influenza is based upon the pillars of preparedness and communication, surveillance and detection, and response and containment.[80]

There are several tools available for pandemic preparedness, including *vaccines, antiviral medications, infection control measures,* and *community mitigation measures.* **Vaccines** can be highly effective.[81] Even if the vaccines are available, sufficient quantities to be distributed to the entire population may not be available. In this situation, public health officials must determine which persons will receive vaccine priority. Usually, first responders and healthcare workers receive some of the first available vaccines.[82] This was the case with the COVID-19 vaccines.

Infection control is another tool available for pandemic preparedness. Much of this involves simple and commonplace measures, such as encouraging standard hygiene practices such as hand washing. Personal Protective Equipment (PPE) such as N95 masks and surgical masks have been shown to be effective when properly used.[83]

Community mitigation techniques are also used for pandemic preparedness, such as *social distancing.* This mandates that people maintain a minimum physical distance between others to limit the opportunity for disease transmission.[84] For flu and COVID-19, a distance of six feet was recommended. Other community mitigation measures include remote work and flexible work schedules to reduce disease spread.[85]

In terms of community mitigation, practicing isolation and minimizing mass gatherings could be used.[86] These techniques were used extensively during the COVID-19 pandemic and proved to be controversial.

In order for pandemic plans to be successful, training is essential.[87] The federal government has taken the lead in this area. Since the Post-Katrina Emergency Management Reform Act in 2006, all-hazards exercises must be conducted annually.[88] The **TOPOFF (Top Officials)** exercise and the **NEP (National Exercise Program)** provide training in the release of chemical, radiological, and biological agents.[89] Plans made by emergency managers at any level must be exercised regularly and should be revised based on new information and lessons learned.[90]

Communications during a pandemic and the recovery from a pandemic must be addressed. The PIO (Public Information Officer) of both health authorities and emergency management agencies must provide clear and timely information to the public about the scope of the epidemic and cautionary protections to take. Information about where to take those who are ill and with what steps to take regarding those who have died must be effectively communicated. Social media applications can help in this regard. At all costs, pandemic communications should be used to calm and reassure the public. These things will reduce anxiety and panic.

Recovery is also an issue that should be considered. Pandemics exert a powerful psychological and economic toll on the population. Pandemics change the way that people live, work, and interact.[91] Continuity of Operations (COOP) plans, such as **Continuity of Operations-Essential (COP-E)** and the Dept. of Homeland Security's *Pandemic Influenza Preparedness, Response, and Recovery Guide for Critical Infrastructure and Key Resources* provide information about suggested recovery activities following an epidemic.[92]

COVID-19 proved that pandemic preparedness is vitally important to American communities. Pandemic preparedness must involve both government construct and private entities such as nonprofits, businesses, and faith-based organizations.[93]

Community Disaster Resilience in the United States

This section examines the importance of resilience as a pre-disaster mitigation measure. To the extent that communities are able to mitigate, prepare for, respond to, and recover from disasters, resilience will be increased.[94]

Community disaster resilience is based upon **systems theory**, which is an approach to understanding complex human relationships holistically in terms of how internal and external factors affect their functioning. In this context, systems theory examines how outside factors, such as man-made or natural disasters impact the functioning of complex human relationships, and in turn, how the internal dynamics of complex human relationships can affect the impact of disasters. Resilience can help a system to positively adapt when it is faced with a disaster or emergency.[95]

It is important to become familiar with the concept of *community resilience.* **Community resilience** refers to the factors that are associated the ability of a geographical area to cope with and adapt to challenges effectively.[96]

It is noted that the present design and focus of emergency management in dealing with disasters and emergencies has limitations for achieving more widespread community disaster resilience. Specifically, the focus on the **all-hazards approach** and the **all-agencies approach** utilized by emergency management agencies can actually hinder community resilience.

The *all-hazards approach* to emergency management is very broad and encompasses all possible hazards that could be faced by a community, even though the probability of certain events is highly unlikely.[97] An *all-agencies approach* to emergency management requires that all possible government and nonprofit agencies plausibly connected with emergency management to engage in the four phases of emergency management.[98]

Both the all-hazards approach and the all-agencies approach are traditional. They each possess both advantages and disadvantages towards achieving the overall goals of emergency management. However, it is dependent upon command and control management supported by governments. For that reason, it is costly due to labor and resource commitments. It has not been as effective in building community resilience as intended.[99]

The argument is made that the all-hazards and all-agencies approaches tend to exclude community stakeholders. Rather, the focus is on agencies, its employees, and their capabilities. In addition, the visibility and funding of emergency management and first responder agencies lead individuals to falsely conclude that such agencies will resolve disasters and emergencies quickly without community involvement.[100]

Based upon the perceived limitations of the all-hazards all-agencies approach to building community disaster resilience, an argument has been made that a new approach is needed. This is the **All-Hazards, All-Agencies, All-People Approach**. This approach requires the involvement of emergency management agencies directly with communities to build community disaster resilience together. The synergy between the community and emergency management agencies working together toward common goals will achieve community disaster resilience, according to the "all-hazards, all-agencies, all-people" approach.[101] If this could be achieved, communities would be safer and better able to deal with disasters and emergencies. However, achieving this is difficult. Some suggestions follow with regard to how this approach might be brought to fruition.

As a first step, emergency management agencies must assess community disaster resilience. This must include obtaining meaningful feedback from the community.[102] Census data, information from nonprofit organizations like the American Red Cross, and data from service providers to at-risk populations can be utilized for this purpose. In addition, there are several online resources available to assess community resilience including the Community Resilience: Learn and Tell Toolkit published by the RAND Corporation.

Obtaining data is a necessary first step in this process. But obtaining the data is not enough. This is true because locating cooperative community leaders willing to "take up the torch" of community resilience can be an issue. This situation is worsened because some communities possess a strong distrust of government agencies.[103]

Some ways to overcome these challenges include building working relationships with nongovernmental organizations (NGOs) and working through and with volunteer networks. Emergency managers should realize that NGOs are often comprised of well-connected group individuals with close links to their communities. For this reason, NGOs can be more effective than government agencies in locating and assisting citizens during disasters or emergencies.[104] For example, the American Red Cross, charities like the United Way, and health care providers can assist in this endeavor. Disaster resilience can also be enhanced through the provision of volunteer opportunities.[105]

Such engagement between emergency management agencies and the community can be an effective strategy for cooperatively building disaster-resilient communities. Such a partnership can pay dividends in preventing, dealing with, and responding to emergencies and disasters.

Characteristics of At-Risk Populations

In order to plan to deliver health resources to at-risk populations following disasters or emergencies, it is first necessary to define what is meant by the term. Some segments of the population are more vulnerable than others to disasters. These are referred to as the **at-risk populations**. It is noted that certain people in a population are more vulnerable than others. Predictors can offer clues that tend to show which parts of the population are more vulnerable to disasters and emergencies than others. Indicators based on age, gender, income, education, and ethnicity can point to social vulnerability.[106] While all individuals are at risk when exposed to natural and man-made disasters, at-risk populations are potentially at **greater** risk due to age, income, access to resources, and physical condition.

At-risk persons are those with functional and access needs of sufficient magnitude that their ability to access or medical care may be hampered during an emergency or disaster.[107] Approximately twenty percent of the population of the United States has some form of recognized disability. This often results in diminished ability to respond to emergencies and to deal effectively with the aftermath or emergencies.[108] In particular, at-risk individuals may have difficulty receiving and understanding emergency broadcasts due to hearing difficulties of English proficiency. Those living in poverty often do not have access to transportation needed to evacuate. Individuals with mobility issues may not be able to evacuate as well.[109] For example, New Orleans officials were unable to effectively communicate with members of the Vietnamese community during and after Hurricane Katrina in 2005 due to language barriers. Similarly, the Hispanic community was unable to connect to emergency services for the same reason.[110]

According to a 2006 federal law, "at-risk individuals" refers to senior citizens, children, pregnant women, and individuals who have special needs.[111] More recent research indicates that minorities, those with limited English proficiency, and immigrants are also "at risk."[112] More broadly, "at-risk" individuals are conceptualized as those that lack financial, physical, and social assets.[113]

At-risk populations are often discussed in the context of functional needs and access needs. **Function-based needs** (or functional needs) involve limitations or restrictions that a person has that require assistance from others during a public health emergency or disaster.[114] **Access-based needs** mandate that vital resources are useable by all persons, which includes accommodations, social services, transportation, medications, and information.[115]

The first responder, healthcare, and emergency management communities identify *vulnerable*, *at-risk*, and *special populations* based upon chronic disability and health status as defined in disaster scenarios.[116] These disaster scenarios and frameworks have been produced from definitions used by FEMA, the U.S. Department of Justice, and the U.S. Department of Health and Human Services (HHS). Fire services, emergency management agencies, public health agencies, and emergency medical providers base their definitions of "at-risk" populations on these frameworks.[117] Many federal laws defining at-risk populations and accommodating persons with functional and access needs include the Americans with Disabilities Act (1990), the Rehabilitation Act (1973), the Pandemic and All-Hazards Preparedness Act (2006), and the Post-Katrina Emergency Management Reform Act (2006).

There are also executive orders and federal agency policies and regulations that require accommodation of persons with functional needs. For example, FEMA issued its *Guidance on Planning for Integration of Functional Needs Support Services in General Population Shelters.* It provides requirements to make evacuation shelter accommodations for individuals with functional needs. This is required by the ADA and was also written to integrate all persons in FEMA shelters.[118]

As noted above, risk and vulnerability are not equally distributed. In addition to functional needs, demographic and social characteristics of a community may also impact resilience.[119] Gender, income, age, education, and ethnicity are associated with vulnerability as well.[120] Those 65 and older, race, and poverty are disproportionately affected by emergencies and disasters.[121] Recognizing this, the CDE produced the **Social Vulnerability Index (SVI)** to assist practitioners and planners in identifying vulnerable populations. The SVI makes predictions based on socioeconomic status, household composition, disability, language, minority status, housing, and transportation.[122]

In particular, populations with low levels of income and wealth are less likely than others to possess the resources to prepare for and respond to disasters. Low-income populations have a higher proportional cost of replacing lost property and may lack the ability to access and respond to government warnings. The lack of English proficiency can also result in the failure to understand and act upon warnings.[123]

From the perspective of emergency management planning, the numbers and percentages of a local population "at risk" be determined by the SVI and other means. Some communities have developed and maintained registries of persons "at risk" or with functional needs. These registries have been constructed through both voluntary identification or by organizations who deliver services to clients with special needs. These can include utilities and home health care agencies.[124] Also, U.S. Census data, web-based population monitoring, and other government databases can be utilized.

The goal of these methods is to estimate the numbers and needs of the at-risk population within a particular geographic area. For example, the North Carolina Department of Health and Human Services devised a method (the **Hazard-Based Framework**) to identify at-risk populations in terms of three major hazard categories. This approach assesses risk of vulnerable populations with reference to three major hazards: (A) communicable disease, (B) natural disasters (including extreme weather), and (C) contaminating events, such as hazmat. By employing this framework, at-risk populations can be identified to facilitate outreach and response efforts on them during times of disasters or emergencies.[125]

In addition to functional needs individuals, children, and the elderly, at-risk populations include prisoners and transient populations. After planners have identified at-risk populations within a community, additional steps must be taken. High concentrations of at risk populations for each hazard category require that plans be made to contact them during times of disasters or emergencies. Community groups and partner agencies can also be engaged to provide resources and services to these individuals.[126] Taking these actions helps to build resilience to assist the at-risk population.[127]

The Hazards-Based Framework includes a five-step process: (1) identification of potential hazards to the jurisdiction, (2) enumerate and map at-risk populations, (3) contact partner state and local government agencies who work with at-risk populations, (4) reach out to community partners associated with at-risk populations, and (5) plan and coordinate preparedness and response efforts in conjunction with partners.[128]

The methods thus far discussed in this section are a good starting place for emergency management estimation of at risk populations in a particular jurisdiction. However, all of these approaches have limitations. For one thing, the registries may not be accurate. Individuals may move and or their vulnerabilities may improve.[129] In addition, the methodologies may incorrectly include populations that are not at high risk or incorrectly exclude populations are actually at high risk.[130]

Despite these limitations, it is the duty and responsibility of emergency management and first responder agencies to make plans to care for at-risk populations in emergency situations. This requires making emergency response plans based upon the best information available.

Response Factors to Consider with High-Risk Populations

This leads us to the **response factors to consider with high-risk populations**. There are eight (8) factors to consider as an emergency management planner to serve the needs of the identified at-risk population: (1) access, (2) sensory deficits, (3) availability of durable and consumable medical goods, (4) power supplies, (5) language and cultural competency of messages, (6) food services, (7) intellectual and cognitive conditions, and (8) service animals.[131]

Once the components of a response have been chosen and a strategy for implementation of those components has been selected, emergency management agencies are in a stronger position to serve the needs of at-risk populations in emergency situations. Hazard assessments allow for emergency management and public health officials to make realistic plans with which to assist at risk populations.[132]

Anticipating Human Behavior in Emergency Situations

Social science research findings can be utilized in an effort to explain and predict how people behave during disaster situations. The emergency responder and emergency manager must know how all people truly react during a disaster so that they can plan their responses appropriately. Having a correct understanding of the way that human beings behave during disasters is a vital skill for a law enforcement officer and for a first responder to possess. It makes tasks easier and facilitates effective and recovery operations.[133]

Not all human behaviors can be predicted. But because we can predict many behaviors, it is important that emergency managers develop plans to respond to those predictable behaviors. Knowing this makes your job easier in stressful situations. It seems everybody has an opinion about how people act during disasters. People who have never actually been in a disaster often hold beliefs about how people will respond to disaster. Many of these beliefs are false or based on myths.[134]

A **myth** is a widely held false belief. Myths are either totally false, or overgeneralized rare events related to disasters. Myths are sometimes hard to get people to disbelieve. A **misconception** is easier to get people to discard. A misconception is simply an incorrect idea based upon incomplete or misunderstood information. It is about something that is perceived inaccurately. When correct information is given, misconceptions are corrected. For example, some people blame first responders for failing to prevent a disaster. However, preventing disasters is not their job. When this is explained, the blame tends to diminish.[135]

Incorrect assumptions are more difficult to get people to discard, because they are more difficult to detect. **Incorrect assumptions** happen when people draw conclusions based upon hastily obtained and incorrect information.[136] For example if someone states "Everybody knows that the government does not care." Or "Everybody knows looting happens after all disasters." Many individuals do not bother to do research or to verify the true facts, because they "know" that what they think is true.

Misconceptions are the easiest to refute. Myths are in the middle, and incorrect assumptions are the hardest. This is true because people's incorrect assumptions are held close in their minds. However, incorrect assumptions, misconceptions, and myths produce incorrect information. First responders must know how people truly react in a disaster instead.[137]

The Psychology of Disaster Response

The **psychology of disaster response** examines how human beings behave during disasters. In this sense, it is based on **behavioralism**–the approach to social science that tries to measure real-world actions of human beings in order to explain and predict human behavior. Behavioralism tries to systematically observe the way that people act in given situations from a "scientific" or "objective" point of view. Then, explanations for that behavior or for those actions are made. Based on observing systematic regularities over time, human behavior in the future can be predicted and anticipated generally.

To work towards rationality, one should ideally base decisions on the best data available. For that reason, a mental separation from myths and misconceptions about human behavior during disasters from observed realities of this behavior is necessary.

Common myths:

- Disaster victims act irrationally.
- Victims panic.
- Victims wander around in shock.
- Victims are helpless and require immediate assistance from government or nonprofit organizations to avoid dying.
- Social order breaks down immediately – looting and violence occur soon after the disaster.

This is the "conventional wisdom" from Hollywood disaster movies and some media depictions. However, behavioral research demonstrates that most disaster victims do not behave in these ways.[138] In reality, few people show shock reactions to disasters. Panic does not occur often. Individuals attempt rationality in that they behave in a manner that they believe is best under the situation according to their understanding. Most individuals seek out information and adjust their behavior accordingly.[139]

A leading emergency management authority found that most disaster victims utilize their available resources to adapt to the situation as much as possible.[140] Research indicates that violence and looting do not occur as often as perceived.[141] Behavioral research shows that these generalizations are true in typical disasters. However, the longer the disaster continues, and the longer the grid is down, antisocial behaviors increase. Hurricanes are an example. Long periods without electricity and potable water can lead to social unrest. People get frustrated when they cannot obtain supplies. Therefore, sometimes they loot stores and commit other property crimes. There is also a correlation between receiving outside aid and antisocial behaviors. The longer it takes for outside help to arrive, the more antisocial behavior such as theft and looting is likely to occur.

It is also possible that people have confused protests with disasters. Protests against the government that involve violent confrontations often result in looting, arson, and other antisocial behaviors. But the typical disaster does not.

Experts argue that the false belief in disaster myths can be dangerous.[142] This is true because when people believe things that are not true, they can make completely wrong decisions. For example, when authorities believe that people will panic, they are likely to fail to warn about a disaster. This can lead to unnecessary death, injury, and property damage.

The **panic myth** in disasters and emergencies will be examined. A pervasive myth regarding human behavior following disasters is the incorrect conclusion that widespread panic will ensue. In other words, the notion that there is widespread panic after disasters is overblown and overstated. Panic is a misused word. *Fear and acute fear* are often described incorrectly as *panic.* Fear is different from panic – fear is generally rational, while panic is generally irrational.

Panic is an intense fear reaction characterized by loss of self-control and flight behavior.[143] It is uncontrollable and irrational loss of composure and logic that causes disordered behavior. *Panic and fear are two different things.* **Fear** is a rational response to danger that causes people to take protective actions.[144] People who experience fear are generally able to function in something approaching a rational manner. Panic causes people to either freeze or to behave in an irrational manner. If fear leads to panic, irrational and antisocial actions can occur.

Fear-based rational actions to danger are often mislabeled as panic for three reasons. First, disaster survivors often describe their protective actions as being motivated by "panic." For example, a person living on the Pacific coast might say, "When I heard the tsunami siren, I panicked. Then I immediately got in the car and drove 3 miles and stopped in a parking lot." This was not panic—this was rational fear that led to the intelligent action of driving to a safe distance. Here, the survivor equated the initial fear with panic, which are not the same thing. If they had actually panicked, they probably would not have taken the protective action necessary to save themselves. Thus, panic is a misused word.[145]

Second, observers who read about a disaster or watch disaster footage sometimes falsely interpret the mental state of disaster victims.[146] People assume that panic occurred due to misconceptions about how they think that people must have felt. People can "armchair quarterback" when they see disaster victims on television or social media. They might think, "They should have done X differently." Making what an outside observer might consider evidence of panic might only be a situation in which a person involved in a disaster made only an error of judgment in a high-stress situation.[147] In addition, it must be realized that Hollywood disaster movies often portray panic responses to disasters. This has at least a subconscious influence over how we imagine that people must feel in a real-world disaster situation.

The third reason is related to the second. When many people watch disaster response and recovery on social media or television or read about it on the internet, observers often interpret the attempt of people who received warnings to evacuate as panic. For example, interstates heading away from the coast are packed solidly with motor vehicles and resemble parking lots. But a reaction to a warning designed to protect people from an imminent disaster is not panic—it is a rational response to avoid harm.[148]

Thus, we can see that panic is a misused word. Panic and fear are not the same thing. Widespread panic is largely a myth. However, that being said, panic does sometimes occur. For panic to occur, behavioral research shows that certain conditions must be present though, as defined in terms of the individual's beliefs at the time:

1. A perception of immediate and extreme danger
2. The existence of a limited number of escape routes
3. A perception that the escape routes are closing, necessitating immediate escape
4. A lack of communication[149]

For example, panic occurred when the Titanic sank in 1912 and there were not enough lifeboats for all passengers and crew. Panic also was noted during the Las Vegas mass shooting in 2017 because there were limited escape routes, a rapid-fire semi-automatic rifle, and a lack of communication. But these are not typical disasters. Panic is not a typical or common reaction to disasters. When panic is observed, it typically involves a small component of the individuals affected by a threat and does not usually last long.[150]

Another disaster myth is the notion of *disaster shock*. **Disaster shock** is characterized by an overwhelming amount of stress resulting from a sudden and catastrophic disaster that causes a person to cease normal functioning. Some disaster victims have gone into psychological shock following a disaster. This psychological shock is characterized by the mental disconnection between the victim and the environment, disoriented thinking, and passivity.[151] Disaster shock can also manifest itself in disbelief, confusion, and indifference.[152] The person who experiences disaster shock typically cannot communicate normally or function normally for a period of time.

There is a widespread misperception that a large portion of disaster victims get disaster shock. This is untrue and exaggerated. True disaster shock affects a relatively small portion of disaster victims. Many disaster victims have stress-related illnesses, such as digestive problems, sleeping problems, depression, and anxiety, but this is not the same thing as disaster shock. Disaster shock, when it occurs, is associated with *sudden* events involving widespread destruction, traumatic injuries, or death.[153] For example, terrorist attacks, severe tornadoes, and tsunamis are associated with disaster shock.

Even when these sudden extreme disasters occur, relatively few people suffer from true disaster shock, a maximum of 14% according to behavioral research conducted over a 40-year period. Much larger percentages of disaster victims suffer from depression, sleep problems, and anxiety.[154]

Those who actually get disaster shock typically recover fairly quickly. Disaster shock tends to persist from a few hours to a few days in its acute form. Long-term effects of disaster shock can include phobia, anxiety, and depression.[155] Those with pre-existing mental health issues are much more likely than the average person to suffer from disaster shock and are much more likely to have lingering stress effects from the disaster.[156]

Another disaster myth is referred to as *homogeneity of victim response*. **Homogeneity of victim response** is the idea that all disaster victims are the same – that every person involved in a disaster is in an identical situation and that they have equal resources and skills. This is obviously a grossly oversimplified myth. Disaster victims are not homogeneous. There is no single "population" or "public" that can be aggregated for the purpose of making all-encompassing generalizations. Individuals and groups possess different hazard knowledge, abilities, and resources.[157] In other words, there are rich people, poor people, people in the middle, different types of houses, different levels of health, and different levels of ability and training. People experience disasters differently based on these things. Some are more vulnerable than others.

In addition to demographics and socioeconomic status, one must distinguish between the characteristics of people who are physically in an area when a disaster strikes: (1) residents, (2) transients, and (3) special facility populations.[158]

Residents are those who live or work in the area hit by the disaster.

Transients are people that are in the disaster area temporarily–passing through on business, visiting friends or relatives, or there for a vacation.

Special facility populations are individuals in K-12 schools, jails, nursing homes, or hospitals in the disaster area.[159]

Law enforcement officers, emergency managers, and first responder agencies. must consider each group separately because their disaster needs are different. Residents have more property to lose. Warnings must be aimed towards not only physical safety but also towards protecting property. Transients can be treated as residents in some cases, as when they are staying with friends or relatives. But so-called "day visitor" transients who come to an area for a special event, like a sports game, a concert, or casino gambling may be disproportionately impacted by a sudden-onset disaster like a tornado or a terrorist attack. Thus, disaster victims are not homogenous.

Human behavior during disasters is based upon different visions or interpretations of the *social fabric*. The **Social Fabric** is a term borrowed from sociology. It is a metaphor for how well the community members interact amongst themselves. If you consider all the individual members as *threads*, the "social fabric" is made by having those members interact, thus "weaving" the threads together. The tighter the weave (the more frequently and positively the members interact with each other), the stronger the fabric is; the looser the weave, the weaker the fabric, and the more likely to tear (have conflicts that pit one group against another), fray (lose members), develop loose threads (criminals), and otherwise suffer. The social fabric then metaphorically "holds society together" and allows society to function. Disasters (both man-made and natural) stress the social fabric. When the social fabric is stressed, people can act out in negative ways. These can include looting, physical violence, and theft. On the other hand, sometimes stresses in the social fabric have a positive result: people come closer together and try to help each other.

The *type* of the disaster and the *duration* of the disaster impact whether or not individuals will act in negative ways or positive ways. The longer a disaster lasts, the less charitable and kind people feel. This is especially true if the grid remains down and people cannot obtain vital resources. People generally do not panic, and often try to help both themselves and others. However, during the immediate impact and during the first few days after disaster impact, antisocial behaviors like looting and increased crime are rare.

However, the longer the disaster lasts, especially in a "grid-down" situation, as in the case of hurricanes, stealing and looting may emerge. In other words, antisocial behavior can be associated with the recovery periods of disasters. But these are not emergency time behaviors: they appear in the early stages of the recovery period. In short, the type of disaster and the length of time the disaster lasts can be associated with antisocial behaviors.[160]

Caring for the Victims of Disasters and Emergencies

One of the most visible and important parts of emergency response operations involves taking actions to care for the injured, distraught, and the dead following a critical incident or disaster. After a terrorist attack, mass shooting, hurricane, tsunami, tornado, earthquake, volcanic eruption, chemical spill, or nuclear or biological event, the public expects a prompt and meaningful response. The goals of this response are to provide medical care to the injured, process dead bodies, and get the infrastructure functioning again.

One generally visualizes first responders, such as police, fire, and EMT personnel engaging in response activities. However, civilian volunteers, hospital personnel, emergency management personnel, and mortuary workers also have roles to play in response to disasters and critical incidents. Both emergency workers and volunteers typically attempt to rescue and render aid at the incident scene to persons injured or trapped by a disaster or emergency.[161]

Both first responder personnel and volunteers become involved in both routine emergency and non-emergency disaster situations. Generally, first responders on a scene will assess the immediate health impacts of a natural or man-made disaster.

In a serious critical incident, a law enforcement Incident Commander utilizing ICS will be present to assess the situation. He or she will then report the seriousness of the situation. At that point the PHO will be notified.[162]

When the Incident Commander (IC) feels that the situation warrants notifying the PHO, public health agencies are contacted so that they can determine the appropriate public health response.[163] Following notification of a serious health-related incident, the first hours after the incident occurs are critical. The Public Health agency will make decisions about how to respond and will coordinate the planned response with the necessary agencies and jurisdictions.[164]

A **Job Aid** can be utilized by Incident Commanders on the scene to assist in delineating the mechanisms with which ICs and Public Health agencies will coordinate the appropriate response.[165] This job aid describes the incident, indicates the personnel needed to deal with the incident and their responsibilities, and delineates the needed supplies.

The scope and type of response appropriate from the Public Health agency depends upon the nature of the threat and by the by the amount of time that has passed following the critical incident.[166] For example, biological, chemical, radiological, pandemic, and hazmat incidents vary in terms of the onset of health consequences and with regard to the specific healthcare interventions that are necessary. There are appropriate PHO actions 0-3 hours after the incident, 3-6 hours after the incident, and 6-12 hours and beyond after the incident.

Emergency management training plans can be implemented involving contract and deployment of the skills of the PHO with regard to natural disasters, hazmat incidents, terrorist attacks, pandemics, and severe storms. PHOs should have plans in place regarding how to best respond to various types of health-related critical incidents.[167]

First responder agencies are often involved in **Search And Rescue** (SAR) operations. Search and Rescue Operations refer to response activities designed to locate disaster victims and remove them from danger. SAR allows disaster victims to receive aid such as medical care or hydration.[168] Search and rescue include (a) looking for missing persons, (b) establishing the locations of victims, (c) rescue of trapped, stranded, or injured persons, (d) providing medical care, and (e) transporting the seriously injured to hospitals.[169]

There are many types of SAR operations. For example, a police officer extracting an injured person from a car crash is SAR. Some SAR operations include the following: (1) **rural SAR**, which involves search and rescue in wilderness areas, (2) **air-patrolled SAR**, which is used to search for shipwreck survivors, etc., (3) **swift water rescue** (employed to locate and bring in persons trapped by flood waters), and (4) **urban search and rescue (USAR)**.[170]

SAR is broadly about saving trapped and injured people. In small accidents involving only a few victims, volunteer bystanders can rescue the victims.[171] But if the damage is widespread and involves reinforced concrete buildings, **heavy rescue** is needed. This involves search and rescue using specially trained responders with specialized debris removal equipment.[172]

Heavy rescue involves **USAR (Urban Search and Rescue)**. USAR refers to teams maintained by FEMA that locate and extricate disaster victims and provide specialized lifesaving support to those trapped in collapsed structures. USAR supports state and local first responder agencies. FEMA maintains USAR task forces across the United States. USAR forces possess the ability to deploy to a critical incident site within six hours and to sustain themselves at the site for 36 hours.[173] Many large cities have fire departments capable of urban search and rescue.

USAR personnel are the most suitable resource to care for the needs of crush victims at a critical incident site.[174] The federal government's lead USAR team was established by FEMA in 1989. It is named the National Urban Search and Rescue Response.

The **National Urban Search and Rescue Response** is comprised of 28 FEMA USAR Task Forces. These task forces are located across the continental United States. USAR Task Forces consist of firefighters, paramedics, physicians, engineers, and canine teams. FEMA requires that each member possess EMT certification. Generally, USAR Task Forces are deployed following a presidential disaster declaration.[175]

The **DRC Typology** (Disaster Research Center) is a component of understanding the actors in emergency management. It was developed to help practitioners to better understand the operations of organizations that deal with disaster response. The DRC typology is based upon tasks and structures. **Structures** are about how the organization is designed or "set up" in terms of its hierarchy and chain of command. Structures can be organized well or spontaneous. **Tasks** deal with the things that the organization does (activities that it performs).[176]

The organizational structure or organizational design of government, private, and nonprofit/volunteer organizations can be described as being either *normal* or *novel*. **The normal organizational structure** follows the typical chain of command – the normal duties and authority relationships that the organization's members encounter routinely. **Novel organizational structure** happens when circumstances require that the members quickly develop new roles and authority relationships.[177]

All emergency management organizations perform tasks and jobs that can be described as either *normal* or *novel*. **Normal tasks** are routine–the organization has done them before–part of expected job duties. **Novel tasks** are kind of unusual tasks performed only "as needed" during disasters.

Established organizations are the easiest to understand and visualize. These use their standard organizational structure to perform normal tasks. For example, paramedics treating disaster victims; police working an accident investigation during an evacuation.

Extending organizations operate under their standard organizational structure to perform novel tasks. For example, Public Works Department employees doing search and rescue work after a bombing or building collapse. The circumstances caused their normal job duties to be extended due to a disaster.

Expanding organizations are created when volunteer organizations get absorbed by government organizations due to the magnitude of a disaster, or when local first responders get "federalized" by FEMA due to a severe disaster. In this situation, organizational members perform their normal tasks within novel organizations.

Emergent organizations also exist. *Emergent* means "to form spontaneously" or "to form without an advanced plan." For example, in a long "grid-down" situation, neighbors form their own "security detail" and block the roads into the subdivision. Or after an earthquake, a group of friends and neighbors form a team to look for trapped survivors. Emergent organizations perform novel tasks within novel organizations.[178]

In a complex disaster, organizations of all types form or are deployed, and they all interact in complex ways. Understanding inter-organizational dynamics better prepares law enforcement officers and other first responders to be more effective by working with other organizations in disasters.[179]

This is part of understanding and predicting human behavior in SAR operations.[180] Realize that untrained civilians will be the first to arrive and will likely attempt SAR on their own using improvised tools and whatever else is available. These civilians will prioritize extracting family and friends over others. Typically, victims will cooperate with each other towards the common good of rescue. After professional first responders arrive, they generally take over SAR operations. Trained personnel may or may not work with volunteers.[181] This depends upon the magnitude of the disaster, the number of victims, and the number of professional first responders available.

In terms of actually **conducting search and rescue operations**, FEMA has outlined a nine-step process. A complex process must be followed to operate a successful SAR operation in a dense urban environment.[182] These steps are abbreviated or truncated for less complex situations, such as a multi-car pileup on the interstate.

Gathering facts is the first step of SAR. This is about using the factual information that is available about the nature of the disaster, the number of victims, and the environment (weather, buildings, the presence of hazmat, etc.) to orient actions.[183] This can also be viewed as part of **situational awareness** in that law enforcement officers and other first responders must constantly monitor the environment and changing conditions. Such changing conditions may arise from secondary hazards produced by the disaster.[184]

The second step of search and rescue involves **assessing damage**. This deals primarily with the built environment and accident scenes. The actions that need to be taken depends upon the level of damage. For example, if structural damage is light, the primary goal is to immediately come to the aid of victims. On the other hand, heavy structural damage requires immediately securing the building perimeter to limit access by untrained and improperly equipped personnel.[185]

In the third step of SAR, emergency managers and first responders must **consider probabilities**. This involves predicting what is likely to happen under different scenarios and casualty levels.[186]

Assessing your situation is the fourth step of search and rescue. This deals with examining the level of risk associated with the SAR and the type of equipment and personnel that will be needed.[187] Effective SAR depends on having access to the appropriate tools and equipment. Safety equipment and the correct clothing are important components of equipment. Improper tools and equipment hinder rescue and puts responders at risk for death or injury.[188]

Next, it is necessary to **establish rescue priorities** as the fifth step of SAR. This means making the determination about who should be rescued or extracted first, second, third, and so forth depending upon the severity of the injury, the stability of the structure or vehicle, the presence of fire, chemicals, etc., and the availability and expertise of first responders at the disaster site. Triage should occur so that the most difficult extractions are performed last.[189]

The sixth step of search and rescue operations involves **making decisions** from a broad-based perspective based on the overall situation and the progress of SAR up to that point. Resources should be deployed to achieve the best results.[190]

Based upon the overall decision-making priorities set in the previous step, the seventh step of SAR is about **developing a rescue plan**.[191] This is especially necessary for complex disasters such as a building collapse caused by tornadoes, earthquakes, or terrorist bombings. Here, it must be established how to enter the structure safely, which personnel will enter the structure, and the procedures used to locate and extract victims. As part of this, steps must be taken to also address rescuer needs and safety. Because SAR is physically demanding, hydration and food must be supplied to involved first responders. Crews should be rotated to reduce fatigue. FEMA recommends that SAR rescuers work in pairs.[192]

Taking action is the eighth step of search and rescue. This is the actual implementation of the rescue plan that was developed. Personnel on the ground systematically cover the entire structure, call out for survivors, and extract them.[193] SAR workers must realize that the passage of time is closely related to locating and rescuing a live victim. The most likely chance of success occurs during the first hour. However, the first 24 hours also provide a good chance of victim survival. In some disasters, it was discovered that trapped victims had an 80% chance of survival if they were rescued within the first 24 hours. After that, there is a rapid decline in the possibility of victim survival. The morbidity and mortality of trapped victims is increased due to the fact that victims often suffer from severe injuries, including broken bones, respiratory failure, loss of blood, and internal organ damage.[194] Due to the high probability of fatalities, SAR operations often become "search and recovery operations."[195]

An important part of taking action is **marking structures** with spray paint. This is done to eliminate duplication of effort so that the same building or house is not searched again unnecessarily. Rescue workers often paint "/"

on the door to indicate that a structure is being searched. Rescue workers then paint an "X" to denote that the building search was completed. When a rescue worker paints an "X" inside a box, danger inside the structure is indicated and persons without protective equipment should not enter.[196]

Evaluating your progress is the final step of SAR. Responders should continually monitor progress and assess the environment for danger to personnel.[197]

As noted previously, this full nine-step process of SAR will generally be followed only for large-scale disasters involving buildings, homes, and other structures. Smaller-scale incidents most often follow an abbreviated process.

The overall goal of search and rescue is to take victims out of harm's way and to provide medical care to the injured. SAR's primary focus is to help the victims by removing them from danger and through first aid, advanced medical care, or hydration.[198]

Emergency Medical Care and Triage

Critical incidents and disasters result in injuries and deaths. The number of injuries and deaths depend on the severity of the incident as well as the proximity of the victim to the disaster or hazard, the presence or absence of protective structures and devices, the age, health, and physical strength of the victim, and the victim's knowledge about how to react to disasters and critical incidents.[199]

Disasters come in many forms. As a result, different injuries can be produced. For example, cold water exposure from flooding can result in hypothermia. Tornadoes and earthquakes can cause fractures and lacerations. Fires can result in respiratory failure and burns. Hazmat spills can result in damage to a victim's nervous system or respiratory problems.[200]

An important dimension to search and rescue activities involves **emergency medical care**. Emergency medical care differs greatly across geographical areas and jurisdictions. In some areas, emergency medical services (EMS) and ambulance services are housed with fire departments. In other areas, EMS and ambulance services are separate and even provided by different organizations. Emergency medical care and triage for persons injured by a of major disaster can come from the following:[201]

1. Emergency medical personnel in the field
2. Local hospitals
3. **Disaster Medical Assistance Teams (DMATs)**–these are composed of medical personnel specially designated to provide emergency medical care during a disaster or named event.[202]

The federal government maintains the **National Disaster Medical System (NDMS)** which is operated jointly by four federal cabinet departments, and it contains eighty DMATs and 7,000 medical support personnel from the private sector.[203]

For smaller-scale and more typical disasters and critical incidents, local EMS personnel are maintained under city and county governments. These and other emergency medical providers should conduct casualty assessments following a major disaster. **Casualty assessments** involve estimating the number and types of injuries. These are conducted to manage medical services and to properly distribute patients. At the scene of a critical incident, **medical management** involves triage, medical treatment, mental health support, and patient transportation to hospitals if required.[204]

In a large-scale disaster, medical care, search and rescue, and transportation of the injured must be coordinated with the Emergency Operations Center (EOC).[205] Large local jurisdictions and FEMA have extensive protocols in place to deal with mass care, sheltering, and human services needs following large-scale disasters.

Whether a large-scale or small-scale disaster, victims should receive medical assessment. This assessment may lead to medical intervention that may lead to emergency rooms and even to in-patient hospitalization.[206] For most disasters and emergencies, local hospitals handle injuries that require in-patient care. The NDMS will only be activated in catastrophic incidents, and then only for the worst cases.

An important task of emergency management involves dealing with the situation in which a disaster of such magnitude occurs that requires large-scale evacuation, disruption of food and water supplies, mass medical care services, shelter provision, and family reunification efforts. The term **mass care** applies to such situations, which may be caused by a variety of incident scenarios, such as hurricanes, earthquakes, bioweapons attacks, large-scale terrorist incidents, significant tornadoes, and widespread contamination caused by hazmat.[207]

Because the nation faces several natural and man-made hazards such as earthquakes, hurricanes, tsunamis, and fires, significant portions of a local population may be displaced from their homes and communities. This will require mass care and sheltering of evacuees in the aftermath of a catastrophic incident. Mass care involves shelter, food and water, and other vital services to displaced persons.[208] During times of extensive and severe disasters, it is a recognized responsibility of local, state, and sometimes national governments to provide mass care, sheltering, and human services. These governmental responses are facilitated by emergency managers.

As part of mitigation, preparedness, and response efforts, emergency managers must anticipate and prepare for these needs if called upon to do so.

The reception and care of disaster victims occurs fairly frequently. Emergency authorities are called upon in such situations to provide food, shelter, and medical care following catastrophic events.[209]

FEMA is the lead agency in mass care. The American Red Cross and the Salvation Army play volunteer support roles in the provision of mass care.

In both routine critical incidents and mass care situations, the first component of medical care for multiple victims is **triage**. The objective of triage is to allow emergency responders to sort victims into categories for the purpose of concentrating medical resources most effectively to save lives. Emergency medical workers in the field utilize *triage tags* to indicate the correct patient condition classification.[210] This is macabre, but necessary: dead/dying, immediate, delayed, and minor.

Medical personnel set up treatment areas at some distance from the immediate danger area. On-scene medical treatment is focused initially upon addressing basic life support. In the case of biological or chemical exposure, on-scene medical treatment might also involve providing antidotes. If radiological exposure has occurred, the on-scene medical treatment may involve administering potassium iodine. In addition, practice dictates that designated areas should be identified at the medical treatment scene to separate victims that must be transported to hospitals.[211]

Depending of the scope and magnitude of the disaster, the choice may be made to transfer victims on the scene to either hospitals or mass care facilities. Making these assessments is easier for patients in routine disasters. However, if a chemical, radiological, or biological incidents has occurred, victims must be decontaminated before they can be transported.[212]

Several different types of vehicles can be utilized to transport disaster victims to hospitals. This depends upon the condition of the victim and medical need. Ambulances (if available) and multiple occupancy vehicles can both be deployed. If available and urgent need is present, helicopters can be utilized. If the magnitude of the disaster is particularly great, it may be necessary to transport the injured to a NDMS directly.[213]

Each hospital should prepare and maintain a disaster plan. Thus, the response of a particular hospital to a disaster response will be guided by that plan.[214] These plans address vitally important issues with regard to mass casualty events, which can include decontamination, tracking patients, and decisions about where to treat patients on the hospital campus.

Dispatch centers should notify local hospitals that a disaster is in progress. Upon receiving the notification that a mass casualty incident has occurred, most hospitals transition to into *lock-down status*, per their disaster plans. Hospital personnel control access by locking all doors. Hospital staff and physicians are notified of the emergency. In a significant mass casualty incident, hospital procedures may require personnel to open areas outside the hospital to handle the surge of patients.[215] Tents can be set up for this purpose and medical equipment can also be brought into hospital parking decks.

Beyond this, emergency management authorities may need to set up special medical care facilities such as **medical aid stations**. Mass casualty events may overwhelm hospital resources in a jurisdiction. Chemical, biological, or radiological weapons may require antidotes. Exposed victims may also contaminate medical facilities. These may lead to the need to establish off-hospital medical facilities.[216]

Hospitals should expect that disasters will also lead to individuals transporting themselves to the facility to receive medical care. In this situation, hospitals will need to triage, treat, and if necessary, decontaminate these individuals. Due to the potential that victims may be contaminated, medical facility should possess appropriate personal protective equipment (PPE).[217]

Just as hospital medical personnel engage in triage and the determination of patient treatment needs, hospital personnel must also determine the maximum number of patients that can receive care at that facility. If a hospital announces that it has reached its maximum patient load, additional victims should be sent to other hospitals. If the disaster is of such magnitude that all area hospitals are filled to capacity, it is the duty of emergency management authorities to send victims to a NDMS.[218]

Biological attack incidents go beyond the capabilities of most hospitals and require the special expertise of public health agencies. National, state, and local public health departments and agencies are required to monitor hospital and clinic records for evidence of unusual disease patterns such as epidemics. Public health agencies engage in monitoring and investigations to identify and control biological agents. In addition, these agencies specify preventive measures and treatments for those exposed.[219]

Mass Fatalities

Part of the emergency response to mass casualty incidents involves mass fatalities. **Mass fatalities** occur when large numbers of human beings die as result of a disaster or emergency. Dealing with mass fatalities involves receiving human remains, identifying the deceased (DNA, fingerprinting, etc.) producing death certificates, safeguarding personal property of the dead, and releasing remains for final disposition.

Mass fatalities require the involvement of several emergency management actors and institutions, including emergency managers, coroners, medical examiners, forensic investigators, morticians, funeral home employees, mental health personnel, hospitals, and clergy. Public agencies and private companies can recover mass fatality casualties after large-scale disasters.[220]

In the United States, this process is initially a function of county medical examiners and county coroners. The disposal of the dead and the operation of morgues are regulated by statute. Emergency Operations Plans of government organizations address mass fatalities and provide for the location of temporary morgues.[221]

In most American jurisdictions, the medical examiner is delegated the responsibility for managing human remains. In criminal cases or in cases of a suspicious death, the medical examiner is assigned an important place in the chain of custody for evidence. In the event of a mass shooting or act of terrorism, the medical examiner's conclusions and custody of the remains of victims are needed to successfully prosecute these criminal acts. In a mass casualty event, the volume of human remains may exceed the capacity of a local morgues. Capacity can be extended if another morgue facility possesses the utilities and security required.[222] However, if local morgue facilities are overwhelmed, FEMA must be contacted by local and state authorities.

Thus, FEMA can play a needed role in mass casualty events dealing with dead bodies that exceed local capacity.[223] For example, FEMA maintains the **Disaster Mortuary Operations Response Team (DMORT)**. DMORTS are composed of private sector funeral directors, morticians and supporting personnel deployed by the federal government following presidentially declared disasters.

In a mass fatality event caused by terrorism, the site is both a crime scene and a mass care scene. For that reason, law enforcement must be involved to collect and preserve evidence for investigation and criminal prosecution. This is one of the reasons that dead bodies should not be moved immediately. However, once a preliminary investigation has taken place, protocol allows the deceased to be transported to a temporary morgue facility. In extreme circumstances, refrigerated trailers can be repurposed as temporary morgues.[224] Bodies should be photographed, DNA sampled, and fingerprinted to facilitate later identifications.

Mental Health Issues in Mass Casualty Events

Emergency managers and first responders also should not overlook mental health issues and treatment as part of mass casualty incidents. The emotional trauma of a catastrophic event can lead to a litany of mental health problems to both the survivors and first responders.[225] Because law enforcement officers and other first responders often experience high-stress and hazardous conditions on the job, post-traumatic stress and suicidal ideation are higher among these groups.[226]

Witnessing disasters and emergencies or being closely involved in emergencies and disasters can cause psychological stress to individuals. This disaster-related stress affects both members of the general public (including at-risk populations) and the emergency responder community.

Disaster victims over 65 are at risk for diminished cognitive ability. Reduced ability to solve problems and to process information make the elderly susceptible to stress. High-stress situations especially require good decision-making skills. When an elderly person's cognitive abilities are compromised, confusion and delayed responses to threats can emerge.[227]

Victims living in poverty are also at disproportionate risk for mental health problems following a disaster because their lack of resources often manifest in the inability to evacuate. Living in sub-standard housing and lack of transportation also increase stress during and after disaster impacts.[228]

Distrust of authorities and anger at their post-disaster situation can increase stress as well. For example, African-American communities in New Orleans after Hurricane Katrina strongly distrusted government authorities. Many chose to rely upon the community for support, rather than upon the government authorities.[229]

There is a body of literature on critical incident stress and how it affects first responders. The number of emergency responders that have been lost due to stress is unknown. In the law enforcement profession, it has been estimated that suicide results in greater losses of officers than those killed in the line of duty. Many in the first responder community of both active-duty and retired officers have been linked to the trauma resulting from critical incident stress.[230]

Because first responders spend a substantial amount of time at disaster scenes, they interact with victims with varying degrees of physical and emotional injuries. This exposure is associated with stress and long-lasting psychological problems.[231] **Professional suicide**, where a first responder resigns and leaves his or her profession, is another result of critical incident stress. Although some individuals handle stress better than others, all experience stress.[232]

Health and work performance are both adversely affected by stress. This is especially true for those working critical incidents. However, it also affects the victims of critical incidents. When human beings endure threatening events such as fatal accidents, shootings, hazmat episodes, and tornadoes impact and can emotionally scar individuals.[233]

Stress is the body's response to a situation that places special psychological or physical demands on a person. The specific environmental pressures exerted upon a person are called **stressors**. The effect of stressors on the human body may build beyond the ability of a person to adapt effectively.[234]

Several changes occur to the human body due to stress reactions. Heart, brain wave, and breathing rates increase to adapt the human body for anticipated physical exertion. Eyesight and hearing become more acute. These and other physiological changes represent the **fight-or-flight response** in reaction to stressors.[235] Critical incidents can and often do lead to this response. In law enforcement, threats against an officer, working a fatal accident, and death of a victim that he or she attempted to save are major causes of stress.[236]

Each individual is affected differently by critical incident stress. There are several factors that cause stress to manifest itself differently from person to person: (1) the individual's perception of the situation, (2) past experience, (3) the presence or absence of social support networks, and (4) individual differences with regard to stress reactions.[237]

Stress can be manifested in two ways: *acute* and *delayed.*[238] **Acute stress** is severe and typically sudden. It occurs during or immediately after exposure to a traumatic event.[239] Acute stress symptoms can include physical, mental (cognitive) and emotional reactions. Acute physical stress can manifest itself in crying, shaking, and hyperventilation accompanied by increased heart rate. Acute mental (cognitive) stress is evidenced by impaired reasoning, inability to concentrate, and confusion. Acute emotional stress shows itself in fear of event repetition, depression, and withdrawal.[240] **Delayed stress** occurs after the critical incident is over. As with acute stress, physical, mental (cognitive), and emotional manifestations can occur. These include headaches, sleeping problems, substance abuse, intrusive mental images of the event, depression, and apathy.[241]

Civilians involved in disasters or emergency situations can experience these types of stress as well. Psychological trauma can be experienced by victims, witnesses, and first responders.[242] For this reason, law enforcement personnel should be aware of *disaster behavioral health.* **Disaster behavioral health** involves the provision of mental health crisis counseling based upon adverse reactions to critical incidents.[243] This includes first responders, medical personnel, and civilians. Because all disasters result in mental health impacts, disaster behavioral health is an important component of disaster response and recovery.[244]

Law enforcement officers and students of emergency management should be familiar with some of the terminology of disaster behavioral health. PTSD (Posttraumatic Stress Disorder) and CIS (Critical Incident Stress) are both associated with the mental aspects of exposure to disasters and critical incidents. **Posttraumatic Stress Disorder (PTSD)** is a mental disorder caused by experiencing trauma and is associated with excessive anxiety, nightmares, depression, and intrusive thoughts about the traumatic event.[245] For example, it has been found that 80% of rape victims and 30%-40% of direct disaster victims suffer from PTSD.[246] Both combat experience and exposure to major violence are also associated with PTSD.[247] Law enforcement officers and fire personnel also suffer from PTSD due to their extensive exposure to disasters. Empirical research into PTSD among police officers indicates that the condition is reduced among officers that possess strong resilience and social support.[248]

Major Depression Disorder (MDD) is a mental disorder associated with notable mood changes accompanied by significant detachment and sadness disproportionate to the person's circumstances. MDD is manifested in changes in behavior and physiology as well. Among survivors of disasters, MDD is the second most frequently diagnosed mental health condition.[249]

GAD (Generalized Anxiety Disorder) is a mental disorder characterized by high levels of intrusive worry and is not attributable to specific triggers. GAD symptoms include insomnia, irritability, muscle tension, dizziness, and upset stomach. Approximately twenty percent of disaster survivors suffer from GAD.[250]

Critical Incident Stress (CIS) is work-related stress affecting emergency services caused by a trauma-inducing event and that standard coping mechanisms cannot dissipate.[251] It is treated in several ways. **Critical Incident Stress Management (CISM)** is often discussed in the first responder and emergency management community. CISM is a crisis-intervention method utilized for short-term crisis.[252]

CISM can only be provided by certified and properly trained individuals.[253] Emergency response organizations typically have such trained and certified personnel on staff. An important part of CISM is the notion of **debriefing**, in which those impacted by the incident share feelings and experiences in an effort to "take the edge off" trauma. It is for this reason that CISM is mostly heard about in conjunction with uniformed personnel. However, CISM can be applied to the civilian population as well.

First responders can be trained and certified in CISM programs. CISM programs train interested first responders in stress assessment and management, critical intervention, use of peer support techniques, briefings, debriefings, and defusing, and basic workplace violence protocols.[254]

Psychological First Aid (PFA) is a second commonly used stress reduction technique. PFA is a social support-based crisis intervention technique used to reduce the initial psychological trauma caused by of disasters.[255] Because law enforcement officers and other first responders are the first trained personnel at a critical incident scene, they are the officials that make the initial contact with disaster survivors. When first responder agencies train their personnel in Psychological First Aid, the mental health consequences of disaster survivors can be reduced. Law enforcement supervisors should be aware that PFA training and instructions are freely available from the NCTSN (National Child Traumatic Stress Network).[256]

Faith-based counseling and support is another potential resource that can be utilized by the first responder and emergency management community to help deal with the effects of disaster-related stress. Faith-based counseling utilizes he provision of emotional support to first responders and disaster victims based on their religious beliefs.[257]

There are additional strategies that law enforcement and other first responders and their supervisors can utilize to reduce the impact of critical incident stress. None are a substitute for counseling by a licensed mental healthcare practitioner. These should be used when needed. Some overall strategies include thorough planning and training of personnel, building an emotionally supportive team, providing specific instruction to recognize the effects and symptoms of critical incident stress, and making professional counseling available to all personnel.[258]

At the critical incident scene, additional strategies to reduce responder stress include effectively managing the critical incident scene, mandating regular breaks, ensuring that personnel receive food and water during the incident, and rotating personnel regularly. **Defusing** is another stress management technique. Defusing is a widely used technique used in the first responder community. It is based upon setting up a mechanism to allow a first responder experiencing acute stress to speak with someone about that stress immediately.[259]

After the critical incident has been resolved, it is suggested for law enforcement supervisors to see to it that personnel should be strongly encouraged to express their thoughts, feelings, and emotions after the resolution of the critical incident.[260] Also, supervisors should establish and run critical incident stress debriefings quickly after an incident.[261] Beyond this, supervisors should monitor the behavior of personnel that were present at the critical incident scene in order to discern any notable changes in comments or attitudes. Personnel with unusual behavior compared to past norms should be referred for professional counseling.[262]

Critical incident stress is real, and it affects the job performance and the lives of emergency responders and their families. Understanding this is an important part of critical incident management. Law enforcement supervisors should also realize that age, gender, the presence of an underlying mental health condition, and whether or not an officer is full-time or part-time are all factors that can influence the mental health of officers in addition to exposure to critical incidents.[263]

Keep in mind that witnessing disasters and emergencies, or being involved in emergencies and disasters can cause psychological stress to individuals. This disaster-related stress affects both members of the general public and the emergency responder community, including law enforcement.

Sheltering and Mass Care Following Disasters

An important task of emergency management involves the situation in which a disaster of such magnitude occurs that requires large-scale evacuation, disruption of food and water supplies, mass medical care services, shelter provision, and family reunification efforts. The term **mass care** applies to such situations, which may be caused by a variety of incident scenarios, such as hurricanes, earthquakes, bioweapons attacks, large-scale terrorist incidents, significant tornadoes, and widespread contamination caused by hazmat.

A variety of natural and man-made hazards may result in the need for emergency management agencies to provide mass care and sheltering of evacuees following a catastrophic incident.[264] During times of extensive and severe disasters, it is a recognized responsibility of local, state, and sometimes national governments to provide mass care, sheltering, and human services. These governmental responses are facilitated by emergency managers.

As part of mitigation efforts, emergency managers must anticipate and prepare for these needs if called upon to do so. Under American law, government bureaucracies, including FEMA, act on the basis of legal authority. With regard to mass care, sheltering, and human services, six major federal laws and various presidential executive orders provide the legal basis for federal intervention in these areas. Thus, federal agencies have been assigned and equipped for the task of providing mass care if necessary when state and local resources are insufficient.[265]

Part of the Stafford Act (the Robert T. Stafford Disaster Relief and Emergency Assistance Act of 1988, authorizes the president to issue disaster declarations to expedite federal aid to localities impacted by a major disaster. This includes the provision of temporary housing and emergency services. The law also allows financing of these activities through the DRF (Disaster Relief Fund).[266]

The World War II era Public Health Service Act is still in effect and vital to federal mass care, sheltering, and human services efforts. This law allows the federal government to provide emergency services during disasters. The even older (1935) Social Security Act, as amended, allows continuity of services (retirement, disability, survivors, and special veterans payments) during disasters. The Americans With Disabilities Act (1990) prohibits discrimination based upon disability.[267] With reference to sheltering and mass care, this means that all federally-funded emergency facilities are required to accommodate both the general population and those with functional needs.[268] Finally, the 2006 Pets Evacuation and Transportation Standards Act requires that federally-funded emergency shelters must also have accommodations available for domestic animals.[269]

In addition to these laws, Homeland Security Presidential Directives made under the authority of laws enacted by Congress serve as the basis for **disaster response plans**. These are comprehensive and detailed protocols designed to focus resources on reducing the effects of a catastrophic event. The most well-known federal disaster response plan is the 2008 National Response Framework (NRF).[270]

Each disaster response plan, including the National Response Framework utilizes **Emergency Support Functions (ESFs)**. Specifically related to mass care, sheltering, and emergency services is **ESF-6 (Mass Care, Emergency Assistance, Housing, and Human Services)**. The ESF-6 to the National Response Framework stipulates that broad services will be provided to support the immediate needs of displaced disaster victims.[271] ESF-6 contains an "escalating resource request flow," which demonstrates how ESF-6 functions can be escalated depending upon the severity of the disaster.

Under ESF-6, **mass care** in the aftermath of a disaster encompasses feeding, shelter, emergency first aid, distribution of emergency items, and collecting and providing information on victims to family members. **Emergency assistance** deals with evacuation and evacuation support (including registration and tracking), family reunification, provision of aid (including specialized aid and medical shelters to those with functional needs), coordination of donated goods and services, and evacuation, sheltering, and services for service animals and pets.[272]

Housing under ESF-6 includes a variety of federal interventions, such as rental assistance, repair assistance, loan assistance, replacement assistance, and placement of the displaced in "factory-built housing" (trailers).[273] Human services involve the implementation of federal disaster assistance programs to assist in victim recovery of "nonhousing losses," which include personal property such as food, clothing, and furniture. This is achieved through issuing food stamps, disaster unemployment insurance, disaster loans and legal services, and crisis counseling.[274]

Several federal agencies have been mandated to support ESF-6. Similarly, most state, local, and tribal governments have been assigned ESF-6 responsibilities as a condition of receiving federal funds.[275] This support includes mass care services, emergency assistance, housing, sheltering and human services.

In the event of need, mass care services begin at the local government level. Additional support flows from state governments. FEMA then works through a state agency to provide federal resources for mass care operations.[276] These include shelter services, feeding, bulk distribution operations (food, water, etc.), emergency first aid, and disaster welfare information (family tracking and facilitating family communication with relatives outside the disaster area).

Emergency assistance involves mass evacuation support (bus services, emergency medical vehicles, evacuation route planning and implementation), facilitated reunification through **NMETS (National Mass Evacuation Tracking System)**, and providing facilities and support to service animals and household pets pursuant to the Pets Evacuation and Transportation Standards Act of 2006.

Sheltering, or the provision of shelters to disaster victims is an important aspect of ESF-6. A web-based database called **NSS (National Shelter System)** is used to provide information about shelters in use as a result of emergencies and disasters.[277]

The American Red Cross (ARC), faith-based organizations, and non-governmental organizations (NGOs) also provide support to disaster victims housed in shelters. FEMA provides financial support to sheltering operations through the **Individual Assistance-Technical Assistance Contract**. FEMA provides support to NGOs engaging in the provision of shelter services through **FEMA Voluntary Agency Liaisons (VALs)**. The American Red Cross and the Salvation Army provide personnel to support mass care activities.[278]

The federal government's **National Disaster Housing Strategy** describes the scope of disaster housing assistance services.[279] This includes funding for temporary roof repair, general repairs, home replacement assistance, victim housing placement, rental assistance, noncongregate facility placement (temporary housing on cruise ships, barracks, dorms), and relocation.

Human services are also a part of disaster relief under ESF-6. This involves replacement of lost and personal property and other "nonhousing losses," financial assistance (unemployment insurance, food stamps, and disaster loans), and specialized services such as crisis counseling, services for those with functional needs, and disaster legal services.[280]

An important part of implementing ESF-6 is understanding the general *concept of operations*. This is a term used often in emergency management. A **concept of operations** is concise statement specifying which emergency functions will be conducted and how the emergency functions will be accomplished.[281] In connection with this mass care and sheltering, the concept of operations should focus upon addressing the immediate needs of victims, including life and safety issues. Evacuation of persons from danger, the provision of food and hydration, and the provision of shelter are the top priorities. Many evacuees require medical care as well.[282]

Following a catastrophic event requiring mass care, sheltering, and human services, emergency management agencies must establish *evacuation assembly sites*, *local congregate care centers*, and *points of distribution* inside the impact area. An **Evacuation Assembly Site (EAS)** is a local site where evacuees have been directed to receive assistance. An EAS should provide basic food, water, restrooms, and medical care. Evacuees should then be moved to a Consolidated Services Site.[283] **Local Congregate Care Shelters** are established inside the impact zone and are designed for combining mass care and sheltering needs. Local Congregate Care Shelters should be used for victims that require both medical care and sheltering. If medical needs cannot be handled there, they should be transported to a Consolidated Services Site.[284] **Points of distribution** are set up inside the impact zone and are utilized to hand out disaster and survival supplies to victims.

Remaining ESF-6 operations are established outside the impact area. These external to the impact area operations include *consolidated services sites, emergency respite sites, reception processing centers,* and *congregate care centers.*

Consolidated Services Sites provide extensive services to evacuees. These include evacuee processing, the provision of food, water, and personal hygiene items, medical services (including Disaster Medical Assistance Teams if necessary), mental health counseling, and emergency assistance and human services. These large sites are designed to bring together important disaster services in a central location. This also reduces logistical burdens. Evacuation tracking begins at Consolidated Services Sites. After processing, evacuees are transferred to a Reception Processing Center for shelter placement and other additional mass care services.[285] At these sites, some evacuees will be transported to different Reception Processing Centers in other cities.[286]

Emergency Respite Sites are facilities located along evacuation routes between the consolidated services sites and the reception processing center. Emergency Respite Sites provide fuel and water.[287]

Under the ESF-6 concept of operations, *reception processing centers* are the next stop. **Reception Processing Centers** receive evacuees and direct them to places that provide short-term shelter, such as congregate care shelters or other shelters.[288]

Congregate Care Shelters are used to provide shelter for both members of the general population and those with functional needs. Congregate Care Shelters are equipped to provide evacuees with short-term lodging, food, and hydration.[289]

Implementing mass care, sheltering, and human services creates significant logistical issues. Policy and law require certain space requirements for shelters, sources for supplies and equipment, accommodation of service animals and pets, and the provision of services for evacuees with chronic medical conditions. It should be emphasized that various federal laws mandate that mass care and shelters must accommodate the needs of all persons, including those with disabilities. This is actually planned for in FEMA's 2010 **Functional Needs Support Services (FNSS) Guidance.**[290]

Most notably FEMA stipulates *shelter space requirements and layout considerations.* Twenty square feet per person should be available for short-term sheltering and forty square feet per person for sheltering longer than 72 hours is needed according to the American Red Cross. Evacuees that utilize wheelchairs, service animals, lift equipment, and personal assistance services should receive 100 square feet of shelter space.[291] In addition to the square footage required for individual evacuees to sleep, shelters should have as much as fifty percent extra space dedicated to accommodate support services including food storage and preparation, sanitary needs, service animals, communications, mental health services, medical services, medication storage, transportation services and a "quiet area."[292]

Space requirements for use in determining shelter needs must be calculated. These requirements are based upon forty square feet per person for the general population and one hundred square feet for those with disabilities. This allows for a fifty percent size factor to accommodate support services.[293] Emergency managers should have familiarity with these calculations and the methodology upon which they are based.

Thus, we can see that the functions required by ESF-6 are extensive and complex. Significant coordination is required between ESF-6 activities and other ESFs. In the early stages of disaster response extensive coordination between ESF-6 and ESF-1 (Transportation) and ESF-9 (Search and Rescue). During later response operations, ESF-6 activities must be coordinated with ESF-7 (Logistics and Resource Management) and ESF-8 (Public Health and Medical Services).[294]

First responders and emergency managers should keep in mind that the necessity to utilize shelters is a traumatic experience for evacuees. Stress levels will increase and psychological problems will become manifest.

Care and Sheltering of Children Following Disasters

It is noted that persons under the age of 18 years make up about 25 percent of the U.S population. For that reason, planning shelter operations to support the special needs of children is vital.[295] First responders and emergency managers should remember that the needs of children can differ substantially from those of adults. Research has demonstrated that the traumatic effects of a disaster impact children more significantly than adults. This trauma can have long-lasting effects.[296]

In 2010, the **National Commission on Children and Disasters (NCCD)** reported to Congress and the president the results of their comprehensive research. The study examined and assessed the needs of children in disasters. Planning, response, and recovery issues were considered.[297] The NCDD report contains highly relevant information relating to the linkage between emergency management functions and assisting children.

The NCCD report's findings and recommendations significantly impact sheltering and mass care. Several EFSs are affected by the NCCD report, including ESF-5, (Emergency Management), ESF-6, ESF-7, (Logistics and Resource Management), and ESF-8 (Public Health and Medical Services).[298] The NCDD report contained four recommendations:

1. The needs of children must be distinguished and comprehensively integrated across all disaster management services and operations.
2. The NDRF (National Disaster Recovery Framework) must be modified to address both immediate and long-term physical and mental health of children and their housing, educational, and human services needs.
3. FEMA should take the appropriate actions to ensure that vital information necessary to deliver disaster recovery services to children and families is provided to emergency management agencies quickly.
4. Interagency agreements should be established by FEMA to ensure that full resources are provided to state and local child service systems and child congregate care facilities necessary to fully care for the needs of children.[299]

These four recommendations can be most effectively implemented in an ESF-6 mass care, sheltering, and human services deployment. Through modifications to mental health, child physical health and trauma, emergency medical services and pediatric transport, disaster care management, child care and early education, elementary and secondary education, child welfare and juvenile justice, sheltering standards, services, and supplies, housing, and evacuation, the needs of children involved in disasters can be best addressed. Specific recommendations are made to improve these functional areas with regard to children. Emergency managers should be familiar with these recommendations.

From an emergency management standpoint, the most important areas that can be immediately addressed to provide for the specialized needs of children during an ESF-6 situation are (1) **evacuation**, (2) **sheltering standards, services, and supplies**, and (3) **housing**. White the other functional areas are important, these three are under the most direct control of "on the scene" emergency management personnel.

First are evacuation needs of children. Evacuation is much more traumatic to children, who have likely had no experience with either disasters or evacuation. Emergency managers can lessen the stress of evacuation of children through training designed to enhance skills in and to provide services for pediatric disaster mental and behavioral health. These training activities could include psychological first aid and bereavement support. Embedding mental health professionals and persons with extensive experience working with children in shelters could also help.[300]

Additionally, emergency management personnel should work to maximize the effectiveness of the National Mass Evacuation Tracking System so that displaced children can be reunited with their families as soon as possible.[301] Doing so will dramatically reduce the stress of both children and their families and caregivers.

Sheltering standards, services, and supplies must also be modified by emergency management personnel to accommodate the special needs of children. Age-appropriate shelter supplies for children and infants must be obtained and deployed to shelters.[302] To this end, the NCCD Report contains a list of **Supplies for Infants and Toddlers in Mass Care Shelters and Emergency Congregate Care Facilities.**[303]

It is recommended that emergency management agencies have 72 hours' worth of child care supplies necessary to accommodate children up to three years of age.[304] There are lists of "Recommended Perishable Supplies for Immediate Delivery Within 3 Hours" for shelters and "Nonperishable Supplies and Equipment" that shelters serving children will need along with "Other Recommended Perishable Supplies." This information is important for emergency management preparedness and mitigation activities under ESF-6.

Housing is another vital need of children in disasters over and above the sheltering needs. As part of the recovery process, children and families will move from shelters to temporary housing or to housing in need of repair. Some of federally-funded housing assistance programs include rental assistance, referrals, loan assistance, factory-built housing, etc.[305]

Notes

1. Suzet McKinney and Mary E. Papke, *Public Health Emergency Preparedness: A Practical Approach for the Real World*, Burlington, Jones and Bartlett Learning, 2019: 3-4.
2. Ibid: 4. Emphasis added.
3. Ibid.
4. Brett Bailey, "Law Enforcement in Public Health Emergencies," in *The Role of Law Enforcement in Emergency Management and Homeland Security*, Mark. R. Landal and Tonya E. Thornton, Eds., Bingley, U.K., Emerald Publishing Limited, 2021: 235.
5. Lindell, Prater, and Perry, *Introduction to Emergency Management*: 178.
6. Bruce W. Clements and Julie Ann P. Casani, *Disasters and Public Health*: Planning and Response, 2nd Edition, Cambridge, Butterworth-Heinemann Elsevier, 2016: Ibid: 14.

7. Suzet McKinney and Mary E. Papke, *Public Health Emergency Preparedness: A Practical Approach for the Real World*, Burlington, Jones and Bartlett Learning, 2019: 4. Emphasis added.
8. Clements and Casani, *Disasters and Public Health*: 14.
9. American Public Health Association, "What is Public Health" www.apha.org
10. Clements and Casani, *Disasters and Public Health*: 1-2.
11. Michel K. Lindell, Carla Prater, and Ronald W. Perry, *Introduction to Emergency Management*, John Wiley and Sons, Inc., Hoboken, 2007: 322.
12. Ibid: 323.
13. Ibid: 322.
14. Clements and Casani, *Disasters and Public Health*: 5.
15. Ibid.
16. Ibid.
17. Michael J. Fagel, *Principles of Emergency Management: Hazard Specific Issues and Mitigation Strategies*, Boca Raton, CRJ Press/Taylor and Francis Group, 2012: 131.
18. https://www.homelandsecuritygrants.info/Grant-Details/gid/17164
19. Clements and Casani, *Disasters and Public Health*: 5.
20. Ibid: 6.
21. Ibid.
22. Brett Bailey, "Law Enforcement in Public Health Emergencies:" 236-237.
23. U.S. Department of Justice, Office of Justice Programs, *The Role of Law Enforcement in Public Health Emergencies: Special Considerations for an All-Hazards Approach*, September 2006.
24. Clements and Casani, *Disasters and Public Health*: 11.
25. https://www.cdc.gov/orr/readiness/capabilities/index.htm
26. Clements and Casani, *Disasters and Public Health*: 11.
27. Ibid: 14.
28. Ibid: 19-56.
29. Clements and Casani, *Disasters and Public Health*: 20.
30. McKinney and Papke, *Public Health Emergency Preparedness*: 4.
31. Clements and Casani, *Disasters and Public Health*: 20.
32. Ibid.
33. Ibid: 14.
34. Ibid: 21.
35. Ibid.
36. Ibid: 22-23.
37. Ibid: 23.
38. Ibid: 11.
39. Ibid: 26.
40. Ibid: 54.
41. Ibid: 53.
42. Clements and Casani, *Disasters and Public Health*: 249.
43. Ibid: 262.
44. McKinney and Papke, *Public Health Emergency Preparedness*: 64.
45. Ibid.

46. Clements and Casani, *Disasters and Public Health: Planning and Response*: 261
47. Ibid: 254.
48. Ibid: 257.
49. McKinney and Papke, *Public Health Emergency Preparedness*: 72.
50. Ibid: 73.
51. Ibid: 74.
52. Ibid: 75. Emphasis added.
53. Ibid.
54. Clements and Casani, *Disasters and Public Health: Planning and Response*: 258.
55. Ibid.
56. Ibid: 261.
57. Ibid: 262.
58. Ibid.
59. Lindell, Prater, and Perry, *Introduction to Emergency Management*: 114-115.
60. Ibid: 404.
61. Ibid.
62. Ibid.
63. Ibid: 415.
64. Ibid: 407.
65. Ibid: 410.
66. Ibid.
67. Ibid: 412.
68. Ibid.
69. Ibid: 411.
70. Ibid: 408.
71. Ibid.
72. Ibid: 409.
73. Ibid.
74. Ibid: 410.
75. Ibid: 415.
76. Ibid: 413.
77. Ibid: 14.
78. Ibid.
79. Ibid.
80. Ibid.
81. Ibid: 418.
82. Ibid: 418-419.
83. Ibid: 419.
84. Ibid: 410-420.
85. Ibid: 420.
86. Ibid.
87. Ibid.
88. Ibid: 421.
89. Ibid.
90. Ibid.
91. Ibid: 424.

92. Ibid.
93. Ibid: 425-426.
94. Ibid: 57.
95. Ibid: 58.
96. Ibid: 59.
97. Ibid: 62.
98. Ibid.
99. Ibid,
100. Ibid: 62-63.
101. Ibid: 69.
102. Ibid: 66.
103. Ibid: 74.
104. Ibid: 70.
105. Ibid: 71.
106. Lindell, Prater, and Perry, *Introduction to Emergency Management*: 178.
107. Ibid: 88.
108. Elizabeth M. Webster, "Emergency Planning for People With Disabilities and Others With Access and Functional Needs to Ensure Inclusiveness," *Journal of Emergency Management*, Vol. 12, No. 3, May/June 2014: 211.
109. Ibid: 212.
110. Eric Wood and Tim Frazier, "Disasters, Community Vulnerability, and Poverty: The Intersection Between Economics and Emergency Management," *Journal of Emergency Management*, Vol. 19, No. 3, May/June 2021: 227.
111. Lindell, Prater, and Perry, *Introduction to Emergency Management*: 88.
112. Richard Isralowitz and Patricia Findley, "Emergency Preparedness and Vulnerable Populations: Lessons Learned for Education and Training, *Journal or Emergency Management*, Vol. 7, No. 6, November/December 2009: 29.
113. Garret Dolan and Dmitry Messen, "Social Vulnerability: An Emergency Manager's Planning Tool," *Journal of Emergency Management*, Vol. 10, No. 3, May/June 2012: 161.
114. Lindell, Prater, and Perry, *Introduction to Emergency Management*: 88.
115. Ibid. Emphasis in original.
116. Ibid.
117. Ibid.
118. Ibid: 89.
119. Ibid.
120. Ibid: 178.
121. Dolan and Messen, "Social Vulnerability: An Emergency Manager's Planning Tool:" 161.
122. Clements and Casani, *Disasters and Public Health*: 89. Emphasis added.
123. Ibid: 89-90.
124. Ibid: 90.
125. Ibid.
126. Ibid: 98.
127. Ibid.
128. Ibid: 95.

129. Ibid: 90.
130. Ibid: 91.
131. Ibid: 91-95.
132. Ibid: 100.
133. David A. McEntire, *Disaster Response and Recovery: Strategies and Tactics for Resilience*, 2nd Edition, Hoboken, John Wiley and Sons, Inc., 2015: 98.
134. Lindell, Prater, and Perry, *Introduction to Emergency Management*: 225.
135. Ibid.
136. Ibid.
137. Ibid.
138. Ibid.
139. Ibid.
140. Ibid: 226.
141. Ibid.
142. Ibid.
143. Ibid: 227.
144. Ibid.
145. Ibid: 228.
146. Ibid.
147. Ibid.
148. Ibid.
149. Ibid.
150. Ibid: 229.
151. Ibid: 226.
152. Ibid.
153. Ibid.
154. Ibid.
155. Ibid: 226-227.
156. Ibid: 227.
157. Ibid: 229.
158. Ibid.
159. Ibid.
160. Ibid: 98.
161. Ibid: 164.
162. Fagel, *Principles of Emergency Management*: 132.
163. Ibid.
164. Ibid: 137.
165. Ibid: 136.
166. Ibid.
167. Ibid: 133.
168. Lindell, Prater, and Perry, *Introduction to Emergency Management*: 164.
169. Ibid.
170. Ibid: 164-165.
171. Ibid: 316.
172. Ibid.
173. Fagel, *Principles of Emergency Management*: 304.

174. McEntire, *Disaster Response and Recovery*: 168.
175. Ibid: 168-169. Emphasis in original.
176. Ibid: 69-70.
177. Lindell, Prater, and Perry, *Introduction to Emergency Management*: 246.
178. Ibid.
179. McEntire, *Disaster Response and Recovery*: 71.
180. Ibid: 165.
181. Ibid: 166.
182. Ibid: 170.
183. Ibid: 170-171.
184. Ibid: 167.
185. Ibid: 171.
186. Ibid.
187. Ibid.
188. Ibid: 166-167.
189. Ibid: 171.
190. Ibid.
191. Ibid.
192. Ibid: 167-168.
193. Ibid: 171-172.
194. Ibid: 168.
195. Ibid.
196. Ibid: 173.
197. Ibid: 172.
198. Ibid: 164.
199. Ibid: 174.
200. Ibid: 173.
201. Lindell, Prater, and Perry, *Introduction to Emergency Management*: 318.
202. McEntire, *Disaster Response and Recovery*: 179
203. Ibid: 180.
204. Lindell, Prater, and Perry, *Introduction to Emergency Management*: 319.
205. Ibid.
206. Ibid: 319.
207. Ibid: 317.
208. Fagel, *Principles of Emergency Management*: 444.
209. Lindell, Prater, and Perry, *Introduction to Emergency Management*: 317.
210. Ibid: 319.
211. Ibid.
212. Ibid: 320.
213. Ibid.
214. Ibid.
215. Ibid.
216. Ibid: 320-321.
217. Ibid: 321.
218. Ibid.
219. Ibid: 322.

220. McEntire, *Disaster Response and Recovery*: 184.
221. Lindell, Prater, and Perry, *Introduction to Emergency Management*: 321.
222. Ibid: 322.
223. McEntire, *Disaster Response and Recovery*: 186.
224. Ibid: 185.
225. Ibid: 189.
226. Aidan Peat, "Factors Influencing First Responders' Mental Health During COVID-19," *Journal of Emergency Management*, Vol. 20, No. 9, 2022: 27.
227. Dolan and Messen, "Social Vulnerability: An Emergency Manager's Planning Tool:" 162.
228. Ibid.
229. Wood and Frazier, "Disasters, Community Vulnerability, and Poverty: The Intersection Between Economics and Emergency Management:" 227.
230. Vincent Faggiano, John McNall, and Tom Gillespie, *Critical Incident Management: A Complete Response Guide*, 2nd Edition, Boca Raton, CRC Press/Taylor and Francis Group, 2012: 129.
231. Paula A. Morgan, The Psychological Impact of Mass Casualty Incidents on First Responders: A Systematic Review," *Journal of Emergency Management*, Vol. 14, No. 3, May/June 2016: 213.
232. Ibid. Emphasis in original.
233. Ibid: 130.
234. Don Hellriegel, John W. Slocum, Jr., and Richard W. Woodman, *Organizational Behavior*, 8th Edition, Cincinnati: South-Western College Publishing, 1998: 198-199.
235. Ibid: 199.
236. Faggiano, McNall, and Gillespie, *Critical Incident Management*: 130.
237. Hellrigel, Slocum, and Woodman, *Organizational Behavior*: 199.
238. Ibid.
239. Faggiano, McNall, and Gillespie, *Critical Incident Management*: 132.
240. Ibid.
241. Ibid: 133.
242. Clements and Casani, *Disasters and Public Health*: 107.
243. Ibid: 106.
244. Ibid: 107.
245. Ibid: 106.
246. Ibid: 108.
247. Ibid.
248. Erin C. McCanlies, Ja Kook Gu, Michael C. Andrew, Cecil M. Burchfield, and John M. Violanti, "Resilience Mediates the Relationship Beween Social Support and Post-Traumatic Stress Symptoms In Police Officers," *Journal of Emergency Managemet*, Vol. 15, No. 2, March/April 2017: 109.
249. Clements and Casani, *Disasters and Public Health*: 109.
250. Ibid.
251. McEntire, *Disaster Response and Recovery*: 197.
252. Clements, and Casani, *Disasters and Public Health*: 105.
253. Ibid: 112.

254. Norma S.C. Jones and Kamilah Majied, "*Disaster Mental Health*: A Critical Incident Stress Management Program (CISM) to Mitigate Compassion Fatigue," *Journal of Emergency Management*, Vol. 7, No. 4, July/August 2009: 17.
255. Clements, and Casani, *Disasters and Public Health*: 106.
256. Jordan Pekevski, "First Responders and Psychological First Aid," *Journal of Emergency Management*, Vol. 11, No. 1, January/February 2013.
257. Clements, and Casani, *Disasters and Public Health*: 114.
258. Faggiano, McNall, and Gillespie, *Critical Incident Management*: 134.
259. Ibid: 135.
260. Ibid.
261. Ibid: 136.
262. Ibid.
263. Peat, "Factors Influencing First Responders' Mental Health During COVID-19:" 27.
264. Fagel, *Principles of Emergency Management*: 444.
265. Ibid: 445.
266. Ibid: 446.
267. Ibid: 447.
268. Ibid: 445.
269. Ibid: 447.
270. Ibid: 14.
271. Ibid: 444.
272. Ibid: 444-445.
273. Ibid: 445
274. Ibid.
275. Ibid: 448.
276. Ibid.
277. Ibid: 451.
278. Ibid.
279. Ibid: 452.
280. Ibid: 454.
281. Lindell, Prater, and Perry, *Introduction to Emergency Management*: 336.
282. Fagel, *Introduction to Emergency Management*: 447.
283. Ibid: 466.
284. Ibid.
285. Ibid.
286. Ibid: 467.
287. Ibid: 466.
288. Ibid: 467.
289. Ibid.
290. Ibid: 445.
291. Ibid: 458.
292. Ibid: 459.
293. Ibid.
294. Ibid: 470.
295. Ibid: 482.

296. Ibid: 491.
297. Ibid: 473-474.
298. Ibid: 474.
299. Ibid.
300. Ibid: 475.
301. Ibid: 481.
302. Ibid: 480.
303. Ibid: 481-482.
304. Ibid: 482.
305. Ibid: 445.

Chapter 5

NATURAL DISASTER SCENARIOS AND THE ROLE OF LAW ENFORCEMENT AND OTHER AGENCIES

Chapter 5 provides a survey of common natural hazards and disasters to which we are exposed in the United States. The potential harm of natural disasters and hazards to both law enforcement personnel and the general public must be taken into consideration and discussed. Persons working in the law enforcement or emergency management fields must understand hazards and risks likely to be encountered as a necessary part of mitigation and preparedness. We must first begin by defining some terms: *hazard, vulnerability, risk, and disaster.*

A **hazard** is an intentional or accidental occurrence that can cause destruction or damage to human beings, animals, or property. Hazards can be either natural or man-made.[1] In other words, a **hazard** is an extreme occurrence or a danger source that has the potential to harm human lives, the environment, or property.[2] **Vulnerability** refers to a location's exposure to loss from a hazard.[3] **Risk** deals with the likelihood or probability of a hazardous occurrence.[4] For example, communities near the ocean are vulnerable to tsunamis or hurricanes in terms of risk, while inland areas are not vulnerable to these particular hazards. A **disaster** occurs when hazards, vulnerabilities, and risks converge. FEMA (Federal Emergency Management Agency) defines disaster as "an occurrence of a severity and magnitude that normally results in deaths, injuries, and property damage that cannot be managed through the routine procedures and resources of a government."[5]

It is the responsibility of the jurisdiction's emergency manager to prepare a hazard vulnerability analysis. This document will be used to assess the hazard, vulnerability, and risk scenarios that the community faces. The hazard vulnerability analysis should then be used for planning, training, and exercising emergency management and law enforcement agencies. It must be recognized that when hazards result in disasters, jurisdictional boundaries are usually not recognized.[6] It is for this reason that inter-agency communication and cooperation are vital.

Hazards come in different varieties. **Natural hazards** are caused by weather and other forces beyond human control, such as hurricanes and earthquakes. These are covered in this chapter. **Man-made hazards** are the result of deliberate (such as terrorism or cyberattacks) or accidental (such as chemical spills) actions or inactions by human beings. Man-made hazards can also include things like bridge and tunnel collapse or nuclear power plant leaks (infrastructure failures). These are examined in Chapter 6.

There are many hazard effects of natural disasters such as flooding, lightning strikes, tornadoes, wildfires, earthquakes, winter storms, droughts, heat waves, tsunamis, volcanoes, epidemics and pandemics, and the effects of space weather. It is emphasized that hazards can and often do turn into disasters.

Types of Natural Hazards

Natural hazards are caused by forces beyond human control. These are extreme events that originate in nature. There are three types of natural hazards: **(1) meteorological, (2) hydrological, and (3) geophysical**. **Meteorological hazards** refer to natural weather events that originate in the earth's atmosphere (wind, clouds, rain, etc.). These include hurricanes, tornadoes, severe storms, wildfires, and severe summer weather (heat waves), and severe winter weather (blizzards cold temperatures, and ice storms).[7] **Hydrological hazards** are about water movements on and below the surface of the earth. Hydrology is the study of the earth's water movements in relation to land – rivers, groundwater, lakes, and streams. This includes floods and storm surges. Some experts include tsunamis as well.[8] **Geophysical hazards** are caused by changes in the physical properties of the earth's crust. These include geological phenomena like volcanic eruptions and earthquakes.[9]

These three types of natural hazards do not exist in isolation – one can lead to another, and one can cause another. They are often interconnected. For example, an earthquake (geophysical hazard) can cause a tsunami (hydrological hazard). Heavy rain (a meteorological hazard) can lead to flooding (a hydrological hazard).

Meteorological Hazards

Meteorological hazards are caused by natural weather events that originate in the earth's atmosphere (wind, clouds, and rain). One type is the **severe storm**. A severe storm is defined as one that meets one or more of these criteria: (1) wind speeds exceeding 58 Miles Per Hour (MPH); (2) hail with a diameter of ¾ inch or greater, or (3) produces a tornado.[10]

There are several threats from severe storms. One is **hail**, which is ice that falls with force from the atmosphere. Hail rarely causes death or serious injury, but it can lead to traffic accidents due to inability to see and broken windshields, and extensive property damage to roofs, siding, and vehicles. **Flooding** caused by torrential rains has a greater potential to cause death, injury, or property damage. **Lightning** strikes can cause injury, death, and property damage, both in wet and dry areas. In relatively wet/humid areas such as the Southeastern United States, lightning typically causes death, injury, and property damage, but not fires. In the American West where humidity is much lower and the environment is much drier, lightning strikes are the cause of many wildfires. Severe storms have the potential to cause airplanes to crash due to **downbursts** and **microbursts**. These are rapid wind changes caused by severe storms. A downburst has sudden strong wind blowing briefly for up to 125 mph. A microburst is stronger – up to 150 mph. Both can cause airplanes to crash and lead to mass casualty incidents.[11]

Thunderstorms can be severe storms. Thunderstorms are associated with high winds, hail, flooding, lightning, and tornadoes.[12] They are formed when rising warm air and moisture interact to provide lift. The typical thunderstorm is approximately 15 miles in diameter. Most thunderstorms last approximately thirty minutes.[13] Thunderstorms can cause large hail, which can cause death, injury, and property damage. Winds produced by thunderstorms can be either *straight line* or *rotational*. Thunderstorm-produced winds can be powerful and can cause damage.[14]

Both lightning and tornadoes can be produced by thunderstorms. **Lightning** is a high-voltage, short-duration electrical discharge that is naturally occurring.[15] The thunder that accompanies lightning is caused by the instantaneous heating and cooling of the air through which lightning passes at approximately 50,000 degrees.[16] The majority of lighting-related injuries occur between May and September in the United States. In an average year, approximately 250 people are injured by lightning strikes, and about ninety of these are fatal. Approximately three-fourths of lightning strike survivors suffer from permanent disability. Most of those injured from lightning strikes were engaged in outdoor recreation.[17]

At-risk populations are also vulnerable, especially the elderly. Reducing tornado-related deaths and injuries requires warning, public education, and access to storm shelters.[18] There are commercially available storm shelters available for sale in tornado-prone areas. These are reinforced steel boxes that are bolted to concrete floors, typically on the foundation or in the garage for sale in stores like Home Depot. These shelters will survive a collapsed building and will protect occupants from flying debris. Underground storm shelters are often built into houses in hurricane-prone areas. The best tornado shelters are certified by the National Storm Shelter Association or the American Tornado Shelter Association.[19]

Education and outreach should also be focused on individuals residing in mobile homes. Storm shelters and strong structures are obvious risk-reduction measures in high-risk regions.[20]

Some cities have installed tornado warning sirens capable of voice message warnings around the city. Taking protective actions is associated with the receipt of multiple warnings.[21] These include reverse 911, text alerts, television and radio warnings, and sirens. Public warnings and alerts should contain information about appropriate actions that should be taken.[22] To survive a tornado, a shelter provides the safest option. The next safest location is an interior room on the lowest floor of a structure. Mobile home residents should evacuate to a community shelter.[23]

With regard to response and recovery, post-disaster challenges can be extensive. Large amounts of debris, loss of electricity and possibly potable water, and exposure to the elements can result in health risks.[24] Recovery includes debris removal, restoration of utilities, vaccinations (in many cases), cleanup, and mental health care (in many cases).

During cleanup and debris removal, first responders and emergency managers should realize that homes and businesses with major damage can be hazardous due to debris and the potential of collapse. Disease vectors, such as rodents and mosquitoes can increase. Habitable structures such as homes, schools, and businesses without functioning utilities can pose additional threats. These can include the increased risk of foodborne and waterborne illnesses and carbon monoxide poisoning from improper generator ventilation.[25]

Debris related to a storm can pose multiple health and safety hazards. Such debris includes downed trees, destroyed motor vehicles, appliances, discarded household items such as damaged wood or carpet, and hazardous materials. A temporary debris management site should be established following the ten recommendations of the Environmental Protection Agency (EPA).[26] Additional planning is needed if hazardous materials are involved. Additional requirements include site safety and evacuation plans and regular air monitoring. In addition, designated disposal or holding areas for batteries, ammunition, gas cylinders, and fire extinguishers must be established.[27]

The measures essential to reducing public health threats during recovery include community outreach and education, vaccinations, and mental health services. It is important to promote community health and safety messages throughout the recovery process. These messages should be relayed by as many means as possible including paper flyers, social media, print media, radio, and television. Government authorities should take measures to reduce public health threats during recovery by making announcements that include physical safety protocols for those returning to damaged property, education regarding the carbon monoxide hazards posed by generators, measures to reduce heat stress, advisories about unsafe food and water, personal hygiene, and if needed, vaccinations. In addition, public health measures require that tetanus shots be made easily available for individuals exposed to debris.[28]

Finally, emergency management agencies and public health organizations should keep in mind that exposure to major destructive events can create mental health issues.[29]

Next is **severe summer weather**. This is also known as a *heat wave.* A **heat wave** is unusually hot weather, coupled in the east with high humidity. The desert southwest, the southeastern region, and the Mississippi Valley are the most susceptible to severe summer weather. Severe summer weather causes *heat-related illnesses.* These include heat cramps, heat syncope, heat exhaustion, and heat stroke.[30]

Heat cramps are the least serious – they involve only minor hydration and electrolyte imbalances. *Heat syncope* happens when an overheated individual has a sudden loss of consciousness (fainting). The person recovers after lying down to rest. Most people do not faint and thus go directly from heat cramp to heat exhaustion. *Heat exhaustion* involves disorientation, dizziness, and weakness. The most severe heat-related illness is *heatstroke.* This can lead to becoming delirious or going into a coma. Neurological damage can result, and there is a fatality rate of about 15 percent.[31]

Realize that the very old, small children, and people suffering from serious illnesses are the most likely to suffer from heat-related illnesses. Also, people who work outside in forestry, construction, etc., are at high risk. Even so, heat-related illnesses are more likely to occur in cities than in rural areas because city buildings and asphalt radiate heat, and buildings block breezes.[32]

The combination of either heat or heat coupled with high humidity can lead to these heat-related illnesses. Temperature and humidity are combined to calculate a **heat index**. The heat index quantifies apparent temperatures. Apparent temperatures of 80-90°F can result in fatigue. An apparent temperature of 90-105°F requires extreme caution because heat cramps and heat exhaustion can occur. Above 105°F apparent temperature is dangerous because physical activity and exposure can lead to heat stroke. Above an apparent temperature of 130°F, extreme danger exists because a heat stroke will definitely occur.[33] During a heat wave, both hospitalizations and deaths tend to increase among vulnerable populations. It is noted that heat weaves produce more deaths than several other types of severe weather (tornadoes, and hurricanes) combined.[34]

There are many human health effects associated with excessive heat. Under normal conditions, the lungs and skin can effectively control internal body temperature. Abnormal environmental conditions like excessive heat and some types of physical activity can generate more heat than the human body can effectively regulate. When this occurs, the risk of heat-related illness increases.[35]

The effects of high temperatures on the human body become more severe as humidity rises. Increased humidity reduces the evaporation of moisture from the skin, which in turn compromises the ability of the human body to maintain a normal temperature. The heat index developed by the National Weather Service (NWS) is designed to more accurately reflect the temperature actually experienced by the human body as it is affected by humidity.[36]

The **heat index** is a number in degrees that indicates how hot the body feels when humidity is added to the actual air temperature. The heat index thus factors in the reduced rate of evaporation. Thus, the heat index is considered to be a more accurate measure of temperature as associated with the risk to human health.[37] The U.S. National Weather Service Heat Index (HI) Charts in both Celsius and Fahrenheit are used to make public health heat-related preparedness decisions in the United States.

Heat is considered to be more severe in urban areas due to the built environment.[38] Asphalt, dark roofing materials, concrete, and the lack of vegetation compared with rural or suburban areas cause cities and other built environments to collect and retain heat. For this reason, residents of urban areas are more likely to suffer heat-related illnesses than others. This is described by the phrase **Urban Heat Islands (UHI)**. Urban Heat Islands are used to characterize the higher temperatures contained in urban areas due to the fact that they absorb more heat than rural areas. This is caused by the presence of a greater concentration of building and road materials in urban areas than in surrounding rural areas.[39]

There are several social and physical factors associated with a higher risk of heat-related morbidity and mortality, which include socioeconomic status, urban residence, social isolation, elderly, infants, physically disabled, mentally/behaviorally impaired, users of certain prescription drugs such as antidepressants, high blood pressure medications, users of illegal drugs or alcohol, and those engaged in outdoor work.[40] The prevention of and preparedness for heat-related illnesses by the emergency management and public health communities is fairly straightforward. Deaths from excessive heat are more preventable than is the case with most other types of disasters. Heat waves are predictable. They can be managed relatively simply and inexpensively.[41]

Functioning infrastructure is important in prevention. Electrical and water supplies are vital for extreme heat. In addition, preparedness activities should be engaged in before a heat emergency occurs.[42]

One of the most important steps that can be taken to reduce deaths and injuries associated with extreme heat is for authorities to identify and locate the populations at risk in advance. Then, information and instructions regarding how and when to move those at risk to a safer environment should be disseminated.[43] For example, an effective strategy should include community involvement to establish a *heat wave task force.* Members should be comprised of authorities in addition to individuals representing organizations with a track record of assisting vulnerable populations. Actions such as setting up cooling centers at specified locations for persons who lack air conditioning and establishing a formal process for checking on the elderly should be taken.[44] Officials and community representatives can contact the media to assist in reaching vulnerable individuals.[45]

Public service announcements could be made to reduce the likelihood of experiencing serious heat-related health problems could be made with messages such as "stay hydrated," "wear light-colored clothing," and "use the buddy system." Emergency management and first responder personnel should be familiar with these. Due to climate change, areas that have not had a past history of heat-related emergencies are more likely than others to experience more medical problems during a heat wave.[46]

In terms of the steps that first responder and emergency management agencies should take to prepare for heat-related emergencies, it is important to define the role to be played by each agency. Setting up a warning system is essential with which to communicate with vulnerable populations. Information about the locations of cooling centers and instructions for personal preparedness must be communicated. The number of heat casualties must be measured.[47]

The opposite of severe summer weather is **severe winter weather**. This is extreme cold, especially when accompanied by snow, ice, and low temperatures. A blizzard is one type and occurs when temperatures are less than 21°F and wind speeds are more than 38 MPH. Ice storms occur when rain freezes, making roads impassable and breaking power lines.[48]

In severe winter weather, there are serious wind chill effects, making the apparent temperature seem much colder than it actually is. Severe winter storms can immobilize travel, trap people at work or at home, deposit large amounts of ice and snow, and bring down electrical lines. This can cause secondary effects, such as a lack of heat, hot water, and cooking facilities.[49] Winter storms most often strike Northern areas of the United States. When winter storms impact Southern states, great disruption can occur because emergency management resources to deal with winter storms are more limited.[50]

Wildfires are another type of meteorological hazard. The combination of fuel, oxygen, and heat (the fire triangle) is the cause of wildfires. The primary fuel of a wildfire is wood and brush in dry areas. These are most often seen in the drier Western states. Fires there often burn significant areas that are controlled only with difficulty. About 13 percent are caused by lightning strikes, but most are caused by human beings, either accidentally or deliberately. Approximately 73,000 wildfires are reported per year, involving about 3 million acres annually.[51]

The particular source of fuel is what distinguishes between the types of wildfires. **Wildland fires** burn only natural vegetation for fuel. **Interface fires** burn a combination of natural vegetation and built structures. Typically, they start out as wildland fires but spread to burn houses and businesses. **Firestorms** are the most severe type of wildfire because they grow so large and consume so much fuel and oxygen that they create their own micro-weather systems. These are the most difficult to extinguish. Every year firefighters die in the West to put out wildfires. Millions of dollars worth of built structures are destroyed every year, and there are also some casualties that occur from smoke and heat.[52]

Wildfires are often caused by lightning strikes. Wildfires can also be caused by human beings either deliberately (arson) or as a result of carelessness. The highest risk areas for wildfires include areas with vegetation (wooded areas, grasslands, scrub) during periods of dry weather and strong winds. When wildfires occur near human populations, death, injury, and property damage can occur from heat, flames, debris, and smoke.[53]

Wildfires can result in the destruction of homes, schools, and commercial structures. This causes loss of housing, death, injury, and economic damages to the affected area. Extensive infrastructure damage to electricity, gas, water, and transportation can occur, along with health-related air quality issues. Severe wildfires can destroy enough vegetation to result in erosion, which can eventually lead to landslides and flooding hazards. Pervasive and severe wildfires can significantly harm the natural ecosystem, which can lead to substantial damage to the timber and tourism industries in a jurisdiction.[54] The U.S. Forest Service has a color-coded **Fire Danger Rating System** that provides the relative degree of wildfire hazard on a given day in a given area, based on weather and satellite data.[55]

In addition to burn injuries, wildfires can cause respiratory damage or death due to smoke. Health-related effects of wildfire smoke can be as simple as irritation or as serious as death, depending upon an individual's level of exposure and underlying medical conditions. Individuals with emphysema, COPD or asthma, the elderly, those with compromised immune systems, and young children are especially susceptible.[56]

Complex particles and gases are contained in wildfire smoke. Some of these gases include nitrogen oxide, including carbon dioxide, carbon monoxide, water vapor, and particulates. The specific chemical composition of the smoke varies between wildfires. Nevertheless, air quality measures taken at the local level are used to assess health risks.[57] This is the Air Quality Index (AQI). The AQI was developed by the EPA (Environmental Protection Agency) and is available online at www.airnow.gov/index.

The Air Quality Index (AQI) measures harmful substances present in the air of a given jurisdiction. The AQI is utilized by weather forecasters and meteorologists to assess the relative purity of the air in a community at a specific point in time. The AQI index indicates air pollution on a scale of 0-500. The best AQI score should be 100 or lower. If the AQI exceeds 100 at a particular location, national standards for key toxic substances have been exceeded. The higher the AQI number, the greater the negative public health impact.[58] The AQI is thus a good measure of health risk associated with both wildfire smoke and volcanic eruptions.[59]

With regard to prevention and preparedness, fire departments and emergency managers should concentrate on the provision of educational materials to individuals living closest to wildfire risk.[60] For individuals living in hazard-prone areas, there are many actions that can be taken to reduce the fire risk to homes and buildings, such as utilizing slate or clay roofing and maintaining a **Home Ignition Zone (HIZ)** around the property. An HIZ refers to a clear 100-foot zone surrounding homes, businesses, and schools at risk of being damaged by wildfires. The HIZ must be free from combustible vegetation in order to reduce the probability that fire will reach the structure.[61]

During a wildfire, public officials should disseminate warnings about the nature of the wildfire threat in addition to weather conditions. If officials have reasons to believe that the wildfire will threaten lives or property, evacuation orders should be issued. For residents close enough to experience smoke exposure but too far away from the wildfire to warrant evacuation, the AQI should be utilized to communicate the level of risk to human health from smoke exposure.[62]

If you encounter a wildfire, the best THING to do is to evacuate the area. If that is not possible, go to an open field (no trees around; little grass around). If you have access to a fire-resistant structure, like an all-brick or all-concrete building, this is a good option as well. Remember that for the general public, there is no access to air-purifying respirators. However, a properly fitted N-95 respirator does offer some protection from smoke particles.[63]

The initial official actions to be taken during a wildfire should include public notification, evacuation instructions and assistance, and setting up suitable sheltering if needed. Once a wildfire passes, persons residing in the area should not be permitted to return to their homes until critical safety and health hazards have been resolved.[64]

Tornadoes comprise another severe type of meteorological hazard. These are a significant risk to the southern and midwestern United States. Each year, approximately 1,200 tornadoes are recorded in the U.S. Approximately 65 deaths occur in a given year as a direct result of tornadoes.[65] The southeastern U.S. is very vulnerable to tornadoes, as are Oklahoma, Kansas, Texas, Missouri, and Arkansas. Half of all tornadoes occur in April, May, and June. Tornadoes are most likely to strike between 4 PM and 8 PM. The vast majority of tornadoes (76%) travel either northeast or east.[66]

A tornado forms when cold air collides with warm air. The cold air descends due to its greater weight. The cold air is replaced by rising warmer air. Rotational flow inside the air mass is then produced. Pressure drops and wind speed increases as the tornado forms. The high wind speeds thus produced can cause death and property damage. Tornadoes can be caused by a warm front hitting a cold front. They can also be a byproduct of a hurricane.[67]

Property damage is the most often result of tornadoes. Contrary to popular belief, the average tornado does not cause deaths. Approximately three percent of tornadoes actually result in deaths. About half of tornado deaths occur among residents of mobile homes due to their weak construction.[68]

The **Fujita Scale** is used to measure the strength of a tornado, which is based on the rotational wind speed. F0 is the weakest tornado, with a maximum wind speed of 40 MPH. F5 is the strongest, with maximum speeds in excess of 261 MPH. Two-thirds of all tornadoes have wind speeds of 112 MPH or less, which is a category F1. In terms of the speed at which a tornado moves across the ground, most go about 30 MPH. The typical tornado covers a path of about four miles before it dissipates.[69] An F2 tornado has rotational winds of 113-157 MPH. F3s are 158-207 MPH. F4s are 208-260 MPH. The vast majority of tornadoes are F1s.

Tornado sightings have been increasing in recent years. Some of this is due to better radar; some of this is due to global climate change. Tornadoes have distinct physical cues that one can observe: Dark cumulonimbus clouds, intense lightning, hail and strong downpours, and rumbling noise like a train.[70]

With modern technology, sirens warn of approaching tornadoes in urban areas. Radio, internet, and television media warnings are also used. The federal government's **National Oceanic and Atmospheric Administration's (NOAA)** *weather radio* provides tornado warnings as well.[71]

To survive a tornado, the best available action is to shelter in a specially constructed safe room. If this is not available, the next best option is to shelter in an interior room on the lowest floor. Those that live in mobile homes should go to a community shelter. If one is outside, he or she should seek refuge in a low spot.[72]

Thunderstorms and tornadoes are examples of *severe weather*. Scientists have noted that more severe weather events occur in the United States than any other nation. In a typical year, more than 100,000 thunderstorms, 5,000 floods, 1,000 tornadoes, and two deadly hurricanes impact the United States. On average, approximately 500 deaths and $15 billion in damage occur. Most federally declared disasters are the result of severe weather.[73]

Tropical Storms and Hurricanes

Most tropical storms and hurricanes that affect the United States form in the Atlantic Ocean and strike either the eastern seaboard from Virginia to Florida or in the Gulf of Mexico from Texas to Louisiana to Mississippi to Alabama to the west coast and panhandle of Florida. There are other tropical storms that have impacted Hawaii and California, but these are much less frequent than the Gulf and Atlantic storms.

Hurricanes and tropical storms are major hazards. An average of ten to eleven tropical storms develop annually. In an average year, approximately six of these turn into hurricanes. In a typical three-year period, an average of five hurricanes make landfall in the United States. Approximately 50 to 100 people are killed.[74] Keep in mind that these are averages. Some years have more hurricanes than others. For example, between 1950-1969, 33 hurricanes occurred. But from 1970-1988, only six hurricanes occurred.[75]

Tropical storms and hurricanes are related, in that a hurricane is a stronger tropical storm. Both are low pressure systems (storms) that form in the tropics (between the Tropic of Cancer and the Tropic of Capricorn). In the Northern Hemisphere, both hurricanes and tropical storms rotate counterclockwise. Several factors must coalesce to form a tropical storm. Weather disturbances with moisture such as thunderstorms, ocean waters of at least 80° F, and winds. If these conditions combine, a tropical storm or hurricane can form.[76]

In the Atlantic and Gulf of Mexico, hurricane season runs from June 1 to November 30. Tropical storms and hurricanes often result in extensive property damage, injuries, and deaths. High winds, strong rains, storm surges, and potential tornadoes are responsible for the damages from tropical storms. Although the majority of the impact is upon coastal areas, effects from hurricanes can impact conditions hundreds of miles inland.[77]

Tropical disturbances exist at three levels of intensity, from the lowest to the highest: (1) tropical depression, (2) tropical storm, and (3) hurricane. Hurricanes also exist at different levels of intensity and strength. A **tropical depression** is the weakest of all. It usually brings only rain and some moderate waves. Tropical depressions have a well-defined pattern of rotation but with winds of 38 MPH or less.[78] A **tropical storm** is stronger with sustained winds of 39-73 MPH.[79] A **hurricane** has a *well-defined* pattern of rotation coupled with sustained winds of 74 MPH or higher. They appear circular from space. At the center is the **eye**, which is a 10–20-mile area of calm conditions surrounded by rain and high wind.[80] The typical hurricane moves at a 12 MPH speed. Hurricanes weaken as they hit land because the land cuts the hurricane off from its fuel, which is the warm water it traverses over, and because the land surface itself interferes with the rotation.[81]

Hurricanes have categories depending on wind strength and potential damage. Hurricanes are categorized by the **Saffir-Simpson Hurricane Scale**.[82] Much like the tornado scale, the Saffir-Simpson Hurricane Scale also classifies storms by their wind intensity. Category 1 is 74-95 MPH with a 4-5 ft. storm surge. These cause mild damage to mobile homes, some damage to vegetation, etc. Category 2 is 96-110 MPH with a 6–8-foot storm surge. Category 2 storms result in significant damage to mobile homes, cause some small and medium trees to blow down, cause some street sign damage, and some damage to roofs and windows. Category 1 and Category 2 hurricanes comprise 80% of all hurricanes.[83]

The remaining hurricanes account for only 20% of landfalls but 80% of all damage.[84] Category 3 is 111-130 MPH and 9-12 ft storm surge. Mobile homes are destroyed, large trees are blown down, most street signs are blown down, and structural damage to buildings and houses occurs. Category 4 winds are 131-155 MPH and are accompanied by 13-18 feet of storm surge. Extensive structural damage occurs, most windows are blown out, and all street signs are down. Category 5 winds are 156 MPH and higher, and storm surge is greater than 18 feet. The damage is almost total, all houses are destroyed, some commercial buildings are destroyed and the remainder have structural damage.[85]

The destructive power of hurricanes depends upon the strength category. Hurricanes produce 4 specific hazards: (1) storm surge, (2) high winds, (3) flooding, and (4) tornadoes.[86] A **storm surge** is seawater pushed by the wind and rotation of the hurricane. This wall of water ranges from 4 feet to 18+ feet and causes major destruction. High winds are self-explanatory. They can lead not only to roof damage, window breakage, and structural damage, but they can injure or kill human beings due to flying debris from the high winds.[87] Flooding is caused by the torrential rains and storm surge that accompany hurricanes. During Hurricanes Harvey and Irma, more than four inches of rain fell per hour. This overwhelmed the drainage runoff and sewers.

Hurricanes may or may not cause large loss of human life. It depends on the strength of the storm and the extent to which evacuations and precautions took place. The worst hurricane mass casualty event in American history took place in 1900 when a hurricane killed an estimated six thousand people.[88] However, the only warning system that then existed was barometers.

Hurricane casualties have increased substantially during the past fifty years when compared with the historical norm due to the fact that American coastal areas have experienced substantial explosive population growth. In addition, economic losses from hurricanes continue to grow, because more and more property is being built in vulnerable areas.

Today, the public receives advanced warnings about hurricanes. This is due to satellite imagery and aircraft monitoring. Predicting the path and landfall of a hurricane improves every year. However, this is not an exact science due to numerous variables. At present, science can predict a path and landfall within 200 miles three days in advance of impact, and within 75 miles one day in advance.[89]

Uncertainties exist regarding the strength that a hurricane will have when it strikes land and its exact landfall. One problem with this uncertainty involves planning for evacuation of the affected population. Evacuations often require more than one or two days to be completed. This is true because many coastal cities take three days or more to evacuate. For example, the population of Miami was told to evacuate in 2017, but Hurricane Irma traveled south of Miami and made landfall on the West coast of Florida. This did not provide sufficient time for those communities to fully evacuate. In addition, it is difficult to predict the rate at which hurricane windspeed will reduce upon land impact, which makes the safe distance hard to determine in advance.

Nevertheless, the appropriate protective actions for hurricanes are well-known. Ideally, one should evacuate. This is especially true if a Category 3 or above is predicted to strike. Evacuation should occur before flooding or high winds occur. Sheltering in place in an area that could be affected by the storm surge should be avoided. If it cannot be avoided one must shelter in an *elevated* concrete building on the second floor or higher.

Outside of storm surge areas, survival is likely if one is in a permanent building or house with solid construction. Brick is preferred, but in any case, windows should be taped or boarded. Evacuation is a must for mobile homes.

Hydrological Hazards

Hydrological hazards are caused by water movements on and below the surface of the earth. Hydrology is the study of the earth's water movements in relation to land (rivers, lakes, and groundwater). This includes floods and storm surges.

The **flood** is the most obvious hydrological hazard. A flood is an event in which abnormally large amounts of water accumulate in areas in which water is not usually found. Floods cause more deaths each year than any other hazard produced from severe weather-related events.[90] More people are killed by flooding (an average of 99 per year) than by tornadoes (54 per year) and hurricanes (49 per year). Flooding causes many problems – death, property damage, and contamination from water-borne illnesses. The vast majority of presidential disaster declarations are due to flooding.[91]

Flooding is caused by excessive precipitation (rain or snow). When too much rain or snow falls too fast to be absorbed by the soil and that cannot be effectively carried away by rivers and streams, flooding results. Flooding is caused primarily by precipitation. But flooding is also affected by surface runoff (how quickly water flows into streams and rivers and soaks into the soil).[92] Obviously, where there is no soil (asphalt, cement, etc.), there is no way for water to soak in. Gravel and sand absorb the most water. This is a real problem in urban areas with lots of concrete and asphalt (hardscape). **Hardscape** refers to impermeable surfaces like roads, streets, driveways, and roofs.[93] Houston, Texas and New Orleans, Louisiana have extensive hardscape. Because both cities are located in low-lying coastal areas, the hardscape makes them very vulnerable to flooding. Undeveloped areas with less asphalt experience less flooding unless they are adjacent to overflowing rivers.

Surface runoff is also affected by **slope**, which refers to the steepness of the surface of the ground. Flatter areas are more likely to flood. Areas downstream from levees are more likely to flood because this channels water under higher than natural pressure to other areas. The intensity of floods is measured by either *discharge* or *stage.*[94] **Discharge** measures flooding in a geographic area by the volume of water per unit of time.[95] For example, fifteen inches of rain fell in seven hours; 28 inches of rain fell during the hurricane, etc. **Stage** measures flooding in rivers and in the areas immediately surrounding rivers. In this sense, stage is the height of water above a defined level, usually the normal river level.[96] For example, the Missouri River could be six feet above flood stage.

It is possible to convert discharge to stage following the rating curve methodology. Doing so is necessary because stage is the unit needed by emergency managers to standardize flood disasters. Stage determines the level of damages and casualties. Discharge in cubic feet per second determines the flood stage. The slope affects the state at a given discharge. In other words, valleys flood faster that flat areas because the valley walls confine the water and make it more dangerous.[97]

Flood risk areas in the U.S. are measured by the **100-Year Flood Standard**. This is a flood event that is hypothetically supposed to occur every century and theoretically has a one percent chance of happening in a given year. This risk is used for zoning and insurance decisions on property.[98]

There are several types of flooding that can occur: riverine, flash floods, alluvial fan, ice/debris dam failures, surface ponding, fluctuating lake levels, and control structure (levee or dam) failure. **Riverine flooding** is caused by water overflowing the banks of rivers. This is the most common type of flood. These are usually caused by large-scale weather events that generate precipitation over a large geographical area.[99]

Alluvial fan flooding refers to flooding in the delta-shaped area below a mountain range where a river flows into flat lands and breaks into channels. Alluvial fan flooding occurs when all branches of the river overflow their very shallow banks of only a few inches and flood the entire plain. Because the banks disappear and all the water combines, large debris such as whole trees can be carried into the plain.[100] For example, there was a flood in Venezuela in 1999 that killed 19,000 people. The alluvial plains were built upon because it was the only flat land between the ocean and the mountains.

Ice/debris dam failures are not human-constructed structures but rather dams that form *accidentally* from the accumulation of debris like wood, fallen trees, and ice in a river or stream. Ice/debris dam failures occur when an accumulation of debris or ice collects, jams, and temporarily blocks the flow of water and raises it above the bank of the stream, flooding surrounding areas.[101]

Surface ponding happens when water accumulates in very flat areas in terms of no slope – runoff cannot carry the water away fast enough, so flooding occurs.[102]

Fluctuating lake levels involve lakes that are landlocked and have few outlets to let water drain. Such lakes are prone to overflowing their banks and flooding surrounding areas.

Control structure (levee or dam) failure occurs when a human-made structure designed to contain or control water breaks or fails. This can lead to sudden, rapid flooding similar to a flash flood.[103]

A flash flood is rapid, sudden flooding. Water rushes over an area in high volumes and the water flows with visible velocity. Flash floods occur when a control structure fails or when torrential rain occurs rapidly. This is most often seen in hilly areas with little vegetation. This can also be seen in arid areas.[104]

Floods are predicted by the National Weather Service based on precipitation forecasts (radar) and actual rainfall measures (rain gauges). There are also river and stream gauges that measure water depth in real time.

Evacuation is a good precaution to take to protect human beings from floods. In flat areas, evacuation should be oriented toward moving away from the river or ocean. In steep canyons or valleys, it is better to climb up rather than trying to parallel a river. Persons should avoid attempting to cross running water or flooded roadways because one can be swept away easily.

Storm surge is another hydrological hazard. Storm surges are connected with hurricanes. A storm surge is seawater pushed by the wind and rotation of the hurricane. This far exceeds the normal high tide for the area. The higher the category of hurricane, the higher the storm surge. Low slope makes the storm surge more destructive. Storm surges range from four feet to more than eighteen feet. Before the 1970s, storm surge was responsible for most hurricane deaths. Today, with satellite imagery and computers, areas can be well estimated that are likely to be hit by storm surge so that evacuation can occur. For this reason, inland flooding is the major killer in terms of hurricanes. The best protective action is evacuation. If this is not possible, sheltering on the third or fourth floor of a reinforced concrete building can provide some protection.[105]

The flood-related health threats include drowning, traumatic injuries, electrocution, heart attacks, carbon monoxide poisoning, and infectious diseases.[106] Fully 70% of flood-related deaths are due to drowning, while 12% are due to traumatic injuries.[107] The primary cause of death from a flood is drowning in a motor vehicle.[108] Flood-related injuries generally consist of bruises and skin lacerations. Flood-related illnesses include gastrointestinal problems, skin rashes, and respiratory issues.[109] Mold in houses and other buildings is a danger following floods, as is contaminated water.

Water and sewer systems often become incapacitated during flooding. This often causes contaminated drinking water. In addition, researchers have noted that a so-called "toxic soup" consisting of liquid water, sewage, and chemicals is generally created. This "toxic soup" poses dangers to both first responders and survivors. "Toxic soup" can contain both toxins and bacteria that can cause illness or death when absorbed through cuts or accidentally ingested. In addition, large amounts of stagnant water remaining after a flood can serve as a mosquito breeding ground. Mosquitoes are recognized vectors for serious diseases including West Nile Virus and Zika.[110]

Mold typically grows during and after floods.[111] Mold can pose a major health hazard. Areas and items covered by flood water (such as sheetrock and flooring materials) should be removed and replaced. Taking these actions is expensive in terms of money and labor. For that reason, persons in low-income areas may find that removal and replacement of water-damaged items is unaffordable. This often leads to lingering health effects over a period of months and years.[112]

Ideally, construction in flood-prone areas should include reinforced and elevated structures. In addition, appliances such as water heaters and heating, cooling, and ventilation units should be elevated inside dwellings and businesses.[113]

The ability of first responder agencies to provide services during severe floods may be impaired by submerged and blocked roads. The necessity of travel by helicopter or watercraft will substantially reduce response time. In addition to deaths, floods often lead to large numbers of persons displaced from their homes. This requires additional planning by emergency managers and health professionals. Emergency management personnel must select shelter sites and place them into operation.[114]

Once the flood begins to recede, decisions must be made by government officials based on the observed environmental impact. Homes, businesses, and other buildings have been destroyed or damaged. In addition, human beings and animals may have died due to drowning or illness. Additional public health risks are posed by decaying human and animal remains.[115]

Decaying bodies, exposed sewage, and chemicals may have contaminated potable water sources. These items must be removed. The water sources must be treated with chlorine to enable it to be consumed safely. In addition, it must be recognized that floods can also result in food shortages due to transportation problems, and the losses of livestock and crops. The lack of electricity typically leads to the destruction of refrigerated foods.[116]

There are many ways to protect at-risk populations from foodborne and waterborne threats, chemical threats, physical threats, mold, and wound infections.[117] Once flood waters have receded, government officials should utilize the media to send messages to evacuees and those who remain in the community about when to return and how to do so safely. If appropriate, information on disaster services and sheltering should also be provided.[118]

The final hydrological hazard is the **tsunami**. Tsunamis are large sea waves that are generated by undersea earthquakes or volcanic eruptions. Tsunamis are much higher and more dangerous than storm surges. They can be as high as 100 feet.[119]

Tsunamis originate in the deep ocean and can travel as fast as 400 miles per hour. Thus, tsunamis have immense force when they strike land. However, in the middle of the ocean, large ships cannot generally sense a tsunami passing under. Tsunamis are also not usually visible from the air. The destructive force of tsunamis comes when they impact shallow water near land. The pressure of the water against the shallow seafloor does two things: (1) it slows down the tsunami to between 25 and 40 miles per hour, and (2) it forces the water upwards into a towering high wave.[120]

The force and volume of rapidly moving seawater often produce strong currents. This water and these currents sweep vehicles, structures, trees, and human beings away rapidly. The force of the water causes structural damage to homes and businesses. In addition, infrastructure damage to roads and utilities occurs and large amounts of debris are generated. Tsunamis cause mass casualties, contamination of drinking water, hazmat incidents, and long-term electricity outages. Disease risk also increased due to mold and contaminated water.

The primary risk areas of the U.S are in the Pacific Ocean areas of Hawaii, California, and Alaska. For example, Hilo, Hawaii was hit by tsunamis in 1946 and 1960. California was impacted by a major tsunami during the 1960s. During the 2004 Indian Ocean tsunami over 220,000 people were killed, and 1.7 million more were displaced by water and damaged homes.[121]

In terms of warnings, various governments have placed *seismic buoys* in the ocean to detect tsunamis. Seismic sensors provide international organizations with information about undersea earthquakes. It is possible then to predict the severity of the tsunami and its estimated time and place of impact. The further the earthquake is away from a landmass, the more warning is possible. Earthquakes closer to land can result in the arrival of a tsunami in as little as 15 minutes. Survivors have reported that the ocean water recedes substantially before the tsunami hits. Hawaii and other Pacific coastal areas have tsunami warning sirens based on the Pacific Tsunami Warning Center on Oahu.[122]

The best defense against a tsunami is for individuals to rapidly evacuate to an area at least one-half mile inland or climb a hill or travel up the side of a mountain quickly. Climbing to the fourth floor or higher in a reinforced concrete building is likely to offer protection as well.

Geophysical Hazards

Geophysical hazards are caused by changes in the physical properties of the earth's crust, such as geological phenomena like volcanic eruptions and earthquakes. The basis of this is plate tectonics. Tectonic processes result in the two most important geophysical hazards in the United States: earthquakes and volcanoes.

Earthquakes are movements of the earth's crust in the form of seismic waves. The crust is composed of many sections, which are called tectonic plates. Tectonic plates are constantly in motion due to convective currents caused by the interior heating cycle of the planet emanating from the core. Convective currents cause tectonic plates to move, which releases energy resulting in seismic waves.[123] Energy is released when an earthquake occurs. Earthquakes are generally identified by the **epicenter**, which is the place on the surface directly above the place beneath the earth from which an earthquake emanates (hypocenter).[124]

Earthquakes are measured both in magnitude and intensity. **Magnitude** reflects the amount of energy released at the hypocenter. Magnitude is measured on the **Richter Scale** and does not reflect damage. Damage is measured by intensity. **Intensity** is measured based on observed effects on people, buildings, and natural features. Intensity is measured on the **Modified Mercalli Intensity Scale**. There are ratings from I to XII, ranging in severity. Earthquakes can cause destruction or damage to the infrastructure, mass casualties, fires, hazardous materials incidents, water contamination, and building destruction.[125]

Some of the most devastating recent earthquakes impacted Japan in 1995, killing more than 6,000 people. In 2010, more than 222,000 were killed in a major earthquake in Haiti.[126] California is impacted fairly often by earthquakes. The situation is made worse due to the high population.

Most injuries that occur during earthquakes occur when people are attempting to enter or exit buildings that drop debris or collapse.[127] Research shows that the risk of death from earthquakes is higher among those with disabilities, persons under age 15, and the elderly. Persons at greatest risk of death from collapsing structures tend to occupy lower socioeconomic status.[128]

The most significant morbidity and mortality variables associated with earthquakes include geological factors, timing, weather, geography, built environment, and individual behavior and characteristics. Most earthquake injuries are indirect and are the result of collapsing buildings, fires, and falling debris.[129]

Earthquakes cause numerous secondary disasters, which include fires, collapsed structures, hazmat, mass casualties, contaminated water, and destroyed motor vehicles. Damages are associated with the intensity of the earthquake.[130] Fires caused by broken gas lines and downed electrical wires are common after earthquakes and can be particularly dangerous. Damaged and obstructed roads can make emergency services impossible to obtain in the short term. Damaged water mains can significantly reduce the ability of firefighters to perform their duties.[131]

Exposure to the elements and reduced air quality often occurs in the aftermath of an earthquake. This is especially true for vulnerable members of the population during times of extreme heat or cold. The lack of electricity can create unsafe conditions even among those with intact dwellings. Soil liquefaction can accelerate structural collapse and can harm air quality as well.[132]

Substantial numbers of traumatic injuries may be caused by earthquakes. Crush injuries, fractures, and burns are common. In addition, asphyxiation and respiratory distress can result from debris and dust caused by collapsing structures.[133] A **crush injury** occurs when the human body encounters a high degree of pressure caused by being pressed against the weight of a heavy object. Crush injuries can result in internal injuries, bruising, and fractures.[134] Death can quickly result when a person is extracted without immediate supportive care. Medical experts note that toxic substances are released into the bloodstream upon extraction.[135]

Earthquakes often require the skills of USAR (Urban Search and Rescue) teams, which are specially trained first responders (mostly firefighters). Many large cities maintain USAR teams, who can work collapsed buildings caused by both earthquakes and bombings. Smaller cities typically do not maintain USAR teams, which means such teams will have to be deployed from other areas of the country. However, it is often the case that most victims will have died before remote USAR teams are able to arrive. Research indicates that crush injuries usually result in death within 24 hours. Damaged infrastructure also increases USAR response time.[136]

Because earthquakes usually occur without warning, evacuation is typically not possible. Thus, earthquakes tend to have a higher rate of death and injury than many other disasters.[137] In addition, because the infrastructure is so severely impacted, numerous secondary effects occur. For example, individuals who rely upon oxygen, dialysis, respirators, and other medical devices and procedures are at great risk. The loss of heating and air conditioning can also cause risk to other vulnerable populations. The loss of electricity will quickly destroy perishable food. The risk of foodborne disease is thus increased. The lack of running water and functional sewer systems can also contribute to increased health risks. These risks all increase with time.[138]

From an emergency management perspective, advanced preparation is the key. This is especially true because there is little or no advanced warning with regard to earthquakes. Earthquake-resistant buildings are important to mitigate damage in areas prone to seismic activity. Earthquake preparation is facilitated by the construction of emergency kits that will sustain a person for 72 hours.

Ideally, construction projects in high-risk areas should be minimized. Necessary construction in these areas should incorporate rigorous zoning and construction practices to reduce collapse risk. For existing structures, preparedness based upon education about the risks and safety protocols should be emphasized.[139] For example, emergency management agencies should notify the public to help minimize earthquake injury risks in homes and businesses by taking actions to secure objects that can fall or break, such as heavy items, hazardous materials, and flammable items that can catch fire from fallen electrical wires or broken gas lines.[140] After taking such structural mitigation measures, the population of earthquake-prone areas should identify safe locations inside rooms in homes and workplaces. Such safe locations include the areas under large pieces of furniture and along interior walls.[141]

To best protect vulnerable populations, practicing evacuation and earthquake protection protocols is necessary. In addition, beds should be located away from windows and exterior walls. Hospitals and nursing homes should have special plans in place made in consultation with emergency management professionals to deal with the protection and care of vulnerable populations during a seismic event.

Volcanoes

Volcanoes and volcanic activity are also geophysical hazards. Volcanoes are formed when molten rock (magma) rises from the interior of the earth and erupts at the surface. When molten rock erupts at the surface, it is called **lava**. Numerous eruptions at the same location deposited in layers result in the creation of a mountain. The mountain can be destroyed by major eruptions.[142]

In the United States, all active volcanoes are located on the Pacific Coast. Hawaii has active volcanoes, and twenty other American volcanoes have erupted within the last 200 years. Alaska has 92 volcanoes, Oregon has 22, California has 20, and Washington has eight. Earthquakes can also form as part of the eruption.[143] The most obvious example is the 1980 Mt. St. Helens eruption in Washington, where 57 people died.

Eruptions and their accompanying lava flows can devastate the surrounding environment. Sulfuric acid produced by an eruption can result in localized climate change. Byproducts of eruptions include poor air quality, ash, and volcanic gasses.[144] These also include pyroclastic flows, which is a mixture of hot rock fragments and hot gas. Both lava flows and pyroclastic flows incinerate or bury everything in their paths. This includes utilities, homes, businesses, croplands, and utilities. The toxic gasses emanating from a volcanic eruption presents serious health hazards to both human beings and animals. Respiratory problems, falling ash, and the destruction of homes and infrastructure can lead to mass casualties and require mass sheltering.

Scientists have noted that approximately ten percent of the world's population presently resides in areas prone to volcanic eruptions. Substantial parts of the United States population are also vulnerable to potential volcanic effects.[145]

The **Volcanic Explosivity Index (VEI)** is used to categorize the intensity level of volcanic activity. The VEI contains a methodology designed to provide a composite estimate of the power of a volcanic eruption. The VEI includes quantitative measurements of variables including the approximate amount of materials ejected by an eruption and the cloud height of a given eruption. In addition, tephra and pyroclastic flow are estimated by the VEI. These variables are combined to form an index used to categorize a given volcanic eruption on a scale from 0 to 8.[146] Scientists estimate that more than 4,700 volcanic eruptions have occurred over the past 10,000 years.[147] More than seventy percent of these eruptions have had a VEI of 2. Less than one-tenth of one percent had a VEI of 7 or above. Since 1900, there have been 13 volcanic eruptions with a VEI score of 5 or greater.[148]

First responder personnel should be aware that volcanic eruptions produce substantial airborne health hazards in the form of hazardous particles and toxic gases[149] Ash, rocks, heat, and gases all emanate from a volcanic eruption. Gases in particular (carbon monoxide) can cause respiratory damage to human beings and animals. Boulders can be sent miles from the volcano. Exposure to hot gases, lava flows, and pyroclastic flows can result in burn injuries. Fine ash debris and volcanic gases can also cause asphyxiation.[150]

In addition to these human health effects, animals, crops, and other plants can also be adversely affected as a result of a volcanic eruption. The critical infrastructure can also be damaged or rendered inoperable. Electrical power can be interrupted by broken power lines and dry ash accumulation. Wet ash accumulation poses additional dangers because it conducts electricity. This can short out power systems and poses electrocution danger to first responders, emergency workers, and the general public. Medium-term and long-term electricity loss place persons dependent upon medical devices at substantial risk. Food will spoil without electricity. In addition, roads and bridges can be made impassible by ash and lava accumulations. Visibility is also greatly diminished by falling ash.[151]

Beyond this, other infrastructure, such as potable water and sewer systems, are generally impacted. Water reservoirs can be contaminated by volcanic ash, as can sewer treatment facilities. Sewage systems can become blocked due to the accumulation of wet ash. Morbidity and mortality will likely be affected by such critical infrastructure damage.[152]

Due to the vast panoply of human, animal, and crop effects that can result from a volcanic eruption, evacuation is the best protective measure and it should be implemented whenever possible.[153]

Members of the public living and working near active volcanoes should be encouraged by the emergency management community to prepare disaster kits. These kits must include an N95 respirator. Effective preparation and mitigation also involve contingency plans to shelter in place if evacuation is not possible. A plan for providing emergency services and debris management is vital. Emergency management personnel should also develop feeding and sheltering plans. Public works departments and utilities should work with law enforcement agencies, emergency managers, and other first responders to plan which roads will receive first priority to be cleared and opened.[154] For example, in the state of Hawaii, Hawaii County Civil Defense (www.hawaiicounty.gov) exemplifies what emergency management agencies can achieve in the face of volcanic eruption emergencies.

Death, injury, and property damage related to volcanic eruptions can be reduced by taking planning measures involving warnings, evacuation, and recovery, coupled with individual and family preparedness. Post-eruption recovery operations can be enhanced by making specific plans to restore critical infrastructure following a volcanic eruption.[155]

Notes

1. Michael J. Fagel, Editor, *Principles of Emergency Management: Hazard Specific Issues and Mitigation Strategies*, Boca Raton: CRC Press/Taylor and Francis Group, 2012: 88.
2. Michael K. Lindell, Carla Prater, and Ronald W. Perry, *Introduction to Emergency Management*, Hoboken, John Wiley and Sons, Inc., 2007: 2. Emphasis in original.

3. Fagel, *Principles of Emergency Management*: 88.
4. Ibid.
5. Ibid.
6. Ibid.
7. Lindell, *Introduction to Emergency Management*: 108 and 125.
8. Ibid: 117.
9. Ibid: 125.
10. Ibid: 108.
11. Ibid: 108-109.
12. Bruce W. Clements and Julie Ann P. Casani, *Disasters and Public Health: Planning and Response*, 2nd Edition, Cambridge, Butterworth-Heinemann Elsevier, 2016: 424.
13. Ibid: 414.
14. 414-415.
15. Ibid: 413.
16. Ibid: 415.
17. Ibid.
18. Ibid.
19. Ibid: 424.
20. Ibid: 420.
21. Ibid.
22. Ibid: 424.
23. Lindell, Prater, and Perry, *Introduction to Emergency Management*: 111.
24. Clements and Casani, *Disasters and Public Health*: 426.
25. Ibid: 427.
26. Ibid.
27. Ibid.
28. Ibid: 427-428.
29. Ibid: 428.
30. Lindell, Prater, and Perry, *Introduction to Emergency Management*: 109.
31. Ibid.
32. Ibid: 110.
33. Ibid: 109-110.
34. Clements and Casani, *Disasters and Public Health*: 312.
35. Ibid: 313.
36. Ibid.
37. Ibid: 312.
38. Ibid: 314.
39. Ibid: 312.
40. Ibid: 313.
41. Ibid: 316.
42. Ibid.
43. Ibid: 318.
44. Ibid: 324.
45. Ibid: 326.
46. Ibid: 318-319.

47. Ibid: 319.
48. Lindell, Prater, and Perry, Introduction to Emergency Management: 109.
49. Fagel, *Principles of Emergency Management*: 105.
50. Lindell, *Introduction to Emergency Management*: 109.
51. Ibid: 115.
52. Ibid.
53. Clements and Casani, *Disasters and Public Health*: 458.
54. Fagel, *Principles of Emergency Management*: 101.
55. Lindell, Prater, and Perry, *Introduction to Emergency Management*: 116-117.
56. Clements and Casani, *Disasters and Public Health*: 460.
57. Ibid: 459.
58. Ibid: 457.
59. Ibid: 459.
60. Ibid: 462.
61. Ibid: 457.
62. Ibid: 464.
63. Ibid: 465.
64. Ibid: 466.
65. Ibid: 417.
66. Lindell, *Introduction to Emergency Management*: 110.
67. Ibid.
68. Ibid.
69. Ibid.
70. Ibid: 111.
71. Ibid.
72. Ibid.
73. Clements and Casani, *Disasters and Public Health*: 415.
74. Fagel, *Principles of Emergency Management*: 94.
75. Lindell, Prater, and Perry, *Introduction to Emergency Management*: 114.
76. Fagel, *Principles of Emergency Management*: 94.
77. Ibid.
78. Ibid.
79. Ibid.
80. Lindell, Prater, and Perry, *Introduction to Emergency Management*: 111.
81. Ibid: 112.
82. Clements and Casani, *Disasters and Public Health*: 337.
83. Lindell, Prater, and Perry, *Introduction to Emergency Management*: 113.
84. Ibid: 111.
85. Fagel, *Principles of Emergency Management*: 95.
86. Lindell, Prater, and Perry, *Introduction to Emergency Management*: 112.
87. Clements and Casani, *Disasters and Public Health*: 341-343.
88. Lindell, Prater, and Perry, *Introduction to Emergency Management*: 112.
89. Ibid: 114.
90. Ibid: 117.
91. Ibid.
92. Ibid.

93. Ibid: 121.
94. Ibid: 118.
95. Ibid.
96. Ibid.
97. Ibid: 119.
98. Ibid: 121.
99. Ibid: 117.
100. Ibid: 118.
101. Ibid.
102. Ibid.
103. Ibid.
104. Ibid: 118.
105. Ibid: 122.
106. Clements and Casani, *Disasters and Public Health*: 276.
107. Ibid: 277.
108. Ibid: 282.
109. Ibid: 278.
110. Suzet McKinney and Mary E. Papke, *Public Health Emergency Preparedness: A Practical Approach for the Real World*, Burlington, MA, Jones and Bartlett Learning, 2019: 56.
111. Ibid.
112. Ibid.
113. Ibid: 281.
114. Ibid: 56.
115. Clements and Casani, *Disasters and Public Health*: 283.
116. Ibid: 284.
117. Ibid: 287.
118. Ibid: 284.
119. Ibid: 123.
120. Ibid.
121. Ibid: 124.
122. Ibid: 123.
123. Fagel, *Principles of Emergency Management*: 102-103.
124. Lindell, Prater, and Perry, *Introduction to Emergency Management*: 127.
125. Ibid: 127-128.
126. Clements and Casani, *Disasters and Public Health*: 229-231.
127. Ibid: 237.
128. Ibid: 231.
129. Ibid: 229.
130. Fagel, *Principles of Emergency Management*: 103.
131. Suzete McKinney and Mary E. Papke, *Public Health Emergency Preparedness: A Practical Approach for the Real World*, Burlington, Jones and Bartlett Learning, LLC, 2019: 57.
132. Ibid.
133. Clements and Casani, *Disasters and Public Health*: 229.
134. Ibid: 223.

135. Ibid: 230.
136. Lindell, Prater, and Perry, *Introduction to Emergency Management*: 131.
137. McKinney and Papke, *Public Health Emergency Preparedness*: 57.
138. Clements and Casani, *Disasters and Public Health*: 231-232.
139. Ibid: 233.
140. Ibid: 235.
141. Ibid: 236.
142. Lindell, Prater, and Perry, *Introduction to Emergency Management*: 125.
143. Ibid:125.
144. Fagel, *Principles of Emergency Management*: 112.
145. Clements and Casani, *Disasters and Public Health*: 440.
146. Ibid: 440-441.
147. Ibid: 441.
148. Ibid.
149. Ibid.
150. Ibid: 443.
151. Ibid: 446.
152. Ibid: 448.
153. Ibid: 449.
154. Fagel, *Principles of Emergency Management*: 114.
155. Ibid: 452.

Chapter 6

MAN-MADE DISASTER SCENARIOS AND THE ROLE OF LAW ENFORCEMENT AND OTHER AGENCIES

Chapter 6 examines various man-made hazards and disasters that may be encountered by law enforcement personnel. As was noted in the previous chapter, a **disaster** occurs when hazards, vulnerabilities, and risks converge. FEMA (Federal Emergency Management Agency) defines disaster as "an occurrence of a severity and magnitude that normally results in deaths, injuries, and property damage that cannot be managed through the routine procedures and resources of a government."[1]

It is vitally important that both emergency managers and law enforcement personnel develop a thorough understanding of the hazards in their communities. This understanding recognizes the need to understand the potential that any given hazard or disaster can have cascading effects.[2]

It was also pointed out that it is the responsibility of the jurisdiction's emergency manager to prepare a hazard vulnerability analysis. This document will be used to assess the hazard, vulnerability, and risk scenarios that the community faces. The hazard vulnerability analysis should then be used for planning, training, and exercising emergency management and law enforcement agencies. It must be recognized that when hazards result in disasters, jurisdictional boundaries are usually not recognized.[3] It is for this reason that inter-agency communication and cooperation are vital.

Man-made hazards are the result of deliberate (such as terrorism or cyberattacks) or accidental (such as chemical spills) actions or inactions by human beings. Man-made hazards can also include things like bridge and tunnel collapse or nuclear power plant leaks (infrastructure failures).

Hazardous Materials (Hazmat)

Hazardous material (hazmat) spills and exposure can be the result of negligence, due to other hazards (tornado, tsunami, earthquake, etc.) or they can be deliberately placed (terrorism). **Hazmat** refers to any solid, liquid, or gas that can cause long-lasting health effects, injury, or death. A hazmat includes any chemical or other substance incorrectly released from its container that can cause death, injury, environmental damage, or property damage.[4] More than one billion tons of hazmat are produced in the United States and Canada annually. Hazmat poses significant dangers to first responders and the general public. Dealing with hazmat requires education and training for both emergency managers and first responders.[5]

The threats posed by hazmat include fires, explosions, and health effects. Law enforcement officers and other first responders must have basic knowledge of hazmat so that appropriate actions can be taken at a critical incident scene.[6] Many hazardous materials possess the potential to become WMDs (weapons of mass destruction) if used for nefarious purposes.[7]

Hazardous materials are transported via truck, rail, and air along the nation's transportation routes every day. For that reason, there is no area in the country that is not exposed to the potential of a hazmat incident.[8] These hazmat groupings are regulated by several federal agencies, including the U.S. Department of Transportation and the Environmental Protection Agency (EPA). These agencies, along with the U.S. Coast Guard, also have responsibilities for emergency response to hazmat incidents.[9] Natural gas, chlorine, gasoline, hydrochloric acid, and sulfuric acid are the most common chemical releases. The vast majority of hazmat incidents involving these substances occur on highways.

Different organizations categorize and measure chemical health threats in different ways. Because different organizations have different purposes (transportation safety, occupational health safety, medical treatment, etc.), there are several different ways to categorize the threats posed to human health from chemicals.

The U.S. Department of Transportation groups hazmat into nine different classes. The primary mission of the organization is transportation safety. These include explosives, compressed gases (flammable and nonflammable), flammable liquids, flammable solids, oxidizers and organic peroxides, toxic chemicals, infectious substances, radioactive materials, corrosives, and miscellaneous dangerous goods.

A placarding system is utilized by the U.S. Department of Transportation to identify hazmat stored in containers and in transport. These placards are diamond-shaped. Federal regulations require that these placards be placed on both ends and both sides of trucks, shipping containers, and railcars that transport hazardous materials. The placards assist government regulators to ensure that safe shipping practices are being followed. In addition, the placards assist first responders by labeling the type of hazardous substance involved in a critical incident. This facilitates taking protective actions to keep first responders and members of the public from harm.[10]

First responders are at the greatest risk for hazmat exposure due to their sustained presence at critical incident sites. For that reason, placarding and other warning systems are imperative for first responder health and safety.[11] Law enforcement officers should know that many hazmat transporters utilize the National Fire Protection Association (NFPA) System of Communicating Hazards in addition to the U.S. Department of Transportation placards.

Under the NFPA system, an easy-to-understand symbol is placed upon a container for the purpose of indicating the nature of the substance located inside. First responders will thus be able to take the proper precautions prior to getting closer to the substance during a critical incident. The NFPA system utilizes a diamond sign ("fire diamond"), which comprises four smaller diamonds. Each of the four smaller diamonds displays a different primary color. A number ranging from 0 to 4 is placed in at least one of the diamonds for the purpose of indicating the level of risk or danger to first responders. Higher numbers indicate greater risk. The color blue indicates health hazards. Red indicates flammable hazards. Yellow indicates reactive hazards, and white denotes special hazards.[12] Black and white indicates corrosive hazards, and green denotes nonflammable gas. Orange indicates explosives.[13]

Keep in mind that while the placards identify the presence of hazardous materials, they cannot always be relied upon because improper placards may be displayed. "Flip-type" placards may not actually display the incorrect identification number due to an accident impact or human error. This can result in incorrect actions being taken by first responders due to misidentification of the hazmat. In addition, hazmat stored in buildings typically do not display placards.[14]

Since this is true, law enforcement officers should pay attention to the types of trucks and railcars that typically transport hazardous materials.[15] Many critical incidents have the potential to become hazmat scenes.[16] Even calls for service can uncover illegal drug labs, which are both hazmat and a crime scene. Even retail stores and industrial plants can contain hazmat risks.[17]

Hazmat releases from a road accident, such as a truck wreck or a train derailment, are likely to contain relatively small quantities of toxic substances. The risk to human and animal health depends upon the type of hazmat substance, the quantity of the substance released, weather conditions, and how the proximity of the spill or release to populated areas.

A more dangerous situation involves an *industrial* hazmat incident because the amounts of toxic substances that can be released from an industrial facility can cause serious death and mass casualties. For example, the 1984 Bhopal (Union Carbide) chemical leak resulted in the accidental release of the pesticide gas, methyl isocyanate. Officially, 3,800 people were killed. Large numbers of livestock were killed, and serious illnesses and premature death harmed thousands more.

For industrial hazmat, the U.S. Occupational Health and Safety Administration (OSHA) employs categorical descriptors based on the damage that would result to employee organ systems from their unsafe exposure to toxic substances. For example, hepatotoxins cause liver damage and teratogens cause birth defects.[18]

Also, for industrial purposes, the United Nations Economic and Social Council adopted the Globally Harmonized Systems of Classification and Labeling of Chemicals (GHS). This system represents an effort at cross-national standardization of chemical hazards in order to facilitate international recognition.[19] The GHS Classes involve acute toxicity, skin corrosion, respiratory sensitization, and others.

From a healthcare perspective, different classifications are used in the United States. This is true because healthcare differs from transportation and workplace safety. For that reason, the American healthcare profession commonly separates hazardous chemicals by their composition or structure. For example, metals and solvents are commonly utilized. The healthcare profession also classifies chemicals according to the physiological damage that exposure does to the human body. The Centers for Disease Control and Prevention employs CDC Hazardous Chemical Categories, which include blister agents, biotoxins, blood agents, respiratory agents, caustics, and incapacitating agents.[20]

Wind speed, wind direction, and atmospheric stability affect the dispersion of a chemical. Also, individual human beings vary in their susceptibility to hazmat by age (the young and old are most susceptible), physical condition (suppressed immune systems), and general health. In addition, hazmat substances vary their effects based on their exposure pathways. Inhalation, absorption, and ingestion of hazmat toxins will lead to different health outcomes.[21] Inhalation rapidly gets the chemical absorbed via the lungs, which leads to the bloodstream and organs within minutes. Ingestion results in the toxic chemicals affecting the body more slowly. Absorption through the skin is of greater concern than ingestion. By whatever exposure pathway, alteration of cellular functions results from exposure to toxic chemicals.[22]

Law enforcement personnel working critical incidents should be familiar with **chemical toxicity**. This is the ability of a chemical to damage living cells and applies to human beings, animals, and plants. **Response** is the measure of harmful reaction to a living thing caused by chemical exposure. **Dose** is the amount of a chemical to which a living thing is exposed. When the damage to a living thing caused by chemical exposure is assessed, it is called the **dose-response relationship**.[23]

When human beings are exposed to toxic chemicals, the rate and route of the exposure determines the dose. Such exposure can result in *chronic poisoning* and *acute poisoning.* **Acute poisoning** is more serious and is caused by rapid absorption. **Chronic poisoning** is less serious and is associated with prolonged exposure.[24]

There are several ways to measure the level of chronic poisoning and acute poisoning in human beings. OSHA does so with Permissible Exposure Limits (PELs). The EPA uses Acute Exposure Guideline Levels (AEGLs). Other measures include Temporary Emergency Exposure Limits (TEELs) and Emergency Response Planning Guidelines (ERPGs). All but the OSHA method measure levels based on the expected body response of a population at a given level of exposure to a chemical substance. For first responders, the AEGL is the most appropriate choice because it provides an immediate hazard assessment. The next best choice is the ERPG.[25]

Prevention is the first line of defense from hazmat. To facilitate this prevention, the U.S. Department of Homeland Security developed fifteen national preparedness scenarios. Some of these scenarios involve chemical contamination incidents, including how to respond to chlorine tank explosions and toxic chemical releases. Others involve chemical decontamination scenarios and a scenario involving terrorist use of nerve agents upon the civilian population.[26]

A 1986 federal law requires that Local Emergency Planning Committees (LEPCs) be established for the purpose of making local emergency preparedness plans for chemical and other hazmat disasters. These plans must be updated annually and involve first responders, emergency managers, public health agencies, local industry representatives, and the local transportation industry.[27]

Law enforcement agencies should take particular note of the vulnerability posed by outdoor air intakes to buildings. Most building air intakes are easily accessible and not carefully secured. This makes the building susceptible to attack by a terrorist. Chemicals and other harmful substances could be delivered to the occupants of a building by means of a hand sprayer. In addition, because many toxic chemicals stay close to the ground following an industrial leak or hazmat incident, they can be drawn in to the air intake system. For these reasons, the provision of physical security to outdoor air intakes of important buildings is an important mitigation and prevention measure.[28]

Another potential hazmat involves radiological material releases. Medical diagnostic facilities utilize small quantities of radiological materials. Nuclear power plants use much larger quantities of radiological materials to drive electrical generators.[29] For this reason, the greatest risk in this area can potentially occur in areas with nuclear power plants. The radioactive fuel for a nuclear power plant is sealed in a containment building that is constructed of reinforced concrete. The seals for pipes and control cables can be damaged during a terrorist attack or an accident. Such an attack or accident could result in the escape of radioactive material into the environment.[30]

If a severe failure or accident involves the loss of water used to cool a nuclear reactor, the nuclear fuel can melt through its protective cladding and containment building 45-90 minutes later. A melted radioactive core can cause severe health effects from radiation sickness.[31] Examples of such occurrences include Chernobyl, Ukraine in 1986, and Three Mile Island in 1979. The NRC (Nuclear Regulatory Commission) imposes safety and monitoring regulations on nuclear power plants. In a nuclear power plant incident, evacuation is best. The radiation exposure risk is directly related to distance and wind direction.

Terrorism can result in deliberate hazmat release. Such a situation can be described as "Weaponized Toxic Chemicals," "Radiological Material Releases," and "Biological Hazards" – deliberate exposure to disease agents.

Weapons of Mass Destruction

Terrorists have a wide range of potential targets and methods from which to choose. One is **conventional explosives and secondary devices**. Conventional explosives such as those used to construct improvised bombs are relatively easy to obtain and use. Such a device can be used to cause death, injury, or property damage locally. Improvised bombs can also be used to disperse a chemical, radiological, or biological agent. The materials and instructions to construct an improvised bomb are readily available.[32] For example, the Boston Marathon bombers in 2013 used conventional "homemade" explosives.

Such explosives are also called **Improvised Explosive Devices (IEDs)**.[33] IEDs can deliver explosives by a variety of methods. Pressure-cooker bombs and other small explosive devices can be placed in lockers or suitcases and left in public areas for later detonation. This will provide a terrorist with the opportunity to leave the scene prior to the explosion and to time the explosion to inflict the most possible damage.[34]

IEDs are becoming smaller and more sophisticated with the passage of time. For example, American intelligence sources have discovered IEDs small enough to fit into a laptop battery compartment. To inflict greater damage, large quantities of explosives can be delivered to a terrorist's target through car or truck bombs.[35] These strategies need to be incorporated into the Terrorism Annex to a jurisdiction's EOP (Emergency Operations Plan).

Emergency managers should be aware of the potential that a terrorist or terrorist organization might in the future employ a **Weapon of Mass Destruction (WMD)** inside the United States. A WMD is broadly defined as a weapon designed to cause death or serious bodily injury via the release of fire, explosion, toxic chemicals, disease organisms, or radioactivity.[36]

Terrorists may also use **chemical agents**. Chemical agents are the toxic component of an intentionally released substance. These are specially prepared substances that are designed to kill or seriously injure human beings with toxic substances. Deployment of a chemical agent by a terrorist requires immediate reactions from emergency responders. Police, fire, hazmat teams, EMS, and hospital staff thus require the training and equipment necessary to respond.[37]

It should be realized by law enforcement personnel and emergency managers that most chemical attacks have only a local impact.[38] One must also recognize the difference between **persistent chemical agents** and **nonpersistent chemical agents**. The former are long-lasting and remain in the area for hours, days or weeks. Nonpersistent chemical agents evaporate quickly and rapidly disperse. Generally, nonpersistent chemical agents do not cause casualties after 15 minutes.[39]

Chemical agents can be dispersed via aerosol devices, covert dissemination, or breaking containers. A chemical attack could also involve the release of a chemical weapon, such as nerve gas, blistering agents, or industrial chemicals.[40] Indicators of a chemical agent attack include dead or dying animals and fish, unexplained casualties, unusual spray, vapor, powder, devices, or packages.[41]

Biological agents also must be considered as part of planning the Terrorism Annex to the EOC. A **biological agent** is a disease organism that is purposely utilized as a weapon. Biological agents could be aimed at either human beings (anthrax, smallpox, etc.) or at the food supply (animals and plants). The initial detection of a biological attack is likely to be made by medical providers or public health officials rather than law enforcement officers or other first responders.[42]

From the perspective of law enforcement, the deployment of a biological weapon can be recognized in several ways. These include diagnostic reports from medical providers, identification of a threat from a perpetrator, and discovery of bioterrorism evidence. Many indicators of the use of biological agents are similar to those involving chemical agents.

Nuclear/radiological agents must also be considered as being potential terrorist threats, and should therefore be part of the Terrorism Annex to the EOC. Nuclear/radiological agents are atomic-based energy-emitting substances that cause death or damage to living things. Radiological materials are capable of releasing energy, including gamma radiation.[43] Because radiation cannot be detected using human senses, first responders will be unable to ascertain the presence of a radiation hazard unless personnel possess radiation detection equipment.[44] In other words, it may or may not be obvious that radioactive material is involved in a given explosion.[45]

Rather than nuclear bombs (at present only possessed by nation-states), terrorists are most likely to utilize uranium or plutonium obtained from spent nuclear fuel rods or from nuclear medical device waste. Such uranium or plutonium will not be of a quantity or purity to make a "weapons-grade" bomb. Rather, terrorist groups will likely attempt to disperse these radioactive materials using a "dirty bomb" by utilizing an IED as a **Radiological Dispersal Device (RDD)** to spread radioactive materials. It is also possible to simply release radioactive material in an area without an explosive. In any event, these materials will cause contamination, injuries, and possible deaths. Cleanup will be difficult as well due to the radioactivity.

It is possible for a terrorist group to obtain radioactive materials from old medical equipment, or radioactive materials from a rogue government in quantities insufficient to make a nuclear weapon but large enough to make a **dirty bomb**. This is a bomb made of conventional explosives that is used to disperse radioactive materials over a limited area. Such a dirty bomb could lead to radiation contamination of human beings through the lungs or skin, causing death and injury. Also, a dirty bomb would result in extensive property damage and distress due to the long-term cleanup of the radioactive material. The U.S. Department of Homeland Security (DHS) believes that terrorist use of a dirty bomb is a real possibility.

Biological hazards could also be employed by a terrorist – this is the deliberate release of a germ agent into the air, food, or water supplies. For example, a terrorist group could spread microbe-based diseases by deliberately contaminating the food or water supply.[46] This is known as **agroterrorism**. In addition, it is also possible for a terrorist to disperse biological agents in aerosol clouds, which could cause human inhalation exposure. For example, an aerosol containing anthrax could be released either in a public place or through the heating and cooling system of a building.[47]

It can take some time for the disease agent to incubate after exposure. That is why emergency rooms and walk-in clinics have reporting systems in place designed to warn authorities about a suspected attack. The U.S. Department of Agriculture (USDA) and state agriculture departments also monitor and test the food distribution system.

There also exist **weaponized toxic chemicals** – when a terrorist uses poisons or toxins against a civilian population. For example, the deployment of nerve gas, mustard gas, or cyanide could occur. All such weaponized toxic chemicals are very deadly and do not require high dosages to cause death, injury, and mass casualties. They can not only affect those targeted but can also contaminate first responders and medical personnel.

First responders will be the personnel who first notice and report the attack when they respond to reports of mass casualties. The attack scene has to be handled both as a hazmat site and as a crime scene. Access has to be controlled, and the victims must be decontaminated and treated or transported for treatment to a medical facility.[48]

Each type of hazard has certain characteristic causes and effects. Emergency managers and first responders need to know how to identify hazards, how to prepare for them and to respond to them.

If a law enforcement officer or other first responder is exposed to a hazardous agent, both short-term and long-term effects are likely. First responders must complete an **exposure report**. This is true even though many types of hazmat do not cause immediate symptoms. However, if symptoms are noticed later, healthcare officials and the agency's chain of command must be able to identify the precise date of exposure.[49]

Chemical exposure is more difficult to assess than traumatic injuries. In the case of traumatic injuries, triage is based on the initial appearance of a victim. In chemical exposures, the effects are not immediately visible due to delayed effects on the human body.[50]

In a hospital context, victims of a suspected chemical should be held outside until the healthcare personnel dress in personal protective equipment and the emergency department can be prepared. Victims should be screened for contamination before patient entry is allowed into the medical facility.[51]

In a typical chemical hazmat incident, the primary medical tasks involve victim evacuation, decontamination, and the provision of care. If nerve or cyanide agents are involved, unique antidotes must be administered. In a mass casualty critical incident, it may be challenging to acquire sufficient unique antidotes.[52]

Recognize that chemical exposures affect at-risk populations disproportionately. Children and infants are more vulnerable to the effects of hazmat exposure via the skin and lungs than others.[53]

Once a chemical hazmat critical incident is over, workers and residents should not be allowed to return to the area until authorities give clearance. Making this determination involves public health agencies and sometimes environmental teams.[54]

Critical Incident Management of Hazmat Scenes

Law enforcement and fire personnel must work together at hazmat incidents because they require a multidisciplinary response.[55] Most hazmat critical incidents begin with a police response only. Then, EMS personnel are typically contacted for triage, treatment, and removal of affected individuals. After that, the critical incident is usually handled by fire personnel. Once it is determined that hazmat is present, criminal investigation and scene security will be taken over by law enforcement personnel. This is especially true if terrorism is suspected. Utilizing NIMS and ICS protocols with a unified command containing representatives from each agency is necessary and helps to ensure the effective and efficient handling of the critical incident.[56]

At a hazmat scene, law enforcement officers should park patrol vehicles away from the incident. Traffic cones and barrier tape should be utilized to secure the hazmat scene. Flares should never be used. Smoking, eating or drinking should never occur at a hazmat scene. Victims should be isolated until cleared by medical personnel.[57]

Police researchers have noted the tendency of on-scene law enforcement personnel to transfer hazmat scene control to fire units immediately. However, this is not always the correct course of action. For example, if the fire responder is more experienced with hazmat than law enforcement officers on the scene, control should be relinquished. However, law enforcement should maintain control until more experienced fire personnel arrive if the fire personnel on the scene have little hazmat expertise.[58]

Emergency managers and first responders should realize that several levels of hazmat certification exist. Each level of certification is designed to ensure that the individual is competent to perform various duties at a hazmat site.[59] These levels of certification range from Level 1 (First Responder) all the way up to Level 5 (Scene Commander).

Federal regulations from both the Environmental Protection Agency and the Occupational Health and Safety Administration (OSHA) require hazmat responders to (1) use ICS, (2) appoint a Safety Officer, and (3) use the "buddy system" in which every two responders must be supported by two additional "suited and prepared" responders. This is called "two in/two out."[60]

Bioterrorism

Bioterrorism is a potential public health threat. **Bioterrorism** is defined as the use or threatened use of biological organisms and agents as weapons designed to instill fear in the targeted individuals in support of political or social goals.[61] The use of a disease agent as a terrorist weapon to cause mass casualties is bioterrorism.

Biological material used in an act of terrorism can come in a variety of both lethal or nonlethal forms. Such biological material could include pathogens, a common virus or bacteria, or a rare organism.[62] The use of a biological weapon is an example of a WMD.[63]

Bioterrorism is different from other man-made disasters for several reasons. First, bioterrorism can potentially impact a much larger area than other terrorist attacks because the biological agents can result in a delayed surge of a large number of injured victims across a large geographical area. Biological agents can be released in the air or in deliberately contaminated water and food sources. Some biological agents have long incubation periods. For that reason, it may be difficult for healthcare agencies to locate and treat exposed persons quickly. Those infected may transmit the agent to others, resulting in a large disease outbreak away from the site of the terrorist act.[64]

Second, bioterrorism places medical providers in the position of being at the spearhead of the response. Public health and healthcare personnel support first responders and emergency managers. However, in a bioterror attack, most response efforts will be directed at identifying and treating those that have been exposed.[65]

Third, it is possible to successfully intervene in the immediate aftermath of a bioterrorism attack to avert further disease spread. It is also possible to treat those exposed prophylactically to reduce symptoms. This is not true with most other types of attacks or disasters. However, the longer that treatment is delayed, deaths and illness caused by the biological agent increase rapidly due to incubation.[66] These differences from other man-made disasters are the reason that bioterrorism comprises such a difficult critical incident to resolve.[67]

Finally, bioterrorism events (like other acts of terrorism) are both crime scenes and public health incidents. The necessity for law enforcement investigation of such attacks makes bioterrorism different from a naturally occurring disease.[68] Medical and public health professionals have different orientations and frames of reference than law enforcement personnel. For example, law enforcement officers tend to see those attacked as *victims*, and the person who intentionally released the biological agent as a *perpetrator*. But to a health care provider, those attacked are seen as *patients*.[69] In addition, members of the public often react differently to law enforcement personnel than to healthcare workers, especially with regard to sharing healthcare information that may be needed to support a criminal investigation.[70]

Developing protective measures and response and recovery plans to protect at-risk populations from a biological attack requires the emergency management student to understand the **route of infection and chain of transmission** of these agents. The manner in which a biological agent enters the human body depends upon the method of release and the characteristics of the biological agent.[71]

Bioterrorism infection control interventions are designed to break the chain of transmission. Medical professionals look for opportunities after an individual has been exposed to a biological agent to intervene for the purpose of breaking the chain of transmission. This may require medical intervention in several stages. Such intervention can involve vaccinations (to boost immunity and to reduce susceptibility), using personal protective equipment (PPE) to prevent contact, or making efforts to destroy vectors such as rats and mice.[72]

Human beings react differently to exposure. Some individuals display more symptoms than others due to variations in immune systems and the level of exposure to the biological agent.[73] This is why a range of human variations to the exposure can be expected – some will die, others will become sick, and others will display no symptoms.[74]

Potentially, almost all viruses, biological toxins, or bacteria can potentially be weaponized.[75] However, some are more dangerous and toxic than others to at-risk populations. It is for this reason that bioterrorism threats must be categorized so that appropriate planning and response can be initiated.

A **public health assessment of potential biological terrorism agents** was developed in 1999 for this purpose. Both civilian and military health experts devised a typology of biological threats based upon their potential impact as weapons. Both classified and publicly available research were utilized to develop the typology. The typology consists of three categories of pathogens: Category A, Category B, and Category C.[76]

Category A pathogens are the most dangerous to public health and are considered to be the most likely biological agents to be selected by terrorists in a biological attack on at-risk populations. Category A pathogens include **anthrax**, **plague**, **smallpox**, **viral hemorrhagic fevers (like Ebola)**, **botulism**, and **tularemia**. These are associated with the greatest risk of death and injury. It is believed that mass casualties and public panic would also result from the intentional deployment of Category A pathogens. All Category A pathogens can be distributed over a large geographical area. Some can be transmitted easily through contact. For these reasons, aggressive actions must be taken by public health and healthcare organizations to contain the damage.[77]

Category B agents are also dangerous to human health, but they are either not as toxic or as easy to weaponize. Category B pathogens include **ricin**, **Q fever**, **brucellosis**, **glanders**, **typhus**, **viral and equine encephalitis**, **and certain food safety threats**, among others. Medical experts indicate that Category B agents are more easily managed than Category A agents by means of health care monitoring and laboratory testing.[78]

Category C pathogens describe "emerging" emerging infectious diseases and organisms which might become available for use by bioterrorists at some point in the future.[79] These include **hantavirus** and **two types of encephalitis: Hendra and Nipah**.[80]

The concern with bioterrorism in the United States increased substantially following the September-October 2001 anthrax-contaminated letters that killed five people and sickened 17 others.[81]

Prevention, Detection, Response, and Recovery from Bioterrorism

Government public health preparedness efforts at all levels increased significantly following the 9/11 terrorist attacks. Greater efforts were undertaken to plan for and address potential public health emergencies. Infrastructure and methods with which to prepare for a bioterror attack were developed and implemented. Some of these have been used to respond to other public health emergencies.[82]

The first step in preventing bioterrorism lies in laws and regulations designed to prevent the acquisition of biological agents likely to be used in a terrorist attack. A second step requires rapid detection of pathogenic releases that may have been released by bioterrorists. Early identification of unusual disease and outbreaks is also essential. To help achieve these goals, Congress enacted several pieces of legislation.[83]

These laws include the 2002 Public Health Security and Bioterrorism Preparedness and Response Act and the 2005 Pandemic and All-Hazards Preparedness Act (PAHPA). Since 2001, governments in the United States have spent billions of dollars on preparedness activities. A substantial part of this spending has taken the form of new epidemiological surveillance software and new detection and monitoring efforts. One of these monitoring efforts is the **BioWatch Program**, which is overseen by the Countering Weapons of Mass Destruction Office within the U.S. Department of Homeland Security.[84] The BioWatch Program is designed to reduce the impact of bioterrorism should it occur. BioWatch utilizes data from air monitoring, risk assessment, analysis, and notification procedures across more than thirty jurisdictions. BioWatch includes many stakeholders in emergency management, public health, law enforcement, and scientific organizations located around the United States. The ultimate objective of BioWatch is to prepare for, detect, and develop a comprehensive response to bioterrorism should it occur.[85]

Disease surveillance is a vital part of the prevention mission of public health agencies at all levels of American government. Actions such as monitoring mandatory disease reporting by healthcare providers, and ongoing analysis by local, state, and regional public health agencies are important components of surveillance.[86] This information is collected and synthesized by the Centers for Disease Control and Prevention (CDC) in its **BioSense Platform**. The BioSense Platform is the collective work of the CDC, public health agencies, and state and local health departments.[87]

The BioSense Platform is cloud-based and is used to allow the rapid sharing of information between American healthcare providers and public health agencies. Information about disease outbreaks is quickly collected, stored, evaluated, and shared. This allows health officials to quickly exchange information for the purpose of facilitating actions to protect public health in the United States.[88]

It is vital that healthcare providers be trained to recognize disease agents and symptoms from the casualties of bioterrorism events. Their ability to do so as a result of preparedness training is a major factor with which to mitigate the effects of a terrorist attack involving biological agents.[89] To facilitate the recognition, there are ten **Bioterrorism Epidemiological Clues** that have been developed to aid in determining the presence of a bioterrorism attack. Emergency management officials, emergency responders, and the healthcare community must be aware of these clues.

After public health officials have detected a biological threat, both the disease agent and the affected population must be identified rapidly. Many severe illnesses that can result from an act of bioterrorism do not have immediate effects due to their incubation period. For that reason, the possibility of providing prophylactic treatment to exposed individuals exists. Even lethal pathogens can often be stopped with immediate treatment postexposure. This necessitates immediate decisions regarding the best measures to utilize with which to provide an immediate response.[90]

In terms of recovery, government officials and members of the public will likely engage in contentious debates regarding decontamination. It must be noted that most pathogenic organisms can be effectively cleaned up. Anthrax is an exception.[91] However, other aspects of recovery from a bioterrorism attack will be more problematic. Getting the local economy operational may be delayed if fear persists. Individuals may be afraid to return to school and work. It is also possible that the infrastructure could have been damaged by contamination. Medical resources may have been depleted. Survivors of the biological attack may also be ostracized by the community out of fear. Survivals may also be disabled from their exposure. Numerous deaths will have occurred. Stress-related illnesses may be pervasive.[92] For all of these reasons, the potential for bioterrorism is a complex public health issue. A strong public health infrastructure, an effective healthcare system, and well-prepared supporting disciplines are necessary for effective response and recovery.[93]

Explosions and Bombings

Bombings and explosions and the effect of these events on the population are discussed in this section. Bombs and intentionally caused explosions are examples of Weapons of Mass Destruction (WMDs). Industrial accidents are unintentional, but can also lead to explosions with substantial consequences. As is the case with other WMD situations, the bombing site is both a mass casualty location and a crime scene. Personnel working bomb scenes should be aware that there are significant differences between a bomb scene and other critical incident sites. Management of the scene requires different steps.[94]

Keep in mind that terrorism is intended to cause catastrophic damage to lives and property. Terrorists also seek to cause public stress, panic, and chaos. Terrorists also wish to force government agencies and first responders to use up their resources.[95] Terrorists have a wide range of potential methods from which to choose. One is **conventional explosives and secondary devices**. These are easy to obtain and to use. Such explosives are also called **Improvised Explosive Devices (IEDs)**.[96]

There are different types of IEDs. These include pipe bombs, suitcase, briefcase, and backpack bombs. In addition, there are different types of vehicle-based IEDs.

The types and severity of injuries to human beings resulting from a blast depends in large measure upon whether the explosive substance was a **high-order explosive (HE)** or a **low-order explosive (LE)**. The former is more powerful and lead to a greater variety and severity of injury. HEs generate supersonic shock waves accompanied by overpressure that moves thousands of feet per second.[97] **Overpressure** refers to the shock wave resulting from the explosion. Examples of HEs include **TNT**, **nitroglycerin, C4, and Semtex**. LEs are more primitive and less powerful. LEs generate little overpressure along with a subsonic shock wave. LE materials include **petroleum products such as Molotov cocktails and black powder-based devices such as pressure cooker bombs or pipe bombs**.[98]

Blast injuries from bombs are usually grouped into four categories. These categories include **primary**, **secondary**, **tertiary**, and **miscellaneous**. All are based on injuries.[99] Sometimes the term **quaternary** is used in place of "miscellaneous" injuries. HEs can cause all four types of injuries, while LEs typically cause secondary, tertiary, and miscellaneous injuries.

The most serious health effect of a HE is blast damage to the lungs, which is the primary cause of death. For LEs, penetrating injuries and blunt trauma injuries are the most serious health effects leading to injury and death.[100] With both HEs and LEs, recognize that explosions involve many variables. All of these variables influence death and injury. The amount and type of explosive, the specific kind of device used, and the victim's distance from the explosion all affect morbidity and mortality. In addition, death and injuries are also affected by the presence or absence of walls or other barriers between the victim and the explosion and whether the explosion occurs outside or inside a building.[101]

Physical security is at the vanguard of protection from bombings and explosions. An important part of risk reduction is to assess security weaknesses. Locations open to the public where improvised explosive devices can be hidden must be located and secured.[102] In addition, physical security is also analyzed in terms of window laminates, parking barriers around buildings, and other "hardening" of potential bombing targets. Part of this involves explosives threat detection, as in x-ray machines and body scanners at airports and sensitive government buildings.

Planning for bombings and explosions requires physical security and situational awareness. Physical security planning must be regularly reviewed and updated. Government agencies should prepare a **bomb incident plan**. A bomb incident plan contains detailed procedures to be followed in the event of a bomb threat or explosion.[103]

Another important part of preparedness involves individual awareness of employees and persons in or near potential bombing targets. Bomb drills should be conducted. If a bomb threat is received and evacuation is required, employees should be trained to exit immediately with personal items such as purses. This will help to reduce the number of items that must be searched by bomb technicians looking for IEDs. Employees should be instructed to use stairs rather than elevators. Also, employees should be told in advance of a meeting place outside the building to congregate for a head count.[104]

In addition to terrorist bombings, industrial explosions can also have catastrophic effects. Although such explosions are almost always accidental in nature, substantial death, injury, and property damage can still occur. Preparing for an industrial explosion is similar to preparing for bombings in many respects. A physical security threat assessment should be conducted along with employee training. Drills and exercises help to reinforce the response actions of employees. Local healthcare and public health organizations should also prepare for the possibility of an industrial explosion.[105]

Law enforcement and first responder personnel should approach a suspected bombing or industrial explosion scene from the perspective of risk. Realize that the bomb or explosion may not be the only one involved in the critical incident: other explosions may occur either intentionally or accidentally. A bomber might trigger a secondary device to cause harm to first responders. It is also possible that residual explosive material remains at the critical incident scene.[106]

First responder and medical personnel should establish a triage for casualties upwind from the critical incident site in order to reduce exposure to respiratory hazards caused by the explosion. If terrorism is suspected, hazards could include chemical, biological, or radiological substances spread by the explosive device. In addition, numerous hazardous substances can be released from buildings by an explosion. These substances can include lead, fiberglass, silica, and chemicals.[107]

Even after the injured are treated, it is important for public health agencies to maintain long-term contact with the survivors to measure the health impact over time. If hazardous materials were released, public health agencies should track survivors long-term to assess their health effects caused by the critical incident. The public health agency can use its database registry to contact survivors about possible new medical treatments.[108] In most states, public health agencies possess the legal authority to close buildings and other areas for the purpose of protecting public safety and health.[109] The appropriate medical responses for most hazmat incidents focus on the diagnosis and decontamination of exposed individuals.[110]

Nuclear and Radiological Disasters

Law enforcement personnel, emergency managers, and other first responders should realize that nuclear power plant accidents, Radiological Dispersion Devices (RDDs) or "dirty bombs," hidden radiological devices, and nuclear attack by a rogue nation or terrorist group are all real possibilities. This section looks at nuclear disasters and radiological disasters in terms of the threats they pose to American society. The dangers posed by a potential radiological or nuclear disaster are significant.[111]

There is a distinction between *radiological events* and *nuclear events.* A **nuclear event** is characterized by a nuclear detonation, such as the explosion of a nuclear bomb.[112] On the other hand, a **radiological event** does not involve a nuclear explosion or a fission reaction. Radiological events most commonly involve hazmat accidents involving the transport of radiological materials or nuclear facility accidents.[113] In addition, radiological events can describe a "dirty bomb" or **Radiological Dispersal Device (RDD)**, in which terrorists spread radioactive material by means of a conventional explosion. Another example of a radiological event could be where a terrorist could hide radioactive material in a place that would expose an unknowing population to danger.[114]

Two types of radiation exposure can occur: irradiation and contamination.[115] **Irradiation** involves the situation in which gamma or x-ray radioactive energy passes through the human body. Irradiation results in immediate cellular damage accompanied by rapid illness. Higher does result in greater illness. Human beings exposed to irradiation can have damaged DNA along with cancer and birth defects.[116] **Contamination** occurs when a person or object has direct contact with radioactive materials. The inhalation, ingestion, or other contact with radioactive materials results in the irradiation of cells as contamination spreads through the body.[117] Of the two, irradiation is the more dangerous. Law enforcement and other first responder personnel are not harmed by having contact with irradiated victims. However, those touching victims contaminated by radiological materials can themselves become contaminated.[118]

There are many serious human health effects associated with radiological and nuclear exposure, including **ARS (Acute Radiation Syndrome)**, which may manifest itself in bone marrow syndrome, gastrointestinal syndrome, and cardiovascular/central nervous system syndrome. More generally, the overall health effect of radiation exposure is called *early fatalities, prodromal effects*, and *delayed effects.* **Early fatalities** refer to deaths that occur during the first days or weeks following exposure. **Prodromal effects** involve early-onset serious health effects. **Delayed effects** specifically refer to cancers that develop over time following exposure.[119] At-risk populations are particularly susceptible to the effects of radiation. Infants, children, the elderly, and individuals with compromised immune systems are most likely to experience both morbidity and mortality in these situations.[120]

Time, distance, and shielding are the best known protective actions for radiological exposure. When possible, evacuation of the affected population reduces the exposure time to radioactive materials. Evacuation also increases the distance from this hazard. Shielding requires surrounding the human body with dense materials such as lead or concrete. The EPA has published **Protective Action Guidelines (PAGs)**, which delineate specific criteria to be used in radiological events for the purpose of initiating protective action with which to protect persons exposed to radiological emergencies.[121] There are PAGs for first responders. Separate PAGs exist for the general public.

Prevention, Response, and Recovery: Nuclear and Radiological Disasters

Control over the possession of radiological material is the primary prevention measure for accidental and intentional nuclear or radiological incidents.[122] This means monitoring the care, custody, and control over nuclear weapons possessed by nation-states in addition to radioactive raw materials and medical/industrial sites that utilize such materials. This is easier to achieve in theory than in reality. Some nations have better controls that others. We must recognize that a rogue nation-state might make radiological materials available to terrorists, or that terrorists might illicitly obtain such materials from medical or industrial sites. Also, nuclear power plants and nuclear medicine facilities have materials that can either escape confinement or be stolen by terrorists.

It is for this reason that the physical security and controls over radiological material is essential. There has been an increased effort by nation-states to enhance security measures in this regard. In addition, nation-states have worked to improve their ability to detect the presence of radiological materials in seaports.[123] For example, **Radiation Portal Monitors (RPMs)** are used at seaports and international borders. Within the United States,

stand-off detectors are employed. These detectors have been deployed at large gatherings such as major sporting events and major political events to detect radioactive materials.[124] At the individual level, smartphone applications are now available to detect radiation.[125]

In terms of response to a nuclear or radiological disaster, first responders, public health personnel, and medical personnel each have a role to play. The first responders will take immediate action depending on the scenario. Many carry equipment to assess the severity of the situation, which will be relayed to public health and medical personnel for further action.

The primary tasks of public health agencies following a nuclear or radiological incident involve the assessment of ongoing public health risks, the development of recommendations to maintain public health protections, and managing the medical needs of victims.[126] International nuclear and radiological emergency response is facilitated by the interaction between the World Health Organization (WHO) and the International Atomic Energy Agency (IAEA).[127]

According to the CDC, the appropriate medical preparation for radiological critical incidents involves five areas: (1) notification and communication, (2) triage, (3) patient management, (4) healthcare worker protection, and (5) community planning.[128] It may be necessary to request state and federal aid, including deployment of medical countermeasures from the SNS (Strategic National Stockpile). These are complex processes that also involve decontamination, specimen management, and other interventions.

With regard to recovery from a nuclear or radiological incident, it is possible that the long-term issues could be worse than the short-term impact. This is due to contamination. The affected areas may need to be abandoned for many years. If this involves a major city, significant human and economic effects could persist for decades.[129] The cleanup could take years and could cost billions of dollars, as was the case with the 1986 Chernobyl nuclear reactor incident. The health effects, both immediate and latent, could cost incalculable amounts in both money and human suffering.

Agroterrorism

An often overlooked aspect of terrorism is the specter of attacks on our nation's food supply. Understanding the potential for agroterrorism is important to both homeland security and emergency management.[130] **Agroterrorism** is a sub-type of terrorism defined as the intentional introduction of a plant or animal disease for the express purpose of generating panic, undermining regime stability, and causing economic losses.[131] The potential for a terrorist attack on the food supply and distribution channels is a very real threat that must be analyzed in the context of mitigation and preparedness in law enforcement, agriculture, and emergency management. In addition to health concerns from contaminated food, substantial economic losses and widespread psychological damage makes the food supply a potential terrorist target.

Because agroterrorism may or may not cause human deaths, be quickly detected by authorities, or possess the visceral impact of more conventional terrorist attacks, the food supply will not generally be a terrorist's first choice of targets. However, certain kinds of agroterrorism could be achieved with relative ease and could also have significant economic and political impacts.[132] Although no foreign terrorist groups have made known attacks on the food supply in the United States, neither government agencies nor private food suppliers have ignored the possibility of such an attack.[133]

Agriculture (growing and raising food, fiber, and livestock) and its associated industries (processors, grocers, shippers, restaurants) comprise 11% of the Gross Domestic Product of the economy of the United States. Approximately 16% of the nation's workforce is comprised of these industries. In recent years, the sales of farm products have exceeded $200 billion. Farming is concentrated primarily in the Midwest and California. Food crops and livestock each comprise approximately half of the gross sales in the United States.[134]

In economic terms, gross farm assets are approximately $1.45 trillion in the United States. The value of land comprises eighty percent of those assets. More than 900 million acres of farmland exist in the United States.[135] Because the United States exports more than $53 billion worth of agricultural products (39% of the world's supply of corn, 38% of the world's supply of soybeans, and 8% of the world's supply of wheat), severe economic costs would be incurred in the event of an agroterrorism disruption to food supplies.[136]

The vast majority of food production (about 75%) occurs on less than seven percent of farms in the United States. Highly mechanized and efficient farming produces an enormous amount of food at relatively low cost.[137] In terms of animals raised for food, poultry and livestock are centered in well-known regions of the nation. In recent years, animal inventory comprised as many as 95 million cattle and 60 million pigs. Poultry sales are approximately 8.5 million birds annually.[138] Thus, the economic losses from an agroterrorist attack could be significant.[139] These losses would include the following:

- Direct economic losses within the United States from damaged or diseased crops and animals, including lost sales, the cost of destroying diseased or damaged products, and the cost of containment, including diagnostics (laboratory and veterinary), drugs, and pesticides.

- Economic losses from exports due to the fact that foreign countries would cease purchasing American farm products. Even the rumor of agroterrorism and the presence of certain diseases or insects in a nation can result in the cesation of all exports of a given commodity, which could last for an extended period.[140]
- Government costs from eradication, containment, subsidies, and crop insurance (and possibly disease control).
- Economic "ripple" or "multiplier" effects such as food processors, restaurants, grocers, food transporters, and farm suppliers that would be harmed from an agroterrorist event.[141]

Even a relatively small-scale agroterrorism event could affect producers whose crops and animals were not directly impacted due to media coverage, which would result in escalating the event to the national scale. This would likely occur even if the pathogen was successfully eradicated or limited to a small geographical area.[142]

The agricultural commodities most vulnerable to agroterrorism attack include fruits, vegetables, and meats. These commodities do not at present receive federal crop subsidies. For this reason, Congress would have to enact special disaster assistance legislation to provide financial assistance to producers in the aftermath of an agroterrorism attack to compensate them for losses.[143] However, economic costs are only one consequence of an agroterrorism attack. Such an attack could also include both human deaths and illnesses and loss of confidence in government. If the disease is transmissible to humans (zoonotic), a public health crisis could ensue. Even in the absence of human casualties, psychological and economic consequences would still ensue.[144]

From the perspective of mitigation and prevention, what can be done to stop an agroterrorism attack? To answer this question, one must first realize that some of the unique characteristics of agriculture present special challenges regarding managing the agroterrorism threat.[145] First, scientists have noted that a wider range and variety of lethal and contagious biological agents are more effective against animals and plants than is the case for human beings.[146] Since most of these biological agents are not harmful to human beings, this makes it relatively easy for terrorists to acquire and deploy these agents.

Second, there is very little security with regard to agriculture in the United States, making it easy to launch an agroterrorism attack. This is true because agricultural production is widely dispersed across large expanses of geographically dispersed land. This makes it challenging to secure from intruders in general and agroterrorists in particular.[147] In addition, poultry, cattle, and pigs are often concentrated in relatively confined locations. Such concentration is necessary for efficient slaughter, processing, and distribution of the animals. This concentration makes it easier for a potential agroterrorist to efficiently harm a large number of animals.[148] If a disease common to foreign countries is deliberately introduced into American agriculture, critical time may be lost as veterinarians and scientists scramble to determine the nature of the pathogen.

Finally, we must recognize that pathogens placed inside agricultural products are often commingled in the processing, transportation, and distribution systems. This fact works against natural barriers that would be present in a less developed society that could slow the spread of diseases or contaminants.[149]

Now that some of the characteristics of agriculture that pose unique security problems from the perspective of threat management have been examined, it is now necessary to turn to a brief history of agricultural bioweapons to get a better idea of what mitigation and prevention strategies can be employed against bioterrorism. From an historical perspective, attacks against the food supplies of enemies are not new. Both nation-states and clandestine groups have conducted attacks against food supplies throughout history. It is known that at least nine nations had bioweapons programs during the past one hundred years.[150]

However, only a few attacks against agricultural or food targets can be rightfully called agroterrorism.[151] Examples include a Kenyan insurgent group's 1952 killing of a herd of cattle using a plant toxin, and the 1984 salad bar contamination of several Oregon restaurants by a cult. On the other hand, several governments (as state actors) have deployed chemical weapons against agricultural targets.[152]

Despite the potential for agroterrorism against the United States, agriculture has generally received little attention in counterterrorism strategies and homeland security. Fortunately, congressional hearings and legislation, coupled with presidential actions enacted subsequent to the September 11 attacks have demonstrated federal recognition of agroterrorism threats.

In the United States, there has been some confusion regarding which federal agency should have primary authority and responsibility for protecting the nation's food supply. Should the Food and Drug Administration (FDA), an independent regulatory agency, or the Department of Health and Human Services (HHS), a cabinet department, have this task? Congress answered this in favor of the FDA with the passage of the **Public Health Security and Bioterrorism Response Act** of 2002. Among other things, this law instructed the Food and Drug Administration to register food processors, provide prior notice of food imports into the United States and to allow for administrative detention of food imports, and imposed record keeping requirements for food supplies.[153]

First, the 2002 law requires that the FDA implement a registration system for all facilities that processes, packs, or manufactures food. This FDA registry comprises a comprehensive list of food processers and distributors that are subject to FDA authority and will enhance the agency's capability to trace contaminated food.[154] An obvious security precaution was contained it the law as well: The required registration documents are not subject to FIOA (Freedom of Information Act) disclosure for security purposes.[155] Second, the law stipulates that food importers must provide advance notice to the FDA before reaching U.S. borders. Electronic advanced notice must be provided to the FDA within a specified period: two hours by road, four hours by rail or air, and eight hours by ship. The FDA utilizes this prior notice to determine whether or not to inspect a given shipment.[156]

The Homeland Security Act of 2002, which set up the Department of Homeland Security, also had an impact on food security in the United States. Specifically, the law transferred part of the **Animal and Plant Health Inspection Service (APHIS)** from the U.S. Department of Agriculture (USDA) to the U.S. Department of Homeland Security's Bureau of Customs and Border Security.[157] Also in 2002, APHIS issued regulations under its authority to help reduce the threat that certain toxins and biological agents might be used in acts of terrorism. APHIS identified "select agents" on its list that possess the potential to pose a severe threat to food products or agricultural production. The plant and animal "select agents" regulations delineate the legal requirements for the possession and use of the named pathogens.[158] Under the 2002 laws, both the FDA and Homeland Security's CBP's (Customs and Border Protection) APHIS subunit integrated their information systems. In addition, the two agencies allow CBP officers to inspect imported foods at ports of entry that do not staff FDA inspectors.[159]

APHIS maintains a subdivision called **Agricultural Quarantine Inspection (AQI)**. Now that both APHIS and its AQI subdivision are under CBP, personnel from the latter agency presently inspect international ships, trucks, containers, and rail cars at the U.S. border. CBP employees also inspect the baggage of passengers at U.S. borders for animal and plant products that have the potential to contain disease organisms or insects. They also inspect packages and mail arriving in the United States from foreign countries.[160] These actions stemmed from congressional action to deal with the safety of the nation's food supply. But there were also *executive* (presidential) actions taken to achieve the same purpose. These stem from *homeland security planning*, two *Homeland Security Presidential Directives*, and the utilization of federal bureaucracies.

Shortly after the 9/11 attacks, the USDA established a Homeland Security Staff for the purpose of developing a plan to coordinate agroterrorism preparedness plans inside the agency. These USDA initiatives are focused upon (1) food supply and agricultural production, (2) USDA facilities, and (3) USDA staff and emergency preparedness.[161] In addition, two Homeland

Security Presidential Directives (HSPDs) (one in 2003 and one in 2004) have addressed agroterrorism. Recall that HSPDs are presidential executive orders that specifically deal with homeland security. HSPD-7 and HSPD-9 both deal with aspects of agroterrorism.

Homeland Security Presidential Directive 7 was entitled "Critical Infrastructure Identification, Prioritization, and Protection" and issued in December 2003. HSPD-7 added agriculture to the Critical Infrastructure (CI) list of the federal government. Federal agencies were instructed to create plans to counter potential terrorist threats to American agriculture among other Critical Infrastructure components.[162] One month later, Former President George W. Bush issued **HSPD-9**, "Defense of United States Agriculture and Food." HSPD 9 goes much further than HSPD-7 because the former directive set up a specific national policy designed to protect the American food and agriculture systems from terrorist attacks.[163] Specifically, HSPD-9 orders integration and coordination of efforts of various federal agencies with regard to agroterrorism, with the ultimate goals of (a) protecting the food supply and (b) recovery from an agroterrorist attack.

HSPD-9 requires that the Secretaries of the U.S. Department of Homeland Security (DHS), the U.S. Department of Agriculture (USDA), the U.S. Department of Health and Human Services (HHS), the Administrator of the Environmental Protection Agency (EPA), the Attorney General, and the Director of Central Intelligence (CIA) engage in actions to protect against, prepare for, respond to, and recover from a terrorist attack on the nation's food supplies in a coordinated manner.[164] In order to implement these goals, HSPD-9 ordered executive branch agencies to develop warning systems with which to monitor animal and plant diseases, food quality, and public health. Food commodity and animal tracking systems are required by HSPD-9 to be included along with integrating intelligence information. HSPD-9 stipulated that vulnerability assessments be conducted across the agricultural sector in order to prioritize mitigation strategies regarding agricultural products.[165] In addition, HSPD-9 directed even more specific actions. It was mandated that the National Veterinary Stockpile (NVS) of vaccine, therapeutic, and antiviral products be developed and stored for deployment where needed within 24 hours of an agroterrorist attack. It was also mandated that a National Plant Disease Recovery System (NPDRS) be established to develop new varieties of crops designed to be disease and pest-resistant within one growing season of an agroterrorist attack for the purpose of resuming the production of crops.[166]

Beyond these two presidential decision directives, there are additional executive actions available with which to combat agroterrorism. For example, the Secretary of Agriculture has the authority to prevent food items containing disease from entering the United States.[167] This delegated authority includes the power to stop imports and exports of diseased or contaminated plant or animal products. Further, the Secretary possesses the authority to seize, eradicate, or quarantine infected plant or animal products to prevent the spread of disease.[168]

Another executive action available in this area lies within the agricultural laboratory and diagnostic infrastructure contained within certain federal agencies.[169] For example, the USDA funds the National Plant Diagnostic Network and the National Animal Health Laboratory Network in collaboration with 19 universities across the United States. This collaborative infrastructure is maintained in order to improve the detection of diseases in food products from either natural or deliberate sources.[170]

In addition to the National Plant Diagnostic Network and the National Animal Health Laboratory, the UDSA also maintains other research facilities, including the Agricultural Research Service (ARS), Plum Island Animal Disease Center, the National Animal Disease Center, and the Southeast Poultry Research Laboratory.

Agroterrorism: Mitigation, Preparation, Response, and Recovery

Scientists have concluded that approximately twenty animal and plant pathogens are the most likely to be utilized by agroterrorists. These pathogens represent the greatest potential for economic disruption of the food supply. It should be kept in mind as well that poultry and livestock are at greater risk of bioterrorism than crops.[171] An additional concern stems from the fact that infected livestock may act as vectors to facilitate the continued spread of the disease organism. This is especially true when live animals are transported across jurisdictions. In addition, certain animal pathogens may be more attractive to terrorists because they are transmissible to human beings (zoonotic). Plant pathogens tend to be less dangerous and are more routine.[172]

From an emergency management perspective, plant pathogens are also more difficult to introduce than are animal pathogens. For example, many plant pathogens must have access to specific environmental conditions such as specific temperature or humidity to cause damage or to spread. In addition, most plant pathogens will not achieve the rapid and widespread destruction sought by most terrorists.[173]

Thus, agroterrorists may choose either *animal pathogens* or *plant pathogens.* Animal pathogens will be discussed first. American classifications of animal pathogens are based on the **World Organization for Animal Health** (formerly known as *Office International des Epizooties* or **OIE**), which is a French-based organization consisting of nation-state members. The goal of OIE is to prevent the spread of animal-based diseases. The 2004 *OIE Single Disease List* includes contagious and transmissible animal diseases that possess the potential for rapid spread and that would have serious social, economic, or public health consequences if they were to spread. Such animal diseases would also exert a substantial detriment to international trade in the event of widespread transmission.[174]

Based to a large degree on the *OIE Single Disease List*, the federal government has developed and today maintains the **Federal Select Agent Program**, which is the official list of animal pathogens that the U.S. government considers to be of greatest concern for agroterrorism.[175] The Federal Select Agent list is prepared jointly by the Center for Disease Control (CDC) and the USDA's APHIS. It is comprised of an APHIS-only list that applies only to animals and an additional list of disease agents selected both by APHIS and CDC that applies to both animals and humans.[176]

The regulations establishing the "select agent" list delineate the legal requirements for the possession and use of named biological agents or toxins for animals. The "select agent" list is designed to facilitate safe handling and to prevent them from being used by agroterrorists. APHIS and CDC determined that the biological agents and toxins on the "select list" may pose a severe threat to food products or agricultural production if improperly handled.[177] The Federal Select Agent list overlaps the *OIE Single Disease List* to a considerable degree.

In terms of plant pathogens, the CDC and APHIS also work in tandem to maintain and publish the federal government's current official list of potential plant pathogens.[178] Several agents cause plant diseases. These include certain bacteria, fungi, and viruses that can have the potential to pose a severe threat to several vital food crops, including rice, soybeans, potatoes, corn, stone fruits such as peaches and cherries, and citrus fruits such as oranges and grapefruits. These plant pathogens are of interest to agroterrorists because the listed organisms could cause widespread crop losses and economic damage.[179]

We must realize that the original goal of the U.S. animal and plant safeguarding system was to mitigate unintentional and accidental food contamination. However, this is not sufficient to defend the food supply from a deliberate and focused attack by an agroterrorist. For that reason, the present system has been undergoing upgrading since 9/11 to address the terrorist threat to the U.S. food supply.[180] To counter the threat posed by agroterrorism, the most appropriate strategy is a combination of (a) deterrence and prevention, (b) detection and response, and (c) recovery and management. These will be discussed in turn.

First is **deterrence and prevention**. This means taking steps to stop an agroterrorist attack before it begins. Some of these deterrence and prevention measures involving foreign insects and diseases involve international standards and treaties, inspection by U.S. officials at ports-of-entry, quarantine, treatment, and tracking of animal and plant products after they have entered the United States.[181]

To facilitate these things, American intelligence services monitor agroterrorists in terms of the capabilities and intentions of foreign terrorist groups. Various federal and state agencies engage in food inspection, monitoring, and quarantine. However, this may not always be enough, because every stage in food production is a potential attack point for agroterrorists.[182] For this reason, an additional component of deterrence and prevention that should be encouraged is **biosecurity**, which deals with farm practices designed to make it more difficult to engage in an agroterrorist attack. This includes enclosures designed to limit entry by unauthorized individuals. In addition, engaging in the systematic inspection, cleaning and disinfection of individuals, supplies, and vehicles entering farms are responsible preventative actions.[183]

Second is **detection and response**. These refer to taking steps to identify an agroterrorism attack as soon as possible and then to immediately take action. We must realize that an agroterrorist attack on plants or animals may take time to be noticed.[184] There is an incubation time for pathogens. For this reason, suitable responses must be developed based on the likely targets and pathogens that an agroterrorist might select.[185]

Farm and food groups have banded together to form the **Food and Agriculture Information Sharing and Analysis Center (ISAC)** to assist each other with detection and response. ISAC information is also shared with the Department of Homeland Security. APHIS has created and published the *Emergency Programs Manual*, which outlines federal response procedures to a reported agroterrorism attack.[186] The most expensive response involves isolating and eradicating an epidemic caused by an agroterrorist attack.[187]

Third is **recovery and management**. This is the process through which things "get back to normal." This involves resuming the planting and harvesting of crops and the breeding and slaughter of animals in the affected areas. This may also involve different breeds or varieties of plants and animals and rebuilding confidence in domestic food supplies.[188]

Active Shooter Situations

This section examines emergency responder and emergency management mitigation, preparedness, and response to an "active shooter" incident. Unfortunately, such "active shooter" incidents are becoming increasingly common in the United States. Emergency management and first responder agencies have been forced to devote increasing amounts of time and resources to mitigation and prevention activities relating to active shooter situations. Active shooter agencies are high-consequence violent events.[189]

The U.S. Department of Homeland Security (DHS) defines **active shooter** as an individual actively engaged in killing or attempting to kill human beings in a populated or confined and populated area with firearms. In most cases, the active shooter does not display a particular pattern or method in his or her selection of victims.[190]

There are numerous examples of active shooter incidents that receive regular media coverage in the United States. For example, on October 1, 2017, a lone gunman shot 615 people, killing 58 in Las Vegas, Nevada. In 2016, 49 people were killed in a nightclub in Orlando, Florida by another lone gunman. In 2012, 20 children and 6 adults were killed in a Connecticut elementary school. In 2007, 32 students were killed by a lone gunman at Virginia Tech University. In 1991, 23 people were killed by a lone gunman at a Luby's Cafeteria in Kileen, Texas.[191] There are also documented cases of disgruntled employees returning to their workplaces and engaging in an active shooter incident against specific targets.

According to an analysis of 280 active shooter cases over a forty-three-year period, it was disclosed that more than 98% of incidents involved a lone gunman, and that both strangers and acquaintances were targeted for killings. In terms of the relationship between the perpetrator and the victims, the plurality of active shooter events was work-based, while the second largest category was academic or "school-based." The third category at 22% was "random" or "none." In terms of location, approximately 49% of active shooter events occurred in office buildings/commercial buildings. Approximately 29% occurred in schools.[192]

We must realize that most analyses and discussions regarding active shooter situations focus almost extensively on the actual law enforcement response.[193] This is true because active shooter incidents require an immediate action deployment of a trained and armed law enforcement officer. The objective of this immediate action deployment is to stop the killing as quickly as possible. In most active shooter scenarios, entry at the critical incident scene is made by the first two to five police officers that arrive. Research has demonstrated that most active shooter situations are operationally resolved within ten to fifteen minutes.[194]

From an emergency management perspective, we need to examine *pre-attack* and *attack response* emergency management activities, in addition to *personal actions when confronting an active shooter.* First, we will examine **pre-attack emergency management activities**, which include *coordination of emergency alerting systems, preparedness planning, and drills and exercises.* These are the areas that increase the effectiveness of emergency management efforts before an actual active shooter incident occurs.[195]

The first pre-attack emergency management activity involves the **coordination of emergency alerting systems**. The term describes the variety emergency messaging systems available to first responders, community leaders, emergency managers, and members of the public that enable the rapid broadcast of emergency notification and alerts.[196] Most universities and large employers have an EAS (Emergency Alert System) that sends out warnings via computer and smartphone about impending danger, for example. An EAS can also utilize sirens, horns, and public address voice alerts. An EAS can be employed for an active shooter incident.

An EAS serves several purposes: (a) to warn those present at the facility that an active shooter event is occurring, (b) to warn those not in the area to stay away, and (c) to indicate where to go for more detailed information.[197] In an active shooter situation, the decision about whether individuals should "lock down" and "stay put" or evacuate must be based upon the location of the shooter at the time and the nearest evacuation route.[198]

Four questions need to be asked in order to assess the functionality of an EAS: (1) How long does it take for an emergency message to be broadcast and received? (2) Who in the organization has the authority to send an emergency message through the EAS? (3) Who is the audience of the emergency message? (4) What specific message(s) will be sent? General or specific warnings?[199] These questions must be answered prior to implementation.

Preparedness training is the second aspect of pre-attack emergency management activity. A primary duty of an emergency manager lies in his or her responsibility to coordinate the jurisdiction's organization's emergency preparedness planning training. This planning should include and encompass preparedness training for an active shooter attack. All employees should be educated about the active shooter threat in addition to the actions that they should take should they be confronted an active shooter.[200] In this regard, preparedness training should include (a) the EAS, (b) procedures to lock down or evacuate a facility, (c) indicators of potential violence, (d) emergency response guidance from local law enforcement, and (e) assurance that the training is consistent with updated active shooter response procedures.[201]

The third pre-attack emergency management activity involves the **coordination of drills and exercises** to validate preparedness and assess procedures. Both the New York City Police Department (NYPD) and DHS have suggested preparedness and training protocols for active shooter incidents. These include (1) conducting a security assessment to determine the facility's vulnerability to an active shooter attack, (2) identifying evacuation routes and conducting evacuation drills, (3) designating shelter locations with solid walls, doors, locks, and minimum window exposure, (4) establishing a central building security location, and (5) training workers to recognize the sound of gunshots and to react quickly to those sounds.[202] Another suggestion is to incorporate active shooter training as part of regular *workplace violence* training. This is true not only for the workplace, but is also true for schools, colleges, and universities.[203]

Next, we move to **attack response** emergency management activities. In other words, what will be the reaction of the emergency manager and the emergency management agency to the active shooter incident? If an active shooter critical incident occurs, the role of the emergency manager will vary based on how long the attack lasted, the number of dead and injured, and the location of the mass shooting incident.[204]

Should the EOC (Emergency Operations Center) be activated during a mass shooting incident? This depends on whether the active shooter has been incapacitated by first responders and the number of casualties from that incident.[205] It should be recognized that a mass casualty mass shooter event may require that the recovery phase last many days or even weeks. The psychological impact of the attack on the responders, survivors, and friends and families of survivors and responders may be substantial. Professional counseling is necessary. It is sometimes necessary to keep the EOC open at a minimum staffing level to support recovery phase activities.[206]

At the very end of the active shooter incident, it is likely that the emergency manager will be tasked with seeing to it that a comprehensive After-Action Review (AAR) for the incident is prepared. The AAR should be written a fair amount of time following the date on which the active shooter attack occurred. This allows time for the recovery phase to continue and to enable first responder organizations and agencies involved in the active shooter incent to conduct their "hot wash" assessments. The AAR requires extensive documentation during response and recovery phases.[207]

Finally, as part of active shooter training to the general public, it bears repeating to teach others to know and follow the **personal actions when confronting an active shooter** recommended by DHS. These are summarized by *run*, *hide*, and *fight*. First, try to escape. If this is not possible, try to hide under a desk or go to a room (ideally without windows) that can be locked. Finally, if all else fails and an active shooter is directly in front of you, fight by attempting to take the active shooter down.[208] Research has demonstrated that the presence of armed security at an active shooter scene substantially increases the likelihood of victim survival.[209]

Special Events

Special events can also result in man-made disasters. **Special events** encompass things like concerts, sports games, visiting dignitaries, holiday celebrations (like the 4th of July), and high-profile meetings and conferences. Special event planning presents unique challenges for law enforcement and emergency management officials.[210] In particular, law enforcement officials have noted that special events result in added burdens to the resources of a jurisdiction over and above normal expectations. Planning in advance for special events reduces the stress and unanticipated issues when it comes time to prepare for and respond to the event when it occurs. Law enforcement agencies and emergency managers should work together in advance to create a secure venue for special events.[211]

Special events are of particular importance for emergency managers and law enforcement professionals.[212] This is true because special events contain the very real potential for a mass-casualty event that could be caused by floods, fires, tornadoes, riots, mass shootings, or terrorism. In particular, the large number of people present at a special event in a venue along with representative of the media provides a target-rich environment for violent terrorist activities.[213]

In addition to the potential for natural or man-made disasters to cause mass casualties at special events, the characteristics the event itself coupled with predictable human behavior at such events also increase danger to those in attendance. This is true because many venues have limited access or egress. This can create compressed crowds entering and exiting the venue. This situation can possibly lead to a significant number of individual injuries from trampling as people attempt a mass exodus in the event that an incident occurs at the venue.[214] An event can be designated as a special event based upon the significance of the event for a community (like a major concert), what the event represents (a holiday like Christmas), or a dignitary in attendance.[215] College of professional games, annual festivals, and visits by celebrities can all be called "special events."[216]

This section is oriented towards *local* special events, not towards national-level special events. In other words, this section is not about handling **National Security Special Events (NSSEs)**, which are major incidents of national significance that are accompanied by large crowds, significant media attention, and political importance. NSSEs are monitored by national security and counterterrorism experts.[217] Such events include national political conventions (Republican National Convention), the Super Bowl, and the Academy Awards. Thus, if an event is classified as an NSSE, it will be managed by highly visible federal agencies including the Secret Service, Federal Bureau of Investigation (FBI), and Federal Emergency Management Agency (FEMA).[218] Due to this federal presence, the oversight duties of state and local agencies are diminished. However, research has demonstrated that effective collaboration between first responder organizations greatly enhances the successful and smooth operations of NSSEs.[219]

The focus of this section is on local-level special events. Nevertheless, major local events still require considerable planning by local law enforcement and emergency managers. Major local events may be planned for months in advance and will require extra law enforcement officers, fire personnel, EMS workers, and possibly first aid facilities. City public works departments may be needed to provide additional sanitation.[220]

Realize that most special events are mandated by elected officials.[221] For example, the mayor or governor typically requests emergency management and law enforcement involvement for an upcoming special event. The elected official may order what he or she believes is the appropriate level of support, or the elected official may delegate this decision to his or her subordinates. Plans may need to be modified due to obtaining credible threat information from law enforcement sources. A change in expected weather conditions may cause modifications to the special event response plan.[222]

While information should be shared between agencies to the extent feasible, it must be recognized that not all information at the disposal of the local government can realistically be completely shared between agencies. For example, law enforcement agencies may possess credible information pertaining to a particular threat to the special event. It is within the legitimate purview of the law enforcement agency to determine the most appropriate way to utilize this information. In other words, all agencies involved understand that certain information is "For Official Use Only" or "Restricted.[223]

Open-source information sources and technology can also facilitate planning for special events and coordination between agencies for these events. For example, Google Earth can assist planners to visualize the special event operations area. Gas mains, fire hydrants, and other pertinent information relevant to special event planning can be visualized by CAMEO (Computer Aided Management of Emergency Operations) software.[224]

Law enforcement officers and emergency management personnel should realize that there are three types of participants involved in planning for special events.[225] These include are *planners, managers,* and *operators.* **Planners** are officials that have utilized factual information and have applied this to the activities and steps necessary to provide security and emergency management services to the event. For example, department heads, chiefs, and commissioners are planners.[226] **Managers** are officials that supervise the first responder, emergency management, and security operations of the special event. They consist of supervisors in the field in charge of special event operations. For example, police lieutenants, sergeants, fire battalion chiefs, and EMS shift supervisors are managers.[227] **Operators** carry out the official tasks "on the ground" at the event on behalf of the public safety and emergency management organizations present.[228]

Training to deal with special event crowd control requires that officials present pay special attention to the venue's access points. Establishing multiple access points helps to reduce the potential for trampling and facilitates the more efficient exit of attendees in the event of a critical incident. However, this has the negative consequence of requiring additional personnel to staff these additional access points. Law enforcement officers should remember in working special events that when most attendees feel threatened, they are most likely to exit by the way in which they entered.[229]

Special event operator training should emphasize the physical layout of the special event venue. Having a solid knowledge of the stadium, building, or topography of the venue helps emergency managers and public safety professionals react quickly in the event that an unexpected event occurs. Medical and fire personnel will know the fastest ways to enter and exit the venue and the most efficient ways to remove injured or sick individuals from the area. Law enforcement personnel can use this knowledge to better manage and protect attendees. Fire personnel will know about the locations of hydrants and building construction. Hazmat personnel be aware of any chemicals present within the venue and be able to react quickly if the need arises.[230]

Event planners and managers must consider some additional factors in terms of the logistics and scope of special events. Specifically, paperwork, communications, command, and volunteers (if any) need to be considered and dealt with in advance in order to have a rational organizational response to a special event prepared.

By "paperwork," this means that both Memorandums of Understanding (MOUs) and Incident Action Plans (IAPs) should be prepared and implemented prior to the special event. A **MOU (Memorandum of Understanding)** is a binding document between agencies that stipulates the duties, responsibilities, and interactions of each. For special events, MOUs should specify which resources have been brought to the event by each agency, how long the event is expected to last, and the signatures of the person in charge of each agency present.[231] MOUs thus help to facilitate interagency cooperation during joint operations such as special events.

An **IAP (Incident Action Plan)** is a document that contains all relevant preplanned information for a special event.[232] It is pointed out that IAPs are basic for special event preparation.[233] In terms of communications, this is a twofold concern with regard to special events. First, it refers to the news media. Second, it deals with communications within and between emergency management and emergency response organizations. In the context of the news media, recognize that the special event will likely receive media coverage (print, television, social media) and thus persons not present will learn about what transpired at the special event.[234] In addition, managers, planners, and operators should keep in mind that ongoing and live media coverage of the event provides real-time feedback to employees present and working at the scene. If a critical incident occurs, live footage of casualties, explosions, and damages will be instantly relayed to a wide audience.[235] The efforts of first responders in a real-world critical incident management situation will be placed on display in this way.

The second component of communications deals with communications within and between emergency management and emergency response organizations. Law enforcement and other first responder agencies should realize that communications equipment is vital in special events. A communications plan linking agencies and employees should be set up and tested prior to the special event. Ideally, the communications equipment should be tested inside the actual venue prior to the day of the special event. Doing so will allow employees, managers, and planners to learn how well the equipment functions. The communications plan must clearly delineate the frequencies that will be used for event communications. Keep in mind that using email or text messages may be necessary as a backup method of communicating in the event that radios fail.[236] The most important thing to remember is that there must be effective communication between emergency responders, emergency management, and within these organizations for successful special events operations.

Command in this context deals with setting up and operating the JOC/CP. The JOC is the **Joint Operations Center**. In this context, a **JOC** is a command and control facility designed to coordinate and monitor the activities of emergency management and emergency responder personnel assigned to a particular incident. Several agencies work together under a single JOC.[237] A **CP** is a **Command Post**, which is an "on scene" incident management facility for small-scale events and incidents. Personnel assigned to a special event JOC/CP should have access to media outlets, maps, communications channels, and the IAP.[238]

It should also be realized that special events often involve volunteers. These are unpaid individuals who provide their time and services to assist in special event operations. Volunteers provide additional manpower to bolster the response to a special event. If they receive minimal training, volunteers can fill certain low-skill positions to assist with the event.[239] Planners and managers can decide how to deploy volunteers to assist operators during the special event.

Notes

1. Michael J. Fagel, Editor, *Principles of Emergency Management: Hazard Specific Issues and Mitigation Strategies*, Boca Raton: CRC Press/Taylor and Francis Group, 2012: 87-130.
2. Ibid: 129.
3. Ibid.

4. Vincent Faggiano, John McNall, and Tom Gillespie, *Critical Incident Management: A Complete Response Guide*, 2nd Edition, Boca Raton, CRC Press/ Taylor and Francis Group, 2012: 111.
5. Joseph F. St. Cyr, "Hazardous Materials and Emergency Management: A Primer on Hazmat Law," *Journal of Emergency Management*, Vol. 2, No. 2, Spring 2004: 47.
6. Faggiano, McNall, and Gillespie, *Critical Incident Management*: 111.
7. Ibid.
8. Lindell, Prater, and Perry, *Introduction to Emergency Management*: 131.
9. Ibid: 133.
10. Fagel, *Principles of Emergency Management*: 118.
11. Bruce W. Clements and Julie Ann P. Casani, *Disasters and Public Health: Planning and Response*, 2nd Edition, Cambridge, Butterworth-Heinemann Elsevier, 2016: 188.
12. Ibid.
13. Karen M. Hess, Christine H. Orthmann, and Henry Cho, *Police Operations: Theory and Practice*, 6th Edition, Clifton Park, NY, Delmar Cengage Learning, 2014: 308.
14. Faggiano, *Critical Incident Management*: 112.
15. Ibid: 116.
16. Ibid: 117.
17. Ibid: 114.
18. Clements and Casani, *Disasters and Public Health*: 192.
19. Ibid: 186.
20. Ibid: 191.
21. Lindell, *Introduction to Emergency Management*: 139.
22. Ibid: 140.
23. Clements and Casani, *Disasters and Public Health*: 183-184.
24. Ibid: 184.
25. Ibid: 196.
26. Ibid: 196.
27. Ibid: 203.
28. Ibid: 207.
29. Lindell, *Introduction to Emergency Management*: 142.
30. Ibid: 143.
31. Ibid.
32. Fagel, *Principles of Emergency Management*: 286.
33. Ibid.
34. Ibid: 288.
35. Ibid.
36. Ibid: 283.
37. Ibid: 283-284.
38. Ibid: 284.
39. Ibid.
40. Ibid.
41. Ibid.

42. Ibid: 285.
43. Lindell, Prater, and Perry, *Introduction to Emergency Management*: 144.
44. Fagel, *Principles of Emergency Management*: 285.
45. Ibid.
46. Ibid: 146.
47. Ibid.
48. Ibid: 141.
49. Faggiano, *Critical Incident Management*: 118.
50. Clements and Casani, *Disasters and Public Health*: 208.
51. Ibid.
52. Ibid: 209.
53. Ibid: 212-213.
54. Ibid: 211.
55. Faggiano, *Critical Incident Management*: 110.
56. Ibid: 120.
57. Hess, Orthmann, and Cho, *Police Operations*: 308.
58. Faggiano, *Critical Incident Management*: 119.
59. Ibid.
60. Ibid: 120.
61. Clements and Casani, *Disasters and Public Health*: 121.
62. Ibid.
63. Fagel, *Principles of Emergency Management*: 283.
64. Clements and Casani, *Disasters and Public Health*: 122.
65. Ibid.
66. Ibid.
67. Ibid: 121.
68. Ibid: 125.
69. Ibid.
70. Ibid.
71. Ibid: 125-126.
72. Ibid: 126.
73. Ibid.
74. Ibid.
75. Ibid: 127.
76. Ibid.
77. Ibid.
78. Ibid.
79. Ibid.
80. Ibid: 128.
81. Ibid: 124.
82. Ibid.
83. Ibid: 145-146
84. Ibid: 147.
85. Ibid.
86. Clements and Casani, *Disasters and Public Health: Planning and Response*: 147.
87. https://www.cdc.gov/nssp/biosense/index.html

88. Ibid.
89. Clements and Casani, *Disasters and Public Health: Planning and Response*: 147.
90. Ibid: 150.
91. Ibid: 152.
92. Ibid: 152-153.
93. Ibid: 153.
94. Ibid: 177.
95. Fagel, *Principles of Emergency Management*: 300.
96. Ibid: 288.
97. Clements and Casani, *Disasters and Public Health*: 162.
98. Ibid.
99. Ibid.
100. Ibid: 163-164.
101. Ibid: 165.
102. Ibid: 171.
103. Ibid: 170.
104. Ibid: 175.
105. Ibid: 177-178.
106. Ibid: 176.
107. Ibid.
108. Ibid: 177.
109. Ibid: 210.
110. Ibid: 208.
111. Ibid: 381.
112. Ibid: 363.
113. Ibid.
114. Ibid: 364.
115. Ibid: 366.
116. Ibid.
117. Ibid: 366-367.
118. Lindell, Prater, and Perry, *Introduction to Emergency Management*: 144.
119. Ibid.
120. Ibid.
121. Ibid: 144-145.
122. Clements and Casani, *Disasters and Public Health*: 372.
123. Ibid: 373.
124. Ibid: 373.
125. Ibid: 374.
126. Ibid: 375.
127. Ibid.
128. Ibid: 377.
129. Ibid: 380.
130. Fagel, *Principles of Emergency Management*: 377.
131. Ibid: 376.
132. Ibid: 378.
133. Ibid: 394.

134. Ibid: 379.
135. Ibid.
136. Ibid.
137. Ibid.
138. Ibid.
139. Ibid: 380.
140. Ibid: 377.
141. Ibid: 380-381.
142. Ibid: 381.
143. Ibid.
144. Ibid: 377.
145. Ibid: 377.
146. Ibid.
147. Ibid.
148. Ibid.
149. Ibid.
150. Ibid: 380.
151. Ibid.
152. Ibid.
153. Ibid: 383.
154. Ibid.
155. Ibid: 384.
156. Ibid.
157. Ibid: 385.
158. Ibid: 384.
159. Ibid.
160. Ibid: 385.
161. Ibid: 386.
162. Ibid: 387.
163. Ibid.
164. Ibid.
165. Ibid.
166. Ibid: 387-388.
167. Ibid: 398.
168. Ibid: 399.
169. Ibid: 397.
170. Ibid.
171. Ibid: 388.
172. Ibid: 388-389.
173. Ibid: 389.
174. Ibid.
175. Ibid.
176. Ibid.
177. Ibid: 391.
178. Ibid: 392.
179. Ibid: 393.

180. Ibid.
181. Ibid: 394.
182. Ibid.
183. Ibid: 395.
184. Ibid.
185. Ibid.
186. Ibid: 396.
187. Ibid: 397.
188. Ibid: 399.
189. Ibid: 317.
190. Ibid: 318.
191. *Time*, October 16, 2017: 27.
192. Fagel, *Principles of Emergency Management*: 318-319, citing *Active Shooter: Recommendations and Analysis for Risk Mitigation*, by the New York City Police Department (NYPD).
193. Fagel, *Principles of Emergency Management*: 318.
194. Ibid.
195. Ibid: 319.
196. Ibid.
197. Ibid: 319-320.
198. Ibid: 320.
199. Ibid.
200. Ibid: 321.
201. Ibid.
202. Ibid: 322.
203. Ibid: 323.
204. Ibid.
205. Ibid: 323-324.
206. Ibid: 324.
207. Ibid.
208. Ibid: 325.
209. Robert Bott, Braiden Frantz, and J. Eric Dietz, "Active Shooter Mitigation Techniques," *Journal of Emergency Management*, Vol. 20, No. 2, March/April 2022: 108.
210. Fagel, *Principles of Emergency Management*: 429.
211. Ibid: 430.
212. Ibid: 431.
213. Ibid:
214. Ibid.
215. Ibid: 430.
216. Ibid.
217. Ibid.
218. Ibid.
219. Chris D. Bertram, "Preparing for Planned Events: National Security Special Events" in *The Role of Law Enforcement in Emergency Management and Homeland Security*, Mark R. Landhal and Tonya E. Thornton, Editors, Bingley, U.K., Emerald Publishing Limited, 2021: 193.

220. Fagel, *Principles of Emergency Management*: 431.
221. Ibid: 432.
222. Ibid.
223. Ibid: 432-433.
224. Ibid: 433.
225. Ibid.
226. Ibid: 434.
227. Ibid.
228. Ibid: 436.
229. Ibid.
230. Ibid: 432.
231. Ibid: 438-439.
232. Ibid: 436.
233. Ibid: 441.
234. Ibid: 432.
235. Ibid.
236. Ibid: 440.
237. Ibid: 432.
238. Ibid: 435-436.
239. Ibid: 439.

Chapter 7

EMERGENCY MANAGEMENT STRATEGIES FOR LAW ENFORCEMENT

Emergency management and law enforcement are closely related. It is important that law enforcement agencies possess an understanding of the strategic objectives behind emergency management so that operations and tactics can be geared toward dealing more effectively with disasters and emergencies.[1] **Strategy** provides the objectives behind planning for law enforcement-based emergency management efforts.

Emergency Planning

This section deals with the fundamental principles of emergency planning. It examines preparing for and responding to a disaster or an emergency. The goal of an emergency manager in a disaster is to prevent casualties and damage. A law enforcement or first responder agency must engage in emergency preparedness actions before a disaster occurs so that the planned actions can be implemented during a disaster.

Federal law and policy require that first responder agencies receiving federal grant funding must engage in emergency planning as a condition of receiving further federal financial assistance.[2] In this way, the federal government induces state and local governments to make strategic decisions regarding emergency management. By means of plans, actions will be oriented toward providing response and recovery to populations adversely affected by disasters and emergencies. The federal government has noted that engaging in planning strategies facilitates both response and recovery. It is recognized that an important way to improve disaster recovery in particular lies with government agencies engaging with community stakeholders prior to disasters.[3] Using similar logic, many American state governments have discovered that the development of state emergency management plans serves to influence actions at local levels.[4]

This chapter examines ways to build community emergency preparedness by taking preimpact actions that establish a state of readiness to respond to extreme events threatening the community. These include (a*) emergency planning principles*, (b) *emergency response functions*, (c) *a comparison of different organizational structures for emergency preparedness and responses*, and (d) *an examination of the purpose and design of EOPs (Emergency Operations Plans)*. These are important concepts in the emergency management field. Law enforcement personnel, emergency response workers, and emergency managers need a working knowledge of these things to be conversant with other agencies.

First are **emergency planning principles**. Planning is based on *rationality*. This is the idea that the human condition can be improved through the use of logic and factual information – that we can take this information and use a sequential process to get from point A to point B. Planning involves preparing for the future. All efforts at *planning* involve thinking about the activities and steps that would be necessary to create a desired future state of affairs, or a method or technique for thinking about purposes or activities in advance. *Planning* involves a systematic effort to improve the quality of decisions. The theory behind planning is to improve the quality of life through the use of logic and factual information. For example, if one *plans* for an emergency response to a disaster, a better outcome will be achieved than would have been the case without such planning.

Planning for emergency management is a sequential information-based process that should follow the following steps:

1. Develop an emergency response plan linked to the hazards faced by the community. Ideally, this should be an all-hazards plan. This can be done with guidance from FEMA (Federal Emergency Management Agency) or from the state emergency management agency. It is typically done under the leadership of the CAO (Chief Administrative Officer)—usually a mayor, city manager, or governor.
2. Identify the individuals and agencies with the skills and abilities to respond to an emergency or disaster. Analyze the ability of these organizations to perform basic Emergency Response Functions and evaluate their training and resources.
3. Write up *Emergency Operations Plans (EOPs)* and implement them. These will identify the types of emergency response actions that are best suited to the hazards faced by the community.
4. Implement the appropriate structures for emergency response (Incident Command System-ICS, Incident Management System-IMS, National Incident Management System-NIMS) as discussed in Chapter 3.
5. Set up protocols to design and staff the *Emergency Operations Center (EOC)*.
6. Recognize the ongoing linkages between disaster mitigation, response, and recovery and the need for continuous planning and improvement.[5]

Following this process will result in better preparedness for emergency response.

Assessing *emergency response functions* will be covered first. These deal with identifying the personnel, procedures, facilities, equipment, materials, and supplies needed to deal with emergency and disaster response. This is part of identifying the skills and abilities of emergency management and first responder organizations. An analysis of a first responder organization's ability to perform essential response functions must be made.[6]

There are four basic **emergency response functions:** (1) emergency assessment, (2) hazard operations, (3) population protection, and (4) incident management.[7] First is **emergency assessment**. Emergency assessment actions include things like using hazard vulnerability analysis and weather warnings to predict the consequences of a disaster. Some emergency assessment is under the control of the local agency, like hazmat. Other organizations such as the federal government engage in emergency assessment as well. Emergency assessment includes **hazard monitoring**. This is about keeping abreast of hazard status and projecting future damage. The technology for hazard monitoring varies by agency and the specific hazard.[8]

The second is **hazard operations**. This means being prepared with the supplies and equipment to respond to a disaster or emergency in the short term. For example, emergency vehicles must be fueled, equipped, and maintained. Keeping an inventory of empty sandbags on hand in case of a flood threat supports hazard operations. Short short-term actions to protect property, such as taping up and boarding up windows is rational preparation prior to the impact of a hurricane.[9]

Third is **population protection** actions, which include actions such as warnings designed to protect human beings from death and injury. For example, issuing a tornado warning or ordering an evacuation facilitates population protection. In addition, population protection actions could involve advising about protective actions to take for each disaster.[10]

Fourth is **incident management** actions, which are things in which emergency management agencies specialize, such as activating the EOC (Emergency Operations Center) and communicating between emergency management agencies.[11]

Engaging in these emergency preparedness practices will make the impact of the disaster less severe. That is why an important part of preparedness for emergency response is analyzing an agency's capability to perform the four basic emergency response functions.

Another vitally important component of planning that must be examined is the purpose and design of *Emergency Operations Plans* (*EOPs*). A very important component of the disaster cycle and planning is the **Emergency Operations Plan (EOP)**, which is a document that stipulates how a facility or agency will respond to and recover from including natural and man-made disasters.[12] All organizations, both public and private, should have an EOP in place as part of sound management practice. EOPs should take an "all hazards" approach to address every known disaster possibility. An organization's EOP is a vital part of an integrated emergency management system. The preparation of an EOP reflects a holistic "all hazards" approach to potential disasters and incorporates all four phases of the Emergency Management Cycle/Disaster Management Cycle. In 2010, the U.S. Department of Homeland Security published its guidance designed to assist law enforcement agencies in developing their EOPs: *Developing and Maintaining Emergency Operations Plans: Comprehensive Preparedness Guide 101.*[13]

EOPs should have 4 components: *(1) the basic plan, (2) functional annexes, (3) hazard-specific appendices, and (4) standard operating procedures (SOPs) and checklists.*[14] The first component of an EOP is the **basic plan**, which is an all-hazards-oriented document that lays out how the organization or facility will respond to and recover from all hazards. The document is generic in that it deals with handling routine natural disasters.[15] The basic plan is the bedrock of the EOP. It consists of 7 parts: *(1) purpose, (2) situation and assumptions, (3) concept of operations, (4) organization and assignment of responsibilities, (5) administration and logistics, (6) plan development and maintenance, and (7) authorities and references.*[16]

The **purpose** simply summarizes the basic plan. The **situation and assumptions** briefly summarize the vulnerability analysis and the authority of the organization. The **concept of operations** lays out the order or sequence in which emergency response activities are planned to occur. The **organization and assignment of responsibilities** shows the structure and design of the emergency response organization. The **administration and logistics** section deals with emergency management resources and the protocol for expanding the organization through combining with other emergency management organizations or volunteers. **Plan development and maintenance** indicates how the EOP will be updated and reviewed. **Authorities and references** cover the legal authority under which the EOP was prepared and will operate. Authorities and references also contain links to other supporting documents, like the hazard vulnerability analysis.[17]

This is the basic plan, which is the foundation of the EOP. Everything else springs from this basic EOP. EOPs should also have attached **EOP Annexes**, sometimes called **functional annexes** for different functions and hazards, such as utilities, continuity of operations, evacuation, terrorism, and others. According to FEMA, "Annexes are the parts of the EOP that begin to provide specific information and direction. Annexes should focus on operations: what the function is and who is responsible for carrying it out. While the Basic Plan provides information relevant to the EOP as a whole, annexes should emphasize responsibilities, tasks, and operational actions that pertain to the function being covered. Annexes should cover, in general terms, the activities to be performed by anyone with responsibility under the function. An annex should identify actions that not only ensure effective response but also aid in preparing for emergencies and disasters. Annexes should clearly define and describe the policies, processes, roles, and responsibilities inherent in the various functions before, during, and after any emergency period."[18]

The planning process for developing an EOC annex should include plan development and validation of these plans using exercises.[19] Some large jurisdictions include **hazard-specific annexes** to EOPs. These are used to provide information about the ways in which the response to a particular hazard differs from the standard response contained in the EOP's basic plan. For example, some of these include chemicals, radiological/radioactive agents, and explosives. Smaller jurisdictions combine these into functional annexes.

In any event, during and after this EOP planning process, the emergency manager "should carefully compare plans for the various response functions within that agency and revise the plans, if necessary, to remove any discrepancies. This will help prevent disconnects between vital functions that support one another and help ensure that each does what the others expect on a timely basis. Similarly, the various departments and agencies within a local jurisdiction should also compare their plans, focusing on issues of consistency and coordination."[20]

Next, **organizational structures for emergency response** will be examined. *These are design and operations components of first responder and emergency agencies used to facilitate effective functioning during emergencies and disasters.* They were invented to help agencies and personnel to integrate and to do their jobs more effectively. They improve functionality and communication during disasters and emergencies. Although they were technically developed as organizational structures for emergency *response*, training in their use counts as emergency *preparedness* as well. One leads to the other. They accompany each other. These organizational structures of emergency response are known by acronyms (ICS, IMS, NIMS, EOC).

A fifth component of an emergency response plan is the Emergency Operations Center (EOC). This is a physical central location utilized by local governments to coordinate their activities and decisions to better facilitate critical incident response and recovery efforts.[21] EOCs do not control first responder actions directly at critical incident scenes. Rather, EOCs coordinate by collecting and analyzing information obtained from first responders, establishing critical incident response priorities, and managing resource utilization and procurement.[22]

EOC decisions are broad-based. First responders conduct tactical operations. The EOC links top elected officials with emergency agencies.[23] It is necessary to establish a primary EOC in order to effectively coordinate first responder actions within the jurisdiction and to connect with other jurisdictions and federal agencies.[24]

There exist FEMA grant programs to provide training for first responders and emergency management personnel, especially with regard to improving organizational structures for emergency response. Examples include the Metropolitan Medical Response System (MMRS) and the Urban Areas Security Initiative (UASI). These are designed first to aid the goal of preparedness, and after a disaster or emergency, this training will aid in response. In addition, FEMA operates the State Homeland Security Program (SHSP) under the Homeland Security Grant Program (HSGP). The SHSP provides grants to state and local governments that are used to bolster response capabilities. Grant funding is allocated on the basis of what is considered to be the optimum level of financial support necessary to achieve the most effectiveness.[25]

The final and never-ending part of emergency response planning is *continuous monitoring and improvement* of the plans that are in place. Things change. Technology evolves. Hazards are ever-present. That is why the EOP and the ability of an emergency management agency to perform the basic emergency response functions have to be monitored, improved and changed to keep abreast with the ongoing hazard situation faced by the nation, state, city, and county.

Assessing Vulnerabilities

This section deals with the subject of *vulnerability assessment* as part of mitigation in emergency management. **Vulnerability** is about an organization's, a society's, or an individual's likelihood of being exposed to risks or attack by outside forces, whether natural or man-made. Therefore, **Vulnerability assessment** efforts have the goal of identifying any weakness present in a facility or a jurisdiction, especially those weaknesses that could potentially be exploited by an adversary such as a terrorist.[26]

Institutions and individuals have numerous vulnerabilities. For example, populated areas are vulnerable to terrorist attacks. Many ocean communities are vulnerable to tsunamis and hurricanes. The electrical and water grids are vulnerable to infrastructure attacks and decay. Vulnerabilities can also result from security weaknesses and personnel behavior on the job.[27]

Under the Homeland Security Act (2002), the U.S. Department of Homeland Security (DHS) was tasked with the responsibility of developing a national plan to secure critical infrastructure and key resources (CIKR) located in the United States.[28] **Critical infrastructure (CI)** refers to physical or virtual assets and systems and assets that are so vital to the economy, public safety and health, the environment, or security that the damage or destruction of such assets may have a debilitating impact across American jurisdictions.[29]

Closely related to CI sectors are **Key Resources (KR)**. Key resources are privately or publicly controlled resources that are essential to the basic operations of the government and the economy of the United States.[30] Critical Infrastructure and Key Resources (CI-KRs) are closely related and interdependent. These include Agriculture and Food, Banking and Finance, Water, Chemical, and Government facilities. CI-KR in the United States is geographically dispersed and of immense size. Much of the actual physical protection of CI-KR is performed by a combination of local government law enforcement officers and private corporations, some of which are international.[31]

The failure of or an attack upon CI-KR would significantly disrupt the functioning of the nation. In addition, the disruption of government and commerce would produce cascading effects that would result in further disruption across American jurisdictions. Both natural and man-made hazards could result in catastrophic losses in terms of deaths, injuries, property damage and destruction, and significant economic losses. Either an attack or a failure of CI-KR would also result in significant damage to public confidence and morale.[32]

It is for this reason that the **National Infrastructure Protection Plan (NIPP)** was published by the Dept. of Homeland Security in 2006. The federal government's NIPP contains a national structure with which to integrate efforts to protect CI-KR. NIPP was also designed to implement Homeland Security Presidential Directive 7 (HSPD-7), "Critical Infrastructure Identification, Prioritization, and Protection." HSPD-7 set up a mechanism for federal agencies and departments to systematically identify and prioritize United States CI-KR in terms of protecting them from attacks by terrorists. The NIPP stressed the need for risk assessments to be conducted and to make efforts to reduce vulnerabilities and mitigate risk.[33]

Risk assessment is also called *vulnerability assessment*. Assessing vulnerabilities is a vital part of mitigation in emergency management, as mitigation is about the *prevention of harm* or the *lessening of harm* before it occurs. Seeing where organizations and communities are vulnerable to hazards, risks, and disasters is a prerequisite to reducing (mitigating) harm. To be done correctly, comprehensively, and systematically, vulnerability assessment should follow a plan.

Vulnerability assessment methodologies comprise four elements of assessment: physical, cyber, operations security, and interdependencies.[34] First is the **physical security assessment**. A physical security assessment is employed to evaluate the physical security systems in place at a facility, including locks, access controls, barriers, passes and badges, intrusion detection cameras and motion sensors, alarms, video monitors used for surveillance, telephones, radios, and other communications equipment, interior and exterior lighting, electrical power sources, signs, protective force, and security system hardware. All of these systems should be regularly inspected and reviewed.[35]

Second is the **cyber security assessment**. Cyber-security assessment is utilized to examine the security features contained in the information networks connected with the critical infrastructure systems of an organization or agency. This assessment should involve an inspection of network operations and connectivity, information assets, communications and information protocols, and the linkage of major components, including information security.[36]

Third is **OPSEC (Operations Security Assessment)**. OPSEC refers to taking appropriate measures to deny adversaries and potential adversaries vital information about the intentions and capabilities of an organization.[37] In other words, OPSEC encompasses things that an organization can do to avoid letting enemies or adversaries know about how the organization operates, the full capabilities of the organization, and what specific activities that are planned by the organization for the future. Effective OPSEC requires an ongoing review of security training programs, personnel policies and procedures, discussions with key personnel, and inspections of facilities. Publicly available information about the organization should also be reviewed as part of OPSEC.[38]

Fourth are **interdependencies**, otherwise known as **infrastructure interdependencies**. This refers to the physical and cyber linkages inside and between the critical infrastructures of the United States.[39] In other words, the KRs and CIs are linked together, so that a failure in one can lead to a cascading failure in others.[40]

These four vulnerability assessment elements are primarily focused upon disruptions caused by terrorism (such as attacks) or human error (man-made mistakes such as chemical spills) that result in disasters. However, this is only one dimension of vulnerability assessment. Natural disasters and technological disasters can also result in the failure of CI-KRs. That is why a broader "all hazards" or "holistic" approach should also be made in order to come closer to a comprehensive vulnerability assessment.

One way to achieve this is by means of a *threat-based approach* to vulnerability assessment methodologies. A **threat-based approach** examines organizations and CI-KRs from the perspective of risk of attack/risk of failure from all causes. Threat-based approaches to vulnerability assessment can either be *asset-based* or *scenario-based*.[41] **Asset-based approaches** consider and plan for the effect on individual assets such as a police substation or the motor pool in the event of an attack.[42] The question is asked here, "If we lost asset x, what would happen? How could we function?" Once this vulnerability has been assessed, plans are then made to mitigate the effect if and when this occurs. **Scenario-based approaches** involve the consideration of several specific hypothetical sequences of events.[43] Thus, hypothetical situations or events are imagined, such as a cyberattack on the electrical grid, a terrorist attack, a tornado, or a pandemic. The vulnerabilities of the organization or its components are then assessed under that scenario. The purpose is to make plans in advance to deal with or work around the issues that would be connected with such an eventuality.

Regardless of the orientation chosen with which to engage in vulnerability assessment, there are commonly used approaches that can be employed "on the job," such as *checklists*, *simple ratings*, *risk matrixes*, and *risk equations*. It is also possible to use a combination of these approaches to vulnerability assessment as a practical matter.

To conduct a vulnerability assessment, a group of knowledgeable practitioners should physically inspect the facility in order to locate vulnerabilities.[44] In other words, vulnerability needs to be assessed "on the job" at the actual facility being examined. The first "on the job" approach to vulnerability assessment is the *checklist*. A **checklist** contains a list of ideal standard criteria utilized by the assessor to compare how the evaluated facility measures up.[45] Here, the asset or facility is assessed in comparison with the criteria.[46] A typical checklist is designed in the following way: On the left side are criteria to be evaluated, and on the right side are simple questions that an evaluator must answer. If any area is not in compliance with the category, this is an indication that a particular vulnerability exists that needs to be addressed.

However, the checklist has a limitation: it typically gives equal weight to each criteria area regardless of significance and importance to the functioning of the system or asset. Simple counting the numbers of "yes," "no," "met," "not met," etc. will provide only a rough idea of vulnerability. For this reason, more advanced measures should be used.

A somewhat more advanced method of vulnerability assessment is the *simple rating*. The **simple rating** provides a numerical assessment of vulnerability in each for a potential correction. The simple rating assigns a number to each asset on each criterion in comparison with the standard. Then the ratings are calculated.[47] The idea behind a simple rating is to base an evaluation on consistent and logical factors so that needed corrective measures can be made.[48]

An even more advanced and quantitative vulnerability assessment tool is the *risk equation*. This is an actual formula used to determine the statistical likelihood of a specific occurrence, such as a disaster. Generally, risk equations are based on actuarial models of probability.[49] Such quantitative data can be used to assess theoretical probabilities of disasters, and system failures.

Data and information obtained from any of these three measures (some more advanced than others) can be placed into another vulnerability assessment tool known as a *risk matrix*. In this context, a **risk matrix** is a chart or graph that illustrates the likelihood of a disaster, attack, or failure against the severity of the consequences that would occur to the organization, asset, or system at differing levels of severity. A risk matrix is premised on the theory that risk depends on the combination of event severity and its likelihood of actually occurring.[50]

A risk matrix will help to illustrate in graphical terms what an organization should focus its mitigation resources on. An event or scenario that is most likely to occur and that carries with it the potential for catastrophic consequences should receive the highest priority, for example. An unlikely event that will result in few consequences should receive the lowest priority according to this approach.

As an example, an outline of the risk management steps designed to assess and mitigate vulnerabilities utilized by the U.S. Department of Energy (DOE) will be examined. The DOE utilizes six steps as part of its "General Vulnerability Assessment Process." These steps and this process can be applied to a wide variety of organizations. This is an asset-based vulnerability assessment methodology.

Step 1 is to **Identify Critical Assets and the Impacts of their Loss**. Estimates are made of the effect of potential consequences associated with failing to mitigate identified vulnerabilities.[51] This involves determining and noting the core or critical functions of the organization and assessing which parts of the organization are most important to this core function. A determination needs to be made in terms of the consequences (in terms of money and/or in terms of human health and well-being) that would occur under various scenarios. Step 1 forces an evaluator to think in terms of **criticality criteria**, which means rank-ordering organizational assets in terms of their importance in fulfilling their core function or reason for existence. Typically, criticality criteria are considered in terms of **functions and assets** (critical assets and equipment controlled by the organization), **impacts of loss** (what would happen in case of a disaster, emergency, or failure), and **asset value** (importance of the functioning asset to other organizations and the larger society).

In Step 2, an evaluator should **Identify What Protects and Supports the Critical Assets**. Here, an assessment is made regarding interdependencies, such as electricity, water, and gas, coupled with an identification of sensitive information about the internal functioning of the organization.[52] The ultimate goal of this data will be to help produce the *vulnerability rating criteria*, as discussed below.

Step 3 involves efforts to **Identify and Characterize the Threat**. Threats can be natural, such as hurricanes, unintentional man-made disasters, such as a chemical spill, a widespread power failure or an airplane crash, or the results of acts of terrorism or sabotage (intentional man-made disasters). In any event, an effort must be made to identify and quantify potential adversaries and threats that may be expected.[53] The intent and capabilities of possible attackers must be considered and evaluated. The probable threats to the organization caused by natural disasters must also be evaluated. For example, what is the probability that a hurricane, tornado, tsunami, or wildfire may adversely impact the organization? This information will be used to help construct a threat rating criteria.

In Step 4, evaluators must take steps to **Identify and Analyze Vulnerabilities**. This means that the specific failures within the organization regarding the provision of the organization's core and essential functions that would result from natural or man-made disasters must be quantified. In other words, what would a pandemic do to the personnel needed to provide the core function of the organization? What would happen if an electrical power loss of 36 hours occurred? What would happen if the security software were to be breached?

Step 5 requires that evaluators **Assess Risks and Determine Priorities for Asset Protection**. Step 5 "ties it all together" in that quantitative and qualitative measures of vulnerability are pooled together and used for the purpose of assessing overall risk in various categories. An index weighting criterion must thus be developed. This will allow a risk rating to be developed.[54]

Specifically, three ratings are generally made and then combined to form a risk rating: (1) asset impact/criticality rating, (2) threat rating, and (3) vulnerability rating.[55] Data from Step 1 are used to construct an **asset impact/criticality rating**. Here, every critical asset identified in the first step is assigned a numerical impact rating value in proportion to its importance in the event of disruption or loss.[56] To summarize this, numerical values should be used to correspond with qualitative measures of "critical," "high," "medium," and "low."[57] Data from Step 2 are used to construct a **vulnerability rating criteria**. This is a numerical value that quantifies the extent to which a given asset is protected against a given threat.[58] For example, four vulnerability levels are listed (critical, high, medium, and low) with values ranging from 1-25 (corresponding with low) to 75-100 (corresponding with critical). Then a **threat rating criteria** is constructed from information obtained from Step 3 based upon the severity of the threat.[59] Often, these three are combined to obtain a **risk rating** to identify the most needed protective areas.[60]

Finally, Step 6 requires the assessor of vulnerability to **Identify Mitigation Options, Costs, and Trade-Offs**.[61] The specific steps that should be taken depend upon the type of organization as well as the specific vulnerabilities identified. Ideally, these decisions will be data-driven as a result of Step 5 and implemented to "harden" the organization and to help the organization become "more secure" and "less vulnerable." The point of the process is to systematically examine vulnerabilities as part of the process of mitigation.

Continuity of Operations Planning (COOP)

Continuity of Operations, or **COOP**, is about the "survival" of organizations, especially government bureaucracies that provide essential services in emergency and disaster situations. COOP can be and is applied more broadly to private organizations as well, especially utilities, for-profit medical providers, and debris removal companies so that they can continue operations during man-made or natural disasters. COOP initiatives prepare government organizations in particular for emergencies that have the potential to disrupt the normal provision of services and overall governmental operations. COOP facilitates the continuity of government operations by identifying legal authority, alternate facilities, and orders of succession in case of a prolonged crisis or critical incident.[62]

This section underscores that continuity of operations requires taking steps in advance to ensure that all essential functions performed by agencies and jurisdictions can be sustained during crises and critical incidents. COOP consists of plans and procedures that specify an organization's essential functions and includes protocols for emergency delegation of authority and succession to office in crisis situations. COOP also includes provisions to ensure the safekeeping of vital databases and other records, alternative operating strategies, and providing for continuous communication. COOP requires testing, training, and exercise (TT&E) programs to ensure that the plans will operate under stressful conditions.[63]

Continuity of operations enables organizations to perform their essential tasks and functions during critical incidents, crises, and emergencies that disrupt normal operations. COOP is imperative for first responder and other government organizations and also for essential private entities.[64] In other words, society would be very much harmed and disaster response and recovery would be impossible without plans in place to address both the continuing and resumed operations of essential government and business services following disasters.

Every organization, both public and private should have a COOP plan as part of sound management practice. The federal government strongly advocates this and attempts to make the U.S. Government an example. COOP is an official policy of the U.S. Government.[65] The need for COOP plans has never been greater than the present due to the potential for no-notice emergencies. COOP should apply to the government especially, but also to vital private businesses. Continuity planning is designed to reduce the consequence of major disruptive events to an acceptable level.[66]

A good continuity plan should attempt to achieve desired goals to ensure the survival and continued operation of the organization. Senior management is responsible for continuity planning. In corporations, it lies with the CEO. In government, it lies with the senior elected official or administrative head of a state, local, or federal bureaucracy. Senior management has a duty to continue the basic services of the organization during times of emergency.[67] Although this is true, realize that emergency managers assist in this endeavor in public sector organizations.[68] In this way, emergency managers are very much involved in COOP.

An organization's ability to survive during and after a disaster (its resiliency) is dependent upon its ability to perform its essential functions under all conditions is called an organization's **continuity capability**. Continuity capability is strongly related to how well management has implemented the pillars and key components of continuity planning.[69]

Of particular COOP relevance to law enforcement agencies during times of crises involves issues relating to (a) communications and (b) personnel continuity. It must be noted that most law enforcement agencies do not possess control over dispatch and the equipment utilized day-to-day. Dispatch is often controlled by other entities, and communications equipment is often actually supported by private corporations. In addition, law enforcement staff shortages can be a serious issue, in that research shows that as much as forty percent of employees may not report for work during a public health emergency. It is for this reason that law enforcement agencies must cross-train personnel so that essential COOP functions can be achieved in extraordinary situations.[70]

The foundation of COOP is comprised of continuity planning and continuity program management. **Continuity planning** is first about taking steps in advance to anticipate disaster scenarios that might impact organizational operations and then consider how to provide key functions under these scenarios. Key or major continuity concepts should be incorporated into continuity planning, including *geographical dispersion*, *risk management*, *security*, *readiness*, and *preparedness*.

The four pillars necessary upon which to build continuity capability are (1) leadership (2) staff (3) communications and (4) facilities. Pillar 1 is **leadership**. This means that organizations must provide a clear line of succession. This includes necessary delegations of authority Pillar 2 is **staff**. In terms of training, staff must have the skills necessary to operate in a continuity environment through cross-training in different jobs. Pillar 3 deals with **communications and technology**. Plans must be made to ensure that vital computers and telephones will function in disaster conditions (be interoperable, robust, and reliable). Pillar 4 is about **facilities**. Organizations must maintain designated locations capable of performing essential functions separate from primary facilities to ensure continuity of operations.[71]

The **Continuity Program Management Cycle** is used to help ensure the continuation of operations across organizations.[72] This cycle should include planning, training, evaluating, and implementation of a blueprint for COOP.

During training, exercises, and simulations of COOP, failures will become apparent in the best made plans. This is why a CAP (Corrective Action Program) must be made and implemented to improve future continuity of operations.[73]

The primary focus of any COOP endeavor must be to keep essential functions operational during a disaster. For government agencies, essential functions during an emergency include the ability to provide essential services, operate civil institutions, maintain law and order to provide for public safety, and to sustain the economic base.[74]

The federal government has taken many steps to ensure COOP, which it calls continuity of government through the **National Continuity Policy Implementation Plan**. This plan contains three categories of essential functions: NEFs (National Essential Functions), PMEF (Primary Mission Essential Functions), and MEFs (Mission Essential Functions) in order of COOP importance.

NEFs are broad and deal with the continuity of the U.S. Government under the Constitution, including national defense, foreign relations, economic stability, and disaster response. These NEFs are the top continuity priorities of the federal government. Of somewhat lesser importance are PMEFs and MEFs, which are oriented toward state governments, local governments, and major business corporations like utilities and petroleum that provide essential services. PMEFs are of vital importance to COOP and include functions and services that either must be continuously operated or resumed within twelve hours after a critical event. PMEFS must be maintained for up to thirty days during an extensive crisis. MEFs are a broader set of essential functions that includes not only an organization's PMEFs, but also all other organization functions that must be continued throughout or resumed rapidly after a disruption of normal activities, but that do not rise to the level of being PMEFs.[75]

The objective is for "nonfederal entities" like essential services corporations and state and local governments to explicitly indicate and identify their MEFs and PMEFs and to take aggressive actions to ensure that these functions can be operated and maintained during the duration of a crisis.[76] Each organization has different functions and responsibilities. For that reason, each organization will have different PMEFs and MEFs.[77]

Planning for COOP requires organizations to first list their PMEFs and MEFs. Then, the organization must determine how often these functions need to be performed. Personnel resources need to be calculated for minimum levels of provision of these services as well. These calculations should be based on different scenarios, such as a one-day, two-day, one-week, and one-month disruption.

In addition, COOP requires that organizations identify *essential services personnel* who can be called upon to provide PMEFs and MEFs during a disaster situation. The plans must incorporate staffing during a continuity situation. This is especially true for government. Large organizations typically establish a "Continuity Planning Team" to coordinate continuity planning.[78]

A related and essential human capital issue involves **Orders of Succession**, or having a mechanism in place to have authority delegated to managers in line from the top to lower level managers involved in running continuity operations under the organizations' chain of command. In other words, who will be in charge of the organization and its functioning operations under a continuity event? Orders of succession facilitate the predefined and orderly transition of organizational leadership.[79]

It is imperative for organizations to delineate and publish a clear line of succession to offices and positions as part of COOP. If organizational leadership roles become empty due to death or illness, someone else must be able to step in and perform the legal and authorized duties of that position.[80] An order of succession should cover the top three positions at a minimum. Ideally, there should be geographical dispersion as well to help ensure that essential functions continue in organizations that operate remotely.[81]

Delegation of authority is another related factor that must be incorporated in an organization's continuity plan. This is the authority given by management to lower-ranking employees to make significant decisions on behalf of the organization in a continuity scenario. There should be an appropriate delegation of authority in advance of any disaster. Delegation should include the subject matter areas in which authority is given, and consideration should be given to the geographical location(s) in which the organization might operate in a continuity situation. In other words, if the organization's primary facility cannot function, alternative sites must operate. Managers at those sites should be delegated authority in the event of a disaster.

Part of sound delegation of authority involves assigning the power to make decisions to field, satellite, and other appropriate organizational levels as part of a COOP. Publication of the delegation of authority plan will notify employees about who will have the legitimate power to make vital decisions during a continuity situation. The delegation of authority plan normally will take effect only when the organization's normal channels of command and control are disrupted.[82]

Continuity plans also need to evaluate organizational facilities. Most organizations operate from a **primary facility**. If and when this primary facility becomes inoperable under a disaster scenario, **alternate facilities** should be identified in advance. Alternate facilities can include virtual operations as well. In the event of a disaster, operations can be relocated to that alternate facility. Two alternative facilities should be identified as part of each organization's

COOP.[83] In order to COOP to be effectively implemented, all employees should be notified about organizational continuity plans, especially those that require relocating employees to alternative facilities or virtual offices. In addition, continuity personnel must be provided with appropriate training with regard to relocation procedures.[84]

Delegation of authority and designating alternative facilities is also related to the concept of **devolution** in continuity planning. Devolution primarily involves government organizations, but it can also apply to large corporations. Devolution is the legal ability to transfer authority and responsibility from an organization's top management to other employees and facilities for an extended period in the event of a crisis or emergency.[85] Thus, devolution is a complex combination of a mixture of succession, delegation of authority and a move to alternative facilities.

COOP efforts must consider how to deal with the organization's vital records and vital resources after a catastrophe. Modern organizations must be able to access vital records and resources needed to support essential functions during a continuity event. Vital records and vital resources include electronic and hardcopy documents, information systems, records, and other materials that the organization needs to perform its functions. Backup copies of vital resources and records needed to operate an organization should be stored at a backup location so that they will be available in the event of COOP activation.

After a major disaster requiring the organization to implement its COOP plan, the ultimate goal will be **reconstitution**. Reconstitution describes how the remaining or new organizational employees will resume normal operations after the crisis has been resolved.[86] Reconstitution means that the organization has "survived" the major disaster/continuity event, and that its COOP plan was successful. An organization should tie all of these principles and elements of its COOP plan together in its overall **Continuity Plan**. This plan will help the organization to quickly resume its essential functions.[87]

Realize that all this theory will not necessarily work as intended without efforts to practice these plans. This is where **Testing, Training, and Exercising (TT&E)** comes into play as part of COOP. In other words, COOP will not occur simply because a written plan exists. A TT&E program is necessary to provide employees with the skills needed to implement the plan. TT&E validates the components of continuity plans, facilities, and systems. Lessons learned from TT&E endeavors inform management how well or how poorly the COOP works. Problems can then be resolved before a crisis event.[88] In the aftermath of TT&E, problems and issues will the COOP plan will become apparent. This is why organizations will have to develop a CAP (Corrective Action Plan). The CAP will be used to fix problems noted in the TT&E program.[89]

Planning for the Future

This section is about the attempt to forecast the types of disaster challenges that emergency responders and emergency managers are likely to face in the future. Doing so will help these professions to be proactive rather than reactive. Being proactive is designed to help us to be ready for future events. It is a long section and contains very important information. It is important for law enforcement officers to think about the challenges that the future might bring to them and their agencies. The frequency of disasters is increasing in the United States, as are their impacts.[90]

Law enforcement professionals can learn from the knowledge gained from prior critical incident response and recovery operations. This will help them to be more effective in performing their first responder duties. This will assist in promoting resilience.[91] Learning in the present and perfecting techniques will allow the emergency manager to be more effective in dealing with future disasters. As a person working in the law enforcement, first responder, or emergency management fields, it is necessary to be able to take the actions necessary to deal with all types of critical incidents and job-related events. This is especially true with critical incidents stemming from natural disasters, technological disasters, and terrorism.[92]

This section also examines some technological hazards (including computer/information hazards), natural hazards, hazards associated with civil conflicts (acts of violence such as mass shootings, war, and terrorism), and hazards resulting from increased vulnerability (population changes, etc.). Several other threats not otherwise covered (such as global warming and asteroid strikes) may at some future time become disasters.

It is the consensus of opinion that natural disasters are becoming more frequent and their effects are becoming more severe in terms of death, injury, and property damage.[93] Natural disasters interact in complex ways with the social and built environments. The **natural environment** is the physical setting for many disasters such as hurricanes, earthquakes, and volcanic eruptions. The **built environment** encompasses the structures and infrastructure created by humans. This includes houses, schools, factories, bridges, tunnels, and roads. The **social environment** includes the political, social, cultural, economic, and demographic activities or characteristics within a jurisdiction or nation-state.[94] For example, a hurricane emanates from the natural environment. It produces winds, tornadoes, rain, and flooding. This in turn harms the built environment of homes, power lines, streets, etc. The harm to the built environment results in damage to the social environment (no electricity, polluted floodwater, spoiled food from lack of refrigeration, economic damage because businesses are not functioning, etc.). In other words, "everything connects." Disasters can lead to far-reaching effects for which emergency managers must plan.

Complex/compound disasters, *cascading disasters*, *synergistic disasters*, and *na-tech disasters* can all stem from a single event and lead to other disasters that magnify the original event. A **complex or compound disaster** is an event involving multiple interconnected factors. For example, a hurricane that is accompanied by destruction of housing and flooding is a complex or compound disaster.[95] There are also **cascading disasters**, which are events that cause other impacts or hazards to occur. For example, on 9/11 hijacked passenger jets impacted the World Trade Center. The buildings burned and then collapsed. The collapse caused the subway system underneath the World Trade Center to be damaged.[96]

A **synergistic disaster** occurs when one event causes other events to magnify in severity. For example, if an earthquake ruptures water mains, firefighters will not be able to use city water to fight fires caused by the earthquake.[97] In a **na-tech disaster**, technology or other complex devices fail due to natural hazards to cause additional adverse effects. For example, if a tornado overturns a train carrying hazmat chemicals, a na-tech disaster has occurred.[98]

The point of these examples and definitions is to stress again that "everything connects." In our complex society, disasters have far-reaching consequences beyond their immediate impact. Every critical incident results in both typical and unusual problems for first responders.[99] This applies to technological and other types of disasters as well. **Technological hazards** occur because of human-controlled endeavors.[100] This includes the built environment (electricity, gas lines, water pipes, explosives, radioactive materials, chemicals, etc.). First responders will often deal with critical incidents brought about by various types of technological hazards. Some technological hazards are similar to natural hazards. For example, whether structure fires were caused by lightning or by faulty electrical wiring, the fire still must be resolved. A fairly common example of a critical incident caused by technological hazards includes train derailments. Hazmat critical incidents are another common technological hazard.[101] Industrial accidents and hazmat incidents have several similarities.

A subset of technological hazards includes **computer/information technology hazards**. This includes cyberterrorism, hackers, worms, and viruses. Cyberterrorism describes the use of computers to carry out attacks.[102] Cyber-terrorists can disrupt critical infrastructure like power grids, pipelines, and utilities. They can also use computers to carry out financial crimes to fund their operations.[103]

Computer/information technology hazards can hinder emergency management response and recovery operations. This is true because both computers and technology are integrated into first responder and emergency management operations. The possibility also exists that cyber terrorists could gain control over utilities such as gas lines, petroleum pipelines, and other critical infrastructure.[104] Much of this is outside the control of emergency managers. However, possessing some knowledge of the risk associated with hackers and cyberterrorism will help emergency managers to foster better preparation and response efforts.

Another future challenge for emergency managers involves hazards associated with *civil conflicts* (acts of violence such as mass shootings, war, and terrorism). These are intentionally caused acts of violence that can and do cause injuries, deaths, and property damage. Civil/conflict hazards include riots, wars, terrorism, and mass shootings. For example, bombings, school, nightclub, and concert shootings, violent protests, and armed conflict are all intentional acts of violence. Dealing with civil/conflict hazards in terms of response and recovery is one of the tasks of law enforcement and components of homeland security in terms of **prevention** (stopping the occurrence of violence through intelligence and border control) and **protection** (increased security and mitigation activities).[105] However, much of dealing with the consequences of violence is up to emergency managers and first responder agencies.

Law enforcement and first responder personnel should always realize that every critical incident that does not involve a natural disaster could actually be caused by a terrorist attack. For example, a building fire could be caused by arson. An explosion may not be the result of a broken gas main, but rather from a bomb. A disease outbreak may not be naturally occurring, but rather a manifestation of bioterrorism. A plane crash may not be due to mechanical error but in fact due to an on-board bomb or due to hijacking.[106]

It is a possibility that a terrorist group could obtain **CRBNs** from a rogue nation or develop such weapons on their own. CRBN stands for **Chemical, Biological, Radiological, and Nuclear** weaponized components. If terrorists actually obtain such materials, the consequences could be catastrophic. Terrorists have demonstrated interest in obtaining CBRN devices.[107] Government intelligence work is the primary line of defense against CBRN weapons.

Due to the specter of terrorism, it is very important for law enforcement personnel and other first responders to possess risk awareness when they are called to the scene of what appears to be an industrial explosion or potential bombing scene. While first responders are focused on the immediate critical incident, terrorists might have placed a secondary explosive device to kill or injure first responders. In the case of a legitimate industrial explosion, residual explosive material may still pose a danger.[108]

If a law enforcement officer is responding to a terrorist incident, he or she should be aware that they are facing between one to six types of harm according to the **TRACEM** acronym.[109] TRACHEM stands for Thermal, Radiological, Asphyxiative, Chemical, Etiological, or Mechanical hazards.

Working terrorist critical incidents requires special skills and technical knowledge. First responders should be familiar with the capabilities of other agencies that can provide assistance in terrorist critical incidents.[110] For example, some states maintain trained first responders to detect WMDs. There are at present more than fifty specialized military units located in different locations around the United States. These specialized military units possess special training in identifying what terrorist weapons have been used and the most effective means of handling these weapons and devices. The federal government operates other teams to aid local first responders in responding to terrorist-related critical incidents. Both the Centers for Disease Control and the Department of Homeland Security assist with the detection of WMDs at critical incident scenes. The FBI is responsible for gathering and protecting evidence to support federal terrorism charges.[111] The federal government has many other additional resources that can be deployed in terrorist events.

Other hazards exist that have the very real potential to cause harm to human beings. Some of these include environmental degradation, climate change, and global warming. All three have resulted and will continue to result in more extreme natural hazards and can also make other types of disasters more severe. An asteroid strike would result in catastrophic consequences.[112] In addition, population changes, poverty, improper land use, improper construction, and failures of emergency management institutions are also hazards.[113]

The **growing population** of both the United States (over 300 million) and the world also impact vulnerability. As more people live in a given area, more people are exposed to various hazards. In addition, increased demand for resources such as food and water make the possibility of famines cause by droughts and other factors increase. In addition, violence between human beings caused by scare resources is another hazard that is likely to increase.[114] Plus, economic opportunity tends to be located in cities, which concentrates the population and makes them more vulnerable to all types of disasters. In addition, many of the world's cities are located in very vulnerable areas, such as coastal areas and seismically active areas.[115] The almost certain result is greater death, injury, and property damage in the future. Increasing population age in developed countries also increases vulnerability because the elderly are more susceptible to morbidity and mortality caused by disasters.[116]

It has been asserted that **increased diversity** also has an impact on vulnerability. Many American cities contain substantial numbers of immigrants from many parts of the globe. Substantial diversity has the potential to impact disaster vulnerability.[117] Cultural differences and language barriers impact emergency management in terms of communication problems and differing attitudes about disaster mitigation, preparation, response, and recovery. Highly diverse nations often have difficulties dealing with disasters.[118]

Increased industrialization is another factor that increases vulnerability. Greater use of chemicals, the presence of nuclear material, increased use of natural resources, increased waste disposal, and increased dependence upon technology all make society more vulnerable to both disasters resulting from industrial accidents and hazmat.

Globalization also increases vulnerability, in that when a crisis occurs in one area of the earth, adverse consequences can affect nations and peoples in other parts of the earth.[119] For example, economic crises in one country or region can affect other countries or regions. Chemical, biological, or nuclear accidents or terrorism in one country can affect others. International travel can lead to more epidemics and pandemics.

Improper land use and construction increases vulnerability as well. This is because human beings had demonstrated the tendency to desire to live and work in hazardous areas, such as in temperate coastal regions. However, coastal land is more susceptible to hurricanes and flooding than other property.[120] Every year, billions of dollars in damage occur to the built environment due to hurricanes and tsunamis. Many people are killed and injured as a result as well. Also, many homes and commercial properties are constructed cheaply and without the full range of precautions necessary to make them strong enough to stand up to natural disasters.

In addition, it can be argued that **weak emergency management institutions** also increase vulnerability. Some experts assert that emergency management is not adequately staffed and funded, though this has been changing. While FEMA recommends that American jurisdictions should hire one emergency manager for every 25,000 people, this has not occurred. Even today many cities lack a full-time emergency manager. A substantial number of jurisdictions fail to adequately finance and equip emergency management agencies.[121] To the extent that emergency management is not prioritized, greater risk for the jurisdiction becomes manifest.[122]

All these sources of increased vulnerability will continue to impact emergency management in the future.

Strategies to Enhance Disaster Resilience

This section examines resilience, preparedness, and ways to increase effective response and recovery operations prior to the impact of disasters. This section also covers creating an emergency management ordinance, establishing a preparedness council or local emergency planning committee, the importance of hazard and vulnerability assessment, and acquiring financial resources to support emergency management agencies through grants and government budgets. The basic steps necessary to establish an EOC (Emergency Operations Center) and to write an Emergency Operations Plan (EOP) are also covered. First responder and organizational training are discussed. Emergency management leadership, professionalization, improvisation, and spontaneous planning are examined, as is the importance of public disaster education. All of these things are designed to tie the materials covered thus far together.

Resilience deals with the ability to respond effectively to disasters.[123] The term **community resilience refers** to the factors used to explain how some communities respond better to disasters than others.[124] Resilience must be promoted by the emergency management community before a disaster strikes a community.[125] Being proactive is about taking steps in advance to achieve an outcome or to ward off difficulties. In terms of emergency management, **preparing your community** for the possibility of a disaster is proactive. Proactive emergency managers engage in **preparedness** activities on an ongoing basis. Preparedness activities improve the capabilities needed to enhance post-disaster response and recovery operations.[126] This involves identifying the most vital functions to perform following a disaster and determining the best ways to deploy organizations and their personnel.[127]

At the local government level, enacting an emergency management ordinance is a vital first step to facilitate the community's rational preparation for future disasters.[128] Doing this, coupled with establishing an EOC and writing an EOP, is important to facilitate rationality.

Public sector emergency managers, like other civilian bureaucrats, act based on legally established authority. For example, FEMA employees get their authority from laws passed by Congress. State emergency managers get their authority from laws enacted by their state legislature. For emergency managers that work for city or county (local) governments, they must obtain their authority from an *ordinance*. An **ordinance** is a specific type of legislation enacted by a city or county legislative body, such as a city council or county commission.[129] Ordinances establish the legal foundation for local emergency management authority.[130]

An emergency management ordinance is divided into sections, which include the **justification** (why the emergency management position/agency is needed), the **relation to state and federal law, the powers, duties, and organization of the position/agency, joint operations and mutual aid authorization, expenditures and contracts** (who has the authority to spend appropriated money and enter into contracts), and **violations and penalties** (who will enforce emergency management decisions and what will be the consequences for noncompliance).[131]

After this, a proactive emergency manager should establish a **preparedness council**, otherwise known as a **local emergency planning committee**. A preparedness council is comprised of the local emergency manager, the mayor and/or the city manager, department leaders from city and county departments, and representatives from utility providers, public health agencies, and nonprofit organizations like the American Red Cross.[132] The purpose of a preparedness council is to hold meetings in which all the stakeholders exchange ideas about how to get the community better prepared for different types of disasters. In this way, the emergency manager can draw upon the expertise of others while simultaneously increasing awareness of the role that emergency management plays in planning.

A **Local Emergency Planning Committee (LEPC)** is a more focused version of a preparedness council. A 1986 federal law requires that the EPA (Environmental Protection Agency) ensure that local governments will be prepared for toxic chemical releases in areas that have substantial amounts of them. LEPCs are composed of emergency managers, elected officials, plant managers, medical professionals, and first responder agencies.[133]

Another aspect of great significance to emergency management and law enforcement personnel involves ways to "play the game" of acquiring financial resources with which to operate his/her agency well so that it can achieve its purposes. This is done through *annual budgets, grants,* and utilizing information obtained about agency operations. Without funding, an emergency management program cannot function, much less engage in response and recovery operations. For that reason, emergency managers must identify their funding sources, whether that be from appropriations made by legislatures or external funding sources.[134] In government agencies, the *budget* is the major source of funding. In the context of emergency management, a **budget** is an appropriation of money for a department or agency allocated by a legislative body.[135] Government budgets are funded by taxes. Budgets "keep the money flowing" to operate emergency management agencies. Budgets fund wages, benefits, and emergency equipment.

Knowing how to prepare an effective budget request is vital to success in emergency management. The budget request should also ask permission to establish a **contingency fund** that will be used in the event of an emergency because emergency management efforts will dramatically increase in that circumstance.[136] Thus, when emergencies and disasters occur, the contingency fund itself can be quickly exhausted due to personnel overtime, use of supplies, and other response and recovery actions. When this occurs, a supplemental budget must be requested from the city or county.[137]

When emergency management administrators make a budget request document each year, it must be justified in writing. This is based upon last year's expenses which must be adjusted for inflation and new needs.

This written justification for an agency's budget request is called a **budget narrative.**[138] This is presented to elected officials.

In addition to budgets, another way that emergency management agencies can obtain money and other resources that they need to operate is through *grants.* **Grants** are funding sources that come from higher levels of government or from nonprofit organizations. Grants are not loans and thus do not have to be repaid by the recipient. Persons working in the emergency management and law enforcement fields should learn about the different kinds of grants and the rules associated with receiving grant funding. Most grants are awarded to encourage or require the recipient to comply with the donor's mandates.[139]

Many grants pertaining to emergency management are provided by the federal government, especially FEMA. The national government funds the Emergency Management Performance Grant (EMPG). This particular grant allocates funding to state governments on the basis of (a) population and (b) the presence of hazards.[140] Other FEMA grants include Fire Suppression Assistance, National Urban Search and Rescue Response System, Predisaster Mitigation Grants, and the State and Local All-Hazard Emergency Preparedness Program. These and other grants typically pay for all or part of first responder and emergency manager salaries during emergencies, in addition to supplies and equipment. For these reasons, grants help both the emergency management agency and its parent government.

Grants are not awarded automatically. There is a complex application process associated with receiving grant funding. Applications must be completed accurately, on time, and with the required accompanying documentation. A grant application must be detailed. Applications must include goals, the personnel that will be involved, the plan to accomplish the work, deliverables, the budget, and information on measuring performance and reporting results.[141] Even if all of these things are completed fully and on time, realize that there is competition between jurisdictions to receive grant funding. That is why learning **grantsmanship**, or the skills associated with writing successful grant proposals is a vital skill to possess in emergency management.[142]

Even if a law enforcement or emergency management agency receives a grant, the agency must maintain extensive records to document the use and expenditure of the funds or equipment that was awarded. Reports must be submitted regularly. The failure to file required reports or fraudulent use of grant funding can lead to loss of funding and criminal sanctions.[143]

Beyond grants and budgets, there are other potential sources for assistance and equipment. These are known as *resource lists* maintained by governments outside an emergency management agency. A **resource list** describes a database of assets (both human and equipment) that could be utilized in disaster response and recovery. Resource lists contain personnel positions, supplies, and equipment. Most items on a resource list include government first responders and their agencies, but can also include nonprofit corporations associated with emergency management. In some jurisdictions, resource lists also contain data relating to private entities that can assist with mass sheltering, disabled vehicle towing and recovery, and generation of electrical power.[144]

Another proactive step that emergency managers should take is establishing the EOC (Emergency Operations Center) if this has not already been done. As we have seen an EOC provides a centralized location from which emergency response, law enforcement, and other agencies coordinate disaster response and recovery.[145] EOCs coordinate through collecting and evaluating critical incident information, establishing priorities for response and recovery, and overseeing the procurement and utilization of equipment and other resources.[146]

An EOC should be located it in a safe area. An alternative location should be established if the primary EOC is damaged. Necessary supplies and equipment to operate the EOC should be acquired. Backup power sources and methods to ensure communications should be arranged, and the criteria to activate the EOC should be determined well in advance of need.[147]

In addition, emergency management personnel must know and anticipate which disasters are most likely to occur in their geographical area. How to address the threats must be carefully considered. A formalized **hazard and vulnerability assessment** will assist in these endeavors. A hazard and vulnerability assessment denotes the major hazards facing a jurisdiction and the capacity to address these hazards. A hazard and vulnerability assessment is often referred to as a Threat and Hazard Identification and Risk Assessment (THIRA). Completing a THIRA for a jurisdiction greatly facilitates rational planning for dealing with future disasters. Based upon the prior history of disasters, and FEMA and state emergency management data, THIRAs help to determine the jurisdiction's EOP content, suitable first responder training, and disaster-related practice exercises.[148]

Hazard and vulnerability assessments should examine all known hazards facing the community (technological, natural, civil) and rank-order them. In addition, extensive demographic data must be collected. The locations and conditions of structures in the built environment must also be noted. Finally, the potential impact of various types of disasters must be estimated.[149] The jurisdiction's EOP should be written following careful consideration of hazards and vulnerabilities.[150]

The jurisdiction's EOP should encompass every function related to anticipated response and recovery operations.[151] The typical sections contained in an EOP include **authority** (the legal basis of the plan such as an ordinance), **purpose** (objectives of the EOP), **situation and assumptions** (list of hazards and how they can interact with each other), **concept of operations** (processes, personnel titles, and strategies to achieve the EOP),

organization and assignment of responsibilities (roles of personnel and departments), **direction and control** (management of the operation), and **plan development and maintenance** (who was responsible for developing the EOC and who will revise the plan).

EOPs must be made in collaboration with relevant stakeholders. It must be distributed and practiced. Failing to do these things will likely result in the failure of the EOC in a real-life emergency or disaster. This is true because there are often gaps between theory (how the EOP looks as written) and reality (how the principles of the EOP work in practice).

This leads to the importance of *training* as part of proactive emergency management. **Training** focuses on teaching personnel how to perform specific tasks utilizing pre-determined methods.[152] Training attempts to apply the theory one has learned to actual practice. This is of special importance to emergency management.

To facilitate training, FEMA operates the **Center for Domestic Preparedness (CDP)** in Anniston, Alabama, and the **Emergency Management Institute (EMI)** in Emmitsburg, Maryland. The FBI and public health agencies provide training courses for the purpose of promoting disaster resilience.[153] But training does not mean as much without practice and exercises. That is why conducting emergency and disaster exercises increases the effectiveness of response and recovery. An **exercise** is a practice simulation of a disaster or emergency that is conducted for the purpose of improving response and recovery operations through practice.[154]

Exercises designed to test theories and plans are a critical part of the success of an emergency management agency. This is true because the purpose of exercises is to *apply* theories to likely scenarios in order to *improve capabilities* and *detect shortcomings.* Effective emergency management agencies must practice their tasks and roles by applying theory to reality in order to achieve their predetermined goals.

Exercises should primarily focus on practice. This focus helps to locate and eliminate problems prior to a real-world disaster.[155] In addition, the focus on practice assists first responders to learn and implement the skills that will be needed in a serious critical incident. Exercises teach first responders about the importance of applying theory to practice through exercises so that our agencies can be better prepared for "all hazards." It also provides specific examples, plans, and methodologies that emergency managers can use to improve their operations to better protect the public.

The best way to test the capability and capacity of an emergency management agency to respond to critical incidents is by means of exercises.[156] In addition, emergency preparedness exercises can be used effectively to foster cooperation between neighboring jurisdictions. Research has shown that neighboring jurisdictions can learn useful practices with which to better deliver response from each other during joint exercises.[157] Exercises serve several purposes for emergency management organizations, including meeting regulatory requirements imposed by the chain of command, clarifying responsibilities and roles, improving communications and coordination, locating performance and resource gaps, and providing ways to improve performance.[158]

It is necessary to distinguish between *discussion-based exercises* and *operations-based exercises.* **Discussion-based exercises** are cheaper and less complex than operations-based exercises. Discussion-based exercises are led by a presenter or director and involve the exchange of dialogue with emergency managers in order to explore disaster scenarios.[159] Discussion-based exercises serve to aid in training, to develop new ideas, and to identify enhancements and improvements to existing plans and procedures. Discussion-based exercises include (1) seminars, (2) workshops, (3) Table-Top Exercises (TTXs), and (4) games. Because discussion-based exercises do not involve sending personnel or equipment to the field, they can be conducted quickly and cheaply.[160] Operations-based exercises, on the other hand, are much more complex and expensive. **Operations-based exercises** involve the deployment of emergency management personnel and resources in order to practice plans and policies in the form of practices and field exercises.[161] Operations-based exercises include (1) drills, (2) functional exercises, and (3) full-scale exercises.

First are **drills**. These are the simplest type of operations-based exercise. A drill is a coordinated, supervised activity usually employed to test a single, specific operation or function within a single entity. For example, if a fire department conducted a decontamination drill.[162] Drills are generally utilized to test personnel, equipment, and facilities on difficult emergency management tasks that are performed infrequently.[163] Drills are necessary to reduce the chance of failure when "the real thing" happens. Drills are conducted by a designated **controller**. Controllers set up and run the scenario. Controllers also often serve as **evaluators**. The primary task of the evaluator is to assess the performance of drill participants and to document shortcomings in EOP or its procedures.[164]

Next are **functional exercises**. A functional exercise examines or validates the coordination, command, and control between various multi-agency coordination centers, such as EOCs and Joint Field Offices. However, a functional exercise does not involve any "boots on the ground" such as first responders pretending to respond to a drill critical incident.[165]

Full-scale exercises are the third type of operations-based exercise. These are the most complex type of exercise. A full-scale exercise is a multi-agency, multi-jurisdictional, multi-discipline exercise involving functional EOCs and "boots on the ground" response such as fire personnel engaging in the process of decontaminating mock hazmat victims.[166] Full-scale exercises are excellent for measuring the full scope of emergency management and emergency response functions simultaneously.[167] Full-scale exercises are very complex and expensive, however.

Whether discussion-based or operations-based, all exercises are designed to channel the thoughts of emergency management participants to think and behave as if they were involved in a real critical incident.[168] This allows capabilities to be practiced prior to an actual crisis or disaster.[169]

The emergency management agency's *Exercise Planning Team* prepares exercise documents in advance of both operations-based exercises and discussion-based exercises. These documents are used to plan and structure the behavior of exercise participants.[170] The Exercise Planning team is also called the **design team.**[171]

In an exercise, the participants include the *design team*, the **players** (the individuals who will be evaluated in the exercise be they first responders or emergency managers), the **victims** (persons who play the role of injured or trapped individuals or witnesses present at a mock critical incident),[172] the **controller** (who runs the exercise), and the **evaluators** (who assess the performance of the players as measured against the EOP or other policies and procedures).[173]

At the conclusion of the exercise, it is time for formal evaluation in the form of an **After Action Report (AAR) and Implementation Plan**. The design team prepares its conclusions and findings of the effectiveness of the exercise to the AAR. This generally includes suggested improvements for future exercises and response efforts.[174] In other words, follow-up is necessary for exercises to be the most effective. The lessons learned must be internalized and changes made to policies and first responder behavior before the next disaster or critical incident.[175] In this way, exercises are a good way to promote resilience.

But so is *public disaster education.* **Public disaster education** is an effort by emergency management professionals to inform members of the public about hazards and vulnerabilities inside the jurisdiction. Public disaster education also involves communicating what to do if a disaster should occur to the public.[176] For example, a public service announcement about what to do in case of a tornado; how and when to evacuate; and the importance of taping or boarding windows prior to a hurricane.

Public disaster education is a mitigation action designed to reduce harm before it occurs. If the general public heeds the advice given, there will be less damage and fewer deaths and injuries when and if a disaster strikes. The converse is also true. When the advice is ignored, or when it is not acted upon due to lack of time or money, public disaster education does little good. Both FEMA and the American Red Cross publish and distribute disaster education materials. Jurisdictions can also develop their own disaster education materials to distribute in utility bills, sporting events, or special events.[177] For example, the Memphis city police and fire departments as well as the city/county emergency management agency distribute substantial information to the community to assist in disaster preparation.[178]

Leadership and Professionalization in Emergency Management

These are all things that public managers can potentially do with their own knowledge, skills, and abilities to enhance resilience. First is leadership. **Leadership** means *to guide or influence* the behavior of others. Or, **leadership** can be thought of as the process whereby one person *influences* others to achieve a goal.[179] Leadership is about gaining *voluntary* compliance from others.

A leader is someone who attempts to exert influence through some sort of power that results in gaining compliance from those being led.[180] Notice the emphasis on *influence* in these definitions. Leadership is that capacity to *influence* the behavior of other people. How this is done and the effective ways this is done have been the subject of many studies and theories. The presence of effective leadership is a significant factor in explaining the success of organizations.

There is a misplaced tendency to equate management with leadership. **Management** is about the day-to-day running of an organization. *Management* is concerned with organizing the workplace, coordinating the activities of employees, and being accountable for success or failure.[181] *Leadership*, by contrast, is something different from management. Leadership goes *beyond* management. A *leader* is someone who *influences* and *inspires* others to achieve a goal.[182]

A leader *inspires* others to reach a goal – a goal based upon the leader's *vision* of the future.[183] So, *management* is more mundane than *leadership* in that *management* is concerned with the day-to-day tasks of operating the organization. *Leadership* is something else: a leader *inspires* and *guides* others towards his or her *vision* of the future. Leaders *stimulate* others to grow and change in new directions.

Management is not synonymous with leadership. A good manager *may not* be a good leader. *Some* managers are good leaders and some are not. Management and leadership require different behaviors, but these behaviors can *sometimes* overlap. Keep in mind that management and leadership are conceptually distinct.[184]

The presence of effective leadership *in addition* to effective management can make a substantial difference in how well an emergency management agency or agency subunit operates during response and recovery. Effective leaders possess disaster response and recovery experience and have a vision.[185]

Another part of effective emergency management leadership is having response and recovery plans in place in advance of a disaster. But this is not always enough. Such plans may need to be modified depending upon the situation "on the ground." This is because unforeseen events may occur to the community during a critical incident. EOPs cannot anticipate every contingency.[186] This leads to the concepts of *spontaneous planning* and *improvisation.*

Spontaneous planning deals with predetermined actions that occur at the scene of a disaster or critical incident designed to improve the situation.[187] Spontaneous planning is based on *improvisation.* **Improvisation** is about immediate adaptation to a changing situation. Spontaneous planning is important in the field of emergency management.[188]

Creativity and flexibility are components of improvisation. **Creativity** is about developing novel ways to achieve goals.[189] **Flexibility** deals with the desire to deviate from standard operating procedures in the event of a compelling need to solve emerging problems.[190] In other words, effective emergency management leadership requires understanding the field, working with others, experience-based decision-making, and the ability to improvise through using creativity and flexibility as part of spontaneous planning.

Professionalism is also very important in emergency management. One of the goals of this book is to assist in the education, training, and development of *professional* emergency managers. Professions must meet certain requirements in order to be properly called by that term.[191] This leads us to the **characteristics of a profession**. The features of a profession involve membership certification, the presence of an organized body of knowledge pertaining to that profession, and written ethical standards.[192] As a profession, emergency management can be evaluated according to these criteria.[193]

First is **membership certification**. The principle behind membership certification is to exclude persons that are unqualified. Membership certification is closely associated with education and training deemed essential by that profession. Education generally is proven by the possession of an earned degree from a regionally accredited college or university.[194]

Training is required for professions for the purpose of demonstrating the ability to engage in currently accepted practices. Training must be updated through continuing education to keep current with the required skills.[195] Training and certification are linked. **Certification** is used to provide assurance that a named individual is qualified to carry out a specific task.[196] To this end, FEMA offers many certification programs for both emergency managers and first responders. Through a combination of education and training, one gains credentials in the emergency management profession. For example, FEMA maintains the Emergency Management Institute. It has a physical location in Emmitsburg, MD and a substantial online presence. The

FEMA Emergency Management Institute offers a *Professional Development Series* and an *Advanced Professional Series* to provide specialized emergency management training.[197] FEMA certificates can be used to maintain or enhance one's credentials.

The highest certification possible to obtain in the emergency management field is the **CEM (Certified Emergency Manager)**. The CEM is offered through the International Association of Emergency Managers (IAEM). The CEM is designed to ensure that an individual possesses competence in integrated emergency management systems.[198]

To obtain the CEM, an emergency manager must have demonstrated knowledge, skills, and experience in the field. First, one must have a bachelor's degree at a minimum. Second, an individual must also possess three years of emergency management work experience. In addition, a person must have either (a) managed a significant disaster event or (b) managed a full-scale exercise. In addition, CEM candidates must have completed one hundred hours each of emergency management training and general management training. CEM certification requires training in all phases of emergency management. Candidates must document six of the following in addition to demonstrating contributions to the emergency management profession: publications, teaching, serving on boards, membership in emergency management professional associations, course development, or giving emergency-management related speeches to the public.[199] CEM applicants must also pass an examination and recertify every five years.[200]

An **organized body of knowledge** is the second characteristic of a profession. A profession must have a body of accumulated knowledge that is agreed as being necessary to practice that profession.[201] In the profession of emergency management, this knowledge is science-based. Such knowledge evolves from experience and analysis. There are journals, textbooks, organizations, and academic programs in emergency management that collect and disseminate this knowledge.

The existence of a recognized and established body of tested knowledge is critical. It lends support to the assertion that emergency management is a critical profession that meaningfully contributes to managing hazards and vulnerabilities.[202] In addition, this body of knowledge orients practice. This established knowledge also maintains a benchmark with which to evaluate the performance of emergency managers.[203]

To be most effective, there needs to be a link between theory and practice. Theory orients action, and provides a framework for understanding disasters and emergency management. Practice is based upon both training and experience. Theory cannot take the place of practice, just as practice cannot take the place of theory. These principles apply very much to emergency management. Training, certifications, academic courses, and degrees help to advance the emergency management profession through disseminating the profession's substantive knowledge.

The third characteristic of a profession is recognized **ethical standards**. Professions collectively teach aspiring member members the ethical standards expected in one's actions. Adherence to ethical standards helps to define the professional culture in that they limit abuse of discretion on the job. Professional ethics are contained in written ethical codes. Ethical codes stipulate compliance.[204] In the emergency management profession, the **IAEM (International Association of Emergency Managers)** is the professional organization that has established and recognized ethical standards.[205] All these things have led to an increased recognition of emergency management as a field and as a profession.

The ultimate strategy of emergency management to effectively respond to and to help communities recover from disasters and emergencies is greatly enhanced when four conditions exist: (1) the community is prepared, (2) first responders are able to improvise solutions to emergencies and disasters when needed, (3) emergency management personnel possess solid leadership abilities, and (4) emergency managers are well trained and educated professionals.[206]

Strategies for preparedness planning in law enforcement are never entirely complete. Plans and initiatives that are published by law enforcement agencies and emergency management organizations must be exercised and modified based on past experience in order to have a meaningful impact on disaster response and recovery.[207] The U.S. Department of Homeland Security recognizes this. For that reason, it developed and published the Homeland Security Exercise Evaluation Program (HSSEP) in 2020. The HSSEP is designed to help ensure that first responder agencies keep their plans "alive" through exercises and modified as a result of lessons learned.[208]

In order to comply with HSSEP, first responder agencies receiving federal funds under several DHS grant programs must follow the Multi-Year Training and Exercise Plan (MYTEP). MYTEP requires that agencies utilize a building-block approach and sequence exercises accordingly, employ capability-based planning, and taking measures to foster continuous improvement.[209] The HSSEP covers both discussion-based and operations-based exercises. Each must be coordinated through the use of a building-block approach in order to meaningfully affect the performance of first responder behavior when a real emergency or disaster strikes. In addition, problems with EOPs can become known only when exercises demonstrate the shortcomings of plans as they exist on paper.[210]

Notes

1. Willard M. Oliver, *Policing In An Era of Homeland Security*, New York: Oxford University Press, 2020: 103.
2. Andrea M. Jackman and Mario G. Beruvides, "Local Hazard Mitigation Plans: A Preliminary Estimation of State-Level Completion From 2004-2009," *Journal of Emergency Management*, Vol. 11, No. 2, March/April 2013: 121.
3. Dylan Sandler and Gavin Smith, "Assessing the Quality of State Disaster Recovery Plans: Implications for Policy and Practice," *Journal of Emergency Management*, Vol. 11, No. 4, July/August 2013: 281.
4. Ibid.
5. Michael K. Lindell, Carla Prater, and Ronald W. Perry, *Introduction to Emergency Management*, Hoboken, John Wiley and Sons, Inc., 2007: 47-71.
6. Ibid: 267.
7. Ibid.
8. Ibid: 267-268.
9. Ibid: 268.
10. Ibid: 269.
11. Ibid.
12. http://www.calhospitalprepare.org/emergency-operations-plan
13. Mark R. Landhal and Stacy L. Muffet-Willett, "Preparedness and Planning for Law Enforcement Operations," in *The Role of Law Enforcement in Emergency Management and Homeland Security*, Mark R. Landhal and Tonya E. Thornton, Editors, Bingley, United Kingdom, Emerald Publishing Limited, 2021: 183.
14. Lindell, Prater, and Perry, *Introduction to Emergency Management*: 287.
15. Ibid.
16. Ibid: 287-288.
17. Ibid.
18. www.fema.gov/pdf/plan/5-ch-0.pdf
19. Ibid.
20. Ibid.
21. www.chathamemergency.org/eoc/. Emphasis added.
22. Ibid.
23. Ibid.
24. Michael J. Fagel, Editor, *Principles of Emergency Management: Hazard Specific Issues and Mitigation Strategies*, Boca Raton: CRC Press/Taylor and Francis Group, 2012: 297.
25. Lilian R. Butterworth, Steve Riedel, and J. Eric Dietz, "Costs and Benefits of a Typical County's Emergency Response Program," *Journal of Emergency Management*, Vol. 9, No. 4, July/August 2011: 19.
26. Fagel, *Principles of Emergency Management*: 166-167.
27. Ibid: 167.
28. Ibid: 166.
29. Ibid.
30. Ibid.
31. Robert C. Kenter and Michael Goldsmith, "Law Enforcement and the Protection of Critical Infrastructures," in *The Role of Law Enforcement in*

Emergency Management and Homeland Security, Mark R. Landhal and Tonya E. Thornton, Editors, Bingley, United Kingdom, Emerald Publishing Limited, 2021: 15.

32. Ibid: 168-169.
33. Ibid: 166.
34. Ibid.
35. Ibid: 167. Emphasis in original.
36. Ibid. Emphasis in original.
37. Ibid. Emphasis in original.
38. Ibid.
39. Ibid.
40. Ibid: 168.
41. Ibid: 173.
42. Ibid.
43. Ibid.
44. Ibid: 177.
45. Ibid: 173.
46. Ibid: 174.
47. Ibid: 175.
48. Ibid.
49. Ibid: 176.
50. Ibid: 175.
51. Ibid: 178.
52. Ibid: 182-186.
53. Ibid: 186.
54. Ibid: 188.
55. Ibid: 189.
56. Ibid.
57. Ibid.
58. Ibid: 189-190.
59. Ibid: 189.
60. Ibid: 190.
61. Ibid.
62. Robin J. Clark and Adrian Wilairat, "Bringing it all Back Home: Continuity of Government Planning for Local Government," *Journal of Emergency Management*, Vol 7, No. 5, September/October 2009: 19.
63. Ibid: 44.
64. Ibid.
65. Ibid.
66. Ibid: 45.
67. Ibid.
68. Fagel, *Principles of Emergency Management*: 46.
69. Ibid.
70. Landahl and Muffet, Willet, "Preparedness and Planning for Law Enforcement Operations:" 185.
71. Fagel, *Principles of Emergency Management*: 46-47.

72. Ibid: 47.
73. Ibid: 49.
74. Ibid.
75. Ibid: 50.
76. Ibid: 49-50.
77. Ibid: 50.
78. Ibid.
79. Ibid: 56.
80. Ibid: 55-56.
81. Ibid: 55.
82. Ibid: 56.
83. Ibid: 57.
84. Ibid: 56-57.
85. Ibid: 61.
86. Ibid: 62.
87. Ibid: 65.
88. Ibid: 62.
89. Ibid: 65.
90. David A. McEntire, *Disaster Response and Recovery: Strategies and Tactics for Resilience*, 2nd Edition, Hoboken, John Wiley and Sons, Inc., 2015: 395.
91. Ibid: 440.
92. Ibid: 439-440.
93. Ibid: 398. Emphasis in original.
94. Ibid: 400. Emphasis in original.
95. Ibid: 398. Emphasis in original.
96. Ibid.
97. Ibid: 399. Emphasis in original.
98. Ibid.
99. Ibid.
100. Lindell, Prater, and Perry, *Introduction to Emergency Management*: 108.
101. McEntire, *Disaster Response and Recovery*: 405.
102. Ibid: 431.
103. Ibid.
104. Ibid.
105. McEntire, *Disasters and Public Health*: 6.
106. Ibid: 415.
107. Fagel, *Principles of Emergency Management*: 359.
108. Ibid: 176.
109. McEntire, *Disaster Response and Recovery*: 415.
110. Ibid: 418.
111. Ibid.
112. Ibid: 421.
113. Ibid: 432.
114. Ibid.
115. Ibid.
116. Ibid: 433.

117. Ibid: 434.
118. Ibid.
119. Ibid: 435.
120. Ibid: 436.
121. Ibid.
122. Ibid: 437.
123. Ibid: 36.
124. Ibid: 59.
125. McEntire, *Disaster Response and Recovery*: 451.
126. Ibid: 452.
127. Ibid.
128. Ibid.
129. Q.v. "ordinance" in *Black's Law Dictionary*, Abridged 6th Edition, St. Paul, West Publishing Co., 1991.
130. McEntire, *Disaster Response and Recovery*: 452.
131. Ibid.
132. Ibid: 454.
133. Ibid.
134. Ibid: 455.
135. Ibid.
136. Lindell, Prater, Perry, *Introduction to Emergency Management*: 51.
137. Ibid.
138. Ibid.
139. Mary E. Guy and Todd L. Ely, *Essentials of Public Service: An Introduction to Contemporary Public Administration*, Lehigh: *Melvin and Leigh Publishers*, 2018: 249. Emphasis added.
140. McEntire, *Disaster Response and Recovery*: 456.
141. Ibid: 457.
142. Lance T. LeLoup, *Politics In America*, 2nd Edition, St. Paul, West Publishing Co., 1989: 78. Emphasis added.
143. McEntire, *Disaster Response and Recovery*: 457.
144. Ibid: 455.
145. www.chathamemergency.org/eoc/
146. Ibid.
147. McEntire, *Disaster Response and Recovery*: 458.
148. Ibid: 460.
149. Ibid.
150. Ibid: 461.
151. Ibid: 461.
152. Lindell, Prater, and Perry, *Introduction to Emergency Management*: 460.
153. Ibid.
154. Ibid: 464.
155. Fagel, *Principles of Emergency Management*: 226.
156. Ibid: 225.
157. Nicole A. Erret, Shannon Frattaroli, Daniel J. Barnett, Beth A. Resnick, and Lainie Rutkow, "The Use of Exercises to Enhance and Assess Interlocal

Collaboration in Preparedness: A Qualitative Analysis," *Journal of Emergency Management*, Vol. 13, No. 6, November/December 2011: 499.

158. Fagel, Principles of Emergency Management: 226.
159. Ibid: 230.
160. Ibid.
161. Ibid: 230-231.
162. www.calhospitalprepare.org/post/what-difference-between-tabletop-exercise-drill-functional-exercise-and-full-scale-exercise
163. Lindell, Prater, and Perry, Introduction to Emergency Management: 402.
164. Ibid: 403-404.
165. www.calhospitalprepare.org/post/what-difference-between-tabletop-exercise-drill-functional-exercise-and-full-scale-exercise
166. Ibid.
167. Lindell, Prater, and Perry, *Introduction to Emergency Management*: 405.
168. Fagel, *Principles of Emergency Management*: 234.
169. Ibid: 226.
170. Ibid: 231.
171. McEntire, *Disaster Response and Recovery*: 466
172. Ibid.
173. Ibid.
174. Fagel, Principles of Emergency Management: 260.
175. McEntire, *Disaster Response and Recovery*: 466
176. Ibid: 479.
177. Ibid.
178. Sheila M. Huss, Abdul-Akeem Sadiq, and Christopher M. Weible, "Organizations and Emergency Management: Information, Trust, and Preparedness," *Journal of Emergency Management*, Vol. 10, No. 5, September/October 2012: 359.
179. G. Yulk and D. D. VanFleet, "Theory and Research On Leadership in Organizations," in M. S. Dunnette and L. M. Hough, eds., *Handbook of Industrial and Organizational Psychology*, Volume 3 (Palo Alto, CA: Consulting Psychology Press, 1992): 147-198 in Don Hellriegel, John W. Slocum, and Richard W. Woodman, *Organizational Behavior*, Eighth Edition, Cincinnati, South-Western College Publishing, 1998: 301.
180. Michael L. Vasu, Debra W. Stewart, and G. David Garson, Garson, *Organizational Behavior and Public Management*, 3rd Edition, Marcel Dekker, 1998: 90.
181. Ibid, 92 and Don Hellriegel, John W. Slocum, and Richard W. Woodman, *Organizational Behavior*, 7th Edition, South-Western College Publishing 1995: 301.
182. Ibid.
183. Hellriegel, Slocum, and Woodman, *Organizational Behavior*: 301-303.
184. Ibid.
185. McEntire, *Disaster Response and Recovery*: 475
186. Ibid: 469.
187. Ibid. Emphasis in original.
188. Ibid: 470. Emphasis in original.

189. Ibid: 471. Emphasis in original.
190. Ibid. Emphasis in original.
191. Lindell, Prater, and Perry, *Introduction to Emergency Management*: 449.
192. Ibid: 451.
193. Ibid.
194. Ibid: 449
195. Ibid: 450.
196. Ibid.
197. Ibid: 453.
198. Ibid: 459.
199. Ibid: 458-459.
200. Ibid: 459.
201. Ibid: 450.
202. Ibid: 455.
203. Ibid.
204. Lindell, Prater, and Perry, *Introduction to Emergency Management*: 451.
205. Ibid: 463.
206. McEntire, Disaster Response and Recovery: 478.
207. Landahl and Muffet-Willett, "Preparedness and Planning for Law Enforcement Operations:" 188.
208. Ibid.
209. Ralph Reneger and Brenda Granillo, "Developing a Comprehensive, Integrated and Meaningful Multi-Year Training and Exercise Plan," *Journal of Emergency Management*, Vol. 10, No. 5, September/October 2012: 383.
210. Ralph Renger, Jessica Wakelee, Jillian Bradshaw, and Lisle Hites, "Steps in Writing An Effective Master Scenario Effects List," *Journal of Emergency Management*, Vol 7, No. 6, November/December 2009: 51.

Chapter 8

EMERGENCY MANAGEMENT OPERATIONS FOR LAW ENFORCEMENT

Many law enforcement operations designed to support emergency management lie in the transitional area between strategy and tactics. The management of law enforcement agencies engages in a process to transform broad strategies into actions that will have an impact on the real world.[1] Operations involve deploying first responder employees for the purpose of achieving strategic goals by ensuring that they are prepared for all hazards and properly directed on the street.[2] To this end, the importance of effectively utilizing available technology to bring about best practices in response and recovery is covered in Chapter 8. In addition, organizational design structures that have been developed to aid first responders and emergency managers to operate more efficiently and effectively are discussed.[3]

Technology, Law Enforcement, and Emergency Management

Technology can be used along with effective organizational design to increase resilience after a disaster. Technology can be channeled to improve emergency management response and recovery efforts.[4] Technology and effective organizational design assist in the improvement of decision-making, working more effectively with others, assessing disaster impacts, and in the allocation of resources. For example, understanding Incident Command (ICS) principles as well as its limitations helps to increase resilience. Developing the skills to work in and operate an EOC (Emergency Operations Center) is another vitally important skill that can increase resilience.[5] In order to utilize organizational designs and technology to perform one's emergency management-related job more effectively, an employee must understand the NIMS (National Incident Management System), the NDRF (National Disaster Recovery Framework), and the National Response Framework (NRF). Possessing this understanding will help first responders and emergency managers perform their disaster-related tasks effectively and improve working relationships with other jurisdictions at all three levels of the American government.[6]

Law enforcement agencies utilize technology to support criticality and vulnerability assessments in order to prevent and prepare for terrorism. **Criticality assessments** are conducted to identify likely terrorist targets in a geographical area. **Vulnerability assessments** attempt to determine how weak or strong a given target is in relation to a possible terrorist attack.[7]

First, technology is examined. Then, organizational designs oriented toward more effective emergency management will be discussed. Being aware of available technology is very important in order to more effectively carry out emergency management duties.[8] Technology plays a vital role in response and recovery endeavors. Technology is also changing rapidly. New technology will bring about greater effectiveness in disaster operations.[9] Some of these technologies include LIDAR (Light Detection and Ranging), remote sensing, Doppler radar, GPS (Global Positioning System), and traffic signal preemption devices.

GIS (Geographic Information System) is a technology used extensively in emergency management. GIS is a collection of computer software, hardware, and geographic data designed to maintain, update, display, and analyze different forms of geographical information. GIS is used to assist first responder and emergency managers to quickly determine the structures, roads, and other information present at a given location.[10]

GIS data is used in all four phases of emergency management: mitigation, preparedness, response, and recovery. For example, FEMA operates **HAZUS**. HAZUS is a nationwide GIS-based methodology that utilizes models for the purpose of estimating losses in a given area that would occur from floods, hurricanes, and earthquakes. HAZUS employs GIS capabilities to estimate economic, social, and physical impacts of possible future disasters. HAZUS can be used in all four phases of the emergency management cycle. Emergency managers and government planners utilize HAZUS to determine appropriate mitigation efforts based on estimated losses.[11]

GIS programs have also been used extensively to facilitate better post-disaster decision-making with regard to hurricanes and oil spills. GIS can be utilized to showcase structures and other assets that have been destroyed after a disaster. GIS also displays downed utility lines and assists in developing priorities during response and recovery operations.[12] Post-disaster GIS uses include showing the path of tornadoes, assessing the extent of fires, earthquakes, and floods, how to access disaster sites, and viewing which structures have been condemned.

GIS is used to improve decision-making in critical incidents that utilize ICS. For example, GIS data can inform first responders about safe areas to evacuate survivors. GIS information can indicate the best staging areas to support critical incident operations. If police vehicles have been equipped with GPS receiving devices, their real-time locations will be known to the Operations Section.[13]

In addition to GIS, many other software programs exist to assist emergency managers with disaster response efforts. Collectively, these are commonly called **Decision Support Systems (DSS).** These are software programs designed to facilitate the determination of priorities in terms of response.[14] Like Geographical Information Systems, DSSs can be used to support response, recovery, mitigation and preparation.

Several Decision Support Systems relevant to emergency management include E-**Team**, which is used to assist in damage assessment and to better manage disasters. **SoftRisk** aids in critical incident management. **WEBEOC** helps to manage EOCs. **EPlan** and **CAMEO** are used to facilitate better HAZMAT management.

Communications equipment is another important aspect of technology. Because so many agencies are involved in first response and emergency management, communications *interoperability* is vital. **Interoperability** refers to the capability of a device to communicate with and operate across different first responder organizations.[15] **ACU-1000 equipment** is used to facilitate interoperability. ACU-1000 is interface equipment used to link together mobile radios, landline and cellular telephones, and satellite technology in a single communication system during periods of disasters and emergencies. ACU-1000 allows the cross-connection and routing of communications over wide area networks (WAN). State, local, and federal first responder organizations possess the capability to coordinate actions with multiple agencies to facilitate interoperability.[16]

Now that some technology designed to improve emergency management has been reviewed, an examination of organizational structures and designs that have been developed for the same purpose will be examined. Three of these designs are the ICS (Incident Command System), the NIMS (National Incident Management System), and the EOC (Emergency Operations Center). All of these have been covered in previous chapters. NIMS, EOCs, and ICS are viewed as rationally designed organizational structures developed to increase the efficiency and effectiveness of first responder and emergency management organizations.

In large-scale disasters, EOCs and ICS are used to achieve the objective of coordinating disaster response. EOCs and ICS work in tandem to achieve the goals of saving lives, reducing disruption, and protecting property.[17] However, they serve different purposes. It has been said that the primary focus of ICS lies with tactical decisions and operations. The primary focus of EOCs lies on strategic issues.[18] For example, ICS would be used to provide medical care at a mass casualty event, and EOCs would see to it that appropriate medical staff and supplies were dispatched to the critical incident site.

In law enforcement, it must be noted that ICS is generally activated a substantial time after the first officers arrive on the scene. In a typical scenario, officers present make tactical decisions and communicate with dispatch. Only in major critical incidents is the management decision made to transition to ICS in law enforcement.[19] Law enforcement agencies use **ILP (Intelligence-Led Policing)** to obtain information for preventing terrorist attacks. ILP utilizes technology to both supplement intelligence gathering and to analyze this information.[20]

ICS and EOCs are used to work more effectively with different emergency management agencies at the local level.[21] Other ways with which this can be accomplished are through **Memorandums of Understanding (MOUs)** and **mutual aid agreements**. Both are used to facilitate cooperation and assistance between first responder agencies in the same jurisdiction and between jurisdictions.[22]

MOUs are agreements between first responder and emergency management agencies to define shared responsibilities in advance of an emergency or disaster. Mutual aid agreements are more formal and may be legally binding. **Mutual aid** involves the sharing of equipment, facilities, and personnel between jurisdictions. Mutual aid is utilized when a jurisdiction discovers that its own resources are not sufficient to deal effectively with a disaster. This is most often seen when adjacent local governments share resources. In catastrophic disasters that cover a wide area, state governments and even the federal government may also share resources. Mutual aid has proven to be vital after major disasters because many municipalities and counties would not be able to engage in meaningful response and recovery efforts without the assistance of other jurisdictions.[23]

Mutual aid agreements and MOUs allow the acquisition of vitally needed resources after disasters. Indeed, it may be the case that local governments will be required to have activated mutual aid agreements before being legally able to request federal disaster assistance.[24] MOUs and mutual aid agreements have other advantages as well. They resolve issues associated with joint operations in advance of disasters, and they help to reduce friction between first responder agencies and jurisdictions.[25]

Mutual aid agreements of smaller jurisdictions should make an effort to request linkage with the nearest **All-Hazards Incident Management Team**. Large cities and metropolitan areas sometimes maintain All-Hazards Incident Management Teams (AHIMT). These teams are composed of credentialed first responders from various emergency management disciplines. AHIMT teams possess statutory authority to perform emergency functions and are available 24 hours per day if needed. They possess their own command and staff members. AHIMTs often operate at the regional level to assist other jurisdictions during crisis situations.[26]

If a catastrophe overwhelms local resources (even those bolstered by MOUs and mutual aid agreements), jurisdictions can appeal to the state government for assistance. Because all fifty states have a state emergency management agency, each state agency is able to work with other emergency management-related state agencies, FEMA, and local emergency management organizations.[27]

State governors have the authority to declare a state-level state of emergency. If a disaster is of a magnitude that requires assistance that cannot be provided by state emergency management resources, the governor may call up the National Guard and seek additional assistance. National Guard forces can assist police forces, engage in search and rescue operations, and engage in clearing roads from debris. The governor may also elect to request aid from the federal government or from other state governments.[28]

Governors can request assistance from other states through the **EMAC (Emergency Management Assistance Compact)**, which is a mutual aid agreement between states to share emergency management resources during disasters.[29] As an example, the Tennessee state government maintains **TEMA (Tennessee Emergency Management Agency)**. TEMA manages substantial grant funding to facilitate all four phases of emergency management. TEMA also facilitates the flow of special teams, services, supplies, and equipment to disaster areas.[30] In addition, TEMA coordinates mutual aid from other state agencies and channels them to disaster impact areas. This serves as a force multiplier with regard to response and recovery. If necessary, TEMA also requests mutual aid from other states and the federal government.[31]

TEMA established and maintains a State Emergency Operations Center. Tennessee's state EOC has integrated communications systems and other vital equipment and other resources with which to better coordinate state-level response and recovery efforts. TEMA also has a command post bus and several communications trailers to support critical incident management.[32] Despite mutual aid agreements, the addition of state government assets, and MOUs, some disasters are of such a magnitude that even combined local and state resources are insufficient. If this occurs, it is necessary for the federal government to intervene for the purpose of providing additional assistance.[33]

Executive Decision-Making by Senior Agency Managers

This section examines the decision-making process of an organization's senior management (the **Executive Policy Group**) during a critical incident. It deals with the decision-based actions that the senior management should take to enable the organization to continue its operations and to deal with (and ultimately recover) from a critical incident.[34] Even smaller-scale critical incidents sometimes require the decisions and actions of the organization's Executive Policy Group. This section suggests ways to improve the Executive Policy Group's decision-making during critical incidents, both inside and outside an internal Emergency Operations Center.

For the purposes of critical incident management and the involvement of the Executive Policy Group in critical incidents, the Executive Policy Group in first responder agencies should consist of a small number of individuals. The most senior four to six members of the organization are sufficient.[35]

The Executive Policy Group strategically determines the operational goals for the agency's response. When this group meets, it should do so away from the command post or EOC operations. A conference room is an appropriate place for the Executive Policy Group to meet.[36] This is a suitable forum for discussion and interaction designed to make the important decisions that will be transmitted to lower-level organizational employees.[37]

For example, an important task of the Executive Policy Group involves making decisions regarding the need to close nonessential government offices, educational institutions, or businesses due to disasters. In addition, making COOP decisions (Continuity of Operations Planning) during a crisis is another important task of this group. Other important policy decisions made by the Executive Policy Group can include when to release incident information to the public and the timing of notifying affected family members of disaster victims.[38]

Decisions should be made as quickly as possible while maintaining rationality. The failure to make and convey Executive Policy Group decisions in a timely manner harms response efforts and can lead to on-scene incident commanders making too many independent decisions that may be harmful in the long term. This can lead to tension and conflict between hierarchical levels of the organizations, which can also harm response efforts at a critical incident.[39] To avoid this, the head of the agency must take proactive steps about (1) setting up the Executive Policy Group quickly if a critical incident occurs and (2) developing and understanding a *concept of operations* for the organization. Doing these things will bring about a more effective and efficient policy decision process when a critical incident occurs.

For that reason, the Executive Policy Group should take measures prior to critical incidents to prepare for quality decision-making under stressful conditions.[40] In order to prepare, the Executive Policy Group should (a) prioritize the most likely hazards faced by the organization that could lead to a critical incident, (b) project the best policy decisions that will likely have to be made for each type of critical incident, and (c) establish critical event *thresholds* for making each decision. In other words, they should determine the types of scenarios that would necessitate triggering different types of policy decisions.[41]

By anticipating the most likely hazards to which the organization is exposed, predicting the likely consequences of critical incidents related to these hazards, identifying critical event "thresholds" for making decisions, anticipating policy decisions, and recording these for future reference, the Executive Policy Group will be in a much stronger position to make good choices when and if a critical incident occurs.[42] Failing to follow this process typically leads to "traps" in which the Executive Policy Group actually interferes in the critical incident resolution. These "traps" include (1) rushing to the scene, (2) becoming overly involved with the critical incident scene, (3) trying to achieve full consensus on policy decisions during a crisis, and (4) removing the incident commander from the scene in order to answer questions.[43] Each of these "traps" interferes with the rational resolution of the critical incident and results in haphazard "seat of the pants" decision-making.

Rather than attempting to "micro-manage" the scene or taking the Incident Commander "hostage" in the administration building, the more appropriate way for the Executive Policy Group to obtain up-to-date information would be to either (A) send an Agency Representative to the Command Post (CP) or the internal EOC to gather information and intelligence, or (B) to run an **electronic log** that would provide secure "real-time" information to decision-makers.[44] The principle is designed to provide vital incident information to the Executive Policy Group so that they can make vital decisions while avoiding interference with emergency responders and the actions that they have to take "on the ground."

In summary, the Executive Policy Group and the functions that it performs are vital parts of the concept of operations for first responder organizations. Its members make important policy decisions, establish the tone for the response to the critical incident, and help to keep the agency focused on its mission.[45]

In our modern world, critical incidents occur with more frequency than in the past. For this reason, the Executive Policy Group must be formed, trained, and prepared to make policy decisions during a crisis. When a critical incident occurs, its members must know where to report, where to obtain critical information, and be able to effectively communicate their decisions to their employees. Achieving these things requires both preparation and training. Members of the Executive Policy Group must be aware of and understand the organization's EOP and its COOP.[46]

The Importance of Public-Private Partnerships in Emergency Management

Few local emergency management agencies receive substantial funding from state governments or from the federal government. For this reason, carrying out the goals of disaster prevention, mitigation, preparedness, response, and recovery by emergency management organizations is greatly enhanced by outside assistance. This is why Public-Private Partnerships are critical to emergency management organizations and the goals of emergency management agencies.[47]

Public-Private Partnerships (PPPs or P3s) involve structured relationships between government agencies and for-profit and not-for-profit organizations. These latter organizations include NGOs (Non-Governmental Organizations like the American Red Cross) and faith-based groups. Emergency management is more effective when it combines resources with private-sector entities and even interested private citizens.[48]

The federal government recognizes this as well. It is noted that the mandate of the U.S. Department of Homeland Security stipulates that DHS must work with private sector entities to carry out its mission. Keep in mind that more than eighty percent of the Critical Infrastructure (CI) of the United States is operated and controlled by the private sector. Natural disasters are most likely to impact the private sector. Most targets selected by terrorists are civilians who work and live in the private sector. It is for these reasons that preparedness for disasters should focus on this sector.[49]

Law enforcement agencies also engage in partnerships, especially mutual aid agreements with other jurisdictions, to share resources during times of crisis. With regard to terrorism prevention, since 9/11 many fusion centers have been created across the United States. A **fusion center** is a collaborative effort by two or more law enforcement agencies to share resources and information for the purpose of detecting, preventing, and responding to criminal activity, especially terrorism.[50]

Since so much of the economy and the infrastructure of the United States are privately controlled, it is absolutely necessary that emergency managers and private organizations cooperate to provide emergency and disaster services. Both the public and private sectors share many common goals. This is especially true with regard to saving lives and protecting property. Public-private partnerships are one way to solidify this "common ground" relationship. The most successful emergency management programs are those that involve the private sector.[51] This need has increased in recent years.

For example, both public sector and private sector organizations share similar preparedness needs. In both sectors, preparedness, response, and recovery operations should begin with and include evacuation plans, communications capabilities, and a COOP (Continuity of Operations Plan).[52] Examining the private sector response to 9/11 especially demonstrated that most private sector entities are not prepared for a terrorist attack.[53]

The private sector should be more prepared for disasters. The vast majority of the CI (Critical Infrastructure) is owned and operated by private entities. Electricity, communications, and potable water are examples. The United

States relies strongly on private sector CI to sustain the economy, provide food and water, and even defense.[54] However, private sector CI owners are the ones primarily responsible for protecting the services that they create. For that reason, mitigating the true effect of disasters relies to a substantial degree upon private sector preparation and response.[55]

To assist in this endeavor, the **American National Standards Institute (ANSI)** was asked to develop a **National Standard for Preparedness** for private sector organizations. ANSI brought together security, safety, and COOP personnel from across private industry and consulted with local, state, and federal government representatives for the purpose of developing continuity and emergency preparedness standards for private sector businesses and other organizations.[56]

In cooperation with the **National Fire Protection Association**, ANSI recommended that private businesses adopt the National Preparedness Standard based upon the **American National Standard on Disaster/ Emergency Management and Business Continuity Programs (NFPA 1600)**. This document established a common terminology and criteria with which to guide preparedness, disaster response and recovery, and business continuity programs.[57] It is responsible business practice for corporations to adopt the National Preparedness Standard, which is voluntary.

Government emergency management efforts cannot "do it all" with regard to protecting the infrastructure. Thus, government responses will never be sufficient without private sector cooperation. Similarly, private sector organizations must be aware of how government and government-supported first responder agencies will respond. Thus, governments need to collaborate with the private sector to develop and implement response plans for major disasters in order to optimize emergency management effectiveness.[58]

This is why building and maintaining public-private partnerships is so important. Since the government has taken the lead in emergency management efforts, local and state governments are frequently the initiators of PPPs. It is considered the duty of effective emergency managers to engage in the process of developing relationships with disaster management stakeholders in the private and nonprofit sectors.[59] PPPs can help to leverage the emergency management resources of both government and businesses. Therein lies their strength.

In the past, many emergency management PPPs had been oriented mostly towards training and planning. In addition, other common PPPs seen in emergency management involve debris removal, emergency temporary housing, and food, water, and ice supplies for disaster victims. PPP initiatives should be expanded in order to more effectively respond to major disasters.[60]

Next, the types of PPPs will be examined. Many PPPs have operated for decades in both emergency management and under the old Civil Defense apparatus.[61] There are three types of PPP: (1) Joint Public-Private Partnership, (2) Private to Government PPP, and (3) Government to Private PPP.

In a **Joint Public-Private Partnership**, both the government emergency management agency and the business emergency management employees combine resources to pursue a project or to enlist a service. Each entity uses its own resources, including employees, equipment, and funding. Typically, a contract between the entities solidifies this relationship.[62]

A **Private to Government PPP** is funded by the private business but the emergency management services are provided by government agencies – for example, a private corporation paying a municipal fire department to dispose of hazardous industrial materials.[63]

The third type of PPP is the most common public-private partnership, the **Government to Private PPP**. Here, a government purchases services from a private sector organization. The purchase of these services can be funded through legislative line-item appropriations or through grants.[64] Good examples of this are governments contracting with private firms to provide disaster equipment or software, which is continuously supported by the seller. Another example would occur when an emergency management agency has an ongoing relationship with a private ambulance service to take disabled citizens to emergency shelters due to a disaster. These examples are not simply business transactions but involve ongoing dynamic relationships between a government emergency management agency and a private business.

New PPPs can be created to provide emergency management services where none presently exist. To this end, several strategies to help emergency managers to create PPPs have been developed. First, a plan must be established. This plan should address important issues, such as the purpose, goals, expectations, costs, benefits, and other matters to both parties.

Emergency managers should seek PPP support from stakeholders in private businesses. In this context, stakeholders are persons with a personal or financial interest in preventing or responding to disasters. Private sector infrastructure areas include hardware retailers, along with the potential resources they can provide to the public in a disaster situation, such as protective and repair supplies. Finding common ground and shared interests is the key to beginning the PPP conversation.[65]

Once stakeholders are identified, they can then be approached about developing a PPP. The best way to do this is for the emergency manager to convince the private sector stakeholders that such a relationship will be mutually beneficial. In addition, he or she should discuss how a future partnership will benefit the entire community. Asking someone to enter into a one-sided relationship is unlikely to be successful.[66] "Talking points" designed to help convince businesses to enter into PPPs include the mutual benefit that enhanced levels of preparedness will lead to a more effective joint resolution to a disaster would be helpful. In addition, organizations such as FEMA, the NIMSAT Institute, IAEM, and NEMA provide resources to assist emergency managers in establishing, strengthening, and maintaining public-private partnerships.

Emergency managers seeking to develop partnerships with a private sector entity should contact some of the following people with the authority to enter into such agreements depending upon the size of the organization: owner (small businesses), chief executive officer or president (corporations), business continuity planner, risk manager, or security director. The emergency manager will next need to act as a liaison between the private sector decision-maker and decision-makers inside the appropriate government agency regarding the details involved in establishing a partnership.[67] Government officials with the authority to enter into PPPs typically include the emergency management director, the city manager, the chief of police, the fire chief, or the risk manager of that agency or jurisdiction.[68]

Once a PPP has been established, it needs to be maintained. This takes effort by both parties. Meetings can facilitate communication and contact. Drills and exercises involving both the government and the private sector entity can also facilitate the effective maintenance of the relationship. Doing these things will make a more effective response and recovery when an actual disaster occurs.[69]

Utilizing PPPs enables emergency management and first responder agencies to benefit from the financial and technical resources of private sector partners. This will likely enhance the ability of first responder and emergency management organizations to achieve their goals and objectives.[70]

Using Evaluations to Improve Performance

This section examines ways to assess emergency management organizations and teams to see how effectively and efficiently they operate. It is about evaluating and assessing the performance of emergency management organizations and initiatives. The goal is to be able to tell if it is operating well or poorly. Performance appraisals are designed to enhance the collective performance of organizations.[71] To determine if a law enforcement or emergency management agency and its functions are operating correctly, some type of assessment is necessary.

Periodic evaluations improve both employees and organizations in the same way that they help employees. The identification of weaknesses is needed to improve performance. Fundamental principles are utilized to evaluate all organizations. This includes establishing goals and examining the extent to which these goals have been achieved annually. There also exist specific standards with which to evaluate the collective performance of emergency management organizations.[72] Emergency management agencies themselves and the training and services they provide must be evaluated and assessed to determine their effectiveness. It is illogical to set up, run, and maintain emergency management and first responder agencies if they do not accomplish their predetermined goals.

Some of the specific standards established by prominent emergency management and first responder professional organizations that are used to measure and evaluate performance will now be examined. First is the **NFPA 1600 (National Fire Protection Association), NEMA CAR Program (National Emergency Management Association) CAR (Capability Assessment for Readiness),** and **EMAP (Emergency Management Accreditation Program)**. NFPA 1600, the CAR Program, and EMAP set the standard in the emergency management field used to assess organizational performance. NFPA 1600 (National Fire Protection Association) was originally established in 1995. Its actual title is **Standard on Disaster/Emergency Management and Business Continuity Programs**. It was established through the National Fire Protection Agency, which is a worldwide nonprofit organization focused on the prevention of death and property damage.

NFPA 1600 is based upon the "all hazards" emergency management approach and established concrete standards for preparation, response, and recovery for a broad range of hazards and disasters encountered by emergency management agencies. It is important to emergency management and can be effectively used in program assessment for self-evaluation and by external evaluators. It can also serve as a model with which to both create a new program or improve an existing program.[73]

NFPA 1600 standards can be utilized by all three levels of American government. It helps agencies to better manage all hazards. The standards encompass planning and response and recovery operations. The NFPA 1600 standards place emphasis upon mitigation with regard to sound land-use practices, sustainable urban design, effective codes, and strategic community protection efforts.[74]

NFPA 1600 defines an **entity** for the purpose of applying the standards as an organization that has been tasked with emergency management responsibilities or COOP. NFPA requires an organization to possess (a) a written emergency management program, (b) a suitable administrative structure, (c) a named coordinator, (d) an advisory committee, and (e) documented evaluation procedures.[75]

Under NFPA 1600, an entity's documented emergency management program must contain 14 elements, which include laws and authorities, hazard mitigation, mutual aid, planning, direction, control, and coordination, operations and procedures, training, logistics and facilities, exercises, evaluations, and corrective actions, and crisis communications and public information.[76]

Roles and responsibilities are required to be specified under NFPA 1600. Roles must specifically be defined as well for external organizations that will participate in emergency management activities, including preparedness and recovery.[77]

Another evaluation that can be used to improve performance is the **NEMA CAR Program (National Emergency Management Association) CAR (Capability Assessment for Readiness) Program.** This is also used for organizational assessment in emergency management.

In 1997, in collaboration with FEMA, the National Emergency Management Association published the state **Capability Assessment for Readiness (CAR) Program**. The CAR program consists of a self-assessment process for state emergency management agencies (SEMAs). The CAR program is utilized to assess several aspects of SEMAs, which include hazard mitigation readiness, their ability to respond to disasters, and their ability to foster disaster recovery.[78]

CAR is operated by means of a well-defined checklist of objective measurable items that state emergency management agencies can utilize with which to assess its capabilities and readiness.[79]

CAR is based on NFPA 1600, but CAR is more specific. CAR takes the list of Emergency Management Functions from NFPA 1600 and divides each one into **attributes**, which are broad performance criteria. Under CAR, attributes are subdivided into *characteristics*, which delineate specific performance criteria. The purpose of doing so is to allow each characteristic of every attribute to be systematically evaluated.[80]

Under CAR, every attribute and characteristic is evaluated on a numerical scale ranging from 1 to 5: 1 is not capable, 2 is marginally capable, 3 is generally capable, 4 is very capable, and 5 is fully capable. The characteristic scores are added to create an attribute score. Then, the scores obtained from measuring all the attributes within an emergency management function can be combined to create an overall score. This provides an assessment of a state emergency management agency's strengths and areas for improvement.[81]

A third organizational assessment approach in emergency management is **EMAP (Emergency Management Accreditation Program)**. EMAP is a performance-based accreditation program for both local and state level emergency management agencies. EMAP is also based on NFPA 1600. EMAP has 54 measurable performance standards.[82]

After a self-study document is prepared, local and state agencies can apply for EMAP accreditation. Then an on-site visit occurs. If approved, an emergency management agency is given EMPA accreditation for five years. It can be renewed. All these organizational assessment approaches are used to increase the efficiency and effectiveness of emergency management agencies.

In addition to evaluating organizations, *the things that organizations do* need to be evaluated as well. In emergency management, this includes personnel evaluation and evaluation of *drills, exercises, and incident response.*

Exercises designed to test theories and plans are a critical part of the success of an emergency management agency. This is true because the purpose of exercises is to *apply* theories to likely scenarios in order to *improve capabilities* and *detect shortcomings.* Effective emergency management agencies must practice their tasks and roles by applying theory to reality in order to achieve their predetermined goals.

Emergency management and law enforcement agencies should recognize the importance of applying theory to practice through exercises so that they can be better prepared for "all hazards." Exercises also provide specific examples, plans, and methodologies that emergency managers can use to improve their operations to better protect the public.

Emergency Operations Center (EOC) Operational Considerations

The operations of Emergency Operations Centers (EOCs) are discussed in this section. Remember that an **Emergency Operations Center (EOC)** is a central location used to facilitate coordination between agencies to support critical incident response and recovery operations. The EOC serves as a central location from which law enforcement and emergency response agencies coordinate disaster response.[83]

Management decisions made at an EOC are focused on providing guidance about priorities. Strategic and operational information is conveyed through EOC managers, while tactical decisions are still made by field response personnel. EOCs serve as a link between executive branch elected officials in a jurisdiction and first responder and emergency management leaders coordinating critical incident response.[84]

EOCs are necessary for the coordination of emergency management disaster services. An EOC can be viewed as both a physical location and in terms of tasks and functions. The EOC as a physical location can sometimes be confused with the tasks performed by the EOC. Because the EOC is a physical location, it must receive certain resources to operate properly.[85]

From the perspective of operating an EOC's physical location best, one must distinguish between the EOC's *facility management* and its *operational management.* **Facility management** deals with the operation of the physical plant, computers, communications systems, and other services such as food and water needed to support human activities inside an EOC.[86] On the other hand, **Operational management** relates to the procedures and systems that are in place that allow employees inside an EOC team to operate effectively.[87]

Operational management and facility management affect each other, in that both are interdependent. Decisions made in one area affect functioning in other areas. This is why an emergency manager must have a firm grasp of both areas in order to operate an EOC effectively and efficiently. Far too many emergency managers feel that the Emergency Operations Plan (EOP) will deal with any issues related to the EOC. This is an incorrect assumption.[88] The EOC as a physical location is different from the EOC in terms of disaster operations.[89]

In terms of facility management, unlike most office buildings, EOCs must be able to operate continuously in 24-hour mode.[90] Compared with a typical office building (which operates 8 to 12 hours per day), an EOC will typically operate around the clock during a disaster. In addition, EOCs typically have systems in place, such as "overpressure" systems and special air filters to protect against biological and chemical attacks. Some EOCs contain living quarters for personnel stocked for an extended period.[91] These things mean that EOCs cannot be viewed as "garden variety" office buildings because of these things, and due to increased security concerns and parallel systems commonly seen in EOCs but not in other buildings.[92]

In terms of planning and facility management, these things must be considered and maintained in order to achieve optimal emergency operations center efficiency. Plus, emergency managers should keep in mind, that as a facility, an EOC is composed of several systems, including utility, environmental, and safety systems. Because an EOC must have the capability for continuous operation, alternative electrical power arrangements must be made. These can include internal and external generators and alternative commercial power feeds. In addition, parallel systems are required in order to maintain radio, telephone, and computer equipment in a grid-down situation.[93]

Neither custodial services nor security services should be overlooked if the EOC is to achieve its predetermined objectives, especially during a prolonged disaster. It is good operational protocol to designate a specific individual to oversee EOC facility management.[94]

With regard to operational management of the EOC, the needs of the EOC as a facility are not usually systematically addressed by the jurisdiction's Emergency Operations Plan (EOP). That is why there should be a systematic plan and protocol for the "nuts and bolts" of setting up the EOC after a disaster situation. A drill should be utilized to activate the EOC to see how plans work in reality. In addition, officials in the jurisdiction must determine what threshold disaster conditions warrant activation of the EOC along with which officials possess the authority to activate the facility. Protocols for calling in EOC personnel must also be made.[95]

Plans should be made in advance with regard to the initiation of EOC setup following the decision to activate the EOC.[96] One should not assume that the first person or persons who arrive upon EOC activation will know how to actually set up the EOC and get it running.[97]

Once the disaster is over, attention also needs to be paid to shutting down the EOC. Important issues can be missed in the absence of a preplanned deactivation process.[98] The **EOC deactivation process** (shutting down the EOC and placing it "on ready" for the next critical incident) involves both physical and procedural tasks. Physical tasks deal with cleaning the facility, performing maintenance and repairs, and restocking supplies. Procedural tasks involve doing things like preparing AARs (After-Action Reports) and transferring records.[99]

Standard Operating Procedures (SOPs) facilitate the effective operation of all aspects of EOCs. The EOC's Standard Operating Procedures should be written in easy-to-understand language and include the following seven things: (1) activation procedures, (2) notification procedures, (3) setup procedures, (4) procedures for using communications systems, (5) procedures for obtaining additional services and supplies, (6) security procedures, and (7) deactivation procedures. Training in these SOPs is critical.[100] To have an effective EOC organization, two emergency management officials should be appointed before a disaster occurs and before the EOC is activated: (1) an official to serve as EOC Coordinator and (2) an official who will plan overall EOC operations.[101]

First is designating an employee to plan overall EOC operations, including establishing guidelines for both facility management and operational management. Both are vital if the EOC is to carry out its objectives.[102] One should not assume that everything will follow the plan – in a stressful disaster situation, unanticipated problems will become manifest. This is one reason that the "bugs" in the EOC systems and procedures as they exist on paper must be resolved through exercises. Here, the connection between the EOC planner and the EOC manager (the individual who runs the EOC during activation) will become manifest – a well-thought-out plan becomes translated into effective EOC management. In sum, effective EOC management greatly improves the efficiency and effectiveness of what the EOC produces. In addition, effective management reduces stress and ambiguity among EOC employees.[103]

Next, the **EOC operations room**, its function, and "best practices" for its design and operation will be examined. The operations room is the actual place where decisions are made at the managerial level during a critical incident. The operations room is the "brain" of an EOC.[104] Understanding effective EOC management and operations must incorporate how to best run the EOC operations room.

EOC operations rooms began under the 1950s Civil Defense program. The EOC operations room was originally designed as a physical space where key decision-makers met to evaluate and disseminate collected information. Most were designed as bunkers to facilitate survival after a bombing.[105] This reflected the Civil Defense mentality, as the primary fear behind Civil Defense preparations was nuclear war. Under CD, what are now called EOCs were very simple and ascetic. They were viewed as a place suitable to ensure the survival of government officials. Most CD facilities used as EOCs were located in basements or other underground facilities.[106]

After the Cold War ended, the consensus came to be that natural disasters posed a greater threat to the government and the larger society than armed attacks. The focus shifted to increasing staff size to facilitate crisis response and the administration of recovery.[107] Thus, EOCs today are better positioned and better protected from environmental hazards.

Modern EOCs are designed to foster the survival of their occupants and to ensure both continuity of operations and continuity of government. Elected officials have realized that achieving these objectives is even more important than in the past due to interdependency and globalization. The EOC operations room plays a crucial role in crisis management.[108]

The success of government response efforts following a major disaster depends upon several key factors, which include redundant and interoperable communications systems, comprehensive asset utilization, organizational flexibility to deal effectively with various responding entities depending upon event type, in-depth situational awareness, and access to all supporting resources to adapt to different response scenarios that are likely to be encountered.[109]

The EOC should be supported by a well-designed Emergency Operations Plan. This EOP should be built around the most likely hazards likely to be encountered in the jurisdiction. It should be rehearsed through training and exercises. Because predicting the future is problematic, it must be recognized that all EOC personnel, especially the "24-7 watch component" must be qualified to perform their tasks.[110]

The remainder of this section compares and contrasts different organizational structures along with their impacts upon the EOC Operations Room. It must be noted that the management orientation and structure of the emergency management agency will impact the layout and management of the EOC Operations Room. More bureaucratic agencies will most likely follow the hierarchical chain of command approach, otherwise known as the C2 ("Command and Control to word). These organizations are typically designed and operated by either law enforcement officials or officials with a military background. Civilian-oriented emergency management-dominated organizations will tend to be more decentralized and operate along C4 lines (Communicate, Collaborate, Coordinate, Control). The effectiveness of the EOC is affected by the ability of its personnel to coordinate emergency management functions and to effectively transmit vital information to victims.[111]

As noted previously, the EOC Operations Room is the "brain" of the EOC. For that reason, it must be designed to best serve the needs of the jurisdiction and its specific hazards. In addition, consideration must be shown to issues such as proximity to responders, the security of the facility, distance from the hazard, and availability of redundant services. Beyond these things, the EOC Operations Room itself must be laid out in a manner that will maximize efficiency and effectiveness.

Management research has demonstrated that design significantly affects the effective operation of physical workplaces. For example, a comfortable environment helps to reduce the negative effects of stress in workplaces, especially in crisis situations.[112] When circulation, access control, and ergonomics are considered in the physical design of an EOC Operations Room, personnel effectiveness is improved.[113]

To this end, various ways with which to set up the EOC Operations Room should be considered with regard to their effect on personnel working in a high-stress critical incident situation. Research has examined six different room configurations that can be utilized to set up an EOC Operations Room. These configurations include Multipurpose, Cubicle Cluster, Horseshoe, Stadium/Theater, Collaboration Pods, and IRIS. Each has advantages and disadvantages and should be tailored to the specific needs and situation of the jurisdiction.[114]

EOC Operations During Terrorist Incidents

Although terrorist attacks do not occur as frequently as natural disasters, effective EOC management must encompass plans for operations following terrorist attacks.[115] Keeping a local EOC prepared for a terrorist incident should incorporate the potential terrorist threats and targets that were identified during the jurisdiction's planning process into assessing needs should such an attack occur.[116] This will keep the terrorist-specific threats to the jurisdiction under advisement so that the EOC can be specifically configured to address these needs. Planners should orient their actions around the types of attacks most likely to occur, the most likely targets of each type of attack, and an assessment of the risk each type of attack poses.[117]

Keep in mind that although a particular jurisdiction may not directly experience a terrorist attack, there can be "spillover" effects on the jurisdiction from terrorist attacks on other areas. For example, an attack on a fuel pipeline or on an adjacent area's electrical supply could potentially disrupt large areas of the nation. Areas near cities may be adversely impacted by refugees seeking to escape the disruption.[118]

Imagining hypothetical terrorist attack scenarios and how those will likely play out in terms of the jurisdiction's EOP (Emergency Operations Plan) is an important part of sound planning.[119] Other scenarios should be considered by jurisdictions, such as the extent to which the EOP could respond effectively to a biological or chemical attack, a suicide bombing at a sporting event, and similar hypothetical situations. Emergency managers should assess if change may be needed in future EOC operations.[120]

EOPs should have attached **EOP Annexes** for different hazards, including terrorism. In order to better prepare the EOC for terrorism, it is necessary for the emergency manager to examine each EOP Annex to determine if gaps exist that would hamper effective handling of risks. The agency's planning team should assess what components of each hazard-specific annex would or would not work and then make necessary changes.[121]

In addition to considering EOC changes or modifications to prepare for terrorist incidents, it is also sometimes necessary to adapt the emergency management agency's policies and procedures to better prepare for terrorist incidents. This will only be necessary, however, if experience gained from actual incident responses or training exercises indicates that the EOP or the design of the organization would fail to function correctly during a terrorist incident.[122]

Once decisions and corrections have been made, they must be tested to see how they would work in the event of a real terrorist attack. Most agencies begin their training with tabletop exercises before proceeding to functional exercises and full-scale exercises.[123] Only in this way can the plan be evaluated in terms of effectiveness.

The U.S. Department of Homeland Security, its training partners, and state emergency management agencies have many resources available to assist law enforcement agencies and emergency management organizations in preparing the jurisdiction's EOC and local agencies for terrorist attacks and their aftermath.

Managing Information, Donations, and Volunteers

This section deals with an important component of both response *and* recovery: the management of information, donations, and volunteers in the aftermath of a disaster. Interacting with the media, dealing with donations, and coordinating the activities of volunteers are a significant part of disaster resilience. For that reason, they are important to the emergency manager.[124]

Resilience also deals with the ability of a first responder agency to work effectively with people and organizations during and after disasters. First responders will likely encounter media personnel that travel to critical incident scenes to report the news. Many donations sent by well-meaning groups and individuals flow to the scene. Volunteers desire to help the community to recover. However, these donations and individuals can cause challenges to first responders and emergency managers.[125]

The **media** includes individuals such as reporters and camera operators who convey information about critical incidents and disasters to members of the public.[126] Traditional media is comprised of television, radio, and newspapers. The advent of the internet and the development of social media has expanded the definition. The characteristics of different media actors must be understood in order to examine the relationship between first responder and emergency management agencies and the media.[127]

Historically, the **media** have referred to newspapers, radio, and television. With regard to comparing these media, it has been said that "newspapers are cold, radio is warm, and television is hot." This refers to the combination of audio and visual effects portrayed by the media.

Newspapers are published either daily or weekly, and the number of readers depends upon the popularity of the publication.[128] The American newspapers with the largest number of readers include the *New York Times, Wall Street Journal*, and *USA Today*. They are known for providing more detailed coverage than other media types.[129]

Radio has been commercially available since the 1920s. Radio was the first type of media that was capable of communicating "real-time" events across vast distances.[130] As time passed, radio stations became more specialized. Modern radio stations may specialize in news, talk, music, and non-English formats.[131] Radio news deadlines are usually hourly.[132] Radio provides news concisely in ten to fifteen-second "sound bites."[133]

Television became widely commercially available during the early 1950s. Television combined sound with live images. Television provides different types of news, which may include breaking news of critical incidents in progress or regularly scheduled news shows on local television stations affiliated with a major network. These local stations also show national and international news produced by one of the major networks.[134] There are also dedicated news channels such as CNN, MSNBC, and Fox News. In terms of TV news deadlines, these vary depending upon the format of the network and station but are immediate for dedicated news channels and hourly for other networks.[135]

Since the 1990s, the advent of the **internet** (World Wide Web) has changed the **traditional media triad** of newspapers, radio, and television. This led to an explosion in the amount of information available and in the number of websites.[136] The internet brings news and instantaneous access to information to anyone at any time through computers and smartphones. The internet has changed the "rules of the game" in terms of media access.

Traditional media outlets have had to adapt to the internet. Newspapers, television, and radio all have corresponding websites. In addition, **blogs** and **social media** have also entered the mix. Blogs have created "citizen journalists" who post opinions, commentary, and summaries of news and events online. Some bloggers have millions of readers and possess as much influence as famous journalists who appear on television networks.[137]

In addition, the internet developed into a mechanism to communicate and network between individuals. This led to the creation of social network sites. **Social network sites** are web-based services that individuals can utilize to connect with others with whom they share a private or semi-private linkage within a bounded system.[138] If the old adage was "newspapers are cold, radio is warm, and television is hot," to that today must be added, "social media is *red* hot." Recognizing this, traditional mainstream media outlets have had to establish and participate in social media sites as well in order to stay relevant.

The most popular social media platforms at present are Facebook, Twitter (now called X), LinkedIn, Pinterest, and Instagram. Many people first learn of news items through social media. Due to increasing political and social polarization, many people access only social media and websites that reflect their outlooks and orientations. Emergency managers and those responsible for issuing communications from first responder organizations must keep in mind that social media is a major tool (along with traditional media) with which to reach intended audiences.[139] In other words, authorities cannot assume that contacting and dealing with the mainstream broadcast media is sufficient to "get out the message." Attention must be paid to the internet in general and social media in particular in order to be effective at the communication of warnings and disaster information.

No matter the format, the media has vast significance in society.[140] In the context of emergency management, the media helps to educate the public about warnings and preparation, evacuation, sheltering, and protective actions. The media also relays information about government actions, which organizations are providing relief, and can generate support for emergency management programs.

Different media outlets focus upon different audiences. Outlets cater to different parts of society and possesses unique perspectives and audiences.[141] First responders and emergency managers should realize that when the media learns of a critical incident, one can expect it to be immediately reported. When reporters are sent to the scene, they typically place demands on first responders. Realize that the media will also put their own "spin" on the story.

Numerous challenges arise from working with the media at a disaster scene. To maintain positive relations with the media, professional emergency management agencies should appoint a **PIO (Public Information Officer).** PIOs are employees of first responder agencies that possess special training and expertise in cómmunicating with the media.[142] They are often interviewed on television wearing a PIO hat, shirt, or jacket.

The Public Information Officer is assigned the duty to disseminate critical incident of information to the public, which includes the news media. This duty can occur either on a regular or on an as-needed basis.[143] PIOs provide "public information" to those outside the first responder or emergency management organization. *Public information* is a term used to convey vital information to the public for the purpose of taking protective action to save lives, prevent or reduce injury, and protect property from damage. Public information must be both accurate and timely to protect residents and visitors to the jurisdiction.[144]

Due to the importance of the PIO's role in representing emergency management and first responder agencies to the media, FEMA engages in training and development for Public Information Officers. FEMA's "Emergency Management Institute (EMI) Public Information Officer (PIO) training program is designed to provide PIOs with the essential knowledge, skills, and abilities to support proper decision-making by delivering the right message, to the right people, at the right time. The EMI training program provides PIOs with the opportunity to learn and practice the tasks of gathering, verifying, coordinating, and disseminating public information at all levels of government.[145] FEMA operates five courses for PIOs.

An emergency management or first responder agency's PIO must focus on several stakeholders, including members of the public, the agency itself, the media, and other first responder organizations.[146] Emergency managers and high-raking first responder personnel expect that the information that the PIO disseminates will result in action by affected people (such as evacuation), provide information about protective actions or critical incident status, affect attitudes or behaviors of members of the public, and create a positive image of the agency.[147] In order to be effective, Public Information Officers need excellent interpersonal skills and extensive substantive knowledge of the organization that they represent.

PIOs provide a vital connection between the emergency management or first responder agency and the public (members of the population and the media). Examples include warnings to the public in terms of hazards and protective measures, the current status of the incident or emergency, agency responses to the incident, specific evacuation actions or directions, important locations (shelters, water, food), closing information (roads, schools, etc.), and status of the grid (water, electricity, etc.).

Emergency managers should realize that the public "face" of the agency is represented by the Public Information Officer. For that reason, he or she must be media savvy. In communicating with the public through and with the media, trust issues are involved. PIOs not only need a solid knowledge of both social and traditional media, but he or she must take the steps necessary to positively portray the efforts of first responders and the agency in a positive manner.[148]

In major disasters, emergency managers must also deal with large amounts of donations made to assist the victims. Thus, **donations management**, or the tasks associated with receiving, sorting, and distributing funds and goods during response and recovery operations for the benefit of victims is an important skill set needed at major disaster sites such as hurricanes.[149] Donations come in two varieties: **cash donations** (money intended for the victims or nonprofit organizations) and **in-kind donations** (gifts of physical items of value, such as food, clothing, medical supplies, and diapers).[150]

Donations management is necessary due to the outpouring of generosity following media coverage of major disasters. Large quantities of donations flow to the disaster scene, usually even without a formal request. In some cases, donations are both unwanted and excessive. When this occurs, additional work must be performed by emergency management workers which can result in problems associated with logistics.[151]

One suggestion to facilitate efficiency is for the emergency manager to request more cash donations than in-kind donations because the former allows the most flexibility and presents fewer logistical problems. For the inevitable quantity of in-kind donations that will flow into the area, conducting a needs assessment will assist in making the best decisions about how to distribute the items.

A **needs assessment** consists of a formal evaluation of what services or supplies are essential in the aftermath of a disaster.[152] Needs assessment models developed by the U.S. Army Corps of Engineers related to population needs following hurricanes are very helpful guides for emergency managers. Emergency management agencies should work closely with nonprofit organizations in terms of donation management as well. Good management practice also stipulates that donations and donation needs be tracked on-site.[153] Failure to do so can lead to wasted donations and bad publicity for the emergency management agencies involved. Strategies designed to manage the volunteers that inevitably appear during disaster recovery efforts should also be discussed. Many individuals "want to help" their fellow citizens to recover from a disaster from altruistic motives.

Emergency managers must thus be prepared to deal with ordinary citizens who arrive at disaster scenes and wish to donate their labor and sometimes services to help others. As is the case with donations, there are both positive and negative aspects to volunteers. **Volunteer management** involves the processes and procedures that are employed to channel volunteer contributions in a positive way during recovery operations.[154]

First responders from other jurisdictions will often report to disaster sites. This is either because they have been assigned there pursuant to an EMAC (Emergency Management Assistance Compact) or because they chose to volunteer their time. In either event, neither local law enforcement personnel nor local first responder employees will know who these first responders from other jurisdictions are or their qualifications. It was for this reason that **First Responder Authentication Credential (FRAC) cards were invented.**[155]

FRAC cards contain a photo and biometric data on first responders. FRAC cards are linked to computer databases and verify both identity and skill sets. This facilitates both security and assurance of competency in other jurisdictions.[156] In addition, FRAC cards can reduce legal liability to local jurisdictions that utilize the services of outside first responders by allowing them to be considered as local or state agents.[157]

Non-first responder volunteers come in two varieties. The first type of volunteer is associated with either recognized nonprofit organizations like the Salvation Army, the American Red Cross, or with faith-based organizations. Such volunteers generally have recognized skills and experience related to disaster recovery.

FEMA trains volunteers to assist the victims of natural disasters and terrorist attacks through its **Community Emergency Response Team.**[158] CERT is comprised of volunteers who have received training in preparation and response functions. CERT courses are taught in a structured manner by certified trainers. Volunteers are required to complete six training modules, which include disaster preparedness, fire suppression in disasters, medical aid, light search and rescue, disaster psychology, and an exercise designed to simulate a real-world disaster.[159] CERT volunteers, when available, can be a valuable on-scene resource.

The second type of volunteer is known as an **unaffiliated** or **spontaneous** volunteer. These individuals are typically from the impact area or nearby and act from a sense of altruism or devotion for the purpose of assisting in restoring their communities to a pre-disaster state. The level of skill, knowledge, and abilities possessed by spontaneous volunteers vary greatly. Some, such as surgeons, translators, mental health counselors, and electricians have vital skills to apply to the recovery effort.[160] Various tasks that are typically performed by volunteers include sandbagging, staffing shelters, preparing food, and sorting donations. Due to the work they provide, volunteers are crucial to disaster response and recovery.[161]

There are many valuable services that volunteers can and do provide. However, working with volunteers also poses certain challenges to emergency managers. This is especially true with spontaneous volunteers that lack highly specialized skills. Also, large numbers of spontaneous volunteers that appear in the days following a major disaster can be difficult to coordinate and manage. Unless there is a mechanism in place to assess their skill set and assign them tasks quickly, frustration can arise. It has been noted that some volunteers become irritated or hurt emotionally if they feel that they are not needed and are not actually incorporated into organized response activities. This can contribute to negative public relations, especially if volunteers voice their frustrations to the media.[162] Additionally, safety concerns abound with regard to utilizing volunteers due to hazards and debris.

In order to deal with these challenges more effectively, several strategies for volunteer management should be utilized. One of the most important things that can be done is to *register volunteers at a central location.* This will allow either emergency management personnel or nonprofit organization personnel (such as the American Red Cross) to assess qualifications and abilities that the volunteer can contribute and to screen volunteers for criminal records.

To facilitate these things, emergency managers should establish a dedicated telephone line or website that can be utilized by potential volunteers. Through the telephone line or website, they can ask questions about what help is needed and how they can provide that help. A volunteer reception center should also be established in proximity to the disaster scene. This reception center can register volunteers, which will also serve to create a database that can be employed for later operations or for other disasters.[163]

By working with nonprofit and faith-based organizations with disaster experience, the emergency manager can reduce his or her workload and simultaneously manage volunteers more effectively. In addition, emergency managers can build an outreach campaign to notify potential volunteers about the skills needed.[164] This can then be communicated with the media.

Another important suggestion regarding volunteer management involves documenting the number of volunteers that were selected and assigned, what tasks they performed, how many hours they served, and to calculate the approximate dollar value of their labor to the response and recovery effort. This is not only good for public relations, but it is possible that the jurisdiction could be reimbursed for volunteer activities by federal disaster assistance programs.[165]

Taking these actions will facilitate effective response and recovery in the affected area. In so doing resilience is also increased.[166]

Disaster Financial Assistance and Reducing Vulnerability

This section deals with how individuals and governments can go about obtaining outside financial assistance to recover from the impact of disasters and about some ways to reduce the impact of future disasters.

Emergency managers must be aware of government programs that exist to provide financial and other assistance to the survivors of disasters for the purpose of assisting them with recovery.[167] This can involve insurance coverage, employment and housing assistance, and government grants and loans.

Disaster impacts do not only affect individuals and families. Businesses are also affected in terms of loss of revenue and destruction or damage to facilities. The government may itself suffer from disaster impacts. For example, bridges may have collapsed. Roads may have washed away. Government vehicles may have been destroyed by water damage or covered with debris. The destruction of Key Resources (KR) and Critical Infrastructure (CI) will harm the ability of the government to fulfill its essential functions. Thus, state and local governments can themselves be disaster victims who may require financial and other assistance in order to recover.[168]

For individual disaster victims, **insurance** is the first source to which to turn for financial assistance. Property damage insurance is technically a preparedness action since it is purchased prior to disaster impact. If insurance were available to everyone and if everyone paid the premiums, it could theoretically cover the vast majority of disaster recovery costs.[169] But not everyone has insurance. Plus, the availability of insurance depends on the hazard. For example, more than eighty percent of hazard insurance policies cover tornado damage, while only about one quarter of hazard insurance policies cover earthquakes.[170] Plus, relatively few people have flood insurance. This means that persons without adequate insurance must deal with losses in other ways.[171] These other strategies can include obtaining government loans, entitlements, services or grants, spending personal savings, or "doing without" by not replacing damaged or lost items.[172] It must be noted that purchasing insurance is related to income, occupational status, and education. Those with higher incomes, more formal education, and higher occupational status are most likely to have insurance coverage.[173]

Nonprofit organizations like the Salvation Army and the American Red Cross also provide disaster assistance to individuals and families, as do faith-based organizations. Such disaster assistance can include funds to replace belongings and assistance for housing.[174]

Households impacted by disaster losses can utilize three modes of disaster recovery.[175] These are *autonomous recovery, kinship recovery,* and *institutional recovery.* **Autonomous recovery** means that households recover "on their own" using their own resources such as insurance, savings, income, and other assets. These are generally individuals with higher net worth and financial resources. **Kinship recovery** depends upon the financial and other help provided by friends and family to restore the household back to normal. Family members help each other with rebuilding, money, and services.

It relies upon the willingness and ability of family members to help one another. **Institutional recovery** depends upon government and private sector organizations to facilitate household recovery. In other words, government grants and charity facilitate recovery efforts for these households.[176]

Obviously, those with the resources for autonomous recovery are going to be "better off" and recover the most quickly. Those who rely upon institutional recovery are generally the worst off and recover slowly, if at all. Economic recovery occurs more rapidly for households with higher income, fewer members, and more years of formal education. In addition, the households most likely to have insurance are those with higher incomes.[177]

Business recovery is next. Disasters disrupt business operations significantly.[178] This is true because disasters interrupt the economic base. Both direct physical damage and the destruction or interruption of services provided through the infrastructure such as water, transportation, and electricity can force businesses to close.[179]

Much like households, businesses with greater resources "weather the storm" better than those with fewer resources. Large corporations generally have insurance and hazard adjustments.[180] Both retail and wholesale businesses suffer significant sales losses following a disaster. Interestingly, construction and manufacturing firms typically increase sales after a disaster.[181]

Also, it should be pointed out that small, independent businesses are much more vulnerable to disaster disruptions than large businesses in terms of disasters and disaster recovery.[182] This is true because (1) they have fewer resources (sales, insurance, assets), (2) they are more likely to be located in strip malls or non-reinforced buildings, and (3) they are less likely to have hazard management programs in place to reduce their vulnerability.[183] In comparison with large corporations, small independent businesses are more dependent upon local customers. Such small businesses also typically do not possess the financial ability to fully recover from a disaster by using only their own resources.[184]

Population dislocation brought about by a disaster can also harm businesses in the affected area. If a significant portion of the population moves away during disaster recovery or permanently, business sales will decrease. Even households that remain will typically have reduced discretionary income with which to make purchases, which also harms business sales. Many small independent businesses will close following a significant disaster for these reasons.[185]

Some businesses, just as some households, are more vulnerable to disaster aftermath than others. For example, professional services have low vulnerability and are not badly impacted.[186] Large manufacturers and tourist-oriented businesses have moderate vulnerability. After the disaster, their revenues will fall drastically, but they will recover over the medium term. However, small locally owned retail shops are the most vulnerable after a disaster. Many go bankrupt due to population dislocation, inadequate insurance, insufficient savings to survive until recovery is complete, and poorly constructed buildings.

There are also psychological aspects to recovery. Disaster recovery has both social and physical and social dimensions. Injuries and property damage can result in psychological and financial strain. Deaths of family members and friends cause substantial emotional trauma.[187] Research has shown that most victims report feeling mild distress after disasters, but not major mental health problems.[188] Strained family relationships, lack of patience, and frustration from dealing with insurance companies and government bureaucracies were the most common issues. Persons experiencing the death of a family member and those who have lost their homes will experience the most severe effects.[189] As always, individuals with preexisting psychological problems are most at risk from the added stress of coping with a disaster impact.[190] It is for this reason that emergency managers must interact with mental health agencies and organizations in the jurisdiction to care for mental health needs.[191]

As part of institutional recovery, individuals, families, businesses, and even state and local governments may need outside assistance provided by the federal government in the form of loans, grants, entitlements, and services. Following major disasters, federal involvement usually begins after a presidential disaster declaration or after damages and needs have been formally assessed. Federal disaster assistance can provide substantial benefit to disaster victims.[192]

Several federal grants, loans, entitlement benefits, and services are available to individuals, businesses, and certain activities of nonprofit organizations as part of institutional recovery. Reimbursements to government and nonprofit entities that have suffered disaster losses are another part of institutional recovery. Individual institutional aid will be covered first, which is called Individual Assistance (IA).

Individual Assistance (IA) is designed to provide relief benefits to individuals, businesses, and nonprofit organizations harmed by the effects of a disaster. IA is focused on individuals, households, small business owners, and nonprofit organizations that have provided post-disaster relief services.[193]

Both the federal and state governments provide IA. However, even the IA provided by state governments is primarily funded by the federal government. Most Individual Assistance is in the form of grants and loans. **Grants** are funds provided to individuals and institutions that do not have to be repaid.[194] On the other hand, **loans** are supposed to be repaid to the federal government at a later date. For this reason, grants are obviously preferred over loans.

Grant programs include the **IHP (Individuals and Households Program)**. The IHP provides up to $27,200 to persons with dwellings that cannot be used and who also do not possess homeowners' insurance.[195] The IHP program consists of two components: Disaster Housing and Other Needs Assistance (OHA). The **Disaster Housing** component applies to persons who have occupied dwellings that are now uninhabitable due to the effect of the disaster (unsafe conditions). This is a grant that is also utilized by the federal government to provide funding for emergency home repairs, motel rooms, and placement in mobile homes. It is funded entirely by the federal government and is administered by FEMA. **Other Needs Assistance (ONA)** is the second component of IHP. ONA is specifically designed for individuals that lack insurance coverage. ONA provides grant funding for home repair, replacement of items of personal property, and some additional disaster-related expenses. These can include transportation, medical care, and funeral services. ONA is operated by state governments, with the federal government paying 25% of the cost. State governments are responsible for paying the remainder.[196] Due to the availability of these grants, some people argue that there can appear to be a disincentive to purchase insurance.[197] On the other hand, grants do not typically pay nearly as much as would hazard insurance.

Another form of grant is **tax assistance**, which is the situation in which the federal government provides income tax breaks. At present, this federal program allows individuals and families to deduct uninsured losses from their federal income taxes if they comprise over 10% of income.[198] Tax assistance is technically a grant because the federal government is providing a deduction that does not have to be repaid.

Federal IA loan programs include *disaster loans for homes and individuals, disaster loans for businesses, farm service agency loans,* and *economic injury disaster loans.* Remember that loans must be repaid. All but the farm service agency loans are operated by the U.S. Small Business Administration. The farm service agency loans are administered by the U.S. Department of Agriculture.

Disaster loans for homes and individuals are available from the federal government in amounts of up to $200,000 for repair or replacement of a primary residence destroyed or damaged by a disaster. Also, up to $40,000 in loans are available to replace furniture, electronics, and other items of personal property that were destroyed. Loan amounts can be increased by up to twenty percent for the purpose of implementing building mitigation measures to reduce the effect of future disasters.[199]

Disaster loans for businesses are similar to disaster loans for homes and individuals, but they are available to small and medium-sized businesses that have been impacted by disaster. The program allows loans of up to 1.5 million, or up to 1.8 million if mitigation measures are installed as part of repairs or replacement to real estate. **Economic injury disaster loans** are intended to allow small and medium-sized businesses to borrow up to 1.5 million to replace revenue lost from a lack of sales as a result of a disaster.[200] Finally, the U.S. Department of Agriculture offers **farm service agency loans**. This program allows farmers that have lost equipment or crops due to a disaster to borrow from the federal government. A similar emergency conservation program exists with which to allocate federal money to rehabilitate farmland and remove debris.[201]

In addition to grants and loans, the federal government also offers special entitlement benefits to disaster victims. Like grants, entitlement benefits do not need to be repaid. **Benefits** are federal government entitlement programs that are offered to disaster victims.[202] Because disasters often make individuals eligible for benefits due to unemployment, deaths, or disabilities caused by a disaster, entitlement benefits such as food stamps and Social Security Disability are used as part of the recovery process. For example, many victims of disasters qualify for **emergency food stamps** and **emergency unemployment assistance**. The latter provides up to 26 weeks of unemployment insurance to those who have lost their employment income due to a disaster. In the event of death or disability caused by a disaster, **Social Security** provides survivor benefits, death benefits, and disability benefits.[203]

Finally, services provided by state and federal governments are used to foster recovery. **Services** refer to government programs designed to address unique needs caused by a disaster.[204] Services are needed when financial assistance will not meet disaster needs.[205] Most services are either provided directly by the government, or they are provided by nonprofit organizations like the American Red Cross, and the costs associated with providing these services are later reimbursed by the government. Examples include crisis counseling, aging services, and consumer services. Realize that even though the federal government offers many types and forms of assistance this assistance is available only if and when the legal requirements for federal assistance are met.[206]

Also, IA requires an application process, which means that the actual receipt of the aid is delayed. Several weeks may pass to allow federal agencies to review IA funding requests and to disburse the funds.[207] Proper ("approved") procedures must be followed in order to receive federal funding, including IA. Officially, federal aid and state aid are only supposed to be available as a "last resort" and assumes that individuals and businesses will exhaust their own resources first. For this reason, FEMA requires that a four-step process be followed: (1) file for personal insurance and request housing aid from nonprofit agencies, (2) apply for FEMA housing assistance (even if not actually needed), (3) apply for one or more of the loans listed above, and (4) seek unmet needs from nonprofit or faith-based organizations. These conditions must be met prior to the provision of governmental disaster assistance. In addition, because many variables affect the receipt of disaster assistance, not all persons will receive such assistance.[208]

Thus, as an emergency manager, one should understand that many victims become frustrated from the paperwork associated with receiving disaster assistance. The documents can be difficult to understand and can take time. Victims should be told that they can completed applications online through the FEMA website. Victims can also be directed to phone the National Processing Service Center (NPSC) or to go in person to Disaster Recovery Center (DRC).[209]

The preferred way to request federal disaster aid is through the FEMA website (www.fema.gov). A more direct way is through www.fema.gov/assistance/register.shtm. IA can be also be requested from FEMA by calling 1-800-621-FEMA or 1-800-462-7585 (TTY). This will connect disaster victims with a FEMA National Processing Service Center (NPSC). When disaster victims request IA, FEMA personnel at the NPSC utilize the National Emergency Management Information System (NEMIS) computer program. NEMIS is used by FEMA to enter personal information about the disaster victim. Also, losses, damages, and needs are entered. Both this software and FEMA employees make a determination about what kinds of disaster assistance to which the victim is eligible. NEMS indicates if assistance will be available after FEMA employees verify the victim's damages inside the presidentially declared disaster area. At the conclusion of this process, financial assistance will be sent to the eligible disaster victim within days or weeks.[210]

In the aftermath of catastrophic disasters, FEMA (in cooperation with state governments) typically establishes a DRC (Disaster Recovery Center) in the affected area, often powered by generators. A **Disaster Recovery Center (DRC)** is a location set up to allow disaster victims to meet FEMA representatives to discuss assistance programs and associated application requirements.[211] DRCs have generators, telephone capabilities, and satellite internet access even in hard-hit areas. DRCs should be at least 4,500 square feet and have 25-50 tables and 150-250 chairs, in addition to restroom facilities and office supplies. In addition to FEMA personnel, DRCs are staffed by state agency and nonprofit organization employees. This provides relatively easy access to several disaster assistance agencies.[212] DRCs offer "one stop" services to many disaster victims in hard-hit areas.

PA (Public Assistance) will now be examined. PA is primarily oriented towards providing recovery aid to government entities. However, PA can also be provided to nonprofit hospitals, utility companies, and schools that have participated in disaster relief activities.[213]

Public Assistance comes in two varieties: (1) Emergency Assistance and (2) Permanent Assistance. **Emergency Assistance** involves the distribution of financial resources to help state and local governments to handle immediate disaster impacts.[214] The most common Emergency Assistance involves federal funding to reimburse local, state, and nonprofit organizations such as nonprofit utility providers to for debris removal (**debris removal assistance**). Emergency Assistance also includes reimbursement funding for **protective**

measures, which are expenses that were incurred to protect lives and to reduce property damage (sandbags, shoring up damaged buildings, etc.).[215] The second category of PA involves **Permanent Assistance.** Permanent Assistance deals with monetary payments to state and local governments to fund long-term rebuilding efforts.[216] This involves payments to rebuild damaged or destroyed government buildings, government equipment, government-owned and nonprofit utility systems, road repair, and flood control.

In order for a local or state government to obtain Public Assistance, federal guidelines must be followed. Government agencies must formally apply for PA within 30 days of receiving the federal disaster declaration. Applications for PA must contain the following: (1) **notice of interest and request for PA forms** (which document the need for assistance and list damages by category), (2) a **designation of applicant's agent form** (this lists the point of contact for the government entity seeking PA), and (3) a **project worksheet for each category of PA (small project** requests of $66,399 or less; **large project** requests of greater than $66,399); **improved projects** designed to expand a structure or to install mitigation measures on the structure; and **alternate projects** requiring rebuilding a structure in a less hazardous area.[217]

To make this process flow smoothly and to familiarize local and state government personnel with these requirements, both *briefings* and *kickoff meetings* should be held prior to the preparation and submission of the PA paperwork to the federal government. In this context, a **briefing** involves a face-to-face meeting held for the purpose of providing a review to local government officials that covers federal programs available to support the disaster recovery process. The briefing is arranged by state emergency management offices and also includes the State Coordinating Officer. Following the briefing, a kickoff meeting will next be held. The kickoff meeting includes the Federal Coordinating Officer in addition to the participants that were included in the briefing. The **kickoff meeting** examines federal disaster assistance programs and the requirements to apply for them.[218] The kickoff meeting is designed to explain the federal PA process in depth, distribute the application forms, and answer questions.

Once the federal government receives the application forms, both FEMA and state officials are required to complete a **Damage Survey Report (DSR)**. DSRs are used to determine the validity and accuracy of aid requests. A separate DSR is required for each type of federal assistance being requested.[219] FEMA personnel examine the submitted paperwork and compare it with the DSRs. For PA, this occurs at a **Joint Field Office (JFO)**. JFOs are the physical location utilized by FEMA personnel to manage disaster recovery.[220] Once this occurs, FEMA forwards approved DSRs to the appropriate state emergency management department. State emergency management officials then interview the local government applicant. Once approval has been given, cleanup and rebuilding efforts commence. After each authorized recovery activity has concluded, a Project Completion Form must be submitted. The Project Completion Form is required in order for local governments to receive reimbursement. FEMA provides funding equaling 75% of the costs. Typical timeframes involve months or years.[221]

This is also assuming that the requested funds are in compliance with federal environmental legislation. An environmental impact statement is required by federal law prior to beginning substantial disaster recovery projects. An **environmental impact statement** is a complete analysis of how planned recovery actions will affect the air, soil, and water in a given geographical area.[222] These are generally prepared by scientists and state government officials. FEMA denies funding to proposals that lack an environmental impact statement.[223] This is another hurdle that must be overcome in order to obtain federal PA funds.

Federal funding in the form of PA and IA can make a substantial difference in paying for an effective recovery following a disaster. Because so much money is at stake and payments can be made to so many individuals, governments, and organizations, fraud is a distinct possibility. In other words, there may be theft, embezzlement, and fraudulent billing involved in funding and reimbursing disaster responses. If caught, federal law provides for five-year prison sentences and fines of up to $250,000. It is imperative that emergency managers who deal with contracts and money engage in monitoring contractor activities and accounting documents properly. To facilitate this, FEMA maintains a dedicated telephone number with which to report fraud regarding federal disaster funds.[224]

Mitigation

This section briefly looks at some ways to reduce the impact of future disasters. This is **mitigation**, or efforts designed to lessen the vulnerabilities to which the community is exposed and to reduce their future impact. Mitigation is one of the major goals of emergency management. As noted previously, in the past much more effort has been focused upon response and recovery than mitigation or preparedness. But a disaster can change this dynamic. When a disaster occurs, this will get media attention. Using a **focusing event** (an event that draws public attention to the need for mitigation) like a disaster can provide a **window of opportunity** (the time during which emergency managers are most able to influence government policy) to get noticed by government decision makers. This is an intelligent strategy and an effective use of power.[225]

In other words, mitigation deals with things that can be done *now* based on the lessons from the most recent and "fresh" disaster to better plan for *future* recovery actions. This type of forward-looking planning is based on rationality. The recovery process is a suitable opportunity to implement stronger mitigation efforts. This is because support for mitigation is at a high level following a disaster.[226]

Thus, forward-thinking emergency managers should prepare a mitigation action plan in advance. Then, when disaster strikes, he or she can modify the plan based upon the lessons learned from the most recent disaster. A **mitigation action plan** is a document prepared for the purpose of listing the hazards and vulnerabilities of a jurisdiction and indicates measures designed to reduce future harm. Mitigation action plans may include new construction requirements and the addition of warning systems.[227] All these things help to increase resilience.[228]

Notes

1. Willard M. Oliver, *Policing In An Era of Homeland Security*, New York: Oxford University Press, 2020: 139.
2. Ibid.
3. David A. McEntire, *Disaster Response and Recovery: Strategies and Tactics for Resilience*, 2nd Edition, Hoboken, John Wiley and Sons, Inc., 2015: 348-393.
4. Ibid: 349.
5. Ibid.
6. Ibid.
7. Oliver, Policing in an Era of Homeland Security: 144.
8. McEntire, *Disaster Response and Recovery*: 385.
9. Ibid: 349.
10. Ibid: 357.
11. www.fema.gov/hazus
12. McEntire, *Disaster Response and Recovery*: 357.
13. Oliver, *Policing In An Era of Homeland Security*: 155.
14. McEntire, *Disaster Response and Recovery*: 354.
15. Ibid.
16. Ibid.
17. Ibid.
18. McEntire, *Disaster Response and Recovery*: 369.
19. Oliver, *Policing In An Era of Homeland Security*: 144.
20. Ibid: 170.
21. McEntire, *Disaster Response and Recovery*: 359.
22. Ibid: 369.
23. Ibid: 46. Emphasis in original.
24. Ibid: 369.
25. Ibid.
26. Amy K. Donahue, "Toward Robust All-Hazards Incident Management Teams: Progress and Priorities," *Journal of Emergency Management*, Vol. 10, No. 4, July/August 2012: 254.

27. McEntire, Disaster Response and Recovery: 369.
28. Ibid: 51.
29. Ibid and 46.
30. www.tn.gov/tema
31. Ibid.
32. Ibid.
33. McEntire, *Disaster Response and Recovery*: 373.
34. Vincent Faggiano, John McNall, and Tom Gillespie, *Critical Incident Management: A Complete Response Guide*, 2nd Edition, Boca Raton, CRC Press/ Taylor and Francis Group, 2012: 165-177.
35. Ibid: 168.
36. Ibid.
37. Ibid.
38. Ibid.
39. Ibid: 169.
40. Ibid: 171.
41. Ibid: 172-173.
42. Ibid: 173.
43. Ibid: 175-177.
44. Ibid: 170-171.
45. Ibid: 177.
46. Ibid.
47. Michael J. Fagel, Editor, *Principles of Emergency Management: Hazard Specific Issues and Mitigation Strategies*, Boca Raton: CRC Press/Taylor and Francis Group, 2012: 150.
48. Ibid: 6. Emphasis added.
49. Ibid: 152. Emphasis added.
50. Oliver, *Policing In An Era of Homeland Security*: 175.
51. Ibid: 151.
52. Ibid.
53. Ibid: 152.
54. Ibid: 154.
55. Ibid.
56. Ibid: 152.
57. Ibid.
58. Ibid: 154-155.
59. Ibid.
60. Ibid: 156.
61. Ibid: 150.
62. Ibid.
63. Ibid.
64. Ibid: 151.
65. Ibid: 155.
66. Ibid: 158.
67. Ibid: 161.
68. Ibid.

69. Ibid: 163.
70. Ibid.
71. Michael K. Lindell, Carla Prater, and Ronald W. Perry, *Introduction to Emergency Management*, Hoboken, John Wiley and Sons, Inc., 2007: 387.
72. Ibid: 393.
73. Ibid: 398.
74. Ibid.
75. Ibid: 395.
76. Ibid.
77. Ibid: 396.
78. Ibid: 398.
79. Ibid.
80. Ibid.
81. Ibid: 399.
82. Ibid: 400.
83. www.chathamemergency.org/eoc/
84. Ibid.
85. Ibid: 26.
86. Ibid.
87. Ibid. Emphasis added.
88. Ibid: 27.
89. Ibid.
90. Ibid: 26.
91. Ibid.
92. Ibid.
93. Ibid: 26-27.
94. Ibid: 27.
95. Ibid: 28.
96. Ibid.
97. Ibid.
98. Ibid.
99. Ibid.
100. Ibid.
101. Ibid: 29.
102. Ibid.
103. Ibid.
104. Ibid: 30.
105. Ibid.
106. Ibid.
107. Ibid.
108. Ibid: 30-31.
109. Ibid.
110. Ibid: 31-32.
111. Ibid: 32.
112. Ibid.
113. Ibid: 33

114. Ibid: 41.
115. Ibid: 309.
116. Ibid.
117. Ibid.
118. Ibid.
119. Fagel, *Principles of Emergency Management*: 310.
120. Ibid: 310-311.
121. Ibid: 311.
122. Ibid: 312.
123. Ibid: 316.
124. McEntire, *Disaster Response and Recovery*: 204-235.
125. Ibid: 205.
126. Ibid: 205.Emphasis in original.
127. Fagel, *Principles of Emergency Management*: 493-494.
128. Ibid: 494.
129. Ibid.
130. Ibid.
131. Ibid.
132. Ibid: 496.
133. Ibid.
134. Ibid.
135. Ibid: 497.
136. Ibid.
137. Ibid: 498.
138. Ibid: 497.
139. Ibid: 498.
140. McEntire, *Disaster Response and Recovery*: 205.
141. Ibid.
142. Ibid: 210.
143. Fagel, *Principles of Emergency Management*: 502.
144. Ibid.
145. https://training.fema.gov/programs/pio/
146. Fagel, *Principles of Emergency Management*: 502.
147. Ibid: 502-503.
148. Ibid: 502.
149. McEntire, *Disaster Response and Recovery*: 220-221.
150. Ibid: 221.
151. Ibid: 215.
152. Ibid: 221. Emphasis in original.
153. Ibid: 222.
154. Ibid: 223. Emphasis in original.
155. Jillian A. Williams and Aileen B. Xenakis, "Establishing Identity During a Disaster: The Emergency Management Assistance Compact and the First Responder Authentication Credential," *Journal of Emergency Management*, Vol. 6, No. 6, November/December 2008: 11.
156. Ibid.

157. Ibid: 14.
158. Oliver, *Policing In An Era of Homeland Security*: 112.
159. Jessica Jensen and John Carr, "Predisaster Integration of Community Emergency Response Teams," *Journal of Emergency Management*, Vol. 13, No. 1, January/February 2015: 26.
160. McEntire, Disaster Response and Recovery: 223.
161. Ibid: 224.
162. Ibid: 225.
163. Ibid: 227.
164. Ibid: 226.
165. Ibid: 228.
166. Ibid: 230.
167. Ibid: 273.
168. Ibid.
169. Lindell, Prater, and Perry, *Introduction to Emergency Management*: 363.
170. Ibid: 352.
171. Ibid.
172. Ibid.
173. Ibid.
174. McEntire, *Disaster Response and Recovery*: 274.
175. Lindell, Prater, and Perry, *Introduction to Emergency Management*: 354.
176. Ibid.
177. Ibid: 353.
178. Ibid: 357.
179. Ibid.
180. Ibid: 356-357.
181. Ibid: 357.
182. Ibid: 357.
183. Ibid.
184. Ibid: 358.
185. Ibid: 357.
186. Ibid: 358.
187. Ibid: 345-346.
188. Ibid: 353.
189. Ibid: 354.
190. Ibid: 353.
191. Ibid.
192. McEntire, *Disaster Response and Recovery*: 274.
193. Ibid: 275.
194. Ibid: 276.
195. Ibid: 276-277.
196. Ibid: 277.
197. Lindell, Prater, and Perry, *Introduction to Emergency Management*: 363.
198. McEntire, *Disaster Response and Recovery*: 277.
199. Ibid: 276.
200. Ibid.

201. Ibid.
202. Ibid: 278.
203. Ibid.
204. Ibid: 277.
205. Ibid.
206. Ibid: 278.
207. Ibid.
208. Ibid: 282.
209. Ibid: 279.
210. Ibid.
211. Ibid: 301.
212. Ibid: 280.
213. Ibid: 284.
214. Ibid.
215. Ibid: 284-285.
216. Ibid: 284.
217. Ibid: 286-287.
218. Ibid: 286.
219. Ibid: 287.
220. Ibid: 287-288.
221. Ibid.
222. Ibid: 289-290.
223. Ibid: 289.
224. Ibid.
225. Lindell, Prater, and Perry, *Introduction to Emergency Management*: 41-42.
226. McEntire, *Disaster Response and Recovery*: 291.
227. Ibid.
228. Ibid: 300.

Chapter 9

EMERGENCY MANAGEMENT TACTICS FOR LAW ENFORCEMENT

Tactics examine how law enforcement, first responder, and emergency workers are deployed at the scene. After the operational plan has been developed, tactics implement the operational plan to support the broad goals contained in the strategy. Tactics are the actual operations "on the ground" at a disaster or emergency. The law enforcement officer at a hazmat incident, the firefighter extracting an accident victim, the emergency management agency employee coordinating volunteers, and the FEMA (Federal Emergency Management Agency) employee conducting a damage assessment all involve tactics oriented towards working and resolving an actual incident.[1]

Typical Human Behavior in Emergencies

Because law enforcement officers and other first responders must work with members of the public during emergency situations, good tactics require being mindful of typical human behavior in crisis situations. Predictable human behavior during emergencies is associated with the following factors: (1) information, (2) fear, (3) protective action, (4) compliance, and (5) spontaneous protective action.

First is **information**, or rather *access* to information. Individuals who feel threatened by impending disasters or emergencies utilize multiple sources of information. This has never been truer than it is today. But to most people, no one source is considered entirely credible. That is why people search for confirmation of disaster information and warnings from multiple sources, including social media, different websites, television, radio, and face-to-face interaction.[2]

The second is **fear**. People threatened by disaster generally experience fear. Fear and panic are not the same thing. Fear is a rational response to danger, and it motivates protective action. But fear also interferes with logical thinking. It impairs a person's ability to reason through complex and unfamiliar problems. Fear can become acute when individuals do not possess sufficient information regarding the effects of hazard exposure.[3] This is especially true with hazmat incidents and biological incidents.

The third is **protective action**. Most people take protective action when they perceive that they are at risk. Authorities can help in this way. That is why officially broadcast warnings must include recommended protective actions. A warning message broadcast in the absence of protective action recommendations is unlikely to reduce fear.[4]

Fourth is **compliance**. Compliance refers to obedience to the actions that the authorities request. Many members of the population will indeed comply with the requests and recommendations of the authorities. Others will not do so. The level of compliance depends on several factors. The biggest factors involved with compliance are (a) *information source* (is it credible? Is it from a government agency?), (b) *message content* (does the message contain specific warnings?), and (c) *situational characteristics* (what *kind* of hazard warning is being given and what area does it affect?)?[5]

Compliance is highest with terrorist threats and imminent hazards such as tornadoes and hazmat. Research also shows that during the response phase of a disaster, the vast majority of people comply with directives from first responders.[6]

Fifth is **spontaneous protective action**. Certain people are "overcautious" and will take protective actions even without the presence of a warning or the presence of a specific hazard. For example, some people evacuate simply due to the fear that a hurricane might head for the area. In 1979 during the Three Mile Island nuclear event, ten times the number of people warned to evacuate actually did so. Spontaneous evacuation can be both positive and negative from an emergency management and first responder perspective. It is positive that people prepare and take action. It is negative if it leads to an unnecessary mass evacuation with the attendant traffic and associated problems.[7]

In addition to these predictions about human behavior, there are two expectations stemming from household behavior in emergencies: *health consequences* and *adaptive behavior*. First are **health consequences** for those not physically injured during disasters, which are mostly stress-related. The trauma of experiencing and living through a major disaster can manifest itself in the form of psychological problems and stress-related illnesses. Not only are depression, anxiety, and PTSD things that are likely to occur in a percentage of the population, but also physical illnesses such as digestive problems, heart problems, chronic headaches, and associated illnesses.[8]

These things are most likely to happen among two groups of survivors: The first group is made up of those who have witnessed deaths or handled dead bodies, those who have witnessed large-scale destruction, and those who have lost loved ones or had loved ones severely injured by the disaster. The second group is composed of those with pre-existing psychological problems.

The second expectation stemming from household behavior in emergencies is **adaptive behavior**. Both first responders and emergency managers often seem to forget the characteristics of disaster victims. The ability of disaster victims to demonstrate adaptive behavior differs significantly. A significant number of disaster victims possess special skills. For example, ex-military members, survivalists, and people who have had disaster training may possess such special skills. Also, one should not forget the other end of the spectrum: there are many people without financial or other tangible resources. There are others with special needs, including nursing home patients and the disabled.[9]

In sum, law enforcement officers and other first responders should know how individuals are likely to react during a disaster or emergency so that they can plan their actions appropriately.[10]

Tactics For Initial Response

The process of implementing initial response measures in terms of tactics will be analyzed.[11] **Response** is about reaction to a disaster or catastrophic event. Emergency response begins when a critical incident occurs.[12]

The responsibilities of first responders and emergency managers significantly increase during a disaster. Detecting the presence of a hazard is the first step in the response phase. Once a hazard has been detected, the population affected must be warned as soon as possible about the risks they face. A determination must also be made about whether evacuation or sheltering will be necessary.[13]

First is **hazard detection**.[14] Hazards can be detected in many ways: senses, field personnel, social media, dispatch, the media, meteorological services (like the National Weather Service), hospitals, and specialized technology.

First responders must constantly monitor their environment for hazards and emergencies. First responder agencies must have personnel on call 24 hours per day, seven days per week.[15]

In terms of initial steps, emergency managers must implement the jurisdiction's EOP (Emergency Operations Plan). The EOP contains tactics with which to respond to different types of disasters.[16] All organizations, both public and private, should have an EOP in place as part of sound management practice. This is especially true for government organizations and emergency management agencies. EOPs should take an "all hazards" approach to address every known disaster possibility. An organization's EOP is a vital part of an integrated emergency management system. The preparation of an EOP reflects a holistic "all hazards" approach to potential disasters and incorporates all four phases of the Emergency Management Cycle/Disaster Management Cycle.

Another initial step involves **seeking additional information**. When a hazard is about to occur or is actually occurring, seeking additional information is vital. Access to additional information will assist first responders to perform their jobs more efficiently and effectively.[17] Basic answers to seek include (a) the number of casualties, (b) the extent of property damage, (c) first responder needs, and (d) which other agencies need to be notified.

Depending upon the severity of the situation or incident, it may be necessary to activate the EOC (Emergency Operations Center). "An **Emergency Operations Center (EOC)** is a central location from which local governments can provide interagency coordination and executive decision-making in support of incident response and recovery operations. The purpose of the EOC is to provide a centralized location where public safety, emergency response, and support agencies coordinate planning, preparedness, and response activities."[18]

An "EOC does not command or control on-scene response efforts, but does carry out the coordination functions through (1) collecting, evaluating, and disseminating incident information, (2) analyzing jurisdictional impacts and setting priority actions, and (3) managing requests, procurement, and utilization of resources."[19]

"The decisions made through the EOC are designed to be broad in scope and offer general guidance on priorities. Information is disseminated through the EOC Manager and tactical decisions are coordinated from field response personnel. The EOC serves as a coordinated link between the Chief Elected Officer (CEO) of each jurisdiction and the field personnel coordinating the execution of event priorities."[20] "A primary EOC is necessary to properly coordinate response actions within the jurisdiction and to liaise with other jurisdictions and federal agencies."[21] EOCs are necessary for the coordination of emergency management disaster services.[22]

During a disaster, a determination must be made with regard to which personnel and agencies should participate in response operations. For example, will search and rescue be needed? Will firefighting be required? The specific type of disaster or emergency will determine which agencies and personnel will be involved. The number of agencies and personnel will rise and fall as response operations require.[23]

In addition, once imminent dangers to the community have been detected, warning the population is a vitally important function of emergency managers.[24] **Warnings** are notifications made in advance of a disaster that are intended to allow individuals in the public to take actions designed to protect themselves and their homes.[25] Warnings usually contain information about a specific hazard in addition to the notification itself.[26]

Warnings provide vital information to the population of the jurisdiction: (a) when the disaster or hazard will occur, (b) expected duration of the hazard or disaster, (c) likely impact of the disaster or hazard, (d) predicted property damages, and (e) predicted utility outages, street closures, and business closures.[27]

In order for a warning to translate into action, several things have to happen: (1) people must receive information, (2) people must pay attention to the information, and (3) people must understand (comprehend) the information.[28] First, people must *receive* information – there must be warnings put out through the media in order for people to receive the information. Warnings will not be effective if an individual is not online or using TV or radio, or if there is a power failure or grid down situation.[29] Second, people must *pay attention* to the information they receive. This is more challenging. People lead busy lives, and sometimes get distracted. They can also be overwhelmed with other tasks.[30] Third, people must *understand* and *comprehend* the information. Environmental cues have to be interpreted correctly. Not everyone will understand the technical terms that they hear. English warnings will not help Spanish speakers. Tornado sirens or tsunami sirens will not warn people who do not know what the sirens mean.[31]

Several **types of warning systems** exist. Some utilize technology and some do not. Each warning system possesses strengths and weaknesses.[32] Warning system types include media, sirens, reverse 911, the Emergency Alert System (EAS), social media, smartphones, weather radios, loudspeakers, and door-to-door notifications.

Warning considerations are principles behind emergency warning messages. Emergency managers must take these warning considerations into account when making the decision to issue warnings: (1) any warning must be clear and contain accurate information; (2) repeat the warning often with consistent content; (3) warnings must emanate from a credible source, such as a government official, and (4) realize that people will interpret warnings differently based upon their past experiences, interactions with others, and the perceived severity of the threat.[33]

Ideally, the public will heed warnings and will either take **protective actions or evacuate**. A **protective action** involves taking steps to prevent injuries or property damage. When a disaster is expected immediately, members of the public must utilize their own skills and resources to protect themselves. Past experience, things learned from friends, family, and neighbors, and public information regarding safety obtained from the media or the warning itself can all provide guidance on protective actions.[34]

Evacuation is also sometimes necessary in response to warnings. **Evacuation** involves the movement of individuals and families away from dangers and hazards for safety purposes. The purpose of evacuation is to physically move human beings away from danger and to a safe location to prevent death or injury.[35] Several means of evacuation can be utilized, which include automobiles, buses, walking, boats, and aircraft.

State transportation departments, emergency management agencies, state highway patrol agencies, and city public works agencies prepare evacuation plans. This is especially true in areas prone to hurricanes and tsunamis. The predicted strength of tropical storms and landfall predictions in particular guide evacuation strategies.[36]

Behavioral research tells us many things about evacuation and evacuation actions after warnings. First, evacuation only works when there is time to allow people to leave before the disaster hits. Second, evacuation is strongly related to wealth and income. People with more of these things have the money and personal autos and even the types of jobs that make evacuation possible. In a large city, up to one-third of households do not have their own vehicles and are dependent upon public transportation.

In terms of evacuation warnings, *warning compliance* and *spontaneous evacuation* must be differentiated. **Warning compliance** is the percentage of people advised to evacuate who *actually* evacuate.[37] Behavioral research demonstrates that between 12% and 87% of those warned actually comply. The typical warning compliance for hurricanes is between 34% and 65% Government officials cannot assume that there will ever be complete warning compliance.[38]

Warning compliance is affected by the *timing* of the evacuation advice. Evacuation recommendations that occur during the middle of the day when people are at work or school take longer to take effect. This is because people have to get home, pack items, and engage in other preparations. Evacuation advice that occurs at night leads to greater compliance because ninety percent of people are at home after 10 p.m. Research has also shown that as a hurricane approaches landfall, many people stay home from work or school in anticipation of receiving an evacuation recommendation.[39]

On the other hand, there is such a thing as **spontaneous evacuation**. This occurs when people evacuate even without an evacuation warning because they feel that they will be impacted. However, no accurate data exists on numbers or percentages of people who do so.[40]

Once the decision is made to order or recommend evacuation, well-recognized **evacuation procedures** should be followed. These include (1) notifying the at-risk population, (2) providing guidelines, instructions, and directions, (3) directing traffic to avoid gridlock, (4) ensuring compliance, (5) monitoring the progress of the evacuation, and (6) determining when to allow evacuees to return.

To facilitate these evacuation procedures, behavioral research allows emergency managers to estimate the percentage of people who will evacuate and the percentage of privately owned vehicles that will be used in an evacuation. This is very important information to know for planning purposes.

Government databases (including GIS) from the U.S. Census Bureau and from local governments allow law enforcement agencies and others to estimate population size and distribution. With this information, it is possible to obtain something known as *evacuation trip generation.* **Evacuation trip generation** is used to calculate the number of vehicles evacuating from a risk area. This number can be accurately estimated using procedures developed by both disaster researchers and traffic engineers.[41]

Evacuation trip generation can be estimated using five different government databases, three from the United States Census Bureau and two from local governments:

1. Size and distribution of the resident population in the evacuation area.
2. Number of persons per household in the evacuation area.
3. Size and distribution of the population dependent upon public transportation in the area.[42]

These three are obtained from the United States Census Bureau. The other two are obtained from local governments:

4. Size and distribution of the transient population in the evacuation area.
5. Number of vehicles per transient household in the evacuation area.[43]

These five government databases provide a good start towards calculating evacuation trip generation. However, this information is not sufficient. The raw data must be supplemented with estimates from behavioral research.

These estimates must be used to determine:

A. The number of evacuating vehicles per resident household.
B. The number of evacuating trailers, especially boat and camper trailers, per resident household. Making this calculation is important because towing trailers adds to the congestion of evacuation routes.
C. Calculating the percentage of people who will actually comply with the advice (warning compliance) to evacuate.[44]

Behavioral research shows first that the *household* is the basic unit of evacuation. Research shows that law enforcement officers and other agencies can expect between 1.2 and 1.5 vehicles per household to be used in an evacuation.[45] Couple this with the other data, and it is possible to estimate the number of cars and the number of people who will actually evacuate. Once this has been calculated, the issue of *departure timing* must be dealt with for planning purposes.

Departure timing deals with *when* household vehicles will actually enter the evacuation routes. Time of day is what departure timing assesses. Law enforcement agencies and government planners need to know when to expect lines for fuel and at what point the highways will become congested.[46]

Individuals and families do not tend to evacuate immediately after getting a hurricane evacuation order. It takes time to pack and prepare. Research shows that most people make their evacuation decisions early in the morning to allow as much daylight as possible for travel. If an evacuation order stems from a hazmat incident, evacuation times are much shorter.[47]

A final factor about evacuations must be addressed: **Route and Destination Choice**. In hurricane and tsunami-prone areas, emergency management agencies in conjunction with highway departments have installed *evacuation route signs* leading away from danger. Most people will follow these designated routes during an evacuation order.

Research shows that there are several factors that determine a household's Route and Destination Choice. First is **primary evacuation route utilization**. Here, evacuees travel along the designated evacuation route. This is the *percentage* of evacuees who do so. The primary evacuation routes will become congested and will often result in stalled traffic over time. Nevertheless, research shows that people *prefer* these routes, even when they move slowly.[48] To avoid this, some evacuees make **alternative route choices** – they travel away from the danger, but take secondary two-lane roads or even four-lane highways as an alternative. This may or may not take extra time.[49]

Evacuees are traveling towards what amounts to *two* destinations: their *proximate destination*, and, finally, to their *ultimate evacuation destination*. The **proximate destination** is where evacuees are out of danger. The **ultimate evacuation destination** is the place where the evacuees plan to reach to wait out the hazard.[50]

Law enforcement officers must engage in manual traffic control at major intersections during evacuations. Manual traffic control is necessary due to saturated traffic and road conditions caused by the evacuation order. Manual traffic control moves highway and road travel more efficiently during the surge caused by the evacuation.[51]

Regardless of the hazard or the warnings, a certain percentage of the population either cannot or will not evacuate. This is true even when danger to lives and health is a possibility.[52] These reasons include not taking the risk seriously, unclear warnings, lack of transportation, age, fear of looting, size and makeup of family, financial resources, peer behavior, past experience, education, disability, and inconvenience.

What are the choices available to those who cannot or will not evacuate? They can either shelter in place or go to **mass care facilities**, like shelters established in gyms, conference centers, schools, or other facilities operated by emergency management agencies or the American Red Cross. The percentage of people who utilize mass care facility shelters ranges from 5% to 20%. Mass care facility utilization is heavily dependent upon the financial resources of the local population. To a lesser extent, shelter use is related to the sudden onset of severe weather and traffic congestion.[53]

Sheltering refers to the relocation of evacuees to housing or to places of safety.[54] Emergency managers must be aware of the different types of shelters, which include (1) emergency shelter, (2) temporary shelter, (3) temporary housing, and (4) permanent housing.

Emergency shelter is established by government agencies (like FEMA) or by non-profit organizations like the American Red Cross. Extensive emergency management resources at all levels of American government have gone into the planning and operation of emergency shelters. However, most individuals choose not to use sheltering services. Experience has shown that most individuals prefer to move in with friends and family if possible.[55] These are often referred to as *congregate care shelters* or *consolidated services sites* as covered in Chapter 4. Realize that shelter use is higher in urban areas and during hurricanes. Also, large-scale disasters make shelter use more likely. Older people and those from lower socio-economic groups are more likely to utilize emergency shelters.[56]

Temporary shelter is obtained with an individual's own resources, and can include motels or the homes of friends or family members away from the disaster impact site.[57]

Temporary housing can be provided by the government (FEMA trailers) or by individuals renting an apartment or house while waiting for permanent housing. Federal policy allows for temporary housing to be extended for months. Temporary housing is viewed as superior to shelters because the former allows normal household routines to occur in a different residence.[58]

Finally, there is **permanent housing**. Permanent housing involves rebuilding damaged or destroyed dwellings or moving to new ones. Permanent housing is the long-term objective post-disaster.[59]

Disaster Declarations, Damage Assessment, and Debris Removal

Recovery is about getting the impacted area back to normal – to restore it as close to possible to its pre-disaster state. Recovery begins once the effects of the disaster have been stabilized. Recovery may take weeks, months, or years. The first step of recovery is the restoration of infrastructure, including power, water, sewer, communications, and transportation.[60]

Recovery is both short-term and long-term. **Short-term recovery** is about "rehabilitation and relief" which sets up temporary solutions to make life easier and to bring about basic community functioning. For example, engaging in debris cleanup to allow transportation to occur, the provision of temporary housing, and restoring services are parts of short-term recovery.[61] **Long-term recovery** is about reconstruction, such as rebuilding houses, businesses, roads, and bridges, and getting the economy functioning normally again.

We should realize that during recovery, the majority of the supplies and other resources required to restore the community come from outside the jurisdiction. For example, insurance companies, private organizations, state governments, and the federal government provide the majority of recovery resources.[62]

Ideally, a jurisdiction's hazard management strategy should consist equally of efforts to foster mitigation, preparedness, response, and recovery.[63] This is the theory. Reality is often different from theory. Much more emphasis has been placed on recovery and response than on mitigation and preparedness.

Recovery and response are related. Resilience is increased when response efforts involve thinking in advance about recovery. Damage assessment is an important precursor to recovery. Accurate damage assessment helps to precisely discern the impact of the disaster. In addition, an accurate assessment of the damage will be used to make a decision about whether or not a disaster should be declared and whether or not the disaster qualifies for state or federal financial assistance. Disaster debris presents difficult challenges. Both damage assessment and debris removal are important parts of the recovery process.[64]

The recovery phase begins when the emergency caused by the disaster has diminished sufficiently to no longer present a threat to human life and property.[65] In other words, recovery means rebuilding and reconstructing so that the community can get back to normal levels of functioning.

Recovery from disaster has both physical and social dimensions.[66] It involves removing debris, reconstructing or repairing damaged buildings, and getting the grid back up and running. Recovery also involves dealing with the psychological and economic stress of living through the disaster and getting back to normal.

The first step of recovery involves damage assessment. Damage assessment typically commences soon after the emergency created by a disaster has dissipated.[67] **Damage assessment** deals with examining and quantifying the extent of destruction caused by a disaster. Damage assessment is important because it guides response activities. Quantification of damage is also needed to determine the availability and extent of outside disaster assistance.[68]

Five functions are served by the damage assessment process: (1) identifying the immediate needs of disaster victims (food, sheltering, emergency medical), (2) determining the need for specific types of material resources (medical supplies, water, ice, etc.) and financial resources (amount of money, nonprofit organization services, etc.), (3) determining what is required in order to receive federal aid, (4) determining if housing is safe for habitation, and (5) assistance in the designation of hazardous areas.

The *types* of damage assessment and the *methods* of damage assessment should be examined. There are three types of damage assessments that can be conducted: (1) rapid assessment (also called initial assessment), (2) preliminary assessment (also called a PDA-Preliminary Damage Assessment), and (3) technical assessment (also called engineering assessment).

First is the rapid assessment. A **rapid assessment** is a post-disaster examination of damage to a given area for the purpose of quickly determining the extent and magnitude of a disaster impact.[69] It is generally conducted by on-scene law enforcement, fire, or public works employees. Data is collected on the numbers of visible deaths, injuries, and property damage in a rapid assessment. It is conducted one to three hours after the disaster occurred and identifies secondary hazards, if any. Rapid assessment delineates the geographical areas impacted by the disaster and the severity of the damage. It is also used to determine if search and rescue or other lifesaving activities are necessary.[70]

Second is the **preliminary assessment**. Preliminary Damage Assessment (PDA) is conducted days or weeks after the impact of a disaster by government officials. The purpose of a preliminary assessment is to discern the need for outside assistance. PDA must be conducted in most disasters prior to being eligible for a presidential disaster declaration and thus the allocation of federal disaster assistance funds. Some disasters are obviously of significant severity to result in a presidential disaster declaration prior to the preliminary assessment. However, the PDA must still be performed later to comply with federal law.[71] The preliminary assessment is more thorough than any initial assessment and documents the extent of losses more completely.[72]

Third is the **technical assessment**, which is also called an *engineering assessment*. It is conducted in the weeks following a disaster by engineers, FEMA employees and contractors, and insurance adjusters. The technical assessment provides accurate and detailed cost estimates for the repair and replacement of each structure damaged or destroyed.[73]

The **methods of conducting damage assessment** are now examined. Damage assessment methods deal with the techniques used to determine the extent of disaster losses. There are three major methods of conducting damage assessment: (1) "drive-through" assessments, (2) aerial assessments, and (3) site visits ("walk-through" assessments).

In a **"drive-through" assessment**, law enforcement officers or other government employees literally drive down the roads and streets inside the disaster impact zone and visibly observe and record the number of damaged homes and businesses and estimate the scope of that damage. Inspectors only leave their vehicles if streets are blocked by debris.[74] This can lead to inaccurate evaluation due to its speed and the fact that structures are only visually examined in passing.

Next is the **aerial assessment**. As indicated by the name, it is done with aircraft, either airplanes or helicopters. When highways and roads are impassible due to water or debris, aerial assessments are necessary. The media plays aerial assessment footage routinely. Elected officials and high-ranking department heads favor aerial assessment because it reveals the scope of damage more effectively than could be seen through a motor vehicle.[75] They also prefer this as it does not directly expose them to debris, water, and the downed infrastructure.

Third is the **site visit** or **walk-through assessment**. This is an "on the ground" examination to assess damages on foot. This is meant to determine both the structural soundness of homes and businesses and the cost to repair or replace each damaged structure. The initial walkthrough assessment is obviously more detailed and complete than a "drive-through" assessment. Walkthrough assessments are detailed. Structures are assigned tags (red, yellow, or green) based on the level of damage and danger to occupants.[76] A thorough walk-through assessment must be conducted by qualified and trained inspectors such as civil engineers.[77] It is here that engineering assessments or technical assessments are completed. Technical walkthrough assessments are also used to determine precise cost estimates of damage caused by the impact and to make recommendations regarding demolition or repairs.[78]

Damage assessment is a complex process. Since that is true, effective damage assessment takes planning before and during the process. Emergency managers must hold meetings at which assessment personnel are briefed on their geographic areas to cover and the protocols that will be utilized to record results.[79] Several challenges related to damage assessment include problems with accuracy, problems involving working with others, and problems relating to access and safety.

In terms of accuracy (correctly assessing damages), initial estimates are sometimes incorrect. This may be due to damages not immediately visible or due to the fact that not all damage was initially reported. Damages may also be missed entirely due to carelessness, fatigue, or other error.[80] FEMA officials, insurance adjusters, and engineers can differ with regard to the basis for calculating damage: replacement cost or purchase price, for example.[81]

With regard to problems involving working with others, law enforcement officers and other first responders should realize that many organizations such as state and federal officials, public and private sector engineers, insurance companies, and different emergency management agencies will be involved in recovery. Each typically possesses a different agenda. Different organizations may use different methodologies, software, and forms to estimate damages.[82]

There are also problems inherent to accessing affected areas and in terms of safety on-site. This is true due to extensive debris blocking roads, flooded streets, and destroyed bridges. In addition, building collapse potential, fire potential, and exposure to chemicals and contaminated water pose hazards to damage assessors.[83] These also can include pathogens, mold, potential for electrocution, and poisonous snakes, among other hazards.

Finally, it must be recognized that members of the general public in the disaster area are often displeased with the speed of assessment and in the results of the assessments in terms of insurance coverage and the speed and amount of disaster relief funding.

Several purposes are served by conducting damage assessment. Since recovery costs a substantial amount of money, local governments seek to obtain reimbursement for recovery costs from a higher level of government. In addition, local governments seek the actual provision of as many recovery services as possible either by higher levels of government directly (or with the contractors that they hire), or by means of obtaining reimbursement funding from a higher level of government. Remember that one purpose of damage assessment, especially preliminary assessments, is to persuade a higher level of government to issue a disaster declaration. A **disaster declaration** is a statement by an executive elected official that a given jurisdiction or community cannot conduct effective disaster response efforts without receiving outside assistance.[84]

City and county governments desire a state disaster declaration at a minimum if possible, and ultimately hope for a federal disaster declaration. Similarly, state governments desire a federal disaster declaration. Nevertheless, the majority of requests for federal disaster declarations are refused. This is most often the case because the estimated damages from the disaster are judged not to meet the minimum requirements necessary to trigger such a declaration.[85]

Although both federal and state agencies are frequently involved in disaster recovery, most disaster recovery is actually carried out by city and county governments. This makes it all the more vital for local governments to prepare to perform substantial disaster recovery services.[86]

The "ultimate" disaster declaration that can be obtained in terms of obtaining funding and resources is the **PDD (Presidential Disaster Declaration)**. As discussed in previous chapters, a PDD results in the provision of a large number of programs and funds to assist in disaster recovery.[87] This federal funding can be used to pay for overtime of government workers (first responders, public works personnel engaged in debris removal, etc.) and for direct recovery costs incurred. Congress has delegated to FEMA the authority to determine whether to determine if a PDD is warranted and if so, to authorize reimbursement.[88]

Under federal law, the PDD process involves both objective and subjective measures of disaster impact.[89] These include the number of structures damaged or destroyed, the estimated costs, the percentage of disabled or those in poverty in an area, and other measures. In addition, at this time the documents provided to FEMA as part of local damage assessments must indicate at least $3.50 per capita in damages at the county level and $1.39 per capita at the state level in order to support a federal disaster declaration.[90]

Most PDDs are given only after a disaster has occurred and following local and state government requests supported by preliminary damage assessments. In some cases, however, advanced PDD can be made if it appears obvious that a disaster will be of great magnitude, such as a Category 4 hurricane predicted to make landfall.[91] Realize that only about one percent of all disasters receive PDD status. If a disaster fails to meet the PDD threshold, local and state governments must rely upon their own resources. Affected property owners must rely on what insurance (if any) will pay.

Extensive recordkeeping is required in order for local and state governments to be reimbursed for costs associated with disaster recovery in the event that any type of disaster is declared. In addition, handling the large volume of debris produced by disasters is a complex matter. All disasters produce debris, though some produce more than others. For example, Hurricane Katrina in 2005 resulted in 118 million cubic yards of debris. These debris were spread across an area of over 90,000 square miles.[92]

Natural disasters like hurricanes, earthquakes, and tornadoes create a substantial amount of debris – trees, downed power lines, building components, and other items that are destroyed can become debris that must be removed. The debris blocks roads and interferes with first responder and recovery efforts. **Debris management** is the protocol or system used to hire and supervise debris removal, in addition to the actual disposal of debris in accordance with environmental legislation and regulations.[93]

Different types of disasters produce various types of debris. **Vegetative debris** are trees and parts of trees like limbs and leaves. **Aggregate debris** includes concrete and asphalt. **Demolition debris** comes from damaged structures that had to be destroyed or repaired. **Indirect debris** includes spoiled food from a lack of electricity for refrigeration and waste (such as water bottles) utilized in response and recovery operations.[94] Human remains and animal carcasses must also be handled in some disasters. The handling of these remains and carcasses poses additional difficulties over and above normal debris management because human remains usually require analysis by medical examiners and criminal investigators. In addition, special disposal techniques are required for biological remains.[95]

Debris itself can create hazards for first responders and the general public. For example, impassible roads make emergency vehicles unable to respond to calls or perform their first responder duties. The presence of broken glass and sharp pieces of metal on the roads will destroy the tires of police and fire vehicles even if the roads are not blocked or flooded. One of the first priorities in a recovery operation is to clear roads and streets for emergency vehicles.[96] The quantity of debris must also be reduced quickly to foster economic recovery.[97]

Research has shown that debris produced by a hazard can exceed seven times the normal volume of garbage produced by a community during normal times.[98] The volume of debris may overwhelm the capabilities of city and county public works employees. Due to overtime expenses and the need to hire outside contractors, debris management also greatly contributes to the cost of recovery. It has been noted that the total financial cost of debris removal accounts for between fifteen percent to one-third of FEMA disaster spending.[99] Because of the expense, local and state governments desire a disaster declaration so that federal funds can be released for debris removal. However, FEMA funding will only transpire when the local and state governments comply with federal paperwork and documentation requirements. If this is done, FEMA pays for all of the costs associated with the debris removal for the first 72 hours after a natural disaster impact. After the first 72 hours, FEMA pays 75 percent of the debris removal costs paid by county and city governments. This FEMA funding applies only in declared disasters, however.[100]

Thus, it is apparent that debris management is a vital part of the recovery process. The U.S. Environmental Protection Agency (EPA) has provided a 10-step recommendation to assist local and state governments in improving their debris management protocols. Among these suggestions are for local and state governments to enter into mutual aid agreements, select collection and storage sites for debris in advance, prepare contracts in advance for private contractors, have a plan to obtain needed supplies and equipment in the event of disaster, and have the mechanisms in place to provide the documentation needed for FEMA debris removal funding. Beyond this, state and local governments can reduce the volume of debris by burning, chipping vegetative debris, and recycling useable materials.[101] If FEMA debris removal funding is obtained, federal regulations require that the debris be removed and disposed of within 180 days.[102]

In summary, recovery requires that emergency managers estimate and calculate damages and deal with debris removal in order to foster resilience. Documentation is needed to obtain outside funding for these critical tasks.

The Challenges of Response and Recovery

Response and recovery pose many challenges. This section looks at seven typical challenges or issues that often appear during the recovery phase of emergency management. Surmounting these issues or challenges requires properly conducted operations.[103]

Evidence-based emergency management practice teaches us that seven specific challenges have the tendency to arise during the recovery phase following a disaster impact: (1) problems with communication and coordination; (2) decision-making issues, (3) problems with transportation and logistics, (4) issues dealing with the problems of at-risk populations, (5) politics, (6) the potential for lawsuits, and (7) the challenges posed by recordkeeping. This section examines these challenges in addition to ways to overcome them.[104]

The first challenge that often emerges is related to **communication and coordination**. In the context of emergency management recovery, **communication** is the verbal and nonverbal process of sending and receiving important information about disaster response and recovery endeavors.[105] In order for communication to be effective, it must be transmitted and those who receive the communication must understand and act upon the communication.[106]

Coordination goes hand in hand with communication in emergency management response and recovery activities. **Coordination** is the synergy of response and recovery operations to achieve predetermined goals among and between first responders and emergency management personnel.[107]

Effective response and recovery depend upon effective communication and coordination. However, effective communication and coordination are not always easy to achieve due to the nature of disasters, which are extraordinary events that place stress on individuals, responders, and emergency management agencies. Disasters are traumatic and chaotic. For this reason, effective communications can be challenging. Time pressures, loud noises, information overload and the presence of large numbers of employees from many different organizations can interfere with both communication and coordination. Response and recovery equipment may break.[108] In addition, first responders are often called upon to perform unknown jobs, forcing them to work with unfamiliar first responder agencies from different jurisdictions. First responders will often also be required to work with civilians and participants who are not part of any first responder organization.[109]

Problems with communication lead to problems with coordination. There are several ways to improve both communication and coordination. Some of these include holding joint meetings with emergency managers, emergency management agencies, and first responder agencies. These meetings will make the stakeholders familiar with each other and the duties and responsibilities of all. Mutual aid agreements, resource sharing, and the development of ongoing interpersonal relationships will improve coordination and communication when disasters strike.

Decision-making issues comprise a second challenge during response and recovery. Decision-making is about making choices during response and recovery operations. Here, first responders and emergency managers choose from among alternatives and then implement a series of actions designed to achieve those choices. *Decision making orients action.* Making decisions leads to taking actions designed to achieve the choices that were made.

Decisions can be made in many ways: in reaction to a problem, on the basis of emotion, or by attempting to follow a step-by-step process designed to achieve a predetermined goal as efficiently and effectively as possible. The approach to decision-making chosen can make all the difference in the quality of the result. Management theory teaches us that we should aim for *rationality* in decision-making. Rationality describes the attempt to base decisions on logic and factual information. Through attempting to use rationality, emotions and ideological beliefs should be suppressed in favor of factual information, according to the theory.

This leads to **rational decision-making**. Rational decision-making involves the attempt to look for alternative solutions and to choose the best one from among several best suited to deal with the situation.[110]

However, many times in life reality diverges from theory. This makes it difficult if not impossible to follow rational decision-making in reality. This is true because it is all but impossible to separate emotions, biases, personality traits, and politics from one's thought process. Also, it is impossible for human beings to know all of their options and to predict the full consequences of making or failing to make one decision over others.[111]

It has been convincingly argued that rational decision-making is an idealized representation of thought processes. In reality, bounded rationality is the best that can be realistically achieved. **Bounded rationality** means that human beings cannot ever fully achieve rational decision-making due to the limitations that disaster impacts impose on decision-makers.[112] This means that rationality is limited (bounded) by what is possible at the time. Rationality is limited based on incomplete knowledge, the inability to precisely predict the future, the skills and experience of emergency managers, politics, and a host of other issues. Thus, first responders and emergency managers attempt to *approximate* rationality, but they will never be able to achieve *true or total* rationality. Among reasons that these are true include compressed time, tragic choice, fuzzy gambling, strain and stress, and the limitations inherent in group processes.

Experience in working with past disasters helps first responders to make better decisions, as does learning from past mistakes. Redesigning policies and procedures considering past mistakes and experiences will improve decision-making as well.

A third challenge typically encountered in the aftermath of disasters involves **transportation and logistical issues**. As we are all aware, major disasters can and do damage the infrastructure, including electricity, water, roads, bridges, and highways. Also, public transport will be inoperable. These facts make moving goods such as food, fuel, and emergency supplies difficult. **Transportation** involves the carrying or hauling of human beings, animals, or goods from one place to another.[113] Transportation is vital to disaster response and recovery endeavors.[114]

Regarding transportation, the first issue that an emergency manager must deal with is finding alternative means of transportation for search, rescue, and disaster relief. Then he or she can concentrate on taking the steps to remove debris sufficiently to allow emergency vehicles to travel. Boats and helicopters may have to be used for rescue and transport of emergency supplies if streets are impassible.[115] Some private corporations are willing to offer transportation services to support disaster relief.[116]

Transportation is closely related to *logistics*. Simply defined, logistics is about the transportation of supplies and equipment from one place to another. The collection, loading, shipping, and unloading of equipment and supplies are part of logistics. In the context of disaster response and recovery, the moving and distribution of supplies to disaster victims and responders are comprise components of logistics.[117]

Disaster-related transportation problems also cause problems with logistics. However, these issues can be overcome. HELIOS software can assist with logistics. Also, it is very important for emergency managers to plan for transportation and logistical difficulties likely to be encountered in advance of disasters.[118]

A fourth post-disaster challenge that generally emerges involved difficulties encountered with **meeting the needs of at-risk populations**. As was noted in Chapter 4, some segments of the population are more vulnerable than others to disasters.[119] While all individuals are at risk when exposed to natural and man-made disasters, at risk populations are potentially at *greater* risk due to age, income, access to resources, physical condition, and other factors.

The unique needs of special populations must be taken into consideration during response and recovery. At-risk populations require additional or unique assistance and more resources than other victims. At-risk populations are not as resilient. First responders must be aware of the locations and needs of special populations in the recovery operations area.[120]

Suggestions to meet the needs of special populations following a disaster include identifying the special populations in the community, making plans to reach out to these populations in the aftermath of a disaster, identifying the resources needed to assist special populations in advance of the disaster, and by working with nonprofit organizations such as the American Red Cross and faith-based organizations to ensure that the needs of special populations are met.

Politics is a fifth specific challenge that often manifests itself in the aftermath of a disaster. In the context of emergency management disaster response and recovery, this means *Who gets what services, what kind of relief, when, and how.* Different individuals and groups will receive different services, depending upon the degree of damage, how accessible they are, and quite frankly socioeconomic status. Disasters have a political dimension. Politics can be manifested in disaster declarations, the timing and order in which assistance is delivered, blame for actions or inactions, and conflict between agencies.[121]

The botched response to Hurricane Katrina in 2005 is an example of politics in emergency response and recovery. Some local government officials have also been known to overstate the amount of destruction for the purpose of obtaining financial assistance from higher levels of government.[122]

An unpleasant dimension to disaster recovery can be manifested in making decisions about who should receive priority for assistance and aid. Political pressure may be brought to bear on elected officials to prioritize more affluent areas of the jurisdiction and to assist large corporations in the area. Elected officials have been known to prioritize them over less affluent areas due to the political clout possessed by the wealthy and large corporations. Even if this does not actually occur, many people will still have the perception that others have been prioritized unfairly.[123]

The attempt by those affected and by the media to assign blame for perceived mistakes in response and recovery also has a political dimension.[124] This is true because, in our representative democracy, public officials are often blamed both for things that are under their control and for things that are *not* under their control. There is a human tendency to shift responsibility for bad things to others. For that reason, emergency managers and first responders may themselves be criticized and blamed for perceived slowness or failures in response and recovery operations.[125] The media may "scapegoat" emergency managers and first responders as well, especially if they receive large numbers of complaints about a "slow" or "botched" response.

Politics are also exhibited after disasters in terms of **interorganizational conflict**. This term refers to "infighting" among and between emergency management agencies, nonprofit organizations involved in disasters, and first responder agencies. This can impede response and recovery operations and hamper rationality. For example, law enforcement, firefighters, and other agencies have different organizational cultures and prioritize different things.[126]

There are other potential areas for interorganizational conflict. For example, issues may arrive over which agency will oversee a particular task. Disputes over resources and responsibilities also have the potential to arise.[127] These types of issues and the decisions made to resolve them can have a substantial impact on the quality of response and recovery.

It has been found that some agencies become "passive-aggressive" and will reduce their work output due to interorganizational rivalries. It is common for law enforcement agencies and fire departments to exhibit this dynamic. For example, law enforcement officers may want to keep a road open after a major traffic accident, while firefighters may want to temporarily close the road in order to protect their personnel.[128]

Internal politics involves motivation, morale, leadership, interpersonal working relationships, clashing personalities, and similar factors. Anyone who has ever worked a job in a government agency knows and understands this. Government organizations with significant internal politics respond more poorly to disasters. Some employees also have hidden agendas and personality issues that manifest themselves on the job. For example, a low-level first responder may attempt to assume incident command although he or she lacks the experience and temperament to do so effectively.[129]

When groups and teams lack trust, have friction, or do not work well together, the rationality or the organization in terms of the ability of the organization to function and to achieve its predetermined goals are jeopardized. It is the responsibility of senior management to diagnose and resolve these issues.[130]

Interorganizational rivalries typically occur most often at large-scale or more serious critical incidents. One of the main purposes of NIMS (National Incident Management System) and ICS (Incident Command System) is to allow for a more smooth and complete integration of state, local, and federal emergency management and first responder agencies. Interorganizational politics has lessened in intensity in recent years. Agencies are improving at working together to address common tragedies affecting communities and the nation. Evidence-based practice advises us to try to work effectively with first responders from other agencies and jurisdictions.[131]

A sixth issue or obstacle associated with response and recovery concerns the **potential for lawsuits (legal liability)**. First responders and emergency managers must be cognizant of the potential for legal liability. These stem from alleged violations of statutory law or constitutional violations.[132] Lawsuits may also involve allegations of negligence by first responder organizations that resulted in harm to individual citizens.[133]

To sue a first responder or emergency management agency (or its parent government), the issue of sovereign immunity must first be surmounted. **Sovereign immunity** is the legal doctrine or principle that a government may not be sued without its consent. However, this consent has been waived in many jurisdictions. In addition, federal legislation has been enacted to impose liability upon local and state governments for violations of federal constitutional provisions and federal statutory law.

The first type of lawsuit involves taking a first responder organization and its parent government to court for the tort of negligence. A **tort** is a civil wrong other than a breach of contract for which the law provides a remedy in the form of an action for damages. There are several kinds of torts, but the tort of negligence is the most frequently litigated.

Negligence is defined as the *failure* to use such care in one's actions as a reasonable and prudent person would have used under the circumstances. Negligence law imposes a legal duty upon all adult persons to take *reasonable care* that their actions or failures to act do not cause harm to others. In the context of law enforcement and emergency management, negligence is the failure of first responders and emergency managers and responders to do what "a reasonable and prudent person" would have done under similar circumstances. For example, a tort could occur if an emergency management or first responder agency failed to warn the population of a hazmat release. Negligent failure to warn could also involve the failure to warn the local population about an impending natural disaster.[134]

Other examples of responder or emergency management negligence could involve slow 911 dispatch resulting in injury or death, accidents involving emergency vehicles, failure to follow standard operating procedures, and alleged medical mistakes by EMS.[135] Beyond this, if first responder agencies such as law enforcement organizations do not follow statutory law on issues relating to hazmat recordkeeping or improperly spend disaster grants, lawsuits and criminal prosecution could follow.[136] Lawsuits may also be brought against governments and government officials for constitutional or statutory rights violations.[137]

As another example, Congress passed a piece of legislation entitled the **Civil Rights Act of 1871** for the purpose of applying the 14th Amendment to state and local governments. Section 1983 of this law makes any state or local government official liable under federal law or equity when any such official deprives any person in his or her official capacity of any federal Constitutional or statutory right. These kinds of lawsuits are called "1983 suits" or "1983 actions."[138] They account for a substantial amount of litigation in the federal courts, because most laws and most police officers operate at the state and local levels of government. Potential legal issues can also include allegations of discrimination. For example, if a first responder was accused of differential treatment of disaster victims because of race, national origin, or religions, a lawsuit for monetary damages could be brought.[139]

Realize that most lawsuits against governments seek monetary damages. If found liable, the taxpayers ultimately pay, not the individual responders and emergency managers in most cases. The doctrine of **qualified immunity** stipulates that individual government employees cannot be sued personally for their wrongful acts if they were committed in the line and scope of their duties; rather, the government must pay for monetary damages for such acts as awarded by a court. Qualified immunity protects government employees from personal civil liability if it is shown that he or she performed their jobs in accordance with procedures and without intentionally violating a constitutional right.[140]

Supervisors should realize that if a critical incident has received extensive media coverage and public criticism, the first responders involved will be scrutinized. A lawsuit, whether warranted or not, is also likely. However, the lawsuit will likely fail unless it can be shown that the first responder acted unreasonably under the circumstances based on information known at the time.[141]

The final typical challenge encountered involves the **challenges posed by recordkeeping**. Government bureaucracies justify their actions to a substantial degree by maintaining written records of what actions were taken over time. This is often required by law, to justify decisions and actions taken, and to protect government employees from lawsuits.[142]

Recordkeeping is necessary to account for material and human resources. Recordkeeping is also needed for the purpose of recording damages. Recordkeeping is also a requirement to receive reimbursement from a higher level of government for emergency management activities following a disaster.[143] However, obtaining and keeping records can be difficult following a disaster. These reasons include records lost, contaminated, or destroyed by the disaster, lack of time to maintain records, the lack of records from spontaneous organizations, and inaccurate records from common carriers or events. If and when these problems occur, emergency managers and first responders should try to reconstruct events from field notes, dispatch recordings, interviews, police and fire reports, and photographs.[144]

Awareness of the major issues that arise following a major disaster will facilitate resilience.[145] Knowing how to deal with these typical challenges will make the emergency manager's job more effective and will pay dividends in terms of serving the public.

Overview of Critical Incidents

This section provides an overview of critical incidents likely to be encountered in the first responder and emergency management fields. Whether one is a first responder or occupying a management position, an individual in the emergency management field must have knowledge of the nature of critical incidents and how to deal with them effectively.[146]

A **critical incident** is an unusual event that places human lives and property in danger and necessitates the deployment and coordination of resources to resolve.[147] This is a broad definition, and it covers many disasters.[148] A critical incident is beyond a *typical* accident or event. A critical incident requires *additional resources* to resolve. For example, terrorist activities involving WMDs (Weapons of Mass destruction), major natural disasters (hurricanes, earthquakes, and volcanic eruptions), epidemics, pandemics, mass-casualty transportation accidents, serious criminal activities, major fires, and significant hazmat incidents are all examples of critical incidents. A critical incident occurs when first responders cannot resolve the issue with their own resources. Additional resources from other agencies, jurisdictions, and levels of government may be required.[149]

Critical incidents must be effectively *managed.* **Incident management** is "the broad spectrum of activities and organizations providing effective and efficient operations, coordination, and support applied at all levels of government, utilizing both governmental and nongovernmental resources to plan for, respond to, and recover from an incident, regardless of cause, size, or complexity."[150] Incidents range in size, scope, and severity. However, the basic principles of critical incident management are remarkably similar across all situations.[151]

Law enforcement trainers have identified several common issues associated with most critical incidents based upon their own professional experience and upon the experiences of emergency management personnel that they have trained: (1) communications, (2) clarity of command, (3) resources and resource coordination, (4) intelligence gathering and problem assessment, (5) perimeter control, (6) environmental factors, (7) planning and training, and (8) the media.[152]

First is **communication**. This means issues involved with sending and receiving messages at the critical incident scene. Communications issues mainly stem from technological issues, such as poor-quality radio equipment (bad reception and transmission; battery issues), lack of interoperable radios (those that can link state, local, and national agencies), and use of 10-codes (police radio codes for different events that may not be understood by other agencies – this is why the federal government has been discouraging their use for many years). Better equipment and training in its use can overcome these communications issues.[153]

A second issue is **clarity of command**. This deals with who is in overall command at a critical incident scene involving different first responder agencies (a multidisciplinary situation). Should police, fire, or emergency medical personnel going to be in change at a given critical incident? Clarity of command also involves who should be in charge at a combination (**multiple agency**) state, local, and federal incident scene. It is recommended that during the initial crisis response, each first responder discipline should manage its own functional are without attempting to take over from other disciplines.[154]

Resources and resource coordination is a third common characteristic. This deals with a dichotomy: during the crisis phase of a critical incident, there are usually very few resources available. However, once the incident is called in and an initial assessment is made, abundant resources are typically made available very quickly during the scene management phase. First responders must quickly shift from being understaffed to being present at a large response to be effective.[155]

A fourth common characteristic involves **intelligence gathering and problem assessment**. This deals with the first responder's ability to obtain vital information about the critical incident quickly. This requires quickly assessing what occurred, what are the dangers, and what must happen to stabilize and resolve the critical incident.[156] In this regard, decisions made by first responders on the scene will vary in quality and effectiveness based upon the ability to assess the problem and gather information under a confusing and highly stressful situation.[157] One of the goals of this book is to improve problem-assessment skills at a critical incident. Having good intelligence gathering and problem assessment skills at a critical incident is vital to making good decisions.

Perimeters and perimeter control is a fifth common characteristic. This deals with the number of people (both bystanders and emergency workers) physically present at the site of a critical incident. In a critical incident, the person in charge must limit access to the scene to those that have a legitimate need to be present: emergency workers. Failing to do so endangers bystanders, victims, and responders.

A sixth common characteristic deals with the physical **environment** in which a critical incident occurs. This means the physical location and conditions (urban, rural, desert, swamp, parking lot, roadway, sun, snow, rain) present at a critical incident site affects the range of options available and the effectiveness of solutions to resolve the critical incident.[158]

Planning and training comprise a seventh common characteristic. This is about having and effectively implementing an **incident action plan**. This is a strategy for resolving the critical incident in terms of written or oral objectives. An incident management plan should include the allocation of personnel assignments and on-scene resources.[159]

Having an incident action plan is very important. However, they are only effective to the extent that they are understood and utilized. Effective plans cannot only exist on paper. They must be used at an actual critical incident scene in order to make a difference. Plans must be tested and validated though training and real-world use.[160]

The final common characteristic is the **media**. Large incidents, especially if they involve deaths or serious injuries get the attention of television, radio, and newspaper reporters. Social media will certainly display images and commentary. Sometimes inaccurate information is broadcast. In addition, it is possible for media representatives to hamper emergency management efforts at a critical incident site. Effective emergency management and first responder agencies have plans in place to deal with the media, such as a

Public Information Officer (PIO). Having an agency or critical incident spokesperson to work with the media and controlling access to the scene can assist both parties. Being aware of these eight common characteristics associated with critical incident management assists emergency managers and first responders to know what to expect. In this way they can better perform their jobs.

In addition, first responders and emergency managers should also keep in mind the differences between *controllable* and *uncontrollable* factors at the site of a critical incident. Since a critical incident can occur at any time, the speed at which incidents unfold depend on many factors, only some of which are controllable. First responders can only focus upon the critical incident factors within their control.[161]

Uncontrollable factors include time of day (or night), weather conditions, location (rural, urban, landscape), injuries and deaths, the presence of weapons (in criminal or terrorist incidents), and chemicals (hazmat from accidents or terrorist incidents). These things are beyond the control of any first responder.

Important controllable factors include allowing or restricting access to the critical incident scene, evacuating nearby areas, stopping or re-routing traffic flow, requesting additional personnel or resources from dispatch, personnel deployment, and communication.[162] The influence of the incident commander over his or her personnel is crucial as well.[163]

Politics can play a role in the success of critical incident resolution. All types of politics can and do impact the workplace for first responders and emergency managers. The key is how to handle them as a professional.

Regarding elected officials, prominent law enforcement trainers advise first responders to avoid public involvement in their politics. First responders should behave in a professionally competent and politically neutral manner in terms of incident response and leave the larger external political issues to the top management of the agency. This is what is known in public administration as the **politics/administration dichotomy**. Professional behavior on the job will reduce political conflict between the agency and elected officials.[164]

Political issues often occur between first responder agencies at large-scale or more serious critical incidents. One of the main purposes of NIMS and ICS is to allow for a more smooth and complete integration of state, local, and federal emergency management and first responder agencies. Evidence has indicated that interagency politics has lessened in intensity in recent years. Agencies are improving their ability to work together for the purpose of addressing common disasters affecting communities and the nation.[165]

Dealing with internal agency politics is much more complex. Internal politics involves motivation, morale, leadership, interpersonal working relationships, and clashing personalities. Anyone who has ever worked a job knows and understands this. Internal politics is almost always negative in that it diminishes the effectiveness of the first responder agency at a critical incident.[166]

When groups and teams lack trust, have friction, or do not work well together, the rationality or the organization in terms of the ability of the organization to function and achieve its predetermined goals is jeopardized. It is the responsibility of senior management to diagnose and resolve these issues. Failing to do so can harm both the agency and the community.[167]

Response Plans and Tactics

The goal of this section is to discuss the importance of a **response plan** at a critical incident or disaster scene. A response plan provides first responders with strategies and courses of action that will allow the officer on the scene to take control of a critical incident effectively.[168] Analysis of various critical incident scenarios including hazmat, hostage situations, and aircraft crashes demonstrates that similar issues arose in all types. In other words, a uniform set of issues related to the management of critical incident scenes emerged.[169]

It was discovered that each critical incident has a (1) crisis phase, (2) scene management phase, and (3) executive management phase.[170] Just as there are common phases in each critical incident, there are common response strategies to critical incident. The extent to which these actions are taken effectively by the Incident Commander can lead either to success or failure in terms of the fastest critical incident resolution.[171]

Under NIMS and ICS, an **Incident Commander (IC)** is "the individual responsible for all incident activities, including the development of strategies and tactics and the ordering and release of resources. The IC has overall authority and responsibility for conducting incident operations and is responsible for the management of all incident operations at the incident site."[172]

During the crisis phase of a critical incident, the IC's role is of vital importance. The primary objectives of an IC are to prevent the expansion of the critical incident, take actions to ensure the safety of members of the public and first responders, and to stabilize the critical incident.[173]

Several tactics exist to achieve these goals. First, the IC should step into the role of tactical command. This requires the IC to adopt a tactical command presence. The IC should take the initiative, assume command, and announce that he or she has assumed incident command over the radio. In addition, the IC should assess the situation, collect information, and make rational decisions designed to achieve the objective of resolution. During the crisis phase of a critical incident requires that the IC adopt *tactical* leadership rather than *traditional* leadership.[174]

Tactical leadership must be distinguished from traditional leadership. **Traditional leadership** follows typical expectations of what a leader is and how he or she should behave. According to the theory, the manager should behave in a kind and humanistic manner. He or she should delegate authority and act as a "first among equals" or as a "pal" to subordinates. The traditional and conventional management literature bear this out. However, this literature is based upon day-to-day operation of hierarchical organizations. While this may be effective for day-to-day management, in a crisis situation, such as a critical incident, this will lead to failure. What is needed in this situation is what they term *tactical leadership.*

In **tactical leadership**, leadership behavior is authoritative and autocratic. Tactical leaders command confidently. Tactical leaders issue clear and specific orders. In day-to-day situations, this style would cause alienation. However, in a crisis such as the initial stage of a critical incident, autocratic leadership is actually appreciated by subordinates. Persons present at critical incident scenes are reassured by the direction provided by a confident IC.[175]

The **crisis phase** of a critical incident is when the situation is at its worst. There is panic, frantic activity, and confusion among victims and bystanders.[176] For example, people are trapped in burning cars. Poison gas is escaping and has visible clouds with casualties. The first responding scene commander or supervisor to arrive at a critical incident scene must take decisive action to stabilize the situation. He or she must also take actions to render aid to protect property.[177] The most important initial action to take is stabilizing the scene.[178]

After the critical incident scene has been stabilized, the **scene management phase** begins. The scene management phase does not have any time limit. It depends upon the type of incident and the severity of the situation. Scene management shifts away from stabilization towards taking overt actions to resolve the critical incident.[179]

Once a first-first responder has entered the scene management phase, he or she should establish a **command post**. The command post is used to coordinate the on-scene response.[180] Taking this action means that the first responder has now become at least the temporary **Incident Commander (IC)**. This is "the individual responsible for all incident activities, including the development of strategies and tactics and the ordering and release of resources. The IC has overall authority and responsibility for conducting incident operations and is responsible for the management of all incident operations at the incident site."[181] The Incident Commander should remain at the Command Post.

If a higher-ranking first responder arrives at the critical incident site, the IC may shift to that person. This is especially likely if the higher-ranking first responder is from the same functional discipline as the initial IC.[182] In other words, the initial IC may then "hand off" the IC and the Command Post to more senior or a higher-ranking first responder. This is the point where ICS (Incident Command System) comes into play. The IC should deploy specialists as available. Also, the tactical "autocratic" management style should now be substituted with the "traditional" more humanistic management style.

The IC must now engage the overall IAP (Incident Action Plan). As was noted previously, an IAP is "an oral or written plan containing general objectives reflecting the overall strategy for managing an incident. It may include the identification of operational resources and assignments. It may also include attachments that provide direction and important information for management of the incident during one or more operational periods."[183] In terms of outcomes, evidence-based practice indicates that most incidents are resolved during the scene management phase. By the time that the scene management phase is over, the IC should have established unified command and developed an IAP.[184]

If it is determined that the seriousness and magnitude of the critical incident cannot be resolved by those on-scene, substantial outside resources must be brought to bear. Examples include major hazmat incidents, earthquakes, and riots. At that point, the critical incident has moved to the **executive management phase**. The executive management phase requires the activation of the EOC (Emergency Operations Center) and the highest-ranking members of the first responder agency begin to make the important decisions regarding resolving the critical incident.[185]

The job of the IC during the executive management phase is to take actions on the ground to resolve the critical incident. The highest-ranking members of the organization and elected officials have the task of consequence management.[186] Escalating a critical incident to the executive management phase requires opening the EOC and convening the Executive Policy Group. Taking these actions constitutes the fullest expansion of ICS.[187] The executive management phase of critical incident management also marks the shift to the recovery phase of the Emergency Management Cycle. EOC officials have now taken over responsibility for transition to the recovery and normal operations.[188]

As the crisis is resolved, the IC maintains scene integrity. Cleanup and investigation will then occur. Order is gradually restored. Returning to normal or "pre-critical incident" conditions for the jurisdiction continues.[189] The return to normal agency operations involves several steps, including documenting damage and injuries, accounting for all employees, and assigning personnel to normal tasks.[190]

Finally, an **AAR (After Action Report)** must be written. The purpose of an AAR is to analyze the management or response to an incident, exercise or event by identifying strengths to be maintained and built upon, as well as identifying potential areas of improvement. AARs are also called **hotwash.**[191] AARs are intended to be used as a tool by emergency management agencies and organizations. An ARR provides analysis for lessons learned, best practices and recommendations for future planning, training, and exercise development. As improvement actions are identified and addressed, it is important that any relevant plans, policies and procedures are updated accordingly.[192] AAR information will assist future first-first responders and first responders to make better decisions in the future based upon past experience.

Critical Incident Leadership

This section deals with tactical leadership during critical incidents. Specifically, it deals with leadership and the leadership styles most appropriate to utilize during the crisis phase of a critical incident.

Leadership means *to guide or influence* the behavior of others. Or **leadership** can be thought of as the process whereby one person *influences* others to achieve a goal.[193] Leadership is about gaining *voluntary* compliance from others. A leader is someone who attempts to exert influence through some sort of power that results in gaining compliance from those being led.[194] Notice the emphasis on *influence* in these definitions. Leadership is the capacity to *influence* the behavior of other people.

How this is done and the effective ways this is done has been the subject of many studies and theories. The presence of effective leadership is a significant factor in explaining the success of organizations.

There is a misplaced tendency to equate management with leadership. **Management** is about the day-to-day running of an organization. *Management* is concerned with organizing the workplace, coordinating the activities of employees, and being accountable for success or failure.[195] *Leadership*, by contrast, is something different from management. Leadership goes *beyond* management. A *leader* is someone who *influences* and *inspires* others to achieve a goal.[196] A leader *inspires* others to reach a goal – a goal based upon the leader's *vision* of the future.[197]

Management is more mundane than *leadership* in that *management* is concerned with the day-to-day tasks of operating the organization. *Leadership* is something else: a leader *inspires* and *guides* others towards his or her *vision* of the future. Leaders *stimulate* others to grow and change in new directions. *Management is not synonymous with leadership.* A good manager *may not* be a good leader. *Some* managers are good leaders, and some are not. Management and leadership require different behaviors, but these behaviors can *sometimes* overlap. Keep in mind that management and leadership are conceptually distinct.[198]

Managers receive their authority from the organization and the organization's chain of command.[199] *Leaders*, on the other hand, receive their authority from *followers*.[200] Think about what this means: *managers* have the authority to supervise your work, to make you show up on time, and to hold you accountable for results. This is because managers have the *authority* to do so that is granted by the organization.[201] *Leaders*, on the other hand, receive *their* authority from followers. Leaders receive this authority from followers because their followers have accepted them as leaders.[202] This acceptance is conditional. To *maintain* a leadership position, a leader must *give* followers something by enabling followers to obtain things that would not otherwise be available to them.[203] This acceptance given to the leader by his or her followers gives the leader power and prestige. And *some*, but by no means *all* managers are also leaders.[204]

Leadership has been deemed to be worthy of study in organizations because leaders help or enable organizations to carry out their goals more effectively than managers alone.[205] This is based on the principle that no goal gets carried out by itself – it takes the coordinated activities of people to accomplish goals. Many studies of organizational behavior have shown consistently that the presence of leadership inside organizations dramatically increases goal attainment.[206]

It has been observed that, due to the influence of leadership, some organizations are more effective than others in channeling, influencing, and inspiring employees to accomplish the organization's goals. In other words, it has been observed that organizations can collectively behave very differently depending upon the presence or absence of effective leadership inside that organization.[207] This indicates that studying the effect of leadership inside organizations is an important component of management and the way that organizations operate.

Since leadership is important in terms of organizational behavior, certain questions arise: How do leaders operate? How do leaders influence their followers to work towards a goal? Is leadership something that can be learned?[208] The answers to these questions are complex.

On the most fundamental level, leaders operate by appealing to employee needs. *Power* is central to effective leadership. **Power** is simply the capacity to influence the behavior of others. Leaders use power on their followers. Leaders attempt to exert influence on their followers through some sort of power that results in gaining compliance from followers.[209] While this is true, understanding the dynamics of leadership is complicated.

Leadership must be understood in the context in which it occurs. It is difficult to attribute cause and effect to the variables involved in the leadership equation. That is why those who study the effect of leadership upon organizational behavior typically vary some condition of the leader's behavior in an experimental situation and then they attempt to attribute differences in the performance of followers to the leader's behavior.[210]

The research that has been done on leadership in organizations starts out with the assumption that the managers of organizations occupy formal leadership roles in that, inside an organization, managers have been given power and authority over subordinates. And, since managers occupy formal leadership roles, the assumption is that leadership may or may not emerge from the manager. Thus, managers who also possess leadership ability inspire others by going "above and beyond" simply engaging in the practice of management.[211]

Leadership studies begin with certain routine expectations about management behavior. Specifically, leadership studies take it for granted that managers will carry out their specific responsibilities in coordinating and controlling the workplace and the activities of subordinates.

In addition to doing these things, it is also assumed that managers (who also occupy formal leadership positions) will also play several expected *roles* required by the job.[212] A **role** is a behavior expected of a person who occupies a given position in an organizational setting.[213] Roles comprise a significant part of a person's behavior on the job. Managers are expected to play several roles as part of their assigned duties.

Specifically, managers play *decisional roles, informational roles,* and *interpersonal roles.*[214] First, managers play *decisional roles.* In the **decisional role**, the manager allocates resources inside the organization. Here, the manager initiates and oversees new projects and channels human and capital resources toward predetermined objectives.[215] This is the most important role a person can play in critical incident management.

In addition, managers also play *informational roles.* In the **informational role**, the manager receives, collects, and broadcasts information relevant to the organization and its employees. The manager provides information to employees necessary to carry out their tasks.[216] This is also important in critical incident management, but of lesser importance than the decisional role.

In addition to these two roles, managers also play **interpersonal roles**, as when they act as a figurehead in duties that are largely symbolic and ceremonial.[217] Leadership studies inside organizations start from the premise that managers will play these three roles and that managers occupy formal leadership positions. However, as we have seen, not all managers are leaders. Managers who also possess leadership abilities are the most effective. Years of research into leadership shows the most appropriate leadership style depends upon the situation encountered by the leader, the followers, and the organization.[218]

According to advocates of the **Contingency Approach to leadership,** a successful leadership theory must take specific leadership situations into account. In other words, this perspective articulated the position that a successful leader *adapts* his or her behavior to best fit the needs of his or her followers, the organization, and the situation. Leaders must thus alter their leadership style to fit the situation–leadership behavior should be contingent then upon the situation encountered, as what works well in one situation may not work well in another.[219] The Contingency Approach to leadership began during the 1960s.

One of the most famous of the various Contingency Approaches to leadership is the Situational Model of Leadership by Hersey and Blanchard.[220] According to the **Situational Model of Leadership** developed by Hersey and Blanchard, an effective leader must alter his or her leadership behavior by becoming more or less authoritative depending upon the behavior manifested by his or her followers.[221] The Situational Model of leadership is based upon three concepts: *follower readiness, task behavior,* and *relationship behavior.*[222]

Follower readiness deals with how willing and able a leader's followers are to perform a job. Followers can and do have varying levels of readiness. For example, they may be well trained and enthusiastic, or they may be unenthusiastic. In addition, followers can be ready and willing to work, but not possess the proper training to do so.[223]

Task behavior concerns how authoritative and directive the leader behaves towards his or her followers. Task behavior thus deals with the extent to which a leader delineates instructions to his or her followers. To what extent does the leader attempt to direct and control the actions of followers? How closely does the leader supervise followers?[224]

Relationship behavior is the opposite of task behavior. Relationship deals with how kind, supportive, and encouraging a leader behaves towards his or her followers. To what extent does the leader allow for participation from followers? How much authority does the leader delegate to followers?[225]

According to Hersey and Blanchard, an effective leader varies his or her actions by leaning more toward *task behavior* or more toward *relationship behavior,* as appropriate, depending upon the *level* of *follower readiness.* In other words, according to the Situational Model, an effective leader moves from becoming more or less authoritative in reaction to the behavior of his or her followers in a given situation. The principle is that a leader can get more accomplished by altering his or her leadership style to fit the situation.[226] Because follower readiness varies from situation to situation, the level of follower readiness informs the leader which leadership is most appropriate to the situation.

The Situational Model of leadership is highly applicable to critical incident management. This is true because critical incidents vary greatly in type and in impact. Leaders must change their behavior according to what is happening at the scene.[227]

The differences between traditional leadership and tactical leadership must be emphasized. **Traditional leadership** follows classical organizational theory. According to the theory, the manager should behave in a kind and humanistic manner. He or she should delegate authority and act as a "first among equals" or as a supportive co-worker to subordinates. The traditional and conventional management literature bear this out. However, this literature is based upon day-to-day operation of hierarchical organizations. While this may be effective inside an agency for day-to-day management, in a crisis situation such as a critical incident, this will lead to failure. What is needed in this situation is *tactical leadership*. In **tactical leadership**, leadership is assertive and autocratic. Specific and strong orders are issued.[228]

Critical incident management calls for tactical leadership in the beginning. The first responder critical incident scene must adapt the situational model of leadership and move immediately toward tactical leadership during the crisis phase. Once the situation becomes more stable, he or she can move towards traditional leadership.

With regard to situational leadership at a critical incident scene, three variables emerge that affect the style of the leader at the scene: the **subordinate**, the **supervisor**, and the **criticality of the task**. Some subordinates require more supervision than others. If a subordinate is unskilled or unsure about what to do, the leadership style must provide close supervision. If a first responder is experienced or comfortable with taking charge, the task will be easier for him or her. In terms of the criticality of the task, the urgency of the situation (deaths, injuries, extent of the damage) will affect the leader's behavior. More serious problems require more directive leadership.[229]

One should also be aware of differences in initial leadership dynamics between police and fire first responders. Police responders almost always arrive alone at a critical incident scene. Then, he or she calls for additional resources. In contrast, fire responders always arrive in a group or team. This means that law enforcement personnel do not form teams until backup resources arrive.[230]

The police supervisor usually responds alone. After arrival at a critical incident scene, the police supervisor then selects a team from those present and available. The police supervisor makes task assignments. He or she takes the steps to foster that other officers interact at the scene with other police officers and with responders from other disciplines as the incident progresses. In order to achieve these goals, the initial supervisor at a critical incident must employ the tactical leadership style.[231]

At the critical incident scene, the successful tactical leader *evaluates data to assess problems, decides on an appropriate course of action, communicates these decisions to others,* and *maintains a command presence.*[232] All of these are requirements of good decision-making.

Decision-making concerns *making choices.* In making a decision, a person must select from among real or imagined alternatives and then he or she must select one alternative over other alternatives.[233] Decision-making is important, because this is how incident commanders set into motion the actions necessary to resolve the critical incident. Incident commanders should make decisions that are designed to increase the efficiency and effectiveness of the organization or to adapt the organization to changed circumstances as they unfold.

Thus, organizational decision-making purposefully channels the organization toward accomplishing its goals. Making decisions sets this process into motion. Therefore, decision-making presupposes rationality of some sort. Decision-making is based on the idea that by making decisions, the organization and the situation can be somehow improved. This is the idea that organizations attempt to be rational because managers try to choose the alternative that promotes the achievement of the organization's objectives.

The incident commander **evaluates data to assess problems**. This is a vital precursor to decision-making. Effective leadership in a crisis situation requires the ability to assess the situation and to process information under highly stressful conditions. The failure to perform effective leadership in a critical incident can lead to deaths or injuries. Remember that the crisis phase of an incident occurs when the situation is at its worst. Gridlock, panic, noise, and danger interfere with gathering and processing important information. Nevertheless, information must be gathered and assimilated. Risks to the IC and personnel must be assessed.[234]

It is also important not to prejudge the crucial incident scene. Evaluation must be based upon what the first responder actually observes on the ground. Decisions must be made correctly and be based on the true extent of the emergency and upon the specific hazards that the emergency presents. Making decisions correctly leads to stabilizing the scene quickly and correctly. Bad decisions can result in the worsening the critical incident.[235]

Based upon data evaluation to assess problems, the incident commander must **decide upon an appropriate course of action**. The appropriate course of action depends upon the hazard, the number of injured, the number of persons in danger, and many other factors. The ability to assess the situation accurately leads to effective critical incident management decisions that will lead to stabilizing the scene.[236]

Saving the lives of victims is a priority. ICs should see to it that a triage area is established to have survivors assessed according to injury severity. It may also be necessary to set up a temporary morgue area for casualties. ICs and other first responder personnel should keep in mind that survivors and witnesses may be very emotional as a result of the stress and trauma.[237]

Due to the volatility of the critical incident scene, it is necessary for the Incident Commander to employ the **incremental model of decision-making**. When a person employs the incremental model of decision-making, he or she settles upon a limited and realistic objective, examines the options that are immediately available and doable, and then makes a choice (a decision) from among those options. A decision-maker does this, because it is impossible to know, much less rank-order all the alternatives that exist in order to solve a problem according to this model.[238] Thus, since the decision-maker is taking what amounts to "shortcuts" in decision-making by making marginal changes to existing policies, he or she is reducing decision-making to manageable proportions. It is not necessary to know all options, only those that are best under the circumstances.[239]

The overall goal of deciding upon the appropriate course of action is this: the pressing need to stabilize a critical incident site matters more than standard operating procedures, rank, or authority. Trying too hard to follow "on paper" theoretically valid procedures to the letter can result in death, injury, and additional property damage.[240] The first responder that has just arrived at a critical incident scene does not always have the luxury of waiting for a higher ranking official to arrive and take over. In urgent situations, the first arriving emergency responder must take immediate actions to control and stabilize the critical incident scene. Doing so demands rapid decision making with stabilizing the scene as the major priority.[241]

After the Incident Commander has made a decision, he or she must then **communicate them to others by issuing orders and directions**. The Incident Commander should issue instructions, orders, and directions utilizing the tactical leadership style. In-person commands and radio commands must be clear and concise.

During the crisis phase of the critical incident the Incident Commander must maintain a **command presence** to be most effective. This involves *seeming* competent, in-control of the situation, and confident in one's own abilities.[242] Some ICs are more skilled than others in achieving command presence. Some individuals have natural command presence, while others must develop command presence by experience. The ability to suppress emotions and adrenaline-laced actions is very important in maintaining command presence. Appearing to be calm and in control of one's emotions under stressful conditions exudes competence and is likely to be reassuring to first responders under the IC's command.[243]

Notes

1. Willard M. Oliver, *Policing In An Era of Homeland Security*, New York: Oxford University Press, 2020: 187.
2. Michael K. Lindell, Carla Prater, and Ronald W. Perry, *Introduction to Emergency Management*, Hoboken, John W. Wiley and Sons, Inc., 2007: 247.
3. Ibid: 248.
4. Ibid: 249-250.
5. Ibid: 250.
6. Ibid.
7. Ibid: 251.
8. Ibid: 253.
9. Ibid: 254.
10. Ibid.
11. David A. McEntire, *Disaster Response and Recovery: Strategies and Tactics for Resilience*, 2nd Edition, Hoboken, John Wiley and Sons, Inc., 2015: 127-162.
12. Lindell, Prater, and Perry, *Introduction to Emergency Management*: 12.
13. McEntire, *Disaster Response and Recovery*: 128.
14. Ibid.
15. Ibid: 131.
16. Ibid: Emphasis in original.
17. McEntire, *Disaster Response and Recovery*: 131.
18. www.chathamemergency.org/eoc/
19. Ibid.
20. Ibid.
21. Michael J. Fagel, *Principles of Emergency Management: Hazard Specific Issues and Mitigation Strategies*, Boca Raton, CRC Press/Taylor and Francis Group, 2012: 297.
22. McEntire, *Disaster Response and Recovery*: 133.
23. Ibid: 134.
24. Ibid: 135.
25. Ibid.
26. Ibid.
27. Ibid: 136.
28. Lindell, Prater, and Perry, *Introduction to Emergency Management*: 77-78.
29. Ibid: 77.
30. Ibid: 77-78.
31. Ibid: 78.
32. McEntire, *Disaster Response and Recovery*: 137.
33. Ibid: 140-141.
34. Lindell, Prater, and Perry, *Introduction to Emergency Management*: 79.
35. McEntire, *Disaster Response and Recovery*: 142-143.
36. Carol A. Lewis, Sandra Onyejekwe, Garlin Wynn, and Brandon Mosley, "Options for Improving Evacuation: Investigating An Unconventional Strategy and Expanding Route Options Using Transportation Analysis and

Simulation System, *Journal of Emergency Management*, Vol. 13, No. 2, March/April 2015: 173.
37. Lindell, Prater, and Perry, *Introduction to Emergency Management*: 238.
38. Ibid.
39. Ibid: 237-239.
40. Ibid: 236.
41. Ibid.
42. Ibid: 237.
43. Ibid.
44. Ibid.
45. Ibid: 238.
46. Ibid: 239.
47. Ibid.
48. Ibid: 241.
49. Ibid: 241-242.
50. Ibid: 241.
51. Scott A. Parr, Brian Wolshon, and Vinayak Dixit, "Selection and Allocation of Manual Traffic Control Points and Personnel During Emergencies," *Journal of Emergency Management*, Vol. 13, No. 2, March/April 2015: 121.
52. McEntire, *Disaster Response and Recovery*: 145.
53. Lindell, Prater, and Perry, *Introduction to Emergency Management*: 243.
54. McEntire, *Disaster Response and Recovery*: 149. Emphasis in original.
55. Ibid: 151.
56. Ibid: 152.
57. Ibid: 151.
58. Ibid.
59. Ibid.
60. Lindell, Prater, and Perry, *Introduction to Emergency Management*: 13.
61. Ibid.
62. Ibid.
63. Ibid: 14.
64. McEntire, *Disaster Response and Recovery*: 237.
65. Lindell, Prater, and Perry, *Introduction to Emergency Management*: 345.
66. Ibid.
67. McEntire, Disaster *Response and Recovery*: 237.
68. Ibid.
69. Ibid: 264.
70. Lindell, Prater, and Perry, *Introduction to Emergency Management*: 369.
71. Ibid: 239.
72. Ibid: 240.
73. Lindell, Prater, and Perry, *Introduction to Emergency Management*: 369.
74. Ibid.
75. McEntire, *Disaster Response and Recovery*: 240.
76. Lindell, Prater, and Perry, *Introduction to Emergency Management*: 369
77. Ibid.
78. McEntire, *Disaster Response and Recovery*: 240.

79. Ibid: 245.
80. Ibid: 242.
81. Ibid.
82. Ibid: 243.
83. Ibid.
84. Ibid: 248.
85. Ibid: 251.
86. Lindell, Prater, and Perry, *Introduction to Emergency Management*: 360.
87. Ibid.
88. Fagel, *Principles of Emergency Management*: 11.
89. McEntire, *Disaster Response and Recovery*: 250.
90. Ibid.
91. Ibid: 251.
92. Julia Crowley, Disaster Debris Management Best Practice Case Studies," *Journal of Emergency Management*, Vol 18, No. 2, March/April 2020: 171.
93. McEntire, *Disaster Response and Recovery*: 254.
94. Ibid: 255 and 257.
95. Ibid: 255.
96. Ibid: 255-256.
97. Ibid: 257.
98. Ibid: 252.
99. Ibid: 256.
100. Ibid.
101. Ibid: 258 and 260.
102. Ibid: 261.
103. Ibid: 339.
104. Ibid: 308.
105. Ibid.
106. Ibid.
107. Ibid.
108. Ibid: 309.
109. Ibid: 310.
110. Ibid: 313.
111. Ibid.
112. Ibid: 313-314. Emphasis in original.
113. www.dictionary.cambridge.org/us/dictionary/English/transportation
114. McEntire, *Disaster Response and Recovery*: 319.
115. Ibid: 318.
116. Ibid: 319.
117. Ibid.
118. Ibid.
119. Lindell, Prater, and Perry, *Introduction to Emergency Management*: 178.
120. McEntire, *Disaster Response and Recovery*: 321.
121. Ibid: 328.
122. Ibid: 329.
123. Ibid.

124. Ibid: 328.
125. Ibid: 329.
126. Ibid: 310.
127. Ibid: 328.
128. Ibid.
129. Vincent Faggiano, John McNall, and Tom Gillespie, *Critical Incident Management: A Complete Response Guide*, 2nd Edition, Boca Raton, CRC Press/Taylor and Francis Group, 2012: 11.
130. Ibid.
131. Ibid.
132. McEntire, *Disaster Response and Recovery*: 333.
133. William C. Nicholson, Emergency Response and *Emergency Management Law: Cases and Materials*, Springfield, Illinois, Charles C. Thomas Publisher, Ltd., 2003: 303-304.
134. McEntire, *Disaster Response and Recovery*: 333-334.
135. Ibid: 334.
136. Ibid.
137. Ibid: 333.
138. Steven J. Cann, *Administrative Law*, 4th Edition, Thousand Oaks, Sage Publications, 2006: 488.
139. McEntire, *Disaster Response and Recovery*: 333.
140. Mary E. Guy and Todd L. Ely, *Essentials of Public Service: An Introduction to Contemporary Public Administration*, Invine, Melvin and Leigh Publishers, 2018: 412.
141. Faggiano, McNall, and Gillespie, *Critical Incident Management*: 46-47.
142. McEntire, *Disaster Response and Recovery*: 335.
143. Ibid.
144. Ibid: 338.
145. Ibid: 308.
146. Faggiano, McNall, and Gillespie, *Critical Incident Management*: 1-14.
147. Ibid: 1.
148. Ibid.
149. Ibid.
150. U.S. Department of Homeland Security, Federal Emergency Management Agency, *National Incident Management System*, December 2008: 140.
151. Ibid.
152. Ibid: 5.
153. Ibid: 5-6.
154. Ibid: 6-7.
155. Ibid: 7.
156. Ibid.
157. Ibid.
158. Ibid: 8.
159. Ibid: 140.
160. Faggiano, *Critical Incident Management*: 9.
161. Ibid: 12.

162. Ibid: 13-14.
163. Ibid: 14.
164. Ibid.
165. Ibid: 11.
166. Ibid.
167. Ibid.
168. Ibid: 25.
169. Ibid.
170. Ibid: 23.
171. Ibid: 26.
172. U.S. Department of Homeland Security, Federal Emergency Management Agency, *National Incident Management System*, December 2008: 140.
173. Faggiano, *Critical Incident Management*: 27.
174. Ibid.
175. Ibid.
176. Ibid: 40-41.
177. Ibid: 28.
178. Ibid: 29.
179. Ibid.
180. Ibid: 30.
181. U.S. Department of Homeland Security, Federal Emergency Management Agency, *National Incident Management System*, December 2008: 140.
182. Faggiano, *Critical Incident Management*: 30.
183. U.S. Department of Homeland Security, Federal Emergency Management Agency, *National Incident Management System*, December 2008: 140.
184. Faggiano, *Critical Incident Management*: 32.
185. Ibid.
186. Ibid: 33.
187. Ibid.
188. Ibid: 33.
189. Ibid: 34.
190. Ibid: 34-35.
191. Oliver, *Policing In An Era of Homeland Security*: 218.
192. http://www.uh.edu/emergency-management/planning-and-response/after-action-report/
193. G. Yulk and D. D. VanFleet, "Theory and Research On Leadership in Organizations," in M. S. Dunnette and L. M. Hough, eds., *Handbook of Industrial and Organizational Psychology*, Volume 3 (Palo Alto, CA: Consulting Psychology Press, 1992): 147-198 in Don Hellriegel, John W. Slocum, and Richard W. Woodman, *Organizational Behavior*, Eighth Edition (Cincinnati, OH: South-Western College Publishing, 1998): 301.
194. Vasu, Stewart, and Garson, *Organizational Behavior* and Public Management: 90.
195. Ibid, 92 and Hellriegel, Slocum, and Woodman, *Organizational Behavior*: 301.
196. Ibid.
197. Hellriegel, Slocum, and Woodman, *Organizational Behavior*: 301-303.
198. Ibid.

199. Ibid, 302.
200. Ibid.
201. Ibid, 301.
202. Ibid, 302.
203. Ibid.
204. Ibid, 301-302.
205. Ibid.
206. Ibid, 301 and Vasu, Stewart, and Garson, *Organizational Behavior and Public Management*: 89-90.
207. Ibid.
208. Hellriegel, Slocum, and Woodman, *Organizational Behavior*: 306-307 and Vasu, Stewart, and Garson, *Organizational Behavior and Public Mangement*: 92-93.
209. Hellriegel, Slocum, and Woodman, *Organizational Behavior*: 305.
210. Vasu, Stewart, and Garson, *Organizational Behavior and Public Management*: 91-92.
211. Hellriegel, Slocum, and Woodman, *Organizational Behavior*: 301-302.
212. Michael L. Vasu, Debra W. Stewart, and G. David Garson, Garson, Organizational Behavior and Public Management, 3rd Edition, Marcel Dekker, 1998: 92.
213. Ibid: 123.
214. Henry Minzberg, *The Nature of Managerial Work* (New York, NY: Harper and Row, 1975) in Vasu, Stewart, and Garson, *Organizational Behavior and Public Management*: 92.
215. Ibid.
216. Ibid.
217. Ibid.
218. Ibid.
219. Ibid, 106.
220. Paul Hersey and K. H. Blanchard, *Management of Organizational Behavior*: Utilizing Human Resources, Fifth Edition (Englewood Cliffs, NJ: Prentis Hall, Inc., 1988) in Hellriegel, Slocum, and Woodman, Organizational Behavior: 316-319 and Vasu, Stewart, and Garson, *Organizational Behavior and Public Management*: 108-110.
221. Ibid.
222. Ibid.
223. Ibid.
224. Ibid.
225. Ibid.
226. Ibid.
227. Faggiano, *Critical Incident Management*: 37.
228. Ibid: 27.
229. Ibid: 37.
230. Ibid: 38.
231. Ibid: 38-39.
232. Ibid: 40.
233. Michael M. Harmon and Richard T. Mayer, *Organization Theory for Public Administration*, (Burke, VA: Chatelaine Press, 1986): 35.

234. Faggiano, *Critical Incident Management*: 40-41.
235. Ibid: 42.
236. Ibid: 43.
237. Karen M. Hess, Christine H. Orthmann, and Henry Cho, *Police Operations, Theory and Practice*, 6th Edition, Clifton Park, New York, Delmar Cengage Learning, 2014: 300-301.
238. Charles E. Lindblom, "The Science of Muddling Through," *Public Administration Review*, Vol. 19, No.2, Spring 1959: 79-88.
239. Faggiano, Critical Incident Management: 43.
240. Ibid: 44.
241. Ibid.
242. Ibid: 45.
243. Ibid: 47.

BIBLIOGRAPHY

Abutabenjeh, Sawsan, Anguelov, Lachezar, Brunjes, Benjamin M., Dimand Ana-Maria, and Rodriguez-Plesa, Evelyn. "Supplying the Pandemic Response: The Importance of Public Procurement." *Journal of Emergency Management*, Vol. 18, No. 7, (2020): 189-208.

Adams, Lavonne M., Reams, Paula K., and Canclini, Sharon B. "Preparing for Partnerships: Maximizing Surge Capacity Through Service Learning." *Journal of Emergency Management*, Vol. 13, No. 6, (November/December 2015): 557-564.

Adams, Terri M., and Anderson, Leigh R. *Policing in Natural Disasters: Stress, Resilience, and the Challenges of Emergency Management.* Philadelphia: Temple University Press, 2020.

Afshari, Hessam M., Cervone, Paul N., Seaton, Mark J., Taylor, Miley A., and Rudy, Bruce S. "The Effect of Training on Disaster Response: Lessons Learned from Recent Events." *Journal of Emergency Management*, Vol. 6, No. 5, (September/October 2008): 57-63.

Aloyo, Osman O. "Emergency Preparedness is All Local." *Journal of Emergency Management*, Vol. 4, No. 1, (January/February 2006): 11-12.

Banks, William C. *The Legal Landscape for Emergency Management in the United States.* New American Foundation. (February 2011).

Barq, Rose. "Breaking Down Barriers: Collaborative Education Drives Collective Change." *Journal of Emergency Management*, Vol. 2, No. 3, (Summer 2004): 51-55.

Bentley, Emily, and Waugh, William L., Jr. "Katrina and the Necessity for Emergency Management Standards." *Journal of Emergency Management*, Vol. 3, No. 5, (September/October 2003): 9-10.

Besserman, Richard, Peterson, Danny, Johnston, Dan, and Rodabaugh, Lyle. "Disconnects Between Expectations and Deliverables Among Emergency Responders." *Journal of Emergency Management*, Vol. 2, No. 2, (Spring 2004): 17-22.

Blanchard, B. Wayne. "The New Role of Higher Education in Emergency Management." *Journal of Emergency Management*, Vol. 1, No. 2, (Summer 2003): 30-34.

Bott, Robert, Frantz, Braiden, and Dietz, J. Eric. "Active Shooter Mitigation Techniques." *Journal of Emergency Management*, Vol. 20, No. 2, (March/April 2022): 95-109.

Briggs, Lisa T., and Mason, Karen A. "First-Responder Preparedness in Western North Carolina: A Preliminary Analysis." *Journal of Emergency Management*, Vol. 6, No. 1, (January/February 2008): 37-42.

Bullock, Jane A, and Haddow, George D. "The Future of Emergency Management." *Journal of Emergency Management*, Vol. 2, No. 1, (Winter 2004): 19-24.

Bullock, Jane A, and Haddow, George D. "How the Next President of the United States Can Fix FEMA." *Journal of Emergency Management*, Vol. 6, No. 5, (September/October 2008): 13-14.

Bumbak, Andrew K. "Catastrophe Planning and Response." *Journal of Emergency Management*, Vol. 6, No. 3, (May/June 2008): 13-15.

Butterworth, Lillian R., Riedel, Steve, and Dietz, J. Eric. "Cost and Benefits of a Typical County's Emergency Response Program." *Journal of Emergency Management*, Vol. 9, No. 4, (July/August 2011): 19-34.

Buzzelli, Michelle M., Morgan, Paula, Muscheck, Alexander G., and MacGregor-Skinner, Gavin. "Information and Communication Technology: Connecting the Public and First Responders During Disasters." *Journal of Emergency Management*, Vol. 12, No. 6, (November/December 2014): 441-447.

Chang, Crystal, Salerno, Anthony, and Hsu, Edbert B. "Perspectives of Xenophobia During Epidemics and Implications for Emergency Management." *Journal of Emergency Management*, Vol. 18, No. 7, (2020): 23-29.

Clark, Robin J., and Wilairat, Adrian. "Bringing It All Back Home: Continuity of Government Planning for Local Government." *Journal of Emergency Management*, Vol. 7, No. 5, (September/October 2009): 19-31.

Clements, Bruce W., and Casani, Julie, Ann P. *Disasters and Public Health: Planning and Response*, 2nd Edition. Cambridge: Butterworth-Heinemann Elsevier, 2016.

Collins, Matthew L. "A Case Study of the Law Enforcement/Emergency Medical Response to the Virginia Tech Mass Casualty Incident on April 16, 2007." *Journal of Emergency Management*, Vol. 5, No. 5, (September/October 2007): 17-24.

Crowley, Julia. "Disaster Debris Management Best Practice Case Studies." *Journal of Emergency Management*, Vol. 18, No. 2, (March/April 2020): 171-182.

Crowther, Kenneth G., Gradishar, Anna K., and French, Michael A. "Enabling the Homeland Security Enterprise Through Systems Engineering the National Exercise Program." *Journal of Emergency Management*, Vol. 10, No. 2, (March/April 2012): 121-138.

Dekker, Sidney W., Jonsen, Magnus, Bergstrom, Johan, and Dahlstrom, Nicklas. "Learning from Failures in Emergency Response: Two Empirical Studies." *Journal of Emergency Management*, Vol. 6, No. 5, (September/October 2008): 64-70.

Dempsey, John S., Forst, Linda S., and Carter, Steve. *An Introduction to Policing*, 8th Edition, Boston: Cengage Learning, 2016.

Dixon, Zachary, and Drishi, Valecha. Critical Decisions in Hurricane Evacuation Bridge and Roadway Closures." *Journal of Emergency Management*, Vol. 20, No. 4, (July/August 2022): 317-328.

Dolan, Garrett, and Messen, Dmitry. "Social Vulnerability: An Emergency Manager's Planning Tool." *Journal of Emergency Management*, Vol. 10, No. 3, (May/June 2012): 161-169.

Donahue, Amy K. "Towards Robust All-Hazards Incident Management Teams: Progress and Priorities." *Journal of Emergency Management*, Vol. 10, No. 4, (July/August 2012): 253-263.

Dorasamy, Magiswary, Raman, Murali, Marimuthu, Maran, and Kaliannan, Maniam. "Disaster Preparedness: An Investigation of Motivation and Barriers." *Journal of Emergency Management*, Vol. 11, No. 6, (November/December 2013): 433-446.

Drabek, Thomas E. "Don't Blame the Victims." *Journal of Emergency Management*, Vol. 3, No. 6, (November/December 2005): 19-23.

Drabek, Thomas E. "Emergency Managers as Community Change Agents: An Expanded View of the Profession." *Journal of Emergency Management*, Vol. 12, No. 1, (January/February 2014): 9-20.

Drabek, Thomas E. "Theories Relevant to Emergency Management Versus A Theory of Emergency Management." *Journal of Emergency Management*, Vol. 3, No. 4, (July/August 2005): 49-54.

Eksioglu, Burak, Jin, Mingzhou, Capar, Ismail, Zhang, Zhuoxiu, and Eksioglu, Sandra D. "Highway Traffic Management in Incidents of National Significance." *Journal of Emergency Management*, Vol. 6, No.1, (January/February 2008): 23-36.

Elzie, Terra, Frydenlund, Erika, Collins, Andrew J., and Robinson, R. Michael. "Conceptualizing Intragroup and Intergroup Dynamics Within A Controlled Crowd Evacuation." *Journal of Emergency Management*, Vol. 13, No. 2, (March/April 2015): 109-120.

Errett, Nicole A., Frattaroli, Shannon, Barnett, Daniel J., Resnick, Beth A., and Rutkow, Lainie. "The Use of Exercises to Enhance and Assess Interlocal Collaboration in Preparedness: A Qualitative Analysis." *Journal of Emergency Management*, Vol. 13, No. 6, (November/December 2015): 499-508.

Etkin, David. *Disaster Theory: An Interdisciplinary Approach to Concepts and Causes.* Oxford, United Kingdom: Butterworth-Heinemann/Elsevier, 2016.

Fagel, Michael A., Editor. *Principles of Emergency Management: Hazard Specific Issues and Mitigation Strategies.* Boca Raton, Florida: CRC Press/Taylor and Francis Group, 2012.

Faggiano, Vincent, McNall, John, and Gillespie, Tom. *Critical Incident Management: A Complete Response Guide*, 2nd Edition. Boca Raton, Florida: CRC Press/Taylor and Francis Group, 2012.

Glasser, Marc. "Do FEMA's, HSSEEP's, and Green's Progressively Difficult Emergency Exercise Training Concepts Ultimately Lead to Increased Emergency Preparedness?" *Journal of Emergency Management*, Vol. 7, No. 5, (September/October 2009): 33-38.

Glick, Jeffrey A. and Barbara, Joseph A. "Moving from Situation Awareness to Decisions During Disaster Response: Transition to Decision-Making." *Journal of Emergency Management*, Vol. 11, No. 6, (November/December 2013): 423-432.

Guth, David W. "Still Wary of the Web? The Evolution of State Emergency Management Agency Web Sites 2008-2017." *Journal of Emergency Management*, Vol. 16, No. 6, (November/December 2018): 377-386.

Hales, Douglas R., and Race, Peter. "Applying a Framework for Defining Emergency Management Scenarios." *Journal of Emergency Management*, Vol. 9, No. 1, (January/February 2011): 15-24.

Hall, Stacey A., Marciani, Lou, and Cooper, Walter. "Emergency Management and Planning At Major Sports Events." *Journal of Emergency Management*, Vol. 6, No. 1, (January/February 2008): 43-47.

Hellriegel, Don, Slocum, John W. Jr., and Woodman, Richard R. *Organizational Behavior*, 8th Edition, Cincinnati, Ohio: South-Western College Publishing, 1998.

Hertelendy, Attilla J., and Burkle, Frederick M. Jr. "The New Normal: A Catalyst for Leadership Adaptation in a Tumultuous World—Let's Stop Applying 20th Century Solutions to 21st Century Problems in Emergency Management." *Journal of Emergency Management*, Vol. 19, No. 4, (July/August 2021): 323-325.

Hertelendy, Attila J., and Waugh, William L. "COVID-19 Pandemic 3 Years In: We are NOT Ready for the Next Pandemic!" *Journal of Emergency Management*, Vol. 21, No. 7, (2023): 11-14.

Hess, Karen M., Orthmann, Christine H., and Cho, Henry. *Police Operations: Theory and Practice*, 6th Edition. Clifton Park, New York: Delmar Cengage Learning, 2014.

Hildebrand, Sean. "Are We Better Off? Emergency Management Policy Implementation Since September 11." *Journal of Emergency Management*, Vol. 17, No. 6, (November/December 2019): 439-452.

Huss, Sheila M., Sadiq, Abdul-Akeem, and Weible, Christopher M. "Organizations and Emergency Management: Information, Trust, and Preparedness." *Journal of Emergency Management*, Vol. 10, No. 5, (September/October 2012): 359-372.

Isralowitz, Richard and Findley, Patricia. "Emergency Preparedness and Vulnerable Populations: Lessons Learned for Education and Training." *Journal of Emergency Management*, Vol. 7, No. 6, (November/December 2009): 29-34.

Jackman, Andrea M., and Beruvides, Mario G. "Local Hazard Mitigation Plans: A Preliminary Estimation of State-Level Completion From 2004 to 2009." *Journal of Emergency Management*, Vol. 11, No. 2, (March/April 2013): 121-132.

Jensen, Jessica and Carr, John. "Predisaster Integration of Community Emergency Response Teams." *Journal of Emergency Management*, Vol. 13, No. 1, (January/February 2015): 25-35.

Johnson, Candice C., and Aldea, Mirela A. "Impact of COVID-19 Pandemic on Mental Health: Potentially Vulnerable Groups and Comorbidities." *Journal of Emergency Management*, Vol. 19, No. 9, (2021): 9-15.

Jones, Norma S.C., and Majied, Kamilah. "Disaster Mental Health: A Critical Incident Stress Management Program (CISM) to Mitigate Compassion Fatigue." *Journal of Emergency Management*, Vol. 7, No. 4, (July/August 2009): 17-23.

Kahan, Jerome H. "Emergency Management and Homeland Security: Exploring the Relationship." *Journal of Emergency Management*, Vol. 13, No. 6, (November/December 2015): 483-498.

Karakostas, Bill. "Context-Aware Mobile Coordination System for Emergency Response." *Journal of Emergency Management*, Vol. 7, No. 4, (July/August 2009): 57-64.

Kemp, Roger L., Editor. *Homeland Security: Best Practices for Local Government*, 2nd Edition. Washington: ICMA Press, 2010.

Lachlan, Kenneth A., and Spence, Patric R. "Emergency Communication: A Framework for Planning and Targeting Messages." *Journal of Emergency Management*, Vol. 7, No. 4, (July/August 2009): 69-72.

Lakshay and Bonila, Nomesh. "Efficient Evacuation Strategies for Emergency Response Management." *Journal of Emergency Management*, Vol. 20, No. 2, (March/April 2022): 175-196.

Landhal, Mark R., and Thornton, Tanya E., Editors. *The Role of Law Enforcement in Emergency Management and Homeland Security.* Bingley, United Kingdom: Emerald Publishing, Ltd., 2021.

Larson, Dean R., and O'Toole, Michael. "Equipping the Safety Professional With Emergency Management Knowledge and Skills: The Emergency Management Certificate Program." *Journal of Emergency Management,* Vol. 3, No. 1, (January/February 2005): 51-54.

Lee, Clark J. "Addressing Emergency Response Provider Fatigue in Emergency Response Preparedness, Management, Policy Making, and Research." *Journal of Emergency Management,* Vol. 9, No. 5, (September/October 2011): 19-29.

Levinson, Jay and Granot, Hayim. *Transportation Disaster Response Handbook.* San Diego, California: Academic Press, 2002.

Levy, Kirsten. "The Management of Volunteers: Recent Experience with the American Red Cross in Baton Rouge, Louisiana." *Journal of Emergency Management,* Vol. 4, No. 3, (May/June 2006): 53-60.

Lewis, Carol A., Onyejekwe, Sandra, Wynn, Garlin, and Mosley, Brandon. "Options for Improving Evacuation: Investigating an Unconventional Strategy and Expanding Route Options Using Transportation Analysis and Simulation System." *Journal of Emergency Management,* Vol. 13, No. 2, (March/April 2015): 173-181.

Lindblom, Charles E. "The Science of Muddling Through." *Public Administration Review,* Vol. 19, No.2, (Spring 1959): 79-88.

Lindell, Michael K., Prater, Carla, and Perry, Ronald W. *Introduction to Emergency Management,* Hoboken, New Jersey: John C. Wiley and Sons, Inc., 2007.

Long, Maureen. "Just What is it Emergency Managers Do, Anyway?" *Journal of Emergency Management,* Vol. 1., No. 1, (Spring 2003): 13-14.

Losco, Joseph and Baker, Ralph. *AM GOV 2017-2018,* 5th Edition, New York: McGraw-Hill Education, 2017.

Maguire, Brian J. "Current Emergency Medical Services Workplace Issues in the United States." *Journal of Emergency Management,* Vol. 2, No. 3, (Summer 2004): 17-26.

Marion, Nancy E., and Oliver, Willard M. *The Public Policy of Crime and Criminal Justice,* 2nd Edition. Boston: Pearson Prentice-Hall, Inc., 2012.

Martin, Daniel W. "The Shifting Paradigms of a Profession: Calming Conflicts Between Homeland Security and Emergency Management." *Journal of Emergency Management,* Vol. 9, No. 5, (September/October 2011): 11-18.

Merlo, Kelsey, Jones, Kayla C., Conen, Katrina M., Dunn, Elizabeth A., Scott, Blake L., and Marshall, Jennifer. "Engaged, Overextended, or Burned Out? What is the State of the Disaster Response Workforce?" *Journal of Emergency Management,* Vol. 19, No. 9, (2021): 159-168.

McCanlies, Erin C., Gu, Ja Kook, Andrew, Michael E., Burchfield, Cecil M., and Violanti, John M. "Resilience Mediates the Relationship Between Social Support and Post-Traumatic Stress Symptoms in Police Officers." *Journal of Emergency Management,* Vol. 15, No. 2, (March/April 2017): 107-116.

McCann, Joseph T. *Terrorism on American Soil: A Concise History of Plots and Perpetrators from the Famous to the Foreign.* Boulder, Colorado: Sentient Publications, 2006.

McCauley-Bush, Pamela, Jeelani, Mohammad, Gaines, Susan, Curling, Llewelyn, Armbrister, Philip, Watlington, Arturo, Major, Renaldo, Rolle, Lorneska, and Cohen, Sarah. "Assessment of Communication Needs for Emergency Management Officials in High-Consequence Emergencies." *Journal of Emergency Management*, Vol. 10, No. 1, (January/February 2012): 15.

McConnell, Jason B., and Crudo, Christine. "Crisis Behavior: An Exploration of Theories in Concert." *Journal of Emergency Management*, Vol. 13, No. 3, (May/June 2015): 247-274.

McCormick, Lindsey. "Hurricane Katrina and Lessons Learned Utilization: Important Findings For the Emergency Management Community." *Journal of Emergency Management*, Vol. 6, No. 3, (May/June 2008): 39-44.

McEntire, David A. "Emergency Management Theory: Issues, Barriers, and Recommendations for Improvement." *Journal of Emergency Management*, Vol. 3, No. 3, (May/June 2005): 44-54.

McEntire, David A. "Managing Debris Successfully After Disasters: Considerations and Recommendations for Emergency Managers." *Journal of Emergency Management*, Vol. 4, No. 4, (July/August, 2006): 23-28.

McEntire, David A. *Introduction to Homeland Security: Understanding Terrorism With an Emergency Management Perspective.* New York: John Wiley and Sons, Inc., 2009.

McEntire, David A. *Disaster Response and Recovery: Strategies and Tactics for Resilience*, 2nd Edition. Hoboken, New Jersey: John Wiley and Sons, Inc., 2015.

McEntire, David A., and Benavides, Abraham D. "Learning in Emergency Management." *Journal of Emergency Management*, Vol. 5, No. 3, (May/June 2007): 17-18.

McEntire, David A., and Lindsay, John R. "One Neighborhood, Two Families: A Comparison of Intergovernmental Emergency Management Relationships." *Journal of Emergency Management*, Vol. 10, No. 2, (March/April 2012): 93-107.

McEntire, David A., and Souza, Jill. "Responding to Catastrophic Disasters: Lessons from the World Trade Center Terrorist Attacks." *Journal of Emergency Management*, Vol. 7, No. 3, (May/June 2009): 43-58.

McKinney, Suzet and Papke, Mary E. *Public Health Emergency Preparedness: A Practical Approach for the Real World.* Burlington, Massachusetts: Jones and Bartlett Learning, 2019.

Morgan, Paula M. "The Psychological Impact of Mass Casualty Incidents on First Responders: A Systematic Review." *Journal of Emergency Management*, Vol. 14, No. 3, (May/June 2016): 213-226.

Nelson, Jeff, Hristovski Kiril, and Perrerson, Danny. "Mission Possible: A Failure Mode and Effect Analysis of the Federal Emergency Management Agency." *Journal of Emergency Management*, Vol. 5, No. 6, (November/December 2007): 17-28.

Nichols, John K., and Denham, Magdalena. "Implementation and Effectiveness of the National Incident Management System's Incident Command System in Law Enforcement Since 2003." *Journal of Emergency Management*, Vol. 19, No. 4, (July/August 2021): 387-417.

Nichols, Larry D. *Law Enforcement Patrol Operations: Police Systems and Practices.* Berkeley, California: McCutchen Publishing Corporation, 1990.

Nicholson, William C. *Emergency Response and Emergency Management Law: Cases and Materials*. Springfield, Illinois: Charles C. Thomas Publisher, Ltd., 2003.

Nicholson, William C. "Immunity Law: Protection for Emergency Responders." *Journal of Emergency Management*, Vol. 3, No. 1, (January/February 2005): 12-13.

Nicholson, William C. "Integrating Local, State, and Federal Responders and EM: New Packaging and New Controls." *Journal of Emergency Management*, Vol. 1, No. 3, (Fall 2003): 15-23.

Nicholson, William C. "NFPA 1600: The New Standard for Emergency Management." *Journal of Emergency Management*, Vol. 3, No. 2, (March/April 2005): 44-46.

Nicholson, William C. "Personnel-Law Issues in Emergency Management," *Journal of Emergency Management*. Vol. 3, No. 4, (July/August 2005): 13-16.

Nicholson, William C. "Sources of Emergency Management Law: An Overview." *Journal of Emergency Management*, Vol. 2, No. 4, (Fall 2004): 14-15.

Nicholson, William C. "Standard Operating Procedures." *Journal of Emergency Management*, Vol. 3, No. 6, (November/December 2005): 25-26.

North, Carol S., McDonald, Katy, Suris, Alina, and Hong, Barry A. "A Longitudinal Study of Oklahoma City Bombing Rescue and Recovery Providing Qualitative Introspections of Their Experience Nearly a Quarter Century Later." *Journal of Emergency Management*, Vol. 21, No. 1, (January/February 2023): 23-36.

O'Connor, Michael J. "Curriculum-Level Goals in Emergency Management Education: Developing A Common Framework in an Evolving Field." *Journal of Emergency Management*, Vol. 3, No. 6, (November/December 2005): 32-35.

Office of Homeland Security, *National Strategy for Homeland Security* (2002).

Oliver, Willard M. *Policing in an Era of Homeland Security*. New York: Oxford University Press, 2020.

Olszewski, Corey and Siebeneck, Laura. "Emergency Management Collaboration: A Review and New Collaboration Cycle." *Journal of Emergency Management*, Vol. 19, No. 1, (January/February 2021): 57-68.

O'Neil, Patrick D. "Emergency Evacuation Orders: Considerations and Lessons from Hurricane Sandy." *Journal of Emergency Management*, Vol. 12, No. 3, (May/June 2014): 219-227.

Ozguven, Eren E., and Ozbay, Kaan. "Emergency Inventory Management for Disasters: A Review." *Journal of Emergency Management*, Vol. 4, No. 4, (July/August 2014): 269-286.

Parr, Scott A., Wolshon, Brian, and Dixit, Vinayak. "Selection and Allocation of Manual Traffic Control Points and Personnel During Emergencies." *Journal of Emergency Management*, Vol. 13, No. 2, (March/April 2015): 121-133.

Peat, Aidan. "Factors Influencing First Responders' Mental Health During COVID-19." *Journal of Emergency Management*. Vol. 20, No. 9, (2022): 27-37.

Pekevski, Jordan. "First Responders and Psychological First Aid," *Journal of Emergency Management*, Vol. 11, No. 1, (January/February 2013): 39-48.

Pinet-Peralta, Luis M., Bissell, Rick, Hein, Katrina, and Prakash, David. "Emergency Management Policies and Natural Hazards in the United States: A State-Level Analysis." *Journal of Emergency Management*, Vol. 9, No. 2, (March/April 2011): 27-38.

Prasad, Michael. "Recognizing and Mitigating Against COVID-19: Consequence Management Impacts in Emergency Management Organizations." *Journal of Emergency Management,* Vol. 20, No. 7, (2022): 19-37.

Prytz, Eric G., Rybing, Jonas, and Jonson, Carl-Oscar. "Workload Differences Across Command Levels and Emergency Response Organizations During a Major Joint Training Exercise." *Journal of Emergency Management,* Vol. 14, No. 4, (July/August 2016): 289-297.

Rapp, Randy R., and Baroudi, Bassam. "Leadership Success Within Disaster Restoration Projects." *Journal of Emergency Management,* Vol. 12, No. 1, (January/February 2014): 75-81.

Reddick, Christopher G., and Rahm, Dianne. "Perceptions of Emergency Management in U.S. Cities: A Survey of Chief Administrative Officers." *Journal of Emergency Management,* Vol. 8, No. 6, (November/December 2010): 29-43.

Reibestein, Jeffrey L. "Capabilities-Based Planning: A Framework for Local Planning Success?" *Journal of Emergency Management,* Vol. 6, No. 4, (July/August 2008): 11-16.

Renger, Ralph and Granillo, Brenda. "Developing a Comprehensive, Integrated and Meaningful Multi-Year Training and Exercise Plan." *Journal of Emergency Management,* Vol. 10, No. 5, (September/October 2012): 383-392.

Renger, Ralph, Wakelee, Jessica, Bradshaw, Jillian, and Hites, Lisle. "Steps in Writing an Effective Master Scenario Events List." *Journal of Emergency Management,* Vol. 7, No. 6, (November/December 2009): 51-60.

Rojeck, Jeff and Smith, Michael R. "Law Enforcement Lessons Learned from Hurricane Katrina." *The Review of Policy Research,* Vol. 24, No. 6, (November 2007): 589-608.

Sandler, Dylan and Smith, Gavin. "Assessing the Quality of State Disaster Recovery Plans: Implications for Policy and Practice." *Journal of Emergency Management,* Vol. 11, No. 4, (July/August 2013): 281-291.

Saunders, Royce. "FEMA: Change or Die." *Journal of Emergency Management,* Vol. 4, No. 3, (May/June 2006): 6.

Schneider, Robert O. "An Overview of the 'New' Emergency Management." *Journal of Emergency Management,* Vol. 2, No. 1, (Winter 2004): 25-28.

Scott, Clayton S. "Emergency Planning for Municipalities: Emergency Planning 101." *Journal of Emergency* Management, Vol. 4, No. 6, (November/December 2006): 52-54.

Shaffer, Daryl. "The Light Switch Fallacy: Emergency Management and Recovery in an On-Demand World." *Journal of Emergency Management,* Vol. 19, No. 3, (May/June 2021): 245-251.

Shaw, Kelly A., and Winzenberg, Tania "Emergency Planning and Preparedness in General Practice." *Journal of Emergency Management,* Vol. 6, No. 2, (March/April 2008): 45-54.

Shin, Raymond K. "The Federal Government's Potential Power to Coordinate or Take State Assets During Emergencies." *Journal of Emergency Management,* Vol. 9, No. 3, (May/June 2011): 7-10.

Simmons, Geoffrey. "The Deadly Second Wave that Follows Every Disaster." *Journal of Emergency Management,* Vol. 7, No. 5, (September/October 2009): 9-18.

Simon, Neil. "Managing Conflict." *Journal of Emergency Management*, Vol. 3, No. 4, (July/August 2005): 19-24.

Simon, Neil. "Organizational Resistance to Emergency Management Response and Planning." *Journal of Emergency Management*, Vol. 2, No. 2, (March/April 2005): 41-43.

Simon, Neil. "People-Related Aspects of Emergency Management." *Journal of Emergency Management*, Vol. 2, No. 3, (Summer 2004): 14-16.

Simon, Neil. "Part 1: Social Dimensions of Interagency Collaboration." *Journal of Emergency Management*, Vol. 4, No. 1, (January/February 2006): 13-16.

Smith, James F., Waggoner, Sandra S., Rabjohn, Arthur, and Bachar, Avi. "Protecting the Functionality of Airports During Disaster Responses: Humanitarian Responses to Terrorism, War, Civil War, and Riots." *Journal of Emergency Management*, Vol. 6, No. 3, (May/June 2008): 53-62.

Sobelson, Robyn K., Wigington, Corinne J., Harp, Victoria, and Bronson, Bernice B. "A Whole Community Approach to Emergency Management: Strategies and Best Practices of Seven Community Programs." *Journal of Emergency Management*, Vol. 13, No. 4, (July/August 2015): 349-357.

Stallings, Michael and Faust, Whitney. "Drafting, Revising, and Updating Local Emergency Operations Plans: The National Response Framework and the Emergency Support Function Annex Model." *Journal of Emergency Management*, Vol. 7, No. 2, (March/April 2009): 11-18.

Stambler, Kimberly S. and Barbera, Joseph A. "The Evolution of Shortcomings in Incident Command Systems: Revisions Have Allowed Critical Management Functions to Atrophy." *Journal of Emergency Management*, Vol. 13, No. 6, (November/December 2015): 509-518.

Standridge, Steven E. "The Legal Impact of Emergency Responder's Actions and Decisions During Interstate Response and the Need for A National Immunity Law." *Journal of Emergency Management*, Vol. 8, No. 3, (May/June 2010): 23-35.

St. Cyr, Joseph F. "Hazardous Materials and Emergency Management: A Primer on Hazmat Law." *Journal of Emergency Management*, Vol. 2, No. 2, (Spring 2004): 47-51.

Stone, Lori R. "The State of Interoperability in the States," *Journal of Emergency Management*, Vol. 10, No. 1, (January/February 2012): 7-21.

Sturgis, Rhonda. "Strategic Planning for Emergency Managers." *Journal of Emergency Management*, Vol. 5, No. 2, (March/April 2007): 41-48.

Sylves, Richard. "Why Revolutionary Change is Needed in Emergency Management." *Journal of Emergency Management*, Vol. 3, No. 3, (November/December 2005): 15-18.

Thibault, Edward A., Lynch, Lawrence M., and McBride, R. Bruce. *Proactive Police Management*, 6th Edition. Upper Saddle River, New Jersey: Pearson-Prentice Hall, 2004.

Topp, Walter S. "Making the Transition from Law Enforcement to Emergency Management: Organizational, Occupational, and Cultural Issues." *Journal of Emergency Management*, Vol. 17, No. 1, (January/February 2019): 45-52.

Uhr, Christian and Ekman, Olof. "Trust Among Decision Makers and Its Consequences in Emergency Response Operations." *Journal of Emergency Management*, Vol. 6, No. 3, (May/June 2008): 21-37.

Urby, Heriberto Jr., and David, E. McEntire. "Emergency Managers as Change Agents: Recognizing the Value of Management, Leadership, and Strategic Management in the Disaster Profession." *Journal of Emergency Management*, Vol. 13, No. 1, (January/February 2015): 37-51.

U.S. Department of Homeland Security, Civil Defense and Homeland Security: A Short History of National Preparedness Efforts. (September 2016).

U.S. Department of Homeland Security, Federal Emergency Management Agency, National Incident Management System. (December 2008).

U.S. Department of Homeland Security, Federal Emergency Management Agency, National Incident Management System. (October 2017).

U.S. Department of Homeland Security, Federal Emergency Management Agency, We are FEMA: Helping People Before, During, and After Disasters. (2016).

U.S. Department of Justice, Office of Justice Programs, The Role of Law Enforcement in Public Health Emergencies: Special Considerations for an All-Hazards Approach. (September 2006).

U.S. Department of Justice, Office of Justice Programs, Bureau of Justice Statistics, Census of State and Local Law Enforcement Agencies. (2018).

U.S. Department of Justice, Office of Justice Programs, Bureau of Justice Statistics, Federal Law Enforcement Officers. (2016).

Vasu, Michael L., Stewart, Debra W., and Garson, G. David. *Organizational Behavior and Public Management*, 3rd Edition. New York: Marcel Dekker, 1998.

Walker, Samuel and Katz, Charles M. *The Police in America: An Introduction*, 4th Edition. New York: McGraw-Hill Higher Education, 2002.

Walsh, Donald W., Christen, Hank T., Jr., Callsen, Christian E., Miller, Geoffrey T., Maniscalco, Paul M., Lord, Graydon C., and Dolan, Neal J. National *Incident Management System: Principles and Practice*, 2nd Edition. Sudbury, Massachusetts: Jones and Bartlett Learning, 2012.

Waugh, William L., Jr. "Emergency Management Today and Tomorrow." *Journal of Emergency Management*, Vol. 1, No. 1, (Spring 2003): 5-6.

Waugh, William L., Jr. "The 'All-Hazards' Approach Must Be Continued." *Journal of Emergency Management*, Vol. 2, No. 1, (Winter 2004): 11-20.

Waugh, William L., Jr. "The Principles of Emergency Management." *Journal of Emergency Management*, Vol. 5, No. 3, (May/June 2007): 15-16.

Webster, Elizabeth M. "Emergency Planning for People With Disabilities and Others With Access and Functional Needs to Ensure Inclusiveness." *Journal of Emergency Management*, Vol. 12, No. 3, (May/June 2014): 211-218.

Weinerman, Jason. "Conservation Districts and Emergency Management: New Partners for Tight Fiscal Times." *Journal of Emergency Management*, Vol. 9, No. 2, (March/April 2011): 67-72.

Wilen, Saul B. "Crisis Leadership Versus Leadership in Crisis." *Journal of Emergency Management*, Vol. 4, No. 3, (May/June 2006): 15-20.

Williams, Jillian A., and Xenakis, Aileen B. "Establishing Identity During a Disaster: The Emergency Management Assistance Compact and the First Responder Identification Credential." *Journal of Emergency Management*, Vol. 6, No. 6, (November/December 2008): 11-15.

Wojtalewicz, Cliff, Kirby, Adam, and Dietz, J. Eric. "Implementation and Modeling of a Regional Hub Reception Center During Mass Evacuation Operations." *Journal of Emergency Management*, Vol. 12, No. 3, (May/June 2014): 197-210.

Wolshon, Brian, Jones, Joe, and Walton, Fotini. "The Evacuation Tail and its Effect on Evacuation Decision Making." *Journal of Emergency Management*, Vol. 8, No. 1, (January/February 2010): 37-46.

Wood, Erik and Frazier, Tim. "Disasters, Community Vulnerability, and Poverty: The Intersection Between Economics and Emergency Management." *Journal of Emergency Management*, Vol. 19, No. 3, (May/June 2021): 227-233.

Woodbury, Glen L. "Critical Curriculum for Emergency Management Leaders: Three Essential Themes." *Journal of Emergency Management*, Vol. 3, No. 2, (March/April 2005): 27-29.

Young, Richard R., and Peterson, Matthew R. "Emergency Management Logistics Must Become Emergency Supply Chain Management." *Journal of Emergency Management*, Vol. 12, No. 2, (March/April 2014): 171-187.

INDEX